This brave and brilliant book brings me fresh insights into how to be a more effective and happier agent of change. Here Miki Kashtan shows me how the radical interdependence of all things, a worldview long central to my own life and work, can be expressed in more grounded and practical ways for social as well as personal transformation. I am particularly grateful for her stories from the future, showing ordinary people practicing the principles she teaches. In Miki I find a marvelous and rare use of the moral imagination.

> — **Joanna Macy**, teacher-activist and author, *Coming Back to Life: The Updated Guide to the Work That Reconnects*

A potent dose of grounded idealism.

> — **Ocean Robbins**, CEO, The Food Revolution Network

Miki Kashtan describes the complex questions raised in the course of nonviolent movements, provides tools with which to approach them, and is admirably honest in admitting when she doesn't have the answers. I have no doubt that if nonviolent movements adopted the insights contained in this volume, the world would be a better place for all.

> — **Erica Chenoweth**, PhD, co-author of *Why Civil Resistance Works*

Reweaving is one of those books that is feeling out the contours of the transition that is in front of us, written by someone at the forefront of an essential aspect of that transition: the social technologies of nonviolent conflict resolution, the healing of a centuries-old legacy of humiliation, violence, and oppression. I have two favorite parts of the book. The first describes the "Myths of Power-with" — really edgy stuff, given the near-universal acceptance in "conscious" circles of naive concepts of non-hierarchy, radical inclusivity, leaderlessness, and so on. I also enjoyed the vignettes from the future that offer a vivid, practicable glimpse of what an ecological, nonviolent society could be.

> — **Charles Eisenstein**, author, *The More Beautiful World Our Hearts Know Is Possible,* and *Sacred Economics.*

Miki Kashtan's work is prophetic, passionate, precisely argued, and original. Read her.

— **Andrew Harvey**, author, *The Hope: a Guide to Sacred Activism*

Reweaving Our Human Fabric is a roadmap to the world we can live in. … which leads to the highest praise I can offer a fellow societal transformationist: her thinking changed mine.

— **Shariff Abdullah**, author, *Creating a World That Works for All*

I have never read a vision of possibility at once so intimate, articulate, wise, and immediately useful – a raw and powerful innovation in the lineage of Gandhi and Martin Luther King, a gift to us all.

— **Tom Atlee**, founder, The Co-Intelligence Institute, author, *The Tao of Democracy*.

Miki Kashtan brings decades of patient, committed work to bear in this stunningly clear and honest book.

— **Vicki Robin**, co-author, *Your Money or Your Life*, author, *Blessing the Hands that Feed Us*

Kashtan shows how nonviolent social transformation is not only possible, but immensely appealing.

— **David Bollier**, activist and author, *Think Like a Commoner*

I dream about placing this book in the hands of every leader, so they can be nourished by the vision and the radically new tools that Miki provides.

— **Cindy Mercer**, Co-Founder, Planet Heritage Foundation

In Reweaving Our Human Fabric, Kashtan seems to go straight to the "big" questions I ask myself during moments of doubt and wonder. How do I live with integrity while making an impact on the web of life around me? Where do I put my energy as a parent, agency leader, romantic partner, community member, writer, sister, mentor?

— **Elaine Shpungin**, Director, UIUC Psychological Services Center, Psychology Today Blogger

This book is an inspirational guide, a love letter to a world in need.

— **Karen Murphy**, seminary student

In this book, Miki Kashtan blows the lid off of Nonviolent Communication as a personal development resource, expanding its potential to transform the larger systems and norms that govern our world.

— **Lorraine Aguilar**, Chief Engagement Officer, Working Harmony, Inc.

Miki did an amazing thing. She invited me to write a qualified endorsement, stating what I think is valuable about her book but also my reservations. This simple extraordinary act speaks volumes about Miki's living, breathing commitment to connection through dialogue based on mutual regard and the Gandhian principle that we all hold a piece of the truth. Miki Kashtan inspires us find our best selves, and she leads in the best possible way — through example.

— **Steven Wineman**, activist, author *Power-Under: Trauma and Nonviolent Social Change*

This is a very big book. Miki Kashtan weaves her deep wisdom about personal transformation, interpersonal dialogue, and political change into a path to the future we all want — where everyone's needs matter and no one is coerced. And best of all, her stories bring that future to life. Having seen Miki in action now for many months, I believe it can be done!

— **Bruce Peterson**, presiding judge of Hennepin County, Minnesota, Drug Court, Co-Parent Court, and Homelessness Court

This is a book that squarely addresses how to bring into being the lived experience of the positive social change that we all long for but often despair of creating.

— **Peter Gabel**, law professor, therapist, author, *The Bank Teller and Other Essays on the Politics of Meaning*, editor-at-large of *Tikkun*

Miki Kashtan paints a vivid picture of how and why a future of nonviolence for the world can unfold.

— **Marie R. Miyashiro**, author, *The Empathy Factor*

A deep activism that is a prescription for this moment.

— **Matthew Albracht**, The Peace Alliance

Strategic yet principled. Visionary yet pragmatic. Practical yet philosophical. From historical examples of nonviolent movements to fictional visions of what our future could be, from the personal to the global, this book provides a complete and holistic view of the nonviolent philosophy.

— **Kazu Haga,** Kingian Nonviolence trainer

Her vision calls me to action, in my business, and in my relationships, with a balance of power and love. The courage of her thinking is an irresistible invitation to dream on a global-sized canvas.

— **Sarah Wilson-Jones**, CEO, Phoenix Coffee Company

This book is honest. And I'm more honest with myself for having read it.

— **Jim Rough**, author, Founder and President,
Dynamic Facilitation Associates

Reweaving Our Human Fabric is one of the most engaging books I have read in a long time.

— **David Hartsough**, Director, Peaceworkers, author,
Waging Peace: Global Adventures of a Life-long Activist

Miki takes us on a journey to discover how practical and powerful nonviolence is, and how it all starts with deliberate communication.

— **Mathis Wackernagel**, President, Global Footprint Network

I read the stories and the last part about principles and systems first. They were catchy and easy reads for me. The first, and longest part … was very eye opening and interesting. There's a movement in the world now that could benefit tremendously from this book, as becoming aware of these tools, systems and elements will bridge the gap that I see between the high tech oriented and the low-tech oriented. Technical solutions are well and good, but they don't help unless you understand humans, their communication and their feelings and true needs.

— **Harald Sandø**, creator of the movie *Waking Up*

Reweaving Our Human Fabric

Working Together to Create a Nonviolent Future

by
Miki Kashtan

the *fearless* HEART

Fearless Heart Publications

Published by
FEARLESS HEART PUBLICATIONS

55 Santa Clara Avenue, Suite 203,
Oakland, CA 94610
www.thefearlessheart.org

ISBN-10: 0990007324   Paperback
ISBN-13: 978-0-9900073-2-6   Paperback

ISBN subject categories: Social Sciences, Fiction – short stories

Library of Congress Control Number: 2015931323

Cover design: "Weaving the World" by Mili Raj (miliraj.com)

For the people of the future

Table of Contents

Foreword

by MICHAEL NAGLER

Professor Emeritus of Classics and Comparative Literature at UC, Berkeley, Founder of the Metta Center for Nonviolence.[1]

In Plato's dialogue *Protagoras,* some of Socrates' admirers ask him to tell them something about the virtue that makes for a good life *(areté).* "I don't mind," Socrates graciously says, "but do you want it in a straight description *(logos)* or should I tell you a story *(mythos)*?"

One of the reasons *Reweaving Our Human Fabric* is such a timely and important book is that it presents a critical issue, as Plato does, with a compelling combination of *logos* and *mythos,* discursive reasoning and imaginative narrative. We might be tempted to call the latter "fiction," but the stories that make up the last third of this unusual book are so true to experience as to be more like "myth," which, according to another Western philosopher, is a "story that never happened but is always true." Miki's stories portray individual lives molded by and in turn molding a society structured entirely around attending to everyone's needs. Her matter-of-fact style in the stories makes what for most people is unimaginable seem what it should be – the norm.

Reweaving follows *Spinning Threads of Radical Aliveness,* a deeply personal book about the author's journey to nonviolence. Since nonviolence arises from "person power," a term I've added to "people power" (the capacities respectively of the individual and a unified group), the personal approach gives us exactly the right lens to begin with. "Nonviolence," as one section heading tells us, "begins with inner practice." This book takes us further into the ways our

---

[1] Dr. Michael Nagler is Professor Emeritus of Classics and Comparative Literature at UC, Berkeley, where he co-founded the Peace and Conflict Studies Program, and the founder of the Metta Center for Nonviolence. Among other awards, he received the Jamnalal Bajaj International Award for "Promoting Gandhian Values Outside India" in 2007, joining other distinguished contributors to nonviolence as Archbishop Desmond Tutu and peace scholar and activist Johan Galtung in receiving this honor. He is the author of *The Search for a Nonviolent Future,* which received a 2002 American Book Award and has been translated into Korean, Arabic, Italian and other languages; *Our Spiritual Crisis: Recovering Human Wisdom in a Time of Violence* (2005); *The Upanishads* (with Sri Eknath Easwaran, 1987), and most recently *The Nonviolence Handbook* as well as many articles on peace and spirituality.

personal transformations can enable us to collaborate together in any organization and in campaigns of nonviolent social change.

Today there are, at last, a number of good accounts of nonviolent *movements* from historical and political viewpoints;[2] we can use some more glimpses into nonviolent *experience* from the point of view of the person offering it. Miki (for full disclosure, we are close friends and I'd feel awkward using her family name) is well qualified to give us this insight. Much of her adult life has been an "experiment" with Gandhi's truth, and her career as an international trainer in Nonviolent Communication (NVC) and co-founder of Bay Area NVC has honed her analytical skills, which she puts to work here to such good effect. In her own words, "I take the core principles of Gandhian nonviolence and explore how they can be used, through the lens of NVC principles, in living our lives in full integrity, on a daily basis." There are many ways Gandhian principles can be applied in daily life – nonviolence, as Gandhi said, is "not the inanity it has been taken for down the ages" and its applications are limitless – and the set of NVC principles that she herself has honed for many years and describes so vividly in this book give us tools to greatly improve the integrity of our daily relationships, in just about any situation.

We are now at the third anniversary of the Occupy movement, and many of us are wondering – some with regret, others with relief – how Occupy faded so quickly, especially those who do not realize that it has not in fact gone quite away but is seeking constructive ways to reinvent itself. Miki points out all its problems, focusing especially on what many regard as *the* problem with that movement – unless it turns out to be its most useful contribution: in her section on "Dilemmas of Leadership," she asks, "where is the line between authority and authoritarianism?" Wisely rejecting the facile anti-authoritarianism that's often found as ideology in otherwise progressive movements, she proposes "combining the potential efficiencies that arise from the expertise and authority of functional leaders with the wisdom and emergent qualities of sharing power" to arrive at a happy middle ground with "built-in mechanisms for subverting the possibility of power-over."

If I might add something here, the line between authority and authoritarianism might be the line between what Gandhi called

---

[2] The Global Nonviolent Action Database at Swarthmore has recently logged its thousandth example: nvdatabase.swarthmore.edu/.

trusteeship and ownership. Trusteeship was one of the brilliant innovations in Gandhi's economics. Unlike Marx, he did not advocate forcibly dispossessing the wealthy of their excess wealth (the obscene proportions of which sparked Occupy). He advocated that *all* of us should cultivate an attitude of trusteeship rather than ownership toward anything we might have regarded as "our" possessions. In other words, treat them as loaned to us to use, not given to us to enjoy. Like most of his essential ideas, this one was grounded in a spiritual Truth: as the Isha Upanishad (one of his favorites) says, "covet nothing, for who (really) owns anything?"

Most of Gandhi's core principles *can* be understood on the material plane and probably were so understood by many: *svadeshi*, or "localism," played out on the economic field as spinning your own cloth and boycotting British manufactures. Trusteeship *could* be limited to meaning non-ownership of one's material holdings. But both these concepts were – in his mind, at least – never cut loose from their spiritual moorings. In this sense svadeshi meant dealing with our own problems before, or rather than, trying to change others – very much a theme of this book. And trusteeship could be applied not to a thing but a personal trait or endowment – in the present case, one's authority. Let's say I have a certain authority in one area or another. Is it for me to use for the good of others, or take advantage of for myself? (Didn't one of the medieval popes, on his election, say, "Now that we have the papacy, let us enjoy it"?) As Miki wisely points out, in practice this can be a subtle distinction. The minute I start to feel good about "my" authority, the minute I start to think of it as "over others," the minute I get annoyed when someone isn't doing what I say, I am regarding myself as the owner of that authority – and this is authoritarianism. But when I'm saying to myself, "how can we all use this, e.g., to make a decision more smoothly and get on with our work, or resolve a quarrel so we can stay united," I can say that I hold the capacity in trust. This is real authority. And this is the kind of authority that Gandhi employed to such spectacular uses in South Africa and India. If there were any authority "over," it was to be over himself: "If my non-violence is to become contagious and infectious," he wrote, "I must acquire greater control over my thoughts." Miki's writing – and more to the point, her life – is entirely faithful to this principle.

The scope of this book is not limited to Gandhi, of course; it explores the principles of nonviolence itself; but Miki sees it playing out very much in a Gandhian spirit. She writes, for example, "Ultimately what makes a nonviolent strategy unique is the intentionality behind it more than the type of action itself." Elsewhere she refers to "the double courage that defines the passage into nonviolence: the courage to overcome internal habits of reaction, and the courage to face the potential consequences that arise from standing up to those in power, especially when they are fully committed to subjugation of the resisters." Every activist – really, every one of us, because who among us is never involved in disagreement of one kind or another – will agree, once she has pointed it out, that we need the courage to resist our own negative drives, our "internal habits;" *and* the courage to stand up to potentially harsh punishment from others. Nonviolent practitioners often find that once they prevail in the first struggle – once they can deal with their own anger or fear – the second struggle – enduring others' resistance – is relatively easy. Not so easy, but critically important, is not being entangled in getting just the results you want. You could almost say that if you have contained your anger or fear (or both – they so often travel together) and left the results to the Universe or whatever you believe in, you have already won.

This key realization that undesirable internal habits can be converted or "rolled over" to their positive equivalent – by working on our openness to others we can convert anger into compassion – allows Miki to develop a brilliant and badly needed concept of power, that it is not to be shunned, as ideologues often do, but carefully channeled. This has nothing to do with repression; as she puts it (drawing, as usual, from her own considerable experience), "Fear itself doesn't go away as the practice of nonviolence deepens. What changes is the ability to bear it and still choose love and courage." This is why nonviolent actors are frequently surprised at the courageous, courteous things they hear themselves saying and, more important, at how their nonviolent action leads to a successful, creative, and lasting solution.

Miki's main focus is on the middle ground of communication, between the inner struggle just described and its results in the field of social action. But she has plenty to say about the latter – including interesting reflections on the failure of the Kibbutz movement in

Israel – just as she is very clear that intention determines the final quality, and value, of action: her statement that "without love, whatever gains are made will be short lived. Historical examples abound," reminds me of William Law, the influential English mystic and theologian: "love hath no errors, for all errors are a want of love."

As far as social action, and particularly any future for Occupy is concerned, she wisely refrains from proposing a strategy for that movement; her observations are about its *culture*. Given what she (and I) believe about the determining power of intention and culture, of inner motive and attitude, this is exactly where the emphasis belongs.

Reweaving is an extremely rich and extremely practical book. But it speaks for itself, and there is no need for me to paraphrase further, but rather to encourage you to read it. How to move forward with civil resistance (civil both in terms of coming from the citizenry and being civil, or nonviolent, in tone) to the ever-deepening oppression and erosion of democracy, mainly here in the United States – how to replace the culture of alienation surrounding us with one of humanity and belonging – is *the* challenge of our time. This book can help every one of us understand and participate effectively in resolving that challenge.

Socrates' admirers ask him to give them the lesson in the form of *mythos*. The great philosopher proceeds to tell us how Zeus gave the responsibility of creating living things to Prometheus, but he turns the job over to his relatively dull-witted brother Epimetheus, who manages to run out of ways of defense before he gets to mankind. Without sharp teeth or claws or any way to defend themselves, the latter are in a bad way. Fortunately, Zeus steps in and has humanity given two saving graces by which they can form communities, build cities, and flourish. They are justice (*diké*) and a sense of respect (*aidos*). These are the qualities that enable human beings to get along together and thus proceed to their – to our – common destiny. The qualities that Miki Kashtan shows us how to develop and illustrates with her stories in this book – understanding, patience, compassion, and the like – are modern translations of these two capacities. We have never needed them more.

Author's Preface

This book combines the visionary and the practical.

On the visionary plane, it describes what a livable future might look like – a world in which human needs are placed at the center of all systems, institutions, and relationships.

On the practical plane, the book provides concrete guidelines for how to live life and engage in social change work informed by a deep commitment to nonviolence[3] and collaborative practices. There are many details here about how a world that works for all, in Shariff Abdullah's[4] resonant phrase, can actually be implemented, starting with each of us today.

The book was born, along with my other book, *Spinning Threads of Radical Aliveness*, from an assignment I received from the religious scholar and teacher of mystic traditions, Andrew Harvey: to write a book in which I would put out the entirety of my message to the world, without trimming, editing, or holding back. He named, specifically, what he called my "prophetic vision," along with the practical applications, the personal struggles that made me who I am, and everything I know that can be useful to others. I took on the invitation even though calling my ideas about the future "prophetic" sounded grandiose and was therefore extremely challenging.

When that project became unwieldy, I knew I had to divide it into two separate books. The first one, published as *Spinning Threads of Radical Aliveness*, is a sweeping journey starting with how denying and suppressing our needs has brought us to have the world we have inherited and how this legacy of separation and scarcity gets recreated each generation anew. With that understanding, that book guides us to learn what each of us can do as individuals to affirm our human needs. We can start to free ourselves from the legacies of the past, both collective and personal, even while the world around us persists in operating on the basis of separation, scarcity, and powerlessness.

---

[3] Nonviolence is a controversial and paradoxical word. Like others, I was suspicious of it before understanding it fully, and extremely reluctant to let go of it once I got the immense beauty this approach to life represents, for which I know no other one word. To understand more fully how and why I use it, see page 26.

[4] The well-known author, attorney, and professor added a second f to his first name in 2014. See sharif.commonway.org and References, p. 419.

Although in some ways *Reweaving Our Human Fabric* logically follows *Spinning Threads of Radical Aliveness*, I present the material here in such a way that you will not need to read that book in order to make sense of this one.

If your experience of reading this book is what I hope it will be, then everything you do toward social transformation might look different, either in subtle or major ways. This will be so in at least three primary ways. One is that you will have some version of a vision of what is possible, what you are working towards, that I believe will provide immense fuel for doing your work with more resilience and hope. The second is that you might gain more capacity in being able to collaborate with others, individually and within groups and organizations. The third is that you might just find a way to align yourself more deeply with the consciousness of nonviolence, and do your work, however confrontational your path, with love in your heart instead of anger.

Miki Kashtan, Oakland, October 2014

Introduction

... the misery here is quite terrible and yet, late at night when the day has slunk away into the depths behind me, I often walk with a spring in my step along the barbed wire and then time and again it soars straight from my heart – I can't help it, that's just the way it is, like some elementary force – the feeling that life is glorious and magnificent, and that one day we shall be building a whole new world. Against every new outrage and every fresh horror we shall put up one more piece of love and goodness, drawing strength from within ourselves. We may suffer, but we must not succumb.

> – Etty Hillesum, *An Interrupted Life* (Diary entry from a transition camp in Holland, shortly before being taken to Auschwitz and killed, 1943)

The capacity to envision a different reality regardless of our circumstances, so powerfully demonstrated in Etty's words, along with the willingness, together with others, to approach the task of creating it with love, form the core of what I address in this book.

This is no small task. We live in a time in which vision is almost gone, love is absent from many of our interactions, and we have accepted a worldview that says that the only possible change is within individuals.

Even when we do work with others towards social transformation, we often do it from anger rather than love, or aiming for love without knowing how to cooperate, thereby creating movements and organizations rife with conflict. Ultimately, even when we win, we often end up establishing structures not significantly different from what we set out to oppose.

I want to contribute to a different outcome, and believe that having a powerful vision to guide us, along with changing how we do social change work, can do it. This is why I wrote this book.

The premise of both parts is that putting human needs at the center of life, allowing them to guide our inner lives, our relationships, and even be the building blocks of our institutions – provides a key transformational assurance that we can succeed in creating a world that works for all.

Because the concept of "needs" is so fraught with complexity, confusion, and negative associations, this frame bears some fleshing out, the skeleton of which I provide below. At the same time, because the lens of human needs is so foundational to all I do, some of the understanding will, by necessity, come osmotically, through reading the book itself, and, especially, through immersion in the stories of what the world could look like if organized around human needs.

What Do I Mean by "Needs"?

I am forever indebted to Marshall Rosenberg, the man who developed the practice of Nonviolent Communication (NVC) that guides everything I do, both in my work and in my personal life, for placing human needs front and center. This is the aspect of NVC that challenges prevalent theories of human nature; the entry point through which collaboration becomes possible in groups; the engine of the kind of healing that happens through engaging with an empathic presence; the mechanism through which conflict mediation proceeds; the path to personal liberation; and, hopefully, a way in which our largest systems and institutions could be organized.

The simplest way that I frame what I mean by human needs is through the distinction between what we do and how we do it on the one hand, and why we do it on the other. Needs, in that frame, provide the "why" for everything that we do.

Rather than trying to define needs in some abstract way, this distinction between the "what" and the "why" provides a dynamic procedure for moving towards understanding and connection in every moment. Another way of describing this distinction is that human beings have an indefinitely large number of variations of ways to meet a relatively small set of needs which are common to all of us. To use one fundamental example: money, the versatile strategy that now serves as a mechanism for attending to so many of our needs, didn't even exist some number of thousand of years ago, and yet the needs we now use it for were already in place.

Looked at this way, needs are the fundamental motivators for all our actions, as well as what gives meaning to all our experiences. The tragedy of life is that while our needs are so all-important, most of us go through life without cultivating the awareness of our needs or the capacity to distinguish between our needs and our strategies. We rarely ask and answer why we want something, what the meaning of our pain is, or any of the many questions that would lead us to connect with our own and others' needs. Why tragic? Because when we do engage with the "why," so much more becomes possible. Showing those possibilities is a big part of what I attempt to do in this book.

We are habituated to seeing needs as a pure expression of self-interest. If, instead, we come to see needs as *everything* that is required for a human being to thrive and have a meaningful life, the equation of needs with self-interest can become limiting. Just as much as we want to be loved, we long to offer our love, to contribute our gifts, to have a positive effect on others. Remember, the idea is that needs are about thriving, not purely surviving.

None of this is to imply that we don't engage in destructive behaviors, as individuals, groups, and even as the entire species. It only means that any behavior can be traced back to a finite set of needs all of which are, at bottom, life-affirming. There are strategies that really do meet the needs that we consciously or unconsciously adopted them to meet. And there are strategies that meet those needs only partially or not at all. Eating a meal with friends can meet needs for nutrition, energy, companionship, joy, and more. It can also give rise to overeating, drunkenness, anger, or sadness: all indicators of unmet needs.

There are strategies that meet our own needs while at the same time preventing others from meeting theirs. There are strategies that satisfy no one's needs.

My claim, born of a vast pool of experience (my own in working with thousands of individuals and dozens of organizations) and ongoing reading and research, is that when we can drill down together to the shared, life-affirming needs beneath competing or even destructive strategies, an alternative path that attends to many more needs is almost always available. And when that path becomes clear, I find that most people want to walk it.[5]

One way of moving into a livable future is by increasing our capacity to identify and implement strategies that are consciously

---

[5] As one small example, a batterers training program designed and delivered by a fellow NVC trainer, Eddie Zacapa, has produced zero recidivism over the course of five years, an unheard of degree of success, confirmed by the El Dorado County District Attorney's office ("Batterers' intervention recidivism rates lowest known to date" in *The Mountain Democrat*, Placerville, CA, 4-30-14).

designed to attend to everyone's needs and are increasingly *successful* in doing so.

Overall, then, in this book I describe as fully as I know how what a society designed primarily to attend to everyone's needs might look like, and I offer my experience and insight into ways we can live and relate that will move us in the direction of that world even now, when so much of the world operates on dramatically different principles.

With that understanding, let's get on with the book.

The Shape of This Book

Although I believe that vision is the foundation of all the work that we do, providing a sense of purpose, energy, and direction, I nonetheless am starting this book with the practical side of things. There are several reasons for it.

One is that the vision is given through fictional stories, and they may not make as much sense in terms of what they are showing until some of the other pieces are in place. I didn't have any other way to convey the vision of a world that hasn't yet existed aside from fictional stories.

Second, the practical part of the book is also, in some ways, visionary. Learning how to collaborate to attend to all our needs in our current society is critical for being able to do it in the future, since we are using the same tools, and applying the same intentionality, even if it's not at the same society-wide level of challenge. It's a different kind of vision: a vision of how we could work with each other effectively even when the wider changes that would support collaboration are not yet in place. For many people, a practical application that is visionary may work far better than starting with a more distant vision for which some foundations have not been laid down.

Lastly, if you would like to start with the stories, then please do. You might not get all the nuances of what I am trying to show there, and you will still get a lot.

I.   Working for Transformation without Recreating the Past

This first part of the book addresses a paradoxical dilemma. If we prioritize social transformation without attending to the ways in which all of us have internalized the very systems and habits of heart and mind that we aim to transform, then we run the risk of re-creating these systems and habits. At the same time, a commitment to inner work without a continued and singular focus on social transformation runs the risk of being adaptive to the ways of the world, as social structures have phenomenal power to persist despite significant personal awareness. Either path without the other is limited. Put simply, we can't change social structures without changing our individual selves, and we can't do that without changing social structures. To create the world of our dreams, we are called to go forward with both together.

This is why this part addresses both, providing tools and practices for applying nonviolence and interdependence both internally and in how we engage in social transformation. It equips those who want to dedicate energies and resources to working for social transformation with the consciousness and tools necessary to ensure that their work remains aligned with the vision. The challenge is immense: all of us are collectively bootstrapping ourselves, and only partially emerging from our current paradigms. If we want to create institutions that truly embody a transformed consciousness, our *way* of working for change is as important as the change we want to create.

This part does not suggest particular structural-change goals nor campaigns to bring them about. Instead, it offers a new approach to power and leadership, decision-making, and resource allocation that are consistent with the primacy of human needs. Every step of the way, it provides concrete practices that model, on a small and growing scale, the world we want to create. If practiced deeply by even a minority of activists, the insights here can transform every campaign for structural change, reduce the in-fighting within and between campaigns, and transform the relationships between social activists and people in power.

II. Wisdom Tales from the Future

Part Two, "Wisdom Tales from the Future," takes the needs-based perspective and shows what the world could look like when human needs become an organizing principle for creating organizations, social structures, and even global institutions and governance. This entire part is written as if the transformation aimed for in this book has already happened, even when we don't and can't know how.

This is based on my faith that the project of creating a world that we can all love begins with having the vision of what that world would look like.

In such a world, the paradigm shift that is pointed to throughout the book will have taken place. Rather than a theoretical exposition, this part provides a detailed picture of what the world of the future could look like by envisioning institutions and systems of global governance and resource allocation that are consciously and directly responsive to maximizing attending to human needs instead of to profit, authority, or tradition.[6] We don't have many models of anything in our current world that truly embody this deep spirit of making things work for everyone. As a result, much of the detail is provided in the form of fiction: stories that show what working together without separation and what completely voluntary participation in life could look like. This would be a world that we can *all* love. On every level, from the most personal to the most global, these stories show a society resting on a consciousness that life-affirming human needs underlie every emotion, desire, and behavior, and that meeting human needs is both possible and the biggest insurance policy for maintaining cohesion and human sociability.

I want to give concrete and detailed form to the vision I have been carrying within me, getting ever clearer and more refined, for years on end. I want to share it with as many people as possible, in the hopes of managing to inspire enough people to rise up to make it happen.

Everything in this society would be geared toward attending to human needs. We would be treated with care and respect from the moment we were born. We would have every reason to believe that our needs and wellbeing matters. We would have daily evidence that resources were being utilized for everyone's benefit. In small measure, I have been present in situations where these shifts have happened, and the results are nothing less than magical.

---

[6] Clearly, profit, authority, and tradition are strategies that attend to at least some human needs for some people. My reading of history and current events leads me to believe that they do so at the expense of many other needs for many people.

Part One

Working for Transformation without Recreating the Past

Nonviolence and the Future

Non-violence is the greatest force at the disposal of [hu]mankind. It is mightier than the mightiest weapon of destruction devised by ... [human] ingenuity.

– Mahatma Gandhi

Many of us carry a vision of a world that works for all, where everyone's needs matter and people and the planet are cared for. None of us know what will or could bring about our vision. Will it be a miracle of a single leader transforming the cultural assumptions and practices? Will it be a world collapse that will create a void and an opportunity to restructure society? Will it be a critical mass of people who inhabit different forms of human relationship? Will it be a nonviolent revolution? Will it be alternative structures that gradually attract more and more resources and people to them? Or will it be something else none of us can imagine?

Aside from the necessary humility of not knowing, it is my belief that in times like ours, any of us who has been given the gift and privilege of having vision is called into stretching to spell out everything we know, however incomplete and biased our knowledge, and offer it to all our peers, students, and teachers.

The stakes are simply too high to wait for the perfect-enough answer, the wise-enough leader, or anything else that keeps us from speaking fully what is in our heart and mind. Boldly and humbly I therefore choose to put forth all I have learned and imagined that may support us in averting the potential collapse and forging a future that sustains life – ours alongside others who share the biosphere with us.

The path and the destination, as I see them, begin with the legacy of nonviolence[7]. Along with Gandhi and Martin Luther King, Jr., I don't see a way to transform the inheritance of our past except in nonviolent methods. These two men have both taught us so much that we are barely scratching the surface of understanding about the unstoppable power of nonviolent methods to create social change.

---

[7] For a rich history of what nonviolence has brought to the world, see *A Force more Powerful* by Ackerman and Duvall.

Both of them encountered and transcended massive opposition to their vision of liberation, and succeeded in removing immense barriers and establishing previously unimaginable freedoms for the people on whose behalf they struggled.

At the same time, neither one of them succeeded in reaching their true dreams. In the wake of their deaths, their respective movements did not survive. India disintegrated into a brutal war, and the Civil Rights movement lost its nonviolent momentum, its leaders dispersing into multiple causes and movements. Gandhi's and King's deep desire to transform separation into a united future for humanity, what King called "the beloved community," nearly died with them despite their impressive achievements. Although there are many who have initiated and sustain projects inspired by their ideals and methods, few are holding out the large vision along with the sheer size of the mass movements that characterized Gandhi and King's work.

In part, I see this result as expressing the limits of the approach that Gandhi and, to a lesser extent, King used. I think of this approach as relying on the moral force of an individual to call on people to live up to a vision that is not yet possible, even before their consciousness has been transformed. In some instances, Gandhi chose to reject purely political and less-than-ideal solutions to work with practical realities in favor of a grand ideal.[8] People stayed with his ideal because of their faith in him, not because they shared his perspective or could embrace in their own lives the consciousness shift he had gone through.

In this way, I believe Gandhi differed from the Civil Rights movement in the United States, where the attention to practical results was unwavering. It seems to me that Dr. King and his supporters had a more firm acceptance than Gandhi did that despite lack of true change of heart on the part of the white majority at the time, legal-political solutions could make a tangible difference in the lived experience of disadvantaged groups.[9]

---

[8] The most significant example is his refusal to accept a two-tier parliament which was requested by Ambedkar and supported by most of the people on his team. It was his fast unto death that finally got everyone to agree to his wishes, which were guided by a belief in one unified India, hence a more idealized version of what would be possible. To this day, many consider him an enemy of the Dalits because of this choice. See my article "Gandhi and the Dalit controversy: The limits of the moral force of an individual," in *Waging Nonviolence*, February 2012, which expands on this point.

[9] In this discussion I leave aside the question of whether or not the changes to race relations that originated with the Civil Rights Movement have resulted in a substantial change in the lived experience

I see the choice that Gandhi made to get people to agree to do or not do something based on their reverence and care for him as likely one of the reasons why he ultimately failed in his fundamental goal of creating a unified, free, and egalitarian India despite having succeeded in the concrete goal of Indian independence. The moral force of a person is not sustainable. The partial gains made in this way can be short lived.

My own wish is for all of us to learn from their experiences, both from what worked and what didn't work, so that recreating the past is less and less inevitable as we develop more and more understanding and integrate more and more practice. While we may not know what creates social and political transformation, we know some about what maintains nonviolence over time. I am in a deep inquiry about the paradox I see. On the one hand, without mass consciousness transformation, even significant gains can be lost when the inspiring individual dies. On the other hand, consciousness transformation is extraordinarily difficult to achieve individually, let alone on a mass scale, and even more so under conditions of massive separation, war, oppression, and just the grind of life. How can we move forward, then?

Given all this, I doubt I have much to add in this book about nonviolent resistance, the aspect of nonviolence that both Gandhi and Martin Luther King perfected, and which has been emulated by many movements since, with extraordinary success *on the material plane*.[10] I can only add this: nonviolent resistance, as I understand it, is about standing up to those with power who are not ready to dialogue, who are committed to their own power despite our most well-intentioned efforts to engage with them, who contribute, by the very business-as-usual daily decisions that they make, to the ongoing massive destruction of our times. While I feel repeatedly inspired by the power of nonviolent resistance where it has been tried, I derive even more hope from imagining what these efforts would look like supported by the practices and methodology of Nonviolent Communication (NVC)[11], which form the backbone of all that I do

---

of African Americans in the US. The complexity and controversy surrounding this particular question are far beyond the scope of my current focus.

[10] See Erica Chenoweth and Maria Stephan's *Why Civil Resistance Works* for a thorough study about the extent and reasons for the success of nonviolent movements.

[11] It is not my purpose in this book to introduce NVC to those who don't know it. If you are interested in a basic understanding, you can look at the reference materials on the BayNVC website at baynvc.org/reference.php. Beyond that, a number of books already exist that serve that purpose in a

in my work. I would like to see NVC applied within activist organizations, between supporters and opponents, in communication with the public, and within each person participating in the struggle. One way of looking at this part of the book is that it provides practical guidelines for how to minimize the risk of recreating the very structures that we are trying to change.

I have some more to say about the second aspect of Gandhi's legacy, what he called Constructive Program. I want to do this for three distinct reasons. One is that while the principles of nonviolent resistance are fairly consistent across time and space, constructive programs[12], as I understand them, take unique forms depending on context, location, and population; they can only be reinvented. The second is that while nonviolent resistance has been written about and practiced extensively, the constructive aspects of Gandhi's work have not been understood, studied, or integrated nearly to the same degree. The third, and perhaps most significant reason, is that nonviolent resistance is only necessary when power is used in ways that harm life, whereas constructive programs are the very stuff of a world that works for all, and will need to be appreciated and instituted for a livable future to be at all possible.

A third aspect of nonviolence, in addition to nonviolent resistance and constructive programs, is the power of dialogue. Dialogue as a discipline has not been studied or written about by either Gandhi or Martin Luther King, although they practiced it *de facto* with the very people against whose power they mounted nonviolent resistance. Although dialogue has been studied extensively, it wasn't until Marshall Rosenberg began his experiments with Nonviolent Communication that the transformative powers of dialogue within the context of a philosophy of nonviolence began to be investigated. We now have – because of his work as well as the development of other fields – much more knowledge about

---

way I wholeheartedly support, which you can find through Puddle Dancer Press, the NVC publisher, at nonviolentcommunication.com. If you want to learn in person, you can find trainers or local supporters on the website of the global organization that was created by Marshall Rosenberg – the Center for Nonviolent Communication – at cnvc.org, along with other online resources. Lastly, you can learn NVC from home (using phone or internet access) through the NVC Academy, at nvctraining.com, which provides both online and telephone-based instruction in NVC done by various trainers from different places in the world. I myself regularly offer classes through the NVC Academy.

[12] For an overview of both nonviolent resistance and constructive programs I recommend the work of Michael Nagler, both his books and the website he founded: mettacenter.org.

relationships, language, and dialogue competencies than Gandhi and King had access to.

To recap, this book is an examination and exploration of what I see as the full potential of nonviolence to be the underlying philosophy and practice of a world that works for all through the unique lens of human needs, both in terms of the powers of dialogue and in terms of the possibility of creating social structures that aim to serve human needs.

The combination of a family of processes that allow for inner and outer transformation and are fully aligned with nonviolence and with the vision of entirely revamped institutions that reflect those same values, is what gives me hope that we can, if we engage deeply with nonviolence at all levels, move from here to a future we can only imagine.

Here's what you can find in this part of the book.

Foundations of a Practice of Nonviolence

Often, as soon as people hear about nonviolence and social change, they invoke the idea of "being the change." This is, indeed, where this part of the book starts: what it means to apply Gandhian principles in everyday life.

Nonviolence, Gandhi's method and life philosophy, is at the very heart of all that I do and what I invite people to join me in through my writing and teaching. There are many challenges, both expected and surprising, about taking Gandhian principles into everyday living. For one thing, the context creates dramatically different requirements for how love, truth, and courage – its three building blocks that I discuss later – are applied in different contexts.

Gandhi exemplified the kind of nonviolence that is essential for engaging in a social change struggle, an aspect of nonviolence to which I return later. In that context, the primary goal is to transform large-scale systems and policies. The challenge then consists in sorting out the profound questions of how to fight while maintaining a total openness and love towards the very people whose choices and policies are being opposed.

By contrast, the initial context for the first section of the book is the mundane, everyday life of individuals.[13] What does it mean, in this more familiar context, to live nonviolently? How do we simultaneously live within our world and embody the future? If we engage in fighting reality around us, we ultimately recreate what was there before. It takes tremendous love and courage to bridge the gap between today's reality and our vision of tomorrow. In this part of the book I map out the connection between Nonviolent Communication (NVC) and the core principles that guided Gandhi in his work. In this way I illustrate what nonviolence can mean in daily living, outside of the context of specific political campaigns. I trace each principle to Gandhi's own words and actions, and then show how it is applied within the context of NVC practice.

This section then branches out beyond our personal lives, and invites us to consider what the practice of nonviolence looks like when we aim to engage with larger forces.

Collaboration, Power, and Leadership

It is my hope that once we see the ways our institutions are set up that make it so difficult to live a life of integrity, meaning, and love, we will find the motivation to extend beyond our own individual lives into aiming for transforming the social structures that have contributed to our personal suffering in the first place.

Indeed, the premise of this book is that no amount of individual change alone will suffice to change the rules of the game. If we are going to change those social structures, we will need to grapple with them directly, not only with our own internal states, nor even only with our relationships with individuals. Doing this will invariably put us in situations where we are asked to collaborate with others towards shared visions.

This is where the task of living the future in the present becomes urgent. If we want to create institutions that are truly embodying a transformed consciousness, our *way* of working for change is equally important to what change we want to create. As much as we want to collaborate, most of us don't know how. This section delves into some of the consciousness shifts and concrete practices that can help

---

[13] All the while, I want to recognize that many individuals' daily living conditions are anything but mundane. Violence, for some people, *is* a daily occurrence, either because of individual circumstances, or because of belonging to a specific group, or because of living in conditions of war.

us as we aim to collaborate effectively and create groups, communities, and organizations as part of our efforts.

Beyond a certain scale, we also come face to face with the most complex questions about power and leadership. Transforming separation, scarcity, and powerlessness in the context of developing new models of power and leadership is a world unto itself, and the journey of learning how to lead without coercing, how to truly combine power with love, will likely take significant individual and collective efforts to achieve. In this section, you will hopefully find extensive support along the way.

Concrete Actions for Change

Assuming we have managed to create organizations that can work together effectively and use power lovingly and collaboratively, we are still faced with the question of what we can do to begin the movement into the future. Following the framework that Joanna Macy offered, this section first reviews the kind of nonviolence that Gandhi and King lived in their respective efforts for freedom, examining the interplay between dialogue and nonviolent resistance. I then look briefly at what creating alternatives looks like within a context of a nonviolent movement, tying it to Gandhi's focus on creating a constructive program. Lastly, I close the circle of actions to bring about the future by returning to consciousness transformation as an integral part of social transformation, examining how we can invite others into awareness that has a chance of creating change.

The Next Generation

Some people will no doubt be surprised at the inclusion of attention to babies, children, and parenting the next generation within the context of social transformation. Unusual as this focus is, it seems vital to me to consider, just as vital as consciousness transformation can be. Given how much the legacy of separation continues from generation to generation because of our parenting practices, having some clues about different parenting practices can be a contribution to those who want to stop the cycle from continuing, at least in their small circles. This section, therefore, contains suggestions for radically different ways of relating to children, in which their needs and, in particular, their autonomy, are honored, and in which collaboration is modeled from the first days of life.

Case Studies

This section attempts to bring to life some of the earlier work through examining the Occupy Movement and two organizations in India that are applying Gandhian principles in their work for transformation. In addition to making vivid what I discuss before, this section also provides an opportunity to reflect on what's effective and what we can learn from successes and challenges of existing efforts for transformation.

Getting from Here to There

The last section of this part ends with an exploration of some uncharted territory. I raise some unanswerable questions about the mystery of how transformation could actually happen. Since Part Two of the book assumes that a transition has already happened, and since none of us can know how it might, I end this part with a gap, to be filled by our future actions.

Section 1

Foundations of a Practice of Nonviolence

Gandhian Principles for Everyday Living

One of the most frequent questions I hear when I speak about Nonviolent Communication is, "Why Nonviolent?" People often hear the word nonviolent as a combination of two words, as a negation of violence. Since they don't think of themselves as "violent," the concept of "non-violence" doesn't make intuitive sense, and appears foreign to them.

For some time, I felt similarly. I was happier when I heard people talk about Compassionate Communication instead of Nonviolent Communication (NVC) because it felt more positive. Like many others, I was unaware of the long-standing tradition of nonviolence to which the practice of Nonviolent Communication traces its origins. Then I learned more about Gandhi's work and the Civil Rights movement. That is when I fell in love with the name Marshall Rosenberg gave to this practice. That love has deepened over the years. Now I am choosing nonviolence as my core approach to life. I can no longer accept "compassionate" as any substitute, because nonviolence, for me, also includes the elements of courage and truth. Compassion, or love, by itself, doesn't point us strongly enough into how much inner work is needed to keep standing for what we fiercely believe in even while maintaining a loving attitude. Nonviolence; this clumsy word, is truly the only one I know that packs so much meaning into only one word.

In this segment[14] of the book, I take the core principles of Gandhian nonviolence and explore how they can be used, through the lens of NVC principles, in living our lives in full integrity, on a daily basis. I take on the task of talking about how nonviolence applies to social transformation in later sections.

---

[14] I want to acknowledge Francisco "Pancho" Ramos-Stierle and Alix Johnson for doing extensive research for stories and quotes from Gandhi's life and writings, Kit Miller for planting the seed of this article in a conversation in 2006, and Michael Nagler for reading this piece from a Gandhian scholar's perspective and offering invaluable suggestions.

Nonviolence as Love

The word nonviolence is the closest literal translation that Gandhi found to the Sanskrit word *ahimsa*. In Sanskrit, negation is sometimes used to suggest that a concept or quality is too great to be named directly. "Ahimsa is unconditional love," writes Eknath Easwaran in his preface to *Gandhi the Man*. "The word we translate as 'nonviolence' is . . . central in Buddhism as well: Ahimsa, the complete absence of violence in word and even thought as well as action. This sounds negative, just as 'nonviolence' sounds passive. But like the English word 'flawless,' ahimsa denotes perfection." As another example, *avera*, which means "love" in Sanskrit, literally translates into "non-hatred."

Hinduism is not the only tradition that honors the unnamable. Judaism has a similar practice. The name of God is unsayable in Hebrew, being letters without vowels, without instructions for how to read them. Some things are beyond words. Nonviolence is one of them.

Gandhi also used other terms for his practice. One word that he commonly used is *Satyagraha*, which translates as "truth force." At times he also used the term "soul force." Whichever term he used, Gandhi made it abundantly clear that nonviolence is a positive force, not a negation.

> "Satyagraha means 'holding to the truth in every situation'. This is ahimsa, which is more than just the absence of violence; it is intense love." (Easwaran, *Gandhi the Man*, p. 53)

> "*A Satyagrahi* has infinite patience, abundant faith in others, ample hope." (Gandhi, *Young India*, Mar 19th, 1931).

Why is nonviolence equated with love? Clearly, it's different from forms of love that sometimes have been the impetus for great violence. (Think of Othello as one such example.) What is this kind of love?

It appears to me that Jesus, Gandhi, Marshall Rosenberg, and those of us following their tradition through the practice of NVC think of love as the full radical acceptance of the humanity of every person, regardless of how unhappy we are with their actions.

Indeed, Gandhi said: "It is nonviolence only when we love those that hate us," (*Gandhi the Man*, p. 108). These words are strikingly similar to a core principle of Jesus' teachings: "Love thy enemy," (Matthew 5:44). Both of them speak to the vision of a heart that is fully open to everyone, especially our enemies. Marshall Rosenberg, too, has said that the practice of NVC emerged from his attempt to understand love.

I understand this love as the commitment to act in ways that uphold everyone's humanity. It means caring for the well-being of the other person even when we are in opposing positions, even when all that we value is at stake. This is one essence of what nonviolence means.

Everything else follows from this principle. I am reminded of a Talmudic story about a pagan man who came to Hillel, one of the famous rabbis, and asked Hillel to teach him the Torah while standing on one foot[15], a way of asking him to summarize it extremely briefly. Hillel is reputed to have said: "What is hateful to yourself, do not do to your fellow man. That is the whole Torah; the rest is just commentary. Go and study it." Similarly both Gandhian nonviolence and the practice of NVC are, in some ways, elaborations on this one key principle: whatever the circumstances, no matter what else is going on, we are committed to caring for the well-being of all.

The practice of NVC, my own path, gives specific form to this commitment. We apply our hearts, focus our consciousness, and bring active attention to transcending and transforming fear and judgment. We excavate underneath our habits to understand our needs, so we can know what longings, dreams, and values inform our reaction to another. This allows us to reach for and maintain an open heart to the needs of another. When we hear others with full empathic presence, their core, irreducible humanity shines forth. I think of this quality of practical open-heartedness, of caring for the well-being of someone regardless of her or his actions, as an essential ingredient of the love I want to live in the world.

---

[15] This reference to "standing on one foot" is a manner of speech designed to show how quick the teaching had to be.

As I am writing this, and listening to music that breaks my heart open, I am filled with grief to recognize that this kind of love is, indeed, going against the grain. Within the dominant culture love often gets tamed, privatized, and circumscribed. This love, the essential love of nonviolence, breaks all barriers between people, goes directly against separation, and equalizes everyone.

I also believe this capacity for loving is at the heart of what's needed for the kind of world transformation that I am so passionately drawn to. I describe this vision in vivid detail in the last part of this book. For now, I continue to use the phrase coined by Shariff Abdullah that has captivated so many of us: a world that works for all. I am writing this book, in large part, as an invitation to everyone who reads it to engage with this vision and to embrace the power to create that world.

As I already said more than once, I am essentially humbled by the prospect and limited in my answers about what it would take to get to this vision. I think we all are. I don't believe that it's possible to "plan" change, though I do think it's possible to create the infrastructure and relationships and strategic thinking that can be ready for the opportunities. I will have more to say about that in a later section of this book. For now I want to tie it back to love, because I have a deep intuitive sense that love is absolutely necessary to create the shift.

To make sense of what I am trying to grapple with, it helps me to think about what it takes to transform an individual relationship. It's clear to me that when both people are committed to honoring their needs within a relationship, and both have the skills for translating their commitment into practical steps, then it takes half the skill and half the love from each of them. I tend to believe that almost all of us are born with sufficient automatic inner resources to participate in this game if everybody else were to participate in it. Almost all of us have enough love and enough skill under such circumstances. By extension, then, I would imagine that almost all of us could care about our own and others' needs if others did, too.

If, however, only one party to a relationship is committed to the vision of everyone's needs mattering, it takes double the love and double the skill because they have to compensate for the fact that the other person is not bringing that much love and skill into it. It's not undoable; it's just that much harder. Being in such a relationship means we would have to do the loving for both parties. We would have to do the skills for both parties. And that requires more love and more skill than if it were mutual because of having to bring in additional love to support the other person's mistrust. Most of us don't have it.

And that is, in sweeping generalizations, the situation into which almost all of us were born. We came into a world where most people are not framing the conflicts between them as dilemmas they are holding together. In those conditions it takes exceptional skill and capacity and love and resilience to try to live the love and the skill in a world that doesn't.

This is, for me, the dilemma of world transformation: Can we find and cultivate enough love and skill to do the work, to do the loving towards and on behalf of those who don't have access to their love? Can a sufficient number of us develop enough capacity and resilience and skills to stand tall in the midst of mistrust, judgment, and even violence from others and maintain our stance of love?

I have faith in that. It's definitely tough. I still have faith.

I see more and more people drawn to becoming agents of love in the world without any sense of fairness, without any sense of what's right and what's wrong, without attachment to outcome, and with full passion and conviction about what we are aiming for.[16] Instead, our love can be motivated by a sense of being so privileged and blessed to have been given the gift of consciousness, and by wanting to share the gift with others, to fill in the holes and the voids of love until other people can do it for themselves – and all this without giving up on ourselves.

That last point is key to me. A love that is at the expense of ourselves is not true love. When we open up to a love so big we can be tempted to give up on others. We can think: "This other person can't hold the love, and this means I'm just going to give them what they want." We can get into an endless cycle of empathizing with

---

[16] Because Gandhi himself *did* use words such as "battle" and "right" and "evil," I feel called to detour a bit and elaborate. I can only rely on my own deep intuitive sense here, although my intuition is also informed by some reading of and about Gandhi. My own sense is that this apparent divergence stems from two sources. One is that in the context of what he was doing, which was visible and public campaigns, where every word he used was designed to contribute to his efforts, it was of paramount importance to be understood easily by others. The other is that, perhaps, the frame of nonviolence that was put together by Marshall Rosenberg, which relies on a true absence of judgment outside of an evaluation of needs attended to, was simply not available to him as a resource. Despite his language, I am quite confident that he would take no issue with anything I am saying here in terms of what nonviolence means, especially in the context of everyday living.

others, hearing them, attending to their needs, and becoming depleted and resentful. I don't see that as true love. For me, true love includes respecting the other person sufficiently to trust that somewhere in them is the capacity to love back, and inviting that love in our direction when the moment is right, no matter how far gone the other person is. Inviting other people to open up, to hear us, to rise to the occasion is every bit as important as hearing them and supporting them. Every time we give up on another person and say they can't do it we compromise the love because in the loving, I want to love the person into their best being.

I know that I'm making a really tall order. I just don't want to compromise on the vision of what's possible. I want us to be completely tender and self-accepting for wherever we are in terms of our own skill and capacity without thereby thinking that nothing can be done more than what I am able to do now. I want to accept myself where I am, and keep my heart and longing open to grow more and more towards taking on more and more of the loving. Until there is enough to turn things around.

Nonviolence as Courage

The history of nonviolence is replete with examples of people willing to endure extreme consequences to live in line with their values. The Gandhian tradition, in particular, includes the willingness to face death in order to maintain the intention and experience of pure nonviolence even when resisting a power structure that has no compunction about using violence.

"Just as one must learn the art of killing in the training for violence, so one must learn the art of dying in the training for non-violence. Violence does not mean emancipation from fear, but discovering the means of combating the cause of fear. Non-violence, on the other hand, has no cause for fear... He who has not overcome all fear cannot practice ahimsa." (Kripalani, *All Men Are Brothers*, p. 104)

"I must obey, even at the cost of my life, the law of love." (Gandhi, *Golden Treasury of Wisdom*, p. 34)

"He/she should not do that which he/she knows to be wrong, and suffer the consequence whatever it may be, this is the key to the use of soul-force." (Gandhi, *Hind Swaraj*, p. 69)

When we look deeper, we see that it is our internal response to the consequences, namely our fear, which stops us from acting on our full truth at all times. I doubt that Gandhi meant to imply that one would have to *feel* no fear. I rather believe the focus is on the willingness to *overcome* the fear. What fuels courage, if we read Gandhi's quotes carefully, is the conviction of truth and integrity, coupled with the abiding trust in love's power. The intensity of love and commitment serves as a form of fire that burns through the perceived danger. This love is not dependent on the behavior of other people. This love continues even in the extreme of enduring violence against self.

Fear itself doesn't go away as the practice of nonviolence deepens. What changes is the ability to bear it and still choose love and courage. With enough practice and commitment, acting based on fear becomes less and less of a draw.

Indeed, Gandhi, who ceaselessly attempted to live the principles of his teaching, time and again walked directly into potential harm's way to carry out his plans. During the civil war that broke out towards the end of the independence campaign between Hindus and Muslims, for example, Gandhi (in his 70s) walked through the most dangerous and violent zones (Bihar state and Noakhali) to "live the truth he went to teach" (*Gandhi the Man*, p. 90).

> "It is not at all impossible that we may have to endure every hardship that we can imagine, and wisdom lies in pledging ourselves on the understanding that we shall have to suffer all that and worse." (*Gandhi the Man*, p. 99)

The practice of NVC applies the principles of nonviolence primarily to relationships and to dialogue. Most people who practice NVC rarely apply it in circumstances where danger to life may be present, although increasing numbers are doing so successfully. Whether or not physical danger is present, practicing NVC invites us to profound emotional vulnerability. It is our emotional self that might be "injured" or "die" as we open ourselves to truth and love in our interactions with ourselves and other humans.

For many, these interactions become a stimulus for intense fear that is *experienced* as a threat to survival. For example, in the context of everyday living, when someone judges us harshly, the threat to our physical survival is highly unlikely. And yet we often rally to defend ourselves as if our survival were at stake. It takes a great deal of practice to remain open and calm and even loving and curious in the face of criticism, blame, or judgment. This practice is what prepares us for the kind of uncompromising love that nonviolence expresses.

At the same time, the practice of opening up to whatever comes our way has an unexpected benefit. As we engage with it, we learn that in fact our emotional self is *not* in any danger. Our soul, our human essence, the truth of who we are, are regularly strengthened by stretching into this vulnerability.

Seeing Others' Humanity

One translation of the word *ahimsa* refers to it as "the state of the heart which has no enemies." And, indeed, Gandhi worked tirelessly to maintain respectful, open, trusting relationships with everyone, regardless of how much he opposed the position, policies, and actions of whoever he was in struggle with. He was uncompromising in this commitment. Here's the way one of his students described the regard Gandhi always held for his opponents: "It was not forgiveness, but whole-hearted acceptance by him of their standpoint as *their* truth which for the time being held the same place in their growth as his truth in his own, and thus entitled to equal respect" (Nayar, *In Gandhiji's Mirror*, p. 10).

As an extreme example, both of Gandhi's letters to Hitler were addressed to "my friend." In the second one, Gandhi starts by saying:

> "Dear Friend, that I address you as a friend is no formality. I own no foes. My business in life has been for the past 33 years to enlist the friendship of the whole of humanity by befriending mankind irrespective of race, colour or creed." (Letter in Mani Bhavan Museum, Mumbai)

Gandhi took explicit pleasure in maintaining this stance towards and with others:

> "It is to me a matter of perennial satisfaction that I retain generally the affection and trust of those whose principles and policies I oppose. In spite of my denunciation of British policy, I enjoy the affection of thousands of Englishmen. It is a triumph of non-violence." (Meghani, ed., *Everyman's A, B, C ... of Gandhi.* June 19 – The Mind of Mahatma Gandhi)

Respectful consideration of opponents, an honoring of their humanity and their value, is a key element of nonviolence, not an accidental by-product. Gandhi expressed this value early on, and included it in his vision of society. Here's just one example:

"Let us honour our opponents for the same honesty of purpose and patriotic motives that we claim for ourselves." (Meghani, *Everyman's*, July 10 – Selections from Gandhi)

The practice of NVC follows in Gandhi's footsteps and provides practical steps for *cultivating* this capacity to see the humanity of each person. The practice is grounded in understanding everyone and every action, belief, and choice in terms of fundamental, core, human needs that are shared by everyone. No matter what action someone takes, there is a human need at the heart of the choice – a dream, a vision, which could be universally understood and usually shared.

The practice of NVC takes a step beyond distinguishing between the action and the person. To see the full humanity of others, we also distinguish between the action and the shared human needs underlying the action. To return to the extreme example, even Hitler had a vision he was working towards and that he articulated. What could his needs have been? I imagine a major element may have been something along the lines of the purity, elegance, and clarity that come from being with people similar to us. This image can strike a chord in many if not most of us. I can easily see, and often experience, that being only with people similar to us is one strategy for the human needs to belong, to have ease in relating, and to have a sense of meaning and connection. Seeing this, I can resonate with Hitler's underlying needs, and thus make *human* sense of Hitler despite of and independent of his actions.[17]

No matter how abhorrent others' actions can be for us, Gandhi urged us to see and connect with their fundamental humanity. In the NVC practice, we do this by reaching for and connecting with their underlying needs, even when we see immense harm done. This does not mean condoning the action – it only means moving beyond right and wrong characterizations into taking full ownership of the values in the name of which we deem the action harmful, recognizing it's our own perspective, without resorting to an implicit external source

---

[17] The issue of why acting on these needs would take the form of such unimaginable actions is covered in more detail in *Spinning Threads of Radical Aliveness*, in the section called "Whence Violence," where I discuss the exploration of the roots of violence given in James Gilligan's book *Violence: Our Deadly Epidemic and Its Causes*. Gilligan discusses, in particular, the role of shame in generating violence and cruelty.

of authority.[18] One of the core practices that serious NVC practitioners employ on a regular basis is what is known as *Transforming Enemy Images*. I offer an example of this practice here to support those who want a deeper understanding of what studying NVC may entail.

Practice: Transforming Judgments and Enemy Images

KEYS:

a.   Judging someone is an indication that a need of ours is not met. The first step in transforming judgments is to recognize and connect with our unmet needs.

b.   The action we're judging is itself an attempt to meet needs. The second step is connecting with the needs of the person we're judging so we can open our hearts with compassion.

c.   When we experience challenge in transforming our judgments, we can reflect on what needs we might be trying to meet by holding on to our judgments. Connecting with this set of needs may be essential to enable the previous two steps to proceed.

1.   Write down a judgment you have of someone else that you would like to explore. This may be something you think about that person that you completely believe is true. You may pick someone in your personal life, or someone who is in some position of political or economic power whose actions affect you.

2.   Think of a time or situation when you are likely to have this judgment come up, and write an observation of what this person is actually saying or doing at that time.

3.   What needs of yours are not met in relation to that person's action? How do you feel when these needs are not met? Explore this sufficiently to experience the relief of self-connection

---

[18] It is my sad belief that resorting to external sources of authority – God, cultural norms and "shoulds," or people in authority – is more likely to lead to war and suffering than the act of taking responsibility for our assessments and evaluations of others by connecting them to our own needs and values.

4. Explore the possibility of opening your heart to this other person. What needs do you imagine this person might be trying to meet by taking this action? How might this person be feeling? Explore this sufficiently to experience the relief of compassion.

5. Check in with yourself about your original judgment. Is it still alive? If yes, return to connecting with your own needs or with the other person's needs – wherever you're experiencing a "charge." If the judgment is still alive after that, consider: What needs might you be trying to meet by holding on to this judgment? What feelings arise in relation to this? Again, connect with yourself sufficiently about these needs to experience some relief.

6. Check in with yourself again about the judgment. If it's still alive, consider the following set of questions:

   a. Is there any way in which you believe the judgment to be "the truth"? If so, explore what needs might be met by this belief, and what needs might be met by letting go of this belief.

   b. Are you afraid to express this judgment? If yes, what needs are you afraid would not be met by sharing it, and what needs might be met?

   c. Are you judging yourself for having this judgment? If yes, explore any way in which you're telling yourself that you should not have this judgment. Connect with your choice about whether or not to work any further on transforming this judgment, and explore any needs that might be met by continuing to work on transforming the judgment, or letting go of working on it.

   d. Reflect on your feelings, needs, and any requests you have of yourself or of the other person in this moment.

Appealing to Others' Humanity

When we see others as evil, unable to care, or in some fundamental way immune to transformation, then, if they can't be ignored, the only available strategy is to overpower and vanquish them. A Gandhian approach that upholds the humanity of our "enemies" leads to other strategies to create change. When opponents, even oppressors, are seen as humans possessing care, dignity, and a heart that can be reached, then it becomes logical to speak to their humanity. This direct approach is often more effective in transforming the situation. In Gandhi's own words:

> "Nonviolence in us ought to soften our opponent, it ought to strike a responsive chord in his heart." (*Everyman's*, August 20 – Harijan: May 13, 1939)

Gandhi's life and work provide some astonishing examples to illustrate this radical concept. Gandhi's great first "experiment with truth" was designed to recover the dignity of the Indian community of South Africa. His chief "enemy" (his word) at the time was General Jan Christian Smuts, head of the South African government in the Transvaal. Here's an account of an early confrontation with Smuts:

> "Gandhi goes to the head of the Transvaal government General Smuts and says: 'I've come to tell you that I am going to fight against your government'. Smuts responds: 'Anything more?' Gandhi: 'I am going to win'. Smuts, laughing: 'How?' Gandhi: 'With your help.' (*Gandhi the Man*, p. 47)

Smuts' secretary provides a rare testimonial about what it feels like to be offered *Satyagraha* by committed, well-trained activists:

> "I don't like your people, and do not care to assist them at all. But what am I to do? You help us in our days of need. How can we lay hands upon you? I often wish that you took to violence like the English strikers, and then we would know at once how to dispose of you. But you will not injure even the enemy. You desire victory by self-suffering alone... and that is what reduces

us to sheer helplessness". (Nagler, *Search for a Nonviolent Future*, p. 64)

As a result of years of such encounters, Jan Christian Smuts himself experienced a complete transformation. As Gandhi said:

> "In a non-violent conflict there is no rancour left behind, and in the end the enemies are converted into friends. That was my experience in South Africa with General Smuts. He started with being my bitterest opponent. Today he is my warmest friend." (*Everyman's*, May 16, "The Mind of Mahatma Gandhi")

Smuts also attested to this shift. Eventually he came to believe that he was "not worthy to stand in the shoes of so great a man" as Gandhi (Radhakrishnan, *Mahatma Gandhi: essays and reflections on his life and work*, p. 226).

A particularly striking example of Gandhi's commitment to seeing everyone's humanity took place in the late 1930s. Gandhi was at a meeting to pressure the local Maharaja to democratize in Rajkot. Thugs came and started beating up the participants. After a short while, Gandhi, who was trembling with revulsion and determination, told all his followers to go home and leave him alone with the thugs. The thugs were completely won over and offered to escort him back to the ashram (Shukla, *Incidents in Gandhi's Life*, pp. 99-101).

British historian Arnold Toynbee summarized the effect of years of *satyagraha*: "Gandhi made it impossible for us to continue ruling India, but at the same time, he made it possible for us to abdicate without rancour and without dishonour" (*Search for a Nonviolent Future*. p. 189).

Similarly, the history of nonviolent movements in the United States contains many moving stories of demonstrators creating powerful human connection with police officers and changing the dynamics of tense moments as a result. Here's one example:

> We went to the Nevada Test Site in 1982 to draw attention to underground nuclear testing. During the season of Lent, we were there daily, standing along the road as the workers drove by us in buses and cars. Each day we spoke to the sheriffs from Nye County and the Wakenhutt Security officers who were there

because we were there. Any idea of "them" and "us" broke down over those days of human connection. At the end of the 40 days of witness, 19 of us committed civil disobedience – walking past the boundaries created for us. Jim Merlino, the head sheriff, instructed his officers as they were arresting us to "treat us like we were his children." Each year we went back during Lent and at other times too. We became friends with several of the officers. We greeted each other with hugs and asked about each other's lives. We always talked to them about what we were doing and why we were there too, and respectfully agreed to disagree. When Terry and I got married in 1986, we invited Jim Merlino to the wedding. He was not able to attend but sent us a gift. He has long since retired, but I still am occasionally in touch with him. To this day, our organization – Nevada Desert Experience – has an exceptional relationship with the security forces at the Nevada Test Site.

– Anne Symens-Bucher, NDE co-founder

Moving from the arena of social change to the challenges of everyday living, the practice of NVC calls on us to remember, even in the midst of intense conflict, that others are more like us than we imagine some of the time. For example, when someone says "no" to a request of ours, we can transcend the habit of believing this means they don't care about us. Nonviolence becomes challenging precisely when people don't do what we want. In those moments we can extend care to others through recognizing and appreciating the needs that wouldn't be met for them if they did what we want. If there's any way that another person will come to *want* to give us what we ask for, it is much more likely to happen through providing the relief of acceptance and care to them, which softens the heart and can create possibilities where none seemed available. Instead of forcing our way or giving up, the practice of NVC entails dialogue that connects with both parties' needs and generates mutual goodwill.[19]

---

[19] In the case of nonviolent resistance, the question of use of force and its consequences and intentions becomes more complex, and I return to this point at "Combining Love with Force: The Power of Nonviolent Resistance" page 197.

Solutions that Work for Everyone

On the one hand (symbolized by a hand firmly stretched out and signaling, "Stop!") I will not cooperate with your violence or injustice; I will resist it with every fiber of my being. And, on the other hand (symbolized by the hand with its palm turned open and stretched toward the other) I am open to you as a human being.

– Ken Butigan

One of Gandhi's core methods was noncooperation. Although noncooperation may appear on the surface as adversarial, Gandhi always maintained that "my noncooperation has its roots not in hatred but in love." (*Gandhi the Man*, p. 56). It was not intended to be at cost to the people he challenged, which is the essence of an adversarial relationship. He was deeply rooted in the Hindu tradition, which holds that all people are one. How did he resolve the apparent contradiction? Even though the British were resisting his efforts, he never wavered in his conviction that what the British were doing in India was not to their benefit. In that way, fighting against their rule was not adversarial *even if it involved force* and even though, by necessity, the British experienced immense discomfort and loss of power.

"We will not submit to this injustice – not merely because it is destroying us but because it is destroying you as well." (*Gandhi the Man*, p. 74)

Gandhi maintained that both the goal of his campaigns and the method of working towards them were to contribute to everyone's benefit.

"Satyagraha is an all-sided sword... it blesses him who uses it and him against whom it is used." (*Hind Swaraj*, p. 74)

"I do not seek to harm [the British]. I want to serve them even as I want to serve my own. I believe that I have always served them. I served them up to 1919 blindly. But when my eyes were opened and I conceived non-cooperation, the object still was to serve them." (*Young India*, Dec 3rd, 1930)

Gandhi especially insisted that the terms of eventual agreement would need to consider the position of others, so that they are livable. Indeed, when the terms of surrender are too restrictive (such as in the case of the WWI Versailles agreements), the level of resentment and powerlessness experienced by the losing side is such that they are likely to erupt later. (Hitler's rise has been in part explained by this national experience of humiliation.)

"A Satyagrahi never yields to panic or hesitancy, neither does she/he think of humiliating the other party, or reducing it to an abject surrender. She/he may not swerve from the path of justice and may not dictate impossible terms. She/he may not pitch them too low." (*Young India,* Mar 19th, 1931)

Embracing the dialogue practice of NVC means that in every situation we consider the needs and well-being of others, even in times of conflict, and strive to reach solutions that maintain everyone's dignity. Even when wanting something with great passion, the deep practice of NVC entails an active unwillingness to accept a solution that would be at the expense of others, including and especially when the protective use of force is introduced as a last resort.[20]

---

[20] See the part "When Dialogue Breaks Down" on page 199

From Opposition to Vision

One of the key aspects of Gandhi's noncooperation was that the campaigns regularly went beyond protest and included an element of what Shariff Abdullah has called "vision implementation" (personal communication, 2003) – the actions themselves prefigure the outcome desired. One clear example is the 1930 Salt March. In response to a law forbidding Indians to make their own salt, Gandhi led a march to the sea to claim the free salt. This wasn't a boycott; it was a clear focus on self-sufficiency and independence, with a strong message of removing the legitimacy of British rule (*Gandhi the Man*, p. 70).

Another example is from the Civil Rights Movement, which was profoundly inspired by Gandhi's example. The young activists went beyond challenging segregation symbolically, for example, by holding placards outside restaurants. In choosing to enter and sit at lunch counters together across racial divisions, they implemented their vision of a world in which racial barriers are removed.

Noncooperation in the form of civil disobedience was only one component of Gandhi's scheme. He saw the struggle for independence as made up of both what Gandhi scholar Michael Nagler calls "Obstructive Program" and a detailed Constructive Program. The role of Obstructive Program was to interfere with the British rulers' ability to carry out their control of the nation. The role of Constructive Program was to create the material and social infrastructure that would provide the foundation for the future society.

Gandhi's program had eighteen elements in it, including abolishing untouchability, establishing gender equality, what he called "village uplift," and achieving economic equality. At its heart was the freeing of India from the imposed economic dependence on the British through the means of re-learning the ancient arts of spinning and weaving cotton. In some ways Gandhi saw this aspect of the program as the most essential. When asked in 1940 "What will it really take to get the British off our backs?" his response was: "Phenomenal progress in spinning" (*Search for a Nonviolent Future*, p. 177). He saw "Constructive programme [as] a Solar System and the charkha [spinning wheel] [as] the Sun" (*Search for a Nonviolent Future*, p. 183).

To my knowledge, a coherent constructive program has not emerged for current nonviolent social movements that identify as such, and their work is primarily focused on obstruction, with a more narrow focus on protest than Gandhi or Martin Luther King, Jr. applied to their work. There are hundreds of movements, communities, groups, and individuals who are participating in creating an alternative future through multiple actions such as different forms of education, providing free health care, permaculture and other forms of sustainable food growing, alternative energy, climate change work, and many, many others. At present, I don't see any of these as forming a coherent, self-aware constructive program rather than a collection of uncoordinated actions. Specifically, one key element that is missing for a constructive program is a core activity with a role similar to that of spinning in Gandhi's days. That role is threefold: an activity that produces concrete material results, that is essential for creating the future, and that *anyone* can undertake.[21]

This principle of nonviolence – the focus on what we want to create, not just what we oppose – is not as widely known as others despite being so foundational to Gandhi's way of thinking and acting.

This principle is also fundamental to the practice of NVC. If others' actions – individuals, groups, or institutions – are to our liking, we can move towards what we want by waking up to celebration and gratitude. At all times, we can move towards what we want by initiating and sustaining actions and projects grounded in our deepest vision. Then we are more prepared to maintain our nonviolence by remembering and staying grounded in what we want when people are doing things we don't like. Knowing what we are working towards allows us to bring all the love we have to our actions and act with care for others' well-being.

Just as much as a constructive program is often absent from social change movements, more often than not in daily life we focus on trying to stop or move away from what's not working rather than reflecting and connecting with ourselves sufficiently to know what is important to us, what we really want, and move towards it by engaging the other party in dialogue.

Indeed, perhaps the heart of the practice of NVC revolves around understanding our needs, being able to get to sufficient

---

[21] More on Constructive Program on pages 220-2.

connection with ourselves to know what matters to us on the most fundamental human level. Once we know the needs, we can then consider what strategies can help meet those needs, and make requests of others to increase the chances of having our needs met. It is through understanding the needs that we move from opposing others or giving up to engaging in dialogue towards creating mutually beneficial solutions.

Nonviolence Begins with Inner Practice

As big and ambitious as Gandhi's campaigns were, he regularly reminded everyone of the very individual nature of his practice. He wrote extensively about his own personal journey being integral to his work, and likened nonviolence to a search for truth, starting from the inside out.

"What I want to achieve – what I have been striving and pining to achieve these thirty years – is self-realization." (Kripalani, *Gandhi's life in his own words*, p. 1)

"The very first step in non-violence is that we cultivate in our daily life, as between ourselves, truthfulness, humility, tolerance, loving kindness." (*Golden Treasury*, p. 41)

Gandhi saw at least three intertwined reasons for the centrality of a personal practice: increasing strength and effectiveness, cultivating acceptance, and finding meaning. As he saw it, the strength and confidence necessary to maintain a loving presence in the face of opposition, oppression, and ridicule could only come from an exacting inner practice.

"Love and *ahimsa...* presuppose self-confidence which in its turn presupposes self-purification." (*Young India* 18-02-1926, *Non Violent Resistance*, p. 345)

Inner practice in the form of a great deal of honesty and humility also served as the reference point for sustaining his commitment to non-judgment.

"It is not for us to sit in judgment over anyone, so long as we notice a single fault in ourselves and wish our friends not to forsake us in spite of such fault. Being myself full of blemishes, and therefore in need of charity of fellow beings, I have learnt not to judge anyone harshly, and to make allowance for defects that I might detect." (*Harijan*, 11-3-1939, p. 47)

The practice of nonviolence also provided Gandhi with unexpected gifts in terms of his own well-being. Gandhi believed in nonviolence for its own sake, whether or not the desired results could be attained. The depth at which he practiced opened up avenues for inner peace and wonder that no doubt sustained him in times of great anguish at the pace of his campaign and at the conflicts within his movement.

> "Whatever may be the result, there is always in me conscious struggle for following the law of nonviolence deliberately and ceaselessly. Such struggle leaves one stronger for it. The more I work at this law, the more I feel the delight in my life, the delight in the scheme of the universe. It gives me a peace and a meaning of the mysteries of nature that I have no power to describe." (*Search for a Nonviolent Future*, p. 101)

Here, again, the practice of NVC follows in the footsteps of Gandhi's own practice. I have already alluded to how essential it is, for practicing NVC, to know intimately our inner landscape and recognize what we need. As simple as this may sound, it can be enormously challenging in moments when we are unhappy with others' or our own actions.

I want to illustrate this with two specific aspects of NVC. The first is about learning to live with and tolerate the experience of unmet needs without getting so agitated that we jump to action. Nonviolence is born of inner peace. If we are out of balance, we are much more likely to be reactive and unable to maintain the strength and clarity necessary for the love and openness that are such a hallmark of nonviolence. This particular aspect of the practice calls for developing a level of non-attachment by remaining in close connection with the needs without focusing on the strategies to get the needs met. In addition to inner peace this practice supports self-connection and creativity in finding alternate strategies for the unmet needs.

The second aspect of the practice of NVC I want to highlight is working on self-acceptance. Just as Gandhi recognized that being honest about his own flaws could be a way to develop compassion for others, so practicing NVC supports non-judgment of others by recognizing and connecting with the needs that lead to any action or thought we don't like in ourselves. Shifting focus from judgment to needs in regard to ourselves increases the chances we may do the same with others. Moreover, the specific focus on needs increases our capacity to see and hear needs, in anyone, even when they are not expressed directly, which for most people is almost all the time. Connecting with needs, our own and others', is surprisingly effective at increasing acceptance and a sense of continuity of humanity between us and others whose actions may be very different from our own.

Expanding Beyond Our Personal Lives

At a certain point in learning and practicing NVC, many people develop a growing interest in the welfare of people and creatures beyond their own personal lives and those of the people nearest them.

Since we don't always know what can create change, and cannot predict what individual actions that we engage in could potentially lead to social change, especially large-scale systemic change, the question often arises about how far the role of personal change extends. Here's how one of my blog readers expressed this challenge: "I don't have the clarity I would like about your distinction between personal growth and social change work. Particularly within the Nonviolent Communication (NVC) framework, where we intend to create change without coercion. We can model the values we want to see; we can invite, request, even try to persuade or instruct when the occasion seems appropriate, but we're not forcing change on anyone. And so a big part of the force for social change that I am imagining comes from being the change that you want to see in the world, which to me sounds like personal development."

This question leads in two directions. This segment of the book addresses one of them: Is "being the change" all that is needed to create social change? I take up the other question, the one that relates to the potential use of force in aiming for a world that works for all, in a future segment (pages 199-208).

Is "Being the Change" Enough?

Organizations, governments, and other social structures are fundamentally based on a set of agreements, almost invariably implicit, to which individuals give their consent, usually unconscious of having done so. In that sense I can imagine the possibility that if enough individuals undergo a personal transformation that wakes them up to their participation in current systems and to the possibilities of having different social arrangements, the result can be structural and systemic transformation. Nonetheless, I have serious concerns about this approach.

My first concern is about numbers. My guess is that in order to create change at the systemic level, "enough" would be millions acting in concert. There are, already, many, many millions of people who are aware of policies, actions, and ways of operating that are damaging life on our planet. Even with their known opposition to significant actions taken by governments and corporations, they have not been able to create significant changes. Cumulative individual actions are not the same as orchestrated collective actions. Even individuals choosing non-cooperation don't make a dent in the systems. It's simply too small. I engage in such actions on a daily basis. Others go further than me and actively and publicly break laws, and still the change doesn't happen.

My second concern is that it is often only people of a certain kind of privilege that have the luxury of dedicating resources to creating personal change. Moreover, such work can inadvertently serve to perpetuate social inequality and privilege. For as long as those who promise us, say, a way to find and live out our true gifts don't, at the same time, have a plan for who will collect the garbage and how that will happen, the result can only be that some people will be barred from access to a meaningful life because someone will need to collect the garbage. Instead, what I want is for us to be able to create systems and structures that work for all people and all life all over the world. For that, I am confident that we need to find ways of operating on all levels at once.

Taking on Larger Structures

My third concern is by far the largest, and I have found it to be challenging for many in the individualized culture of North America to grapple with. Simply put, I see a profound difference between creating personal changes in each of our lives, even in large numbers, and actively taking on the systems that constrain and shape our options, circumstances, and even beliefs. In order to create change at the systemic/structural level, I believe in the essential necessity of thinking and acting on that level.

A full analysis of the role that structures larger than us play in our lives would take me far outside the scope of this current project. Instead, I want to use two examples as cursory illustrations.

As an example, our current economy is based on exchange, competition, and profit. While unusually sturdy individuals find ways of existing outside the money economy (through activities ranging from dumpster diving to living on gifts alone), in general the option of living without exchange is not practical on a large scale. Living within our current economic system clearly affects what choices we make about how to feed and clothe and shelter our bodies, as well as attend to our emotional and social needs. Our economic system also affects our beliefs about people and about what kind of human life is possible. For example, we are less likely to think of people as generous when everything is done as an exchange and when we don't see generosity modeled and practiced on a regular basis. We are also less likely to imagine that anything would get done if a monetary incentive for doing it doesn't exist. We are also less likely to even know that other economic models exist and have existed over human history, or even imagine them as possible.

Similarly, most justice systems in the world are retributive: people are punished for what they have done. Such systems instill and reinforce the notion that when harm is done what's most important is to find out who's at fault and punish them. Restorative justice, the other major form of justice, has existed in many indigenous cultures, and is being reintroduced in many communities around the world. The foundation of restorative justice rests on the notion that when harm is done what's most important is to repair the harm as far as possible and restore the community from the loss of trust that ensues when harm is inflicted. Different models of restorative justice vary in terms of who is involved in sorting through the events, reaching full understanding and responsibility, and coming up with a plan of action to restore the relationships. In some models, the entire community, everyone who is affected, sits at the table to connect and work things out.

An individual, even a community, that wants to handle conflicts in a restorative framework has no avenues for doing so except in rare circumstances, or where pockets of restorative justice systems have been created. This may be even harder to achieve than an individual or community living out a needs-based economics in a sea of money-based transactions.

What Changes Can We Make?

Short of radically transforming the entire structures of the world, what can we actually do in the world that might affect those systems in a direct way, thereby improving lives and our collective chances of surviving these times?

This dilemma is far from trivial. The vision of transformation I have, that some of us have, goes far beyond laws and states. To achieve this vision, the entire apparatus of how the global social order operates would need to be questioned. Capitalism and state communism, the two options we currently know, have failed to create a world that works for all, or even the majority.[22] The world I envision and which I describe later in this book has only a minuscule legal code, and operates through a globally coordinated gift economy.

The gap is so vast that sometimes I do get bouts of extreme despair about how any steps we can make now could be useful change towards that global system change. Nonetheless, I see, for example, that different laws have different effects, and make the lives of many people more livable, allowing for a modicum more dignity or participation. While I continue to maintain the faith that in the end we can transcend the entire paradigm within which we currently operate, I know that many shades of gray exist, and we can move, incrementally, closer to a tipping point. This leads me to accept and embrace the value of creating campaigns to change laws and to achieve specific goals, even if such campaigns do not change the foundations of the social order.

---

[22] Social democracy European-style has fared better than either US-style capitalism or Communism under conditions of stable and growing economies. At present, the systems are being strained under conditions of economic contraction.

Here are a few random examples of what grappling directly with social structures can look like. All of them are real possibilities; some of them are currently being attempted; and some of them have been done and succeeded.

On a Large Scale:

Legislative Change – If not for massive campaigns to create legal changes, women would still not have the vote and slavery would still exist. Currently, for example, a movement exists aiming to change the judicial rulings that have made corporations into people. Such changes are huge for those whose lives they save or transform, even if they are small relative to the vision of what's possible.

Changing Corporate Policies – Throughout the last many decades (and even before), many campaigns have taken on large corporations, and some have been successful. In the 1980s, for example, a concerted effort was put together to create a ban on General Electric, with the successful result of GE stopping their engagement with nuclear production. Several of the campaigns that Greenpeace has mounted over the years have been successful. Vandana Shiva has organized large numbers of farmers in India as well as engaged in legal activities, and has successfully stopped Monsanto from creating patents from certain traditional plants that had been part of the commons for centuries. Given the immense influence that large corporations exert in the world, and the amount of resources available to them to counter any such campaign, I consider getting them to do anything different from their habitual practices a huge accomplishment.

Changing International Agreements – In 1999 protestors staged massive demonstrations, almost entirely nonviolent, which effectively halted the proceedings of the WTO meetings. Although they had only a modicum of success in their goals, their action was focused on a system that exerts unimaginable power in the world that affects the lives of billions.

Regime Changes – In the last few decades, there has been a growth in movements that toppled dictatorial or oppressive regimes successfully using nonviolent methods, ranging from some of the countries in Eastern Europe to South Africa.

On a Smaller Scale:

Although the mainstream media do not usually report on successful local campaigns that create change, the information is widely available, both of successful and unsuccessful attempts. Here are a few examples of such efforts to create change:

Legal: Winning approval for community gardens where they were prohibited (such as in some places in New York City); creating local nuclear-free zones; and a host of others.

Corporate: Local campaigns that have successfully prevented corporations such as Walmart or McDonalds from setting up stores in some locales.

Negotiations: In some areas in the northwest local organizations succeeded in bringing together loggers, environmental activists, and companies to work out collaborative agreements for how to handle certain forests.

In sum, in order to create change on a level beyond our personal lives, I don't see a way other than working with others to transform organizations and systems directly, and to do so in a way that minimizes the risk of getting lost in our internalized version of the very thing we are trying to change.

The questions are deep and complex. The coming sections of the book attend to the challenges that arise as we form groups, communities, organizations, and large scale systems. For the remainder of this section, I explore what I see as the aspects of inner and interpersonal dimensions of nonviolence that take us beyond everyday life and into the kinds of challenges that arise as we aim to transform the world.

The Inner Work of Nonviolent Social Change

Even though "being the change" is not enough, I see it as absolutely indispensable. Without it we do our work in the world with an internalized version of the very structures we are wishing to change. Even if we succeed in "overthrowing" whatever structures are currently there, we are unlikely to create anything that's fundamentally different from what we encounter. For example, if we want to create a world where everyone's needs matter and internally we continue to experience separation and polarization, we will bring this separation into our work and whatever new structures we create will be infused with it.

Because there is so much that needs to be changed on the outside, there is all of that to be changed inside us. This work is not instead of or before working in the world. I see it as continuing to feed our work in the world. It will equally be fed by it.

What changes when we take on doing social change work is the nature of the circumstances within which we operate. The work itself is remarkably similar to what we do in everyday life. Our goal can only be managing to maintain our commitment to nonviolence even in the difficult circumstances of campaigns designed to create change, where the risks are literal and physical. Accepting the call to principled nonviolence and applying it when we are part of a movement for social transformation extends beyond our daily relationships with other people and invites us to a deeper look at the places where we need to transform our consciousness and liberate it from the legacy of separation, scarcity, and powerlessness that have been the mainstay in our world for several millennia. This transformation requires considerable commitment, courage, and love.

Grounding in Vision

In the face of rampant cynicism, despair, and materialism, how can we remain strong in our conviction about the possibility of creating a world based on love, generosity, ecological sensitivity, kindness, peace, and honoring all human beings and life?

I am reminded of a story that my mother told me many years ago. In the story a man comes every day to the plaza at the center of town, stands in the same place, and tells stories. He is all alone, there is no audience, and he does it day in and day out. One day a small child comes to him and asks him why he continues to tell his stories given that no one comes. He responds: "I used to tell my stories in the hopes that others will hear them. Now I tell them to make sure I don't lose them and listen to the other stories."

The lesson I draw from this story is about doing whatever it takes inside me to cultivate a clear vision of what I am working for, and to nourish and sustain it regardless of what else happens.

In the absence of vision, social change work runs the danger of becoming an ongoing struggle *against* whatever the latest horror happens to be. Continually working against something leads both to burnout and to loss of effectiveness.

Even when the actions we take are in and of themselves obstructive in nature, such as acts of civil disobedience, we can model these actions after Gandhi's and King's examples – focusing on civil disobedience that models the world being created rather than being entirely an act of protest. (See the segment called "From Opposition to Vision" in the previous section of the book for more details.)

Vision plays another important role in mobilizing and sustaining our work, and one with which I am intimately familiar on account of writing this book. When we create and work toward a vision, in some small measure we begin to live in the world we are creating, and experience the beauty and sense of possibility that come with that dipping into the future. That, in itself, takes us out of the anguish and grief of living in a world that doesn't work for most people, and buoys us toward a possible future in which we can rest.

Encountering Despair

It is challenging to engage in the ongoing work of opening fully to despair, dread, and other emotional responses that arise in response to what is happening in the world. In the absence of doing this work, many people, including those working for social change, tend to numb out or suppress the depth of their feelings and find it hard to operate based on visionary passion rather than anger and urgency.

I wrote a chapter called "Experiencing Despair" in *Spinning Threads of Radical Aliveness*. The gist of the insight I included there is the one that Joanna Macy brought to all of us: unless we engage with our despair, we are likely to remain disempowered, numb, or angry. When we engage with it deeply enough, we unleash the power of our care and passion as the fuel that motivates our work.

In my experience the deeper layers of despair-work are rarely possible to face alone. This is one of the places where community is essential. Paradoxically, however, communities often unconsciously join forces to make despair-work impossible. Many groups develop an ethos of cynicism and self-righteous indignation, or a tendency to make snide remarks about political opponents, all of which make it harder to slow down and change the pace enough to allow for everyone's despair to arise. Despair is not pretty or comfortable, and the commitment to face it requires conscious choice on everyone's part.

At the same time, I have never once failed to come back from engaging fully with despair or grief much more energized, lighter and full of hope and joy. Nothing changes on the outside, and yet my own capacity to contain it grows.

Non-Attachment to Outcome

If you are an activist, or working to transform external reality in some other way, you may wonder why I am bringing up the idea of non-attachment, and whether such a path would ultimately lead to apathy or lack of engagement with the world.

Non-attachment is not about letting go of wanting. Rather, it's about owning our needs and staying open to the possibility of having them continue to be unmet, which is and has been the reality for so many of us for so many centuries and more.

Those of us who work toward social change often de-personalize our needs and insist on their absolute rightness. We speak about what a government "should" do instead of talking about what we want; we use the language of what "must" happen instead of talking about our pain at what is happening and our longing for a different world. This approach is rooted in a distance from our needs. "It's not about me," we say. We act as if taking personal ownership of what we want would diminish the strength of our message, or as if we would be taken less seriously if we bring our hearts into our work.

Wanting, having a need, is implicitly seen as weak, not strategic, shameful.

In addition, the idea of releasing attachment may seem preposterous when our passion is for the world. What about children's need for food or safety, for example? How can we not insist that these needs be met?

Letting go of attachment is not about giving up on the hope for all the children in the world to be safe and to have sufficient food. Nor is it about giving up on working toward that end. Rather, it is about being able to tolerate internally the possibility that it might not happen that all the children in the world will be safe and have sufficient food. If we cannot tolerate this possibility – which is also the current reality! – then how can we have space inside to interact with life as it is? If our approach is based on what should happen, without this capacity to accept life, what would keep us from trying to force a solution? So many revolutions have turned into a new regime of horror. How would we ensure that we can sustain our vision and openness if we cannot tolerate those who support what is currently happening?

Keeping our hearts open means experiencing the horror of knowing that one child under five years old dies every six seconds (the World Health Organization says almost 19,000 daily in 2011!),[23] mostly from the diseases and conditions of poverty and malnutrition, and then from the effects of wars of all kinds. Without conscious tools to keep our hearts open, many of us do indeed shut down and tune out the plight of the children so we can manage to continue with our own personal lives, while others succumb to anger and desperation that can lead to re-creating domination and horror.

If we accept the possibility that no solution will arise, and at the same time continue to bring our heart and attention and action to working toward a solution, our efforts take on an entirely different flavor. We aim toward our dreams, we embrace the vision and our needs in full, and we remain open in the face of what is happening.

The Courage to Face Consequences

In everyday life, for most of us, the consequences of taking a nonviolent approach to life are mostly relational. However, when we

---

[23] who.int/gho/child_health/en/index.html

take on the world, a host of new potential consequences arise. If we are to engage in social action from a truly nonviolent perspective, facing these fears is indispensable, because fear blocks choice, and choice is core to being able to maintain a stance of nonviolence in the face of immense challenges.

The movie *Police Adjective*, which was written, directed, and produced by Romanian director Corneliu Porumboiu, is a careful study of the limits of courage.[24] The plot is remarkably simple: a police officer follows a teenager who is accused of selling drugs, and faces a major moral dilemma along the way.

I experienced this movie as a rare masterpiece, a profound and subtle exploration of core aspects of what it means to be human. It moves slowly in time, and contains very little action except at the very end. Because of the moral compunction that the main character has about his assignment, he is being presented with an incredibly difficult choice that might have life-changing consequences. The climax of the movie is a conversation between the officer and his boss during which the officer attempts to pull out of this assignment, or change it. Will he follow his conscience and stand up to power, or will he succumb to fear and give up? The reason I see this movie as such a masterpiece is because of that conversation, which lays out the issues of standing up to power so dramatically and compellingly. I couldn't help but imagine myself in the scene, being the person challenged to follow my truth.

How far would any of us go in following our own moral intuition? How much and how often and how far do we each give up on what we know is true for us in order to maintain food on the table, social acceptability, or any other kind of basic comfort? I don't know of short or easy answers to these questions. I do have a deep sense that in some way our future depends on our growing ability to keep reflecting on these questions, and on our collective ability to learn how to move towards deep moral and personal integrity. I want to keep growing in these areas and inspire others to do the same. I want to keep wrestling with my own complicity when it's there. I want to find, accept, and then stretch my limits so I can take bolder and bolder actions in the face of fear. I want to become ever better at

---

[24] The movie is available on Netflix.com in the USA. An interview with the director is available at cinema-scope.com/cs39/spot_peranson_porumboiu.html.

encouraging others to do the same, because I want us to have a future we can look forward to and participate in wholeheartedly.

Seeing Everyone's Humanity

Love is creative and redemptive. Love builds up and unites; hate tears down and destroys. The aftermath of the "fight with fire" method... is bitterness and chaos, the aftermath of the love method is reconciliation and creation of the beloved community. Physical force can repress, restrain, coerce, destroy, but it cannot create and organize anything permanent; only love can do that. Yes, love – which means understanding, creative, redemptive goodwill, even for one's enemies – is the solution...

– Martin Luther King, Jr.

Ultimately what makes a nonviolent strategy unique is the intentionality behind it more than the type of action itself. Jesus, Gandhi, Martin Luther King, and the others who have shaped the practice of nonviolent social change have all advocated seeing the humanity of everyone, including people engaging in behaviors that appear harmful. The terms are uncompromising, and are always about love – loving our enemies, loving those who hate us. Even working to stop people from inflicting harm can be done with love and respect for the person doing the action.

We need tools for ensuring that we approach people as humans rather than as enemies, no matter their positions or actions, whether we are trying to work with them, to organize them, to persuade them to change their mind, or to oppose their actions. I want this capacity to be widespread in movements for social change.

I remember seeing footage from the training of the early Civil Rights activists who were going to engage in lunch counter sit-ins. I can't imagine that the level of self-restraint and inner peace that these young women and men exhibited can be achieved without deep love, enough love to counterbalance the reaction to humiliation, physical taunting, and brutality that were leveled at them. James Zwerg, one of the Freedom Riders who was physically brutalized by a large group of people and almost died, said this: "I asked God to give me the strength to remain nonviolent and to forgive the people for what they might do."

I don't see any shortcuts possible. I doubt that anyone who wants to engage seriously in nonviolent social change could sustain their involvement or be effective without learning to love everyone. It's the best antidote to fear, and therefore also the source of the courage to face consequences.

Empathy for the Oppressor

Perhaps the most challenging act of heart opening and empathy is to direct our open heart towards those who are seen as oppressors, those who hold positions of great power and privilege, and especially when their actions are clearly harmful to others.

While I see the significance of discovering and connecting with outrage and liberating ourselves from the grip of internalized oppression, I think of cultivating empathy as an indispensable second step. Without it, we continue to view at least some people as not fully human. With it, we can embrace the full tragedy of humanity and include violence and injustice in that approach. Like James Gilligan, who spent decades studying violence and working with men who have been violent, I believe that such a focus can actually contribute immensely to a drastic reduction in the incidence of violence.

Empathy for the oppressor calls for an integration of self at a higher level. To use the example of gender, just as much as there is nothing "natural" about women that makes us carriers of connection or gives us a better perspective on reality, there is also nothing about being male or white that gives a group a monopoly over violence or injustice. It is excruciating for any of us to realize that with different birth or social circumstances our group could be engaging in atrocities just as easily as another group now oppressing our own.

So painful is this realization, that for many Israeli Jews it is still impossible to recognize the particular role that Israel is playing in the Middle East, or the fact that Israeli soldiers have engaged in direct torture in the West Bank, or that Israel has been supplying arms and training to some of the most brutal regimes of the world. To be able to integrate that level of understanding means being more fully aware of the entire complexity of what it means to be human.

The attitude of empathy or compassion towards those who are acting in harmful ways is far from common in social change movements, which are usually more focused on images of injustices that must be redressed, or on reparation of past injuries, or on revolution, as the case might be. Many fail to see that such approaches remain trapped within the same structures of domination and oppression that they seek to transform. Where revolutions succeed, much often remains unchanged, except the personnel and the professed values. Such perspectives do nothing to dismantle the psychic apparatus that sustains domination in the first place.

If we take seriously the radical idea that all human beings are indeed human, it becomes immediately clear that defeating others can only reproduce oppression. Empathy for the oppressor, on the other hand, leads to recognition of the full humanity of all, and to an appreciation of the depth of the tragedy that has led some to act in harmful ways. The tragedy in question is the disconnection from our own source of human striving and of beauty. Demonizing "the enemy" leaves no real grounds for hope. It is only a deep understanding that the advantages of privilege come with a package of disadvantages, and that to become an oppressor we must first have been oppressed, that can sustain the hope for a change that will benefit all.

When I read Alice Miller's *For Your Own Good* for the first time, there was a moment somewhere in the description of Hitler's childhood during which I was able to feel, actually feel in my heart, some compassion towards the plight of that child, some understanding of what could have happened that would lead a human being to such unimaginable horrors. Some small part of my anguish over the Holocaust was released in that moment; I felt an unusual sense of hope in being able, as a Jew from Israel, to feel that level of openness in my heart towards that boy.

The absence of empathy is most acute for me in observing the responses to child abuse. The usual reaction is empathy and compassion for the plight of the child whose abuse was just discovered, and outrage and disgust directed at the parent or other adult. For me this response leaves so much out. If we recognize what is by now commonly accepted as true, namely that the "abuser" was also abused as a child, and that the child, now "saved" from further abuse, would otherwise have significant chances of growing up to be an abusive adult, then the absence of empathy towards the adults becomes questionable. Questionable because the root of the problem cannot be identified. Questionable because it perpetuates a social order in which there will always be "bad" people who need to be punished. Questionable because it points to no avenue for true change that is sustainable and lasting. In my understanding and experience, such change emerges from supporting the abusive parent, for example, in coming to terms with their own early suffering, with the shame and trauma that leads them to act against their own love and care for the child in so many instances. As the heart opens to the grief of the original suffering as well as the profound pain of knowing that they are harming their children, the possibility of making different choices opens up in unprecedented ways.

The attitude of compassion and empathy towards oppressors is central in the Buddhist tradition, though the terms used are not political. Metta, the practice of loving-kindness, is an integral part of the Vipassana tradition. Metta meditation starts with a favorite animal, a favorite teacher, or anyone towards whom we easily feel loving-kindness. With increased concentration, our attention gradually shifts from such beings to ever more challenging circumstances, moving through ourselves and someone who is neutral, and finally reaching our enemies. In some versions, the end of the practice involves extending loving-kindness to all sentient beings or the universe as a whole. The purpose is to open our heart ever more fully to embracing the full range of humans. In a way all Buddhist meditation is geared towards cultivation of compassion: by being fully present to our own enormous difficulties in staying present and mindful, an attitude of compassion towards self gradually becomes more and more easily reachable, and with it the increased ability to feel compassion towards another, including at times of strife and conflict.

The final benefit of the attitude of empathy and compassion towards others who act harmfully and in violation of our needs and values is that it enhances the possibility of connection with people whose actions and attitudes we may want to influence. Without such an attitude, it is unlikely that we will be able to have an impact on those whose fears keep them enclosed in their comfort, hence complicit with the structures of domination to a much larger extent. I have so much more hope about nonviolent social change when the premise is an uncompromising presence to everyone's humanity.

The following three pieces – an article, a personal fictive essay, and a poem – are intended to illustrate the potential ramifications of engaging in these inner practices.

No Enemies, No Demands[25]

"If there were more people like you in the left, if I ever felt such true compassion and understanding, I would, despite all the pain involved, (...pause...) consider moving to another place in Israel." After only thirty minutes of receiving empathic listening, Judy (not her real name), a Jewish settler in the West Bank, could imagine moving from the West Bank into internationally recognized Israeli territory.

Secular, left-leaning Jews in Israel often believe that only force will get Jewish settlers to leave the settlements and find their homes within the pre-1967 borders of Israel. Many still remember the traumatic evacuation of Yamit when the Gaza Strip was returned to Egypt, and anticipate, with horror, similar struggles in the West Bank. Jewish settlers in the West Bank are seen as fanatics who are oblivious to the plight of others.

In this heated climate, in the mid-1990's, a different conversation took place between Judy and Arnina, a Nonviolent Communication trainer in Israel. Instead of arguing with Judy, trying to take apart her position, insisting on the moral bankruptcy of her views, or trying to convince her, Arnina simply reflected to Judy her understanding of Judy's deeper feelings and needs. Here are some excerpts from their dialogue:

> **Judy**: "People forget who we are, and our history. ... We go back thousands of years ... We were chosen by God, and given this land. How can they forget this???"
>
> **Arnina**: "So you are feeling devastated, because you would really like to know that the deep meaning of 'settle in this land' is understood and preserved?"
>
> ...
>
> **Judy**: "The secular leftists think we are blind and obstinate, while we are holding on to the most precious symbol of our existence."

---

[25] A shorter version of this piece appeared in *Tikkun* Magazine, September/October 2002

Arnina: "Are you in pain because you so much want to find a way to dissolve the separation between you and leftists, because for you we are all one people?"

Judy: "Yes, yes, yes... Thank you for saying this. This is what's most crucial here for me. This terrible wall between us and ... you. Yes, you said it, we are all one. And I am desperate when I think, again and again, how deep the gap between all of us is, how we only see the external, and judge it, while the important things lie deep inside, for all of us. Don't we all want to keep living, and here? And how do they think this is going to happen, if we give up on this historical land?"

Arnina: "Are you really scared, because your hope for the continued existence of the Jewish people is threatened by the mere idea of losing this land?"

Finally, when Arnina was confident that Judy was fully heard, she stopped, looked at Judy for a long while, then asked gently: "Would you be willing to hear what's going on for me now, and how I see all this?" Judy nodded silently.

Arnina then told Judy how much she shared the deep wish of seeing Israelis living and thriving, and bringing gifts to the world. Then she added: "I want you also to hear just how frightened I am when I see the price we are paying for this. I am wondering if you could conceive of the thought that, if we all really united in our wish, and not against each other, we might find other means of keeping this legacy, while at the same time saving so many lives?" It was in response to this question that Judy expressed her tentative willingness to consider leaving the land she had so tenaciously held on to for so long. It was the experience of being fully heard which made the transformation possible.

The practice of applying empathy in the service of social activism is based on a combination of practical considerations and deep spiritual values. On the practical level, listening with empathy to those with whose positions we disagree increases the chances that they will want to listen to us. Until Judy's needs were acknowledged, she would not have been able to hear and consider Arnina's request. Once Judy's experiences were heard fully, magic happened, her heart opened, and a profound shift took place in her.

When we use force, blame, and self-righteousness instead, even if we manage to create the outcome we want in the short run, we distance ourselves from those whose actions we want to change. Success in the short run does not lead to the transformation we so wish for, neither in ourselves nor in those we are trying to change. Sooner or later, those with more power will prevail, and we are left bitter and defeated. This cycle is a major cause of "burn-out" among activists.

Moreover, on the spiritual plane, listening with empathy to others is one way of putting into practice the fundamental values of compassion and nonviolence. In order to hear Judy with true empathy, Arnina had to transcend thoughts of right and wrong. Indeed, before Arnina was able to listen to Judy, she received a significant amount of empathy from others for her own pain and despair. In cultivating empathy for Judy, Arnina was able to discover behind Judy's statements a human being like herself, with the same basic set of needs. At the end of the dialogue both Judy and Arnina discovered and connected with needs they had not been aware of in themselves or in each other: a deep desire to keep alive the legacy of Judaism, and a longing for unity.

Even when we want to embrace compassion, structures of domination are deeply ingrained in us. According to theologian Walter Wink, we are all indoctrinated in the myth of redemptive violence: the basic belief that violence can create peace. We are trained to enjoy watching the "bad guy" get "what he deserves." Marshall Rosenberg, founder of the Center for Non-Violent Communication, believes that our use of language reinforces "enemy images" of others. When we refer to corporate executives as "profiteers," our use of language implies greed; when we refer to lower-level managers as "bureaucrats," we imply uncaring. Learning to practice empathy requires being able to recognize in others' actions fears and longings similar to our own, and to look for strategies of meeting our own needs that would allow others' needs to be met as well. The alternative to punishing the "bad guys" is NOT passivity, but a subtle dance between genuine empathy for the other's needs and uncompromising expression of our own needs.[26]

---

[26] This example is situated in the context of nonviolence as *dialogue* – the only kind of nonviolence that a single individual can engage in. In the absence of a movement, a single individual cannot mount a nonviolent *resistance* campaign. Some of what I say in this piece would be different if I were talking about the context of a movement.

We all pay a price in the long run when our needs are met at others' expense. Accordingly, the goal of the dance of empathy is to establish enough connection and understanding so that everyone can unite in looking for strategies to meet everyone's needs. When we transcend our own enemy images so that we really experience the humanness of the other, we can truly show people that we care about their needs. When that happens, they are then usually more open to consider ways of meeting their needs that are not at the expense of other human beings' lives, the planet, and other values of theirs.

Let's look at another example. Suppose your mayor decides to invite Walmart to open a new store in your town. Suppose you belong to an organization that seeks to protect local businesses, create sustainable development, and ensure the long term survival of the planet, and thus opposes the building of the store. When you think about your mayor signing an agreement with Walmart to build the new store, what images arise in you? Do you see the mayor as selling out, as breaking her promises, as being cowardly, or as compromising her values in order to aggrandize herself?

Now imagine that you manage to gain access to the mayor's office, and you are given an audience with her. Your organization has not initiated a nonviolent resistance campaign, which if it will happen at all is still a long way away, so your goal for the audience is simply dialogue. What would you say? How would you try to approach her? If any of the above thoughts are racing in your mind, how could you possibly create trust in the mayor's mind that her needs and concerns matter to you? Without a willingness to imagine the mayor as a human being like yourself, who might be open to your concerns, you are likely to see her as an enemy, and speak with anger and mistrust.

The mayor, for her part, is probably frustrated and exhausted, barely listening to you, and annoyed at the interruption in her schedule. She is focused on just how much work she has to do before the end of the day, and wants, more than anything else, a break. She is probably thinking to herself that you are very naïve, and just don't see the realities of life she is so painfully aware of. Perhaps she has her own dreams of what she can create in town, but desperately needs the support of business to be able to get the funds required for some of those innovative projects. She may be completely resigned to the idea of being seen as power-hungry, and unable to imagine that anyone but her closest assistants will be able to understand what she is trying to do. At the same time, she is probably habituated to hiding what is really on her mind and in her heart, for fear of being even more misunderstood.

How is such a conversation likely to end? Short of a miracle, the predictable ending is that each of you will have your enemy image of the other reinforced and confirmed. In your mind: "She's out there to aggrandize herself, she doesn't care about anything except money and power." In the mayor's mind: "He's a fanatic idealist, a danger to the functioning of town." Nothing learned, nothing explored, no connection made.

"Dialogue," says philosopher Martin Buber, "is a conversation between adults the outcome of which is unknown." True dialogue requires valuing the other's needs alongside our own, equally important, not less and not more. This entails a few steps. First, internally, dialogue requires connecting with our needs that give rise to our judgments. Then, when speaking, dialogue requires expressing our needs openly. After expression, sometimes even before, dialogue requires a willingness to listen with empathy. Such listening makes it possible to absorb the difficult messages we hear in a way that maintains the humanness of the other, and without threat to the needs we identify in us. This is what Buber refers to more than any aspect of the dialogue; it is this willingness that enables us to go beyond predictable outcomes and encounter the unknown-ness of the other person.

If you can do this when you talk with the mayor, she is less likely to have to protect herself against your judgments. With empathy, posturing will gradually diminish, and the mayor may allow you and herself access into her inner experience. She might respond to the invitation, implicit in your empathic guesses, to share more of the truth.

Underlying the willingness to persist in identifying and attending to everyone's needs, is a deep well of trust in the possibility of need satisfaction and in the fundamentally benign nature of human needs. The spiritual premise that gives rise to this trust is that human needs, as different from strategies, are universal and shared by all: tenderness, closeness, understanding, safety, the need to be understood, to contribute, to matter to others, to be valued. Our conflicts arise from having different strategies to try to meet the same basic set of needs, not from the needs themselves.

If we want to engage in social activism based on mutuality, trust, compassion, and nonviolence, we are likely to find that social change requires changing ourselves within while working on changing external structures. Because the world around us remains captive to right/wrong thinking, it's likely to take effort for us to find, again, the instinctive faith that I believe we are born with.

We also need to allow for time for organizing a supportive community for our social change efforts. We cannot wait until we are "ready" before embarking on social action, and we cannot wait until we have institutions that truly serve life before we let ourselves take time to attend to our personal struggles and relationships. Combining the two allows us to embody the values we are seeking to manifest in every action we take, even while structures of domination still continue to exist.

Unexpected Visitor

(This is a fictional story I wrote while sitting in a veterans writing group I've been part of since 1994, where I metabolized my own experiences of being in the Israeli army. I wrote more about these experiences in my previous book *Spinning Threads of Radical Aliveness: Transcending the Legacy of Separation in Our Individual Lives*. The quotes from people's introductions are accurate. The visitor never came.)

"I saw a 6-year-old who said we had to kill them there so they wouldn't kill us here," she was wrapping up her opening words. "How have we come to this?" she concluded.

The door opened suddenly and a man stood at the entrance, unsure. Did he really want to walk into this room? Everyone fell silent. Not a comfortable silence. We all recognized him. Many of us weren't sure we wanted him to join either. Some lowered their gaze when they saw him. He looked around. His mouth twitched nervously. His eyes darted around the room. No one held his gaze. His one hand was holding the doorknob; the other was crumpling up a piece of paper, the directions. He looked tired.

No one spoke yet. How did he have the directions? Someone must have invited him, I thought, sad it hadn't been me. He looked around, still not moving. Then a fleeting smile appeared. I traced his eyes. Someone made a gesture as if to say there was room. Then he took a step forward and closed the door quietly behind him.

Everyone was still, so still we could hear a lone fly in the room, buzzing by the window. He stood, blinking, for a few more seconds. Then he walked, a bit unsteady. The woman moved a bit, her face warm, her eyes still welcoming. Her neighbor frowned for a moment, then moved the other direction. Just enough space for the new man to sit. He turned around, facing the circle. Was he welcome? He sat down, trying to take as little space as possible. Tense, he discovered suddenly the piece of paper, still crumpled up in his hand. He looked to his left, nodded nervously, then put the paper in his pocket. He wasn't going to say anything, I realized. Would anyone?

We were still in our opening circle. He wasn't very late. Could we just simply go on? The man made a gesture to invite us to continue. He moved his hand, brushing off some invisible obstacle, as if to say, "Please ignore me." Did he hear what was said before he walked in? Would he have opened the door if he had?

The next person finally opened his mouth, with visible effort. He talked about his girls, about spending some time with older kids in the school, about what those kids know about global warming, the environment. I looked at our new man. His face was almost blank, hard to read. I looked more closely. His eyes were squinting, but there was no source of light. His back was still, his legs very straight, nothing relaxed about him. He caught my glance and looked back at me. For a flash of a second I could see pain in his face. It disappeared so fast, his face resumed its blankness so immediately, I wasn't even sure I saw it. He lingered for another second.

"There was some dog shit on the ground," the story continued, oblivious to my small connection with this man. "And someone had put a little flag with the words 'George Bush' written on it." I fidgeted. Were they really going to continue and ignore our guest? Some people were laughing. Others were squirming, looking embarrassed.

I looked at the man again. There was no mistaking anymore. He was in pain; I wasn't making it up. Will he speak? Will I speak about my pain?

People were still laughing, despite his presence. His face turned slightly pink. Or did I imagine it? This couldn't be comfortable. Why did he come? Could he really take this? Could the group? The laughter died out. He looked relieved. Was I the only one noticing?

The next person spoke about writers' block. The man was breathing more fully, and shifted his position.

The circle continued. Soon it would be his turn. What would he say? Someone spoke of his new granddaughter. The man smiled when everyone else did. He was getting more comfortable.

The next person spoke about being in a vet reunion, feeling alienated, with everyone talking about war from the position of thinking we should fight it. I turned to look at the man again. He was losing his hard-earned comfort. Was he feeling alienated now?

Two more people spoke, and then it was his turn. He cleared his throat, a gesture familiar to all of us. He looked around one last time, then opened his mouth and spoke with visible effort. "My name is George," he said, his voice dry, subdued. No one asked him to speak louder. "George Bush," he added, wincing. "I wish you understood." We waited. He said no more. The circle moved on.

(No, I don't hold the belief that all that's needed to create change is to understand George Bush. I do, however, hold the belief that it is *necessary* to extend human understanding to people in power as part of full engagement with them. I wonder, I keep wondering, at that meeting and elsewhere, often, whether such engagement might conceivably change his heart and mind as well as ours.

This is not idle thinking. While not the common path to change, examples exist. It is, likely, what Nelson Mandela did to help open de Klerk's heart and bring about profound changes to South Africa. It is, explicitly, what a Jewish couple did in relation to a Ku Klux Klan leader in the South as documented in the book *Not by the Sword.*[27]

While creating change through dialogue happens only in the minority of cases, and nonviolent resistance has often been necessary to create significant change, there is no less of a requirement to keep our hearts open to people even when we are fighting, collectively, to change their actions and policies.

I am also left wondering: if more of us could bring forth more love towards people in power, would that result in more change through dialogue, without requiring the much larger investment of resources and risk to human life that arise from mass nonviolent resistance?)

---

[27] See Watterson in the References page 422. I also discuss below, in "When Dialogue Breaks Down" from page 199, the overall question about the desirability of voluntary change on the part of the powerful, as well as the conditions that make it so unlikely. This, in a nutshell, is why nonviolent resistance is necessary instead of only dialogue.

You, Too, Are Human[28]

You are sitting in the cockpit
Behind you dozens in panic
In front of you a building
Approaching you rapidly
Your noble sacrifice
Your sacred act of courage
You will be dying before this thought is complete
You are not afraid

You are sitting in your office
Your report is at the printer
Your boss will be proud of you
You smile
You're thinking of calling your wife
You said unkind words to her this morning
You look out the window
You see an airplane
You run, you run
Your heart is in your neck
    Your ears
             Your eyes
Beating, beating, alive
You cannot comprehend
You will never again speak with your wife
Your unkind words will remain
Bitter memories of love

---

[28] I wrote this poem on September 22, 2001. It was published in *An Eye for an Eye Makes the Whole World Blind: Poets on 9/11*, ed. Allen Cohen, Clive Matson, Regent Press, 2002

Eleven of your friends are gone forever
It's your day off
But you go to the station
A few women are sitting on a couch
Their boyfriends, husbands, brothers missing
Quiet conversation masks the tension
Your tears are ready
Tonight, in your wife's arms,
You will cry inconsolably
Your buddies clench their teeth
Harden their faces
This is not a place to be human
You see so much
You are so alone

You are at home
A little fever, nothing major
Your wife is at her new job
Your children in school
You are not used to being home alone
You turn on the TV
Casually, somewhat restless
Your wife's workplace is on fire
Incredulous, you look at the people
Jumping, escaping the fire

You are walking down the street
You hear footsteps
You turn, facing the eyes of
A young Arab-looking man
It's dark, but he looks nervous
Is he on his way to plan the next attack?
You are scared
You will not let this happen again
You reach for a knife in your pocket

The sense of security
In the country you are serving
Is shattered
You have not had much sleep
Your body is aching
You ignore it, as always
You have decisions to make
Reports appear on the fax,
    The computer
        The phone
People walk into your office
Constantly impinging on your irritated tiredness
No real news
You want action
How will you decide
What is the right thing to do?

Interpersonal Practices for Change Agents

If we are going to create structural change, "being the change" is only one aspect of the work of transforming the world. However we conceive of leverage points for structural change, we would need to organize and act *with others* to create shifts. For that, we need concrete practices to bring our consciousness and practice of nonviolence beyond the personal, inner work.

Inner work doesn't necessarily translate into different relationships or organizational forms. We need interpersonal practices, because otherwise even with a high degree of personal capacity we form organizations that are mired in conflict, mistrust, and inefficiency.

In addition, becoming visible and effective when working for change also involves building alliances with other groups and organizations, as well as connecting with people who may be skeptical about or not already in alignment with the goals or strategies of the group. Creating change ultimately necessitates supporting people, especially those with power, in shifting their views and making different choices than the ones they are used to.

Alongside and emerging from the inner work of transforming our inner structures, we discover and learn afresh how to interact with others – our colleagues, our family and friends who may not agree with our vision, and the many people with whom we interact in order to create the change we seek. We learn the art of dialogue in how it applies, specifically, to situations of social change. If we are not going to coerce people to change their minds or their behaviors, dialogue is our key tool for connection and the search for workable solutions for all.

Fundamental Building Blocks for Dialogue

The art of dialogue consists of listening and speaking in ways that support connection, mutual understanding, and even transformation. Dialogue flows between empathic listening that creates and seeds connection, and authentic and caring expression that paves the way for being understood, by making it more accessible to others and humanizing us to others even in the midst of conflict.

Successful dialogue starts inside us. We get there by cultivating openness and curiosity, being relaxed, and letting go of changing the other. Be prepared to be changed. If you are unwilling to be changed by the conversation, on what grounds are you expecting the other person to change?

From Convincing to Listening

For a number of years I was supporting the campaign to establish a federal-level Department of Peace by offering monthly coaching calls to volunteers and activists. One key take-home lesson I got from this work was confirmed many times over since then: activists are trained to speak, and not trained to listen. The idea remains solid in many movements that the path to change involves convincing people to change their minds.

A conversation focused on convincing is dramatically different from a dialogue. Philosophically, entering dialogue entails a willingness, however small, to be changed by the process. Convincing presupposes that my position is right and unchangeable. Dialogue is a conscious invitation into mutuality and exploration, leaving the outcome unknown until sufficient connection has been established.

Practically, the attempt to convince without integrating the other's point of view rarely works to create true and willing change. The other person almost invariably doesn't have a sense of being respected, let alone heard. It may lead to compliance, which can easily lead to resentment and future, even more intense, conflict (think about the 1919 Treaty of Versailles as a dramatic example).[29] We all have experienced someone else trying to convince us, and know how it so easily serves to entrench us in our position. This is what we do to others when we try to convince them. Instead, I have come to believe that listening empathically is, in most situations, a condition for fruitful dialogue. In fruitful dialogue a person may come to accept our point of view, or we may come to accept their point of view, or we may come to discover a new perspective together. Whatever the outcome, the collaborative nature of dialogue

---

[29] Perhaps compliance is accepted by people so readily because the experience of true shift and mutual convergence is, sadly, so uncommon.

reduces or eliminates defensive postures and moves forward as if by magic.

Truly hearing others tends to be challenging for most of us even in the most ordinary of conflicts, and becomes a major obstacle when the conflicts involve political opinions or core values. It's also probably the single most significant skill necessary for productive dialogues, whether with collaborators or opponents.

Even in significant disagreement, the focus on empathic presence can immediately contribute to connection, trust, and mutual respect. The experience of being heard often results in emotional settling, inner peace, and curiosity about the other person. By listening, we support the other person in wanting to listen to us.

Tip: Listen and reflect before expressing your point of view. Focus on reflecting what you believe is most important to the other person. Go as deep as necessary to look for commonalities in your reflection, something the other person expresses in their position that you also want or care about.

Speaking Truth with Care

The most productive kind of dialogue develops when we speak authentically based on what we want rather than on what we consider to be "right" or "fair" or "just." Speaking from the heart of personal experience and need tends to de-polarize difficult situations and opens up a process of shared exploration of strategies, rather than argument about what should be done.

Dialogue is also helped by our expressing care for everyone's needs, perspectives, and opinions, regardless of disagreement. We can consciously focus on transcending separation, scarcity, and mistrust and seek solutions, strategies, policies, and processes that work for both parties to a dialogue.

Tip: When expressing your position, link it to you instead of making it what should be. What is in your heart, what do you value, what matters to you that is expressed in your position? Articulate that, as vulnerably as possible, and the other person will have an easier time listening to you.

The Power of Dialogue to Create Change

I wish I could point to many concrete examples of significant political transformation that happened through dialogue, especially of the kind that I just described. Unfortunately, most of the people who have applied themselves to the study of Nonviolent Communication (NVC) didn't come from activist circles, and haven't put their learning to use toward social transformation. I am not the kind of researcher who has a fount of such stories at her fingertips from the experience of communities and eras other than my own, nor do I believe that such dialogues occur with any frequency.[30]

As a result, some of the examples below took place in role-plays rather than with the real individuals in question. Nonetheless, I believe strongly that the dialogues that I have seen transform individuals and small groups can scale up. The future of applying the specific lessons of this book to social change is ours to create. I'd like to believe that in ten years we can have a multiplicity of stories to tell from many who will endeavor to engage in transformative dialogues.

The following three snippets of political dialogue took place during a training about the use of NVC for social change. Some of them are real, and some only imagined, role-plays of dialogues as yet to happen. Further below, I also provide a real example of a dialogue across a major divide.

What Is Effective Social Change?

One of the participants in the training was taken aback by the use of the term "social change activist." Her image of an activist was one of holding banners and shouting slogans, and in her experience she didn't see that kind of action as particularly effective. She said she had been involved in humanitarian work within a mainstream organization and she thought that contributed to more effective social change than the activists she saw outside the building. When asked where she had worked, she said it was in the World Bank.

Immediately, I took the moment as an opportunity to demonstrate the power of dialogue across disagreement. I was grateful for the years of practice that allowed me to hear her despite

---

[30] That said, the many processes and experiments *have* taken place, both in the US and elsewhere. Some of the resources that can be consulted for more information are the National Coalition for Dialogue and Deliberation and the Co-Intelligence Institute, in particular the chapters from *The Tao of Democracy* that describe citizen deliberative councils.

my strong disagreement with her. We never even touched on the question of whether or not the World Bank contributes to reducing poverty or, as I believe based on different sources of information from hers, it has, instead, been responsible for massive misery in poor countries. Instead, I focused on reflecting my understanding of what was important to her and keeping my reflection at the level that could stay common to both of us. I have been advocating openness to being changed through dialogue. And I had exactly that experience. What changed was not my opinion about the World Bank. Rather, what changed was my seeing it as possible and even desirable to work with people to create change wherever it would be effective, whether within or outside the mainstream. I felt relief, curiosity, and excitement at recognizing that I had been blinded by an automatic opposition, and that I was now open.

Taking Power by Making Choices

Kris Heydon (her real name), one of the participants in the group, teaches in a public school, where many decisions are made by people in administration. She was confused, because she didn't see how she could apply what I had presented previously given her perception of total lack of power to affect those decisions. She intended to go on from that statement to another part of her question, something about what she can do in her classroom. I didn't want to leave the question of power so quickly, so I probed further. I suggested that she could, if she wanted, get support from others, both teachers and parents, and engage with the decision-makers. At first she didn't see how, and brought up reasons for why this wouldn't work. I told her that was not the point. I wasn't suggesting that she was supposed to do that. It was clear that she didn't want to. My point was only that it was a choice she was making, and she could make it either way, if she wanted. Then she thought for a while, and said she wanted to recap what she had learned. Slowly and carefully she expressed her learning: "I can take power by making choices." In these few simple words she summarized a principle I consider deep and central to the entire project of nonviolence.

To George with Love

In another small group activity a woman, let's call her Claire, wanted to find respectful ways of turning down invitations to participate in a demonstration, rally, or some other political activity when she didn't want to go. We set up a role-play between her and a co-worker who urged her to come to a campus-wide protest against George Bush (this was an event that happened some years ago). Her struggle, as we came to see, was that she had been so deeply trained to maintain harmony, that even when she tried to express herself she didn't really articulate what was going on for her that would lead her to this unpopular choice. She expressed only vague statements such as: "I am not really comfortable going to the demonstration." In coaching her, I invited her to go deeper into her experience, to become vulnerable and assertive, both. Gradually, her passion rose closer to the surface, and her reasons became clear. She *was* troubled by many of the policies that George Bush was putting in place. She *did* want to have her voice heard and for George to receive the feedback. Her real concern was that she wanted that feedback to come with love, so George Bush would be able to take it in. All of us in the room fell silent for a moment. Protest with love was a new concept, especially for the woman in the character who was inviting Claire to the demonstration. She seemed to change, even though she was only a character. Then she expressed, spontaneously, how she has had discomfort with the demonstrations, too, and was glad to have this new idea. For Claire to tell the full truth and remain open and unattached served to create space for the other person to change.

Crossing Divides

> *Jonathan Haidt, a professor at the University of Virginia and author of* The Happiness Hypothesis: Finding Modern Truth in Ancient Wisdom, *found that conservatives could more readily put themselves in the shoes of liberals and understand morally where they were coming from. The reverse was not true of liberals. They have little understanding of those with opposing views to their own....*
>
> *Why are liberals unable to sympathize with conservatives?*
>
> – Helen Smith, psychologist

I mourn the fact that I live in a bubble, with little that would bring me in contact with conservatives. I mourn the fact that in order to teach empathy for conservatives I must conjure up role-plays instead of live dialogues. I mourn the paucity of empathy for conservatives that I see in liberal circles. I still maintain that we can connect across our differences. We may not immediately find ways to come closer on specific issues. I still believe we can see our shared humanity, appreciate the struggles we face in understanding each other, and emerge with more humility and goodwill.

Empathy from Left Field

In the social circles in which I find myself, and in much of the left media, conservatives are regularly referred to as stupid (at best), backward, uncaring, or unevolved. At every opportunity I have, especially in my workshops, I invite people to look at what might be the underlying values behind conservative positions, to imagine how a decent fellow human could arrive at such opposing views. I wish I could contradict Helen Smith, but my experience only confirms what she says.

I see a complete dearth of genuine, open-hearted empathy towards conservatives. I regularly hear jokes at the expense of conservatives in my workshops, and I cringe. I am not conservative myself. Far from it! I find most liberals to be more conservative than me. I cringe because if I were a conservative, I would not experience Nonviolent Communication communities as hospitable. Even more pointedly, activists I have worked with are generally challenged in being able to hear their opponents, to listen with respect and care, to imagine their values and deeper longings and aspirations, and to be open to be affected by what they hear. What is dialogue, after all, if we are expecting others to change their views, positions, or strategies, without a comparable willingness on our part to be affected and changed by what we hear?

Bridging the Divide within Me

To support people in being able to reach a true empathic openness, I have often conducted role- plays in which I assumed the role of a much maligned figure, often George W. Bush, and asked people to enter dialogue with me by offering me empathy and understanding.

Independently of people's success in the activity (spotty), entering these roles has transformed me, because I now have a felt sense of what it might be like to be someone so different from myself. I was most moved when I imagined being the former president just about the time of September 11, 2001. I *felt* the weight of the responsibility, of having to make a decision about how to respond to the situation. I *felt* how awful it was to be hated by half my country.

Another time I engaged in a similar role-play in which I was a soldier returning from Iraq only to face the judgments of others. As this soldier I was able to *feel* the outrage, the experience of not being understood at all for my profound willingness to sacrifice everything in order to protect the way of life of this country that's so dear to me. I was able to *feel* what it was like to be together with others, risking my life, knowing I would do anything to protect theirs.

I feel less separate as a result. My own positions and views have not changed. But I now have a complete appreciation of the shared humanity of people who are far away from me on the political spectrum. I know that we have different worldviews, and I can hold that knowledge without losing understanding for the other worldview, even when I am frightened by the consequences I associate with it. I know that the fear is mutual. Conservatives are just as worried about my views, and what would happen if everyone espoused them, as I am about theirs. Knowing this helps me increase my compassion and understanding.

Empathy, Obama, and Connecting across Differences

Empathy [is] the act of understanding and being sensitive to the feelings and experiences of others. ... Empathy is essential for any president... To be authentically empathetic, however, presidents must consider how policies affect all Americans.

— Gary Bauer, "Obama and the Politics of Empathy"[31]

Empathy calls on us to open our hearts and imagination to others' humanity. It's easy to understand and show care for those similar to us. The challenge of empathy is precisely in the face of differences. How can we show care for others' needs even when we say "no" to what they want? How can we understand and remain

---

[31] politico.com/news/stories/0410/35499.html

open and respectful even when we believe others' positions are potentially harmful? How can we appreciate others' suffering when we believe it's caused by their own actions or misunderstanding? It seems that both conservatives and liberals have failed to step out of being themselves and to enter and understand another perspective.

Beyond understanding, *conveying* empathy to others in the face of disagreement makes the challenge of connecting across differences even more intense. For example, short of agreement with Bauer's policy prescriptions, is there any way that Obama could convey to Bauer and others that their voices matter, and could affect the decisions he makes?

Coming Back to Essential Human Needs

In a country saddled with persistent core disagreements about most fundamental policy issues, connecting across differences seems essential for our continued functioning as a nation. What can we then do as common citizens, public figures, or the President, to cultivate and convey empathy?

My own hope rests on my experience that even in the most intense disagreements we share core needs, values, qualities, and aspirations that inform our opposing views. Here are two examples.

Bauer says: "Conservatives can be just as empathetic. But they believe that, in most cases, it's not government's role to be the primary dispenser of empathy." What I read in this statement is care for people's well-being mixed with a deep respect for individual freedom of choice. Although I disagree with Bauer's *view*, I have no difficulty relating to these *values*, because I share them.

Bauer also says: "our children and grandchildren ... will be saddled with paying for today's unprecedented borrowing." I am touched by our shared desire for the coming generations to be cared about, even though my worry about the next generations comes up in different contexts, not this one.

Can We Work Together?

Shifting attention to *what matters most* to each party to a debate can bridge seemingly insurmountable gaps. I dream of town hall meetings facilitated by skilled people. I want all participants to express the core of what matters to them, and to hear each other across the divide.

This is not a pipedream. Skilled individuals are available. Models of productive citizen deliberation exist and have been successful at finding policies that diverse groups with opposing views can embrace.[32] What would it take for the people of the United States of America to transform their town hall meetings from battleground to an opportunity to shape a shared future?

Dialogue across the Divide

When I talk about crossing the divide I never mean compromising or watering down our approach. I rather mean engaging deeply enough and long enough to where those who disagree experience that their concerns and needs are held dear. Then there is so much more chance that they can be open to hearing from us. I trust that the care for all that I am longing to see in the world lives in each person underneath the fear, shame, despair, and/or confusion that sustain the existing ethos of selfishness. I doubt that anyone immersed in that worldview can truly hear anything different as long as they don't experience being seen and appreciated for who they are and what matters to them. I want to be able to do that, both now and when the world is transformed. I do not and never have sought unity at the cost of integrity. I seek to find the shared core human aspirations that can provide a foundation for strategies that work for people who have opposing views. Relationship, connection, trust, and mutual understanding make that possible.

Having devoted some attention to empathy between liberals and conservatives, and wishing to find ways of facilitating dialogues between the two groups (a project I hope very much to come back to), I decided, as a first step, to try to meet people who identify as conservative. I had the incredible good fortune of stepping out of my bubble and meeting Peeter, who identifies as a "dyed in the wool" conservative, and who is a sympathizer of the Tea Party movement. Unfortunately, this meeting didn't lead to the larger dialogue I was hoping to create. Nonetheless, I learned a lot, I was surprised, and my heart was touched. Out of care and respect, I showed Peeter what I wrote about our meeting before I posted on my blog. I am heartened by what he wrote back: "The whole point of us living in

---

[32] See *The Tao of Democracy* at taoofdemocracy.com/toc.html, especially chapters 12 and 13, which are available online.

this country and society of ours all together is that we accept the inherent differences in our humanity, and deal with them in a civilized manner."

A particularly poignant moment was when I looked in Peeter's eyes and saw just how deeply sacred human life is for him. So deep, in fact, that for him it supersedes freedom, another cherished core value of his, when no strategy exists for upholding both at once. This is the basis of his opposition to abortions. What can I say? I felt deeply connected to him in those moments even though I support women's choice to have an abortion. I had an abortion myself, and what I was left with was just a depth of anguish about how complex, painful, and impossible the dilemma is. I want women to have the choice, and at the same time I completely see that an abortion is the end of a life that could be. I want to live in a world where abortions aren't necessary. What would it take to create good options for women?

Peeter expressed a concern about having people depend on the government for their basic needs. I wanted to understand fully what values informed this view. It's one thing to know in theory that all opinions, views, and strategies stem from shared human needs and values. It's a whole other thing to *experience* this in a moment of conversation with someone whose views are very different from my own. One value that informs Peeter's desire to eliminate dependence on government was his wish for people to take responsibility for the consequences of their choices. Of course I want that, too. I could easily resonate with this wish even though I mix this value with the desire for compassion, so everyone is supported no matter what.

Peeter also expressed a deep faith in the capacity of human beings to take care of themselves and of each other, including those in need, in the absence of government legislation, monitoring, and bureaucracy. This part was completely surprising to me, and goes contrary to my previous semi-unconscious bias, which was that conservatives had a much more negative view of human beings than liberals. Not so for Peeter. Do I have this much faith? I am not so sure. I know I am nervous about leaving the needy without societal guarantees because I am not trusting that all people could overcome their habits of scarcity and greed.

As we were winding down our conversation I asked Peeter if he would join me in trying to organize the dialogue I so want to have.

Peeter was doubtful about it. He didn't see what the point would be. Conflict and differences, he thought, were unavoidable. No dialogue would bring people together, he thought. Did he feel heard by me? Yes, he did. He liked me, and would be happy to meet with me again. Still, he didn't see that mutual understanding between conservatives and liberals could lead to anything. This got me thinking. I have more faith than he does in dialogue. He has more faith than I do in people's ability to care for each other. Am I limited in not trusting that, or is he naïve? Is he limited in not trusting dialogue, or am I naïve? Who is to say?

Transcending Righteousness

Imagine you came to a conference about reconciliation. Imagine you are gay, and you discovered that nothing on the agenda explores this dimension of human life. How would you feel, and what would you do? A dear friend had this experience. This is her story, which I found immensely inspiring.

Her first response was isolation and depression. Sensing the group to be fairly conservative, she felt utterly alone, and quite desperate about it, to the point of almost changing her flight and going home early. She kept meditating and praying, and woke up on the third day with an entirely different orientation. She took the microphone, let everyone know that she was gay, and made herself available to talk with people about anything related to the topic that they wanted. I see this as precisely the core courage of nonviolence that I advocate. She combined, in this act, radical vulnerability with service. Despite her emotional discomfort, she didn't ask for anything, she didn't attempt to justify anything, she only made herself available.

And people started coming. A pastor who wanted to talk with her about how to work with gay people who come out to her, as well as with other members of the congregation who are against homosexuality. A woman who worked closely with someone without knowing he was gay until she learned that his partner had died and was a man. She was so confused she didn't know what to say, and never acknowledged this to anyone, not even her close coworker who had just lost his partner. Over the remaining days of the conference my friend met with a steady stream of people who had no previous context for exploring their feelings and concerns. Instead of trying to get them to agree with her position, as so many of us are wont to do, she connected with the deepest places of caring in each of them, and found communion beyond, or underneath, attachment to position or to being right about anything. With some, no words were exchanged, only a hug, or a smile.

Towards the end my friend experienced a sense of community with people who, for the most part, had an entirely different position on the issues. No matter. They were all human. They all cared about reconciliation and human connection. They all wanted to live in integrity with their values, whatever their values, and they all wanted to find ways of engaging with their uncertainty about their positions, to open up just a little more to the complexity of life. There was no need to agree, which had the surprising effect of creating so much more freedom for my friend. As she said, this was reconciliation in action, more powerful than any learning or methodology she could get from the officially scheduled presentations.

When I shared with her how moved and touched I was by her story, she added that she didn't have a sense of having done something, more that it happened to her through grace. Knowing how easily we don't give ourselves credit, I embarked with her on an exploration of grace and volition. I imagine we all know, intuitively, that we cannot bring grace to us through intention. And yet my friend easily conceded that any one of us could, and she did, make ourselves ready for grace. What does it take? Inner clarity, release of attachment to outcome or to knowing, a kind of ultimate surrender, without resistance, without agenda. Nothing guarantees that grace would then come to us, of course. It only prepares us for receiving. In addition, when grace arrives, as it did for this friend, we still accept or refuse the invitation. My friend accepted, with astonishing results. I hope when called to do so I will, too.

Section 2

Collaboration, Power, and Leadership

We must abandon competition and secure cooperation. This must be the central fact in all our considerations of international affairs; otherwise we face certain disaster.

– Albert Einstein

Social Structures[33]

In *Spinning Threads of Radical Aliveness*, my first book, I included a section I called "The Power of Stories." That section contained a diagram I am reproducing on the next page, with much more explanation.

Every human society is built around a particular dominant "story" of what human beings are like and what life is about. Every human society creates social institutions, based on the story told in that society, to manage its affairs. Examples are institutions for allocating resources (such as market economy, centrally planned economies, or gift economies), institutions for resolving disputes and deviations from the norms of behavior established in the society (such as retributive justice systems or restorative justice systems), institutions of governance (which can be monarchies, representative democracies, totalitarian regimes, and many others), and institutions for caring for the sick (such as socialized health care, insurance-based health care, or community-based health care).[34]

One institution of particular significance is the socialization of the next generation: each society must prepare its young to function within the institutions existing in that society. Based on how children are treated in the society, they grow up to be human beings who, in most cases, act in ways that confirm the story that underlies the society's institutions. The drawing below illustrates the multiple mutually reinforcing relationships that exist between these four elements of every society.[35]

---

[33] I want to acknowledge the immense support I received for this piece from conversations with Serge Marti, author of the forthcoming *Grassroots Leadership and Popular Education in Indonesia*. Our exchanges resulted in significant changes integrated throughout; a true collaboration, in keeping with the content of this piece. I would not have been able to achieve this level of clarity and depth without his input.

[34] Given the endless complexity and variability of human societies, this list is by necessity only an illustrative sample, and is not meant to be exhaustive in any way.

[35] The diagram (on the next page) and the fundamental framing of these notes are directly based on the work of Marshall Rosenberg as given in workshops I have attended, though the specific terms "authority-based" and "collaboration-based" are my own. To my knowledge, this basic modeling of human societies has not been published by Rosenberg.

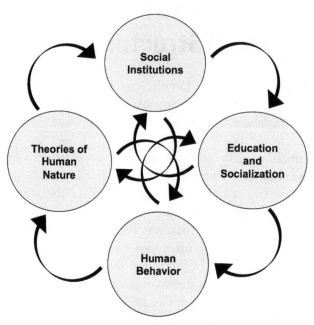

In what follows, I look at two configurations of how societies might operate, placed on two different extremes along the spectrum of how power is used. In actual existing societies, nothing is ever as neatly organized as all that. Even within authority-based societies, there have always existed pockets of full collaboration, such as the governance of the commons in most parts of the world.[36] Similarly, collaboration-based societies are likely to have instances – in some pre-defined situations, during emergencies, or in other as-yet-to-be-defined conditions – where swift action on the part of an individual or a very small group may attend to more needs than the general reliance on collaborative decision-making would. Some examples of this can be seen in the collection of stories about the envisioned future that are included in Part Two of this book.

Despite this complexity in real existing societies, I find it quite helpful to distinguish between authority- and collaboration-based systems, as well as to understand how every society includes the levels described in the diagram above. Merging those understandings to examine how systems operate today at each level, and what fully collaboration-based systems could be, can then provide much more

---

[36] See *The Wealth of the Commons*, more examples and notes below, as well as additional explanations about the commons in the section on governance in Part Two of this book, page 382.

clarity about what we need to do at each of the levels to increase collaboration immediately, and to move towards creating a world that supports humans and the bigger family of life.

For each of these two forms I flesh out what becomes true in each of the circles appearing in the diagram, thereby showing how a society always tends to reproduce itself.

Authority-Based Societies

Authority-based societies operate on one core principle: In the family and in the society at large, some people have the authority to make decisions and others are primarily expected to respect and follow those in authority. In such societies, most often some people have more resources to meet their needs, especially their material needs, while other people's needs are not being met.

Theories of Human Nature ("The Story")

One of the "tasks" of authority-based systems is to create a coherent framework, a theory, or a story that helps explain and legitimize the necessity for authority. This, in itself, is not unique about authority-based systems. Every social form that exists tends to create a coherent story that explains and justifies the existing social order. What is particular about authority-based systems is that, as a matter of practice, human beings have always been unhappy with being coerced, and so a very powerful story has to be created in order for most of us to accept that our fate is going to be governed and established by others. This is so much so, that many of us embrace the position of follower, and even feel a longing to be told what to do, to have someone we can rely on to make things okay.

That very powerful story can be found in sources as diverse as the Bible (Genesis, 8:21 "the imagination of man's heart is evil from his youth"), Thomas Hobbes's notion that humans agreed to the restraints of the social contract because otherwise they would be in a state of constant war with each other, and Freud's *Civilization and Its Discontent*, which is dedicated to the core idea that human beings' own natural urges must be subdued in order for society to function. Here are some of the repeating elements of the more modern version of this story:

- People are selfish and greedy. (Or, at least, everyone but me is.)
- People attend to other people's needs only out of self-interest.
- There isn't enough for everyone.
- We are separate from each other.
- Some people are endowed with more authority (either by virtue of divine decree, familial inheritance, sheer military power, economic power, or certain skills, talents, and expertise).

The invariable conclusion is that some form of authority is needed in order to create and maintain order and safety; that in its absence human life could not function.

Again, in the actual practice of how societies are organized, there are invariably contexts in which generosity, community, trust, and sharing flourish. In much of human history, for example, the commons served this function in innumerable communities where many resources were shared without any state-run rules or private property.[37] Even today, after centuries of losses in the struggle to keep the commons going, there are still roughly two billion people dependent on and living on roughly six billion hectares of commons world-wide. This is no small feat considering how much has been invested by governments and companies to dismantle the commons through the process known as enclosure – the practice of powerful entities literally preventing people from accessing what used to be common resources by enclosing them. Originally, the fences were physical. Today, as the struggle continues, the fences are often virtual, affecting less tangible resources.

---

[37] For a collection of essays ranging from the educational to the heart-wrenching about the role of the commons in the past, present, and future, see *The Wealth of the Commons*. (ed. Bollier and Helfrich). This collection includes much discussion about the findings of Elinor Ostrom that challenge the now-famous concept of the "tragedy of the commons," suggesting instead that commons thrive when governed by a group that establishes its own usually autonomous rules and systems of governance. This means, usually, having a clear membership that participates in designing the rules and sanctions that regulate them, along with institutions to apply benefit-sharing where appropriate and sanctions when the rules are broken. The governance systems in well-managed commons (which are usually locally managed, too) tend to be highly collaborative. Current examples include Wikipedia, lobster fisheries in Maine, community-managed forests in the tropics, and many others. The idea of the commons is often confusing to people, since commons are not private property and operate, traditionally, where no deeds exist, and yet within commons individual users often have specific usage rights (usufruct, as the technical term goes), often including obtaining benefit or profit, along with the right to pass down such rights. Unlike actual ownership, though, sale of these rights is either prohibited or severely restricted.

Because the presence of the commons serves as such a strong counter-example to the dominant story, and because of the intensity of demand by international capital for land, the practice of enclosures continues, disrupting lives, communities, and natural systems. Just in the last ten to twenty years, millions of hectares of land previously held in commons in Africa have been enclosed, seized, and sold to corporate interests supported by local elites and international capital, to meet increasing global demand for, mainly, food, biofuels, and minerals.

Social Institutions

When the prevalent theories of human nature suggest that human beings are separate and selfish and that there isn't enough for everyone, the institutions created are likely to be based on control, domination, and obedience. The implicit theory is that those who are in positions of authority are more capable of making responsible decisions, and everyone else needs to be told what to do for anything to function. Thus the use of power in authority-based societies tends to be *over* other people. (See "Coming to Terms with Power" p. 130).

The authority structure is most apparent and clear in the economic realm, where command and control is still the norm. Even leaders who are committed to collaboration in word and general intention, rarely consider it an option truly to collaborate with, say, the shop floor workers on decisions that may affect a company's future.

Even when the formal arrangements of modern societies have been shifting towards formal equality, it is still the case that power remains concentrated in the hands of a few. The gap created between the formal and the actual is often covered by internalized legitimacy rather than outright coercion. That internalization is a big part of what socialization is about. No one is born, for example, believing that people are poor because of not working hard; that comes from the outside before it becomes a personal belief.

Education & Socialization

Whatever life looks like, it is always the task of parents, teachers, and other adults to prepare the next generation for life as it is. When institutions are based on power-over and control, children get prepared for living in these institutions through training for obedience, with a heavy emphasis on punishment and reward. Indeed, obedience is such a key element in parenting that the notion that children may be human beings in their own right, with their own designs and intentions, is foreign to many. In my previous book, *Spinning Threads of Radical Aliveness*, I discuss at length the process of socialization into existing societies and the toll it takes on our spirit. The bulk of that book is dedicated to the project of recovering from our socialization and reclaiming the fullness of who we are.

Another way that socialization is intertwined with the perpetuation of any social order is that children are always told stories about what it means to be human, what they can expect from others, how they are expected to orient themselves towards others, and what a well-lived human life looks like. This happens both at home and beyond through other institutions, such as schools, religious institutions, and, in current societies, through mass media.

For example, in present-day USA, the prevalent guidelines would include not to trust people, to watch out for oneself, to strive for financial success, and to become entirely self-sufficient. Similarly, while most children grow up hearing of the iconic self-made men (and very few women) who shaped modern capitalism, few, if any, learn about the commons, the role of communities more generally, or stories from around the world that demonstrate instances of extraordinary generosity and people coming together in support of each other.

Human Development: How do people actually act in this society?

When we are raised with reward and punishment, we learn to act based on extrinsic motivation: fear of punishment, desire for reward, obligation, shame, or guilt. As I mentioned in *Spinning Threads of Radical Aliveness*, people who saved Jews during the Holocaust tended to come from non-punitive households – they were able to act on their own intrinsic values rather than simply being guided by the understandable fear of the potential consequences.

Similarly, when we are told not to trust people because they won't care about anything other than their own self-interest, we learn to protect ourselves and live with low hopes, which often leads us to becoming cynical, with reduced capacity to act out of joyful generosity.

The great tragedy I see that is related to the process of reproducing a social order is that how human beings behave ends up confirming whatever theory of human nature exists. This is not because of any kind of magic. It is, simply, because we are creatures of practice and we become what we practice. In the case of our liberal, capitalist societies, since we have internalized the framework of separation, scarcity, either/or thinking, and fear of consequences, our behaviors end up "proving" that humans are selfish, competitive, suspicious, and greedy – the very story that leads to creating and perpetuating authority-based systems.

Collaborative Societies

The primary principle around which collaborative societies can be built is the principle of meeting the most needs for the most number of people possible and for the natural environment. Although this principle may appear as having little consequence, the attempt to apply it changes everything in all the spheres that constitute a human society.

Theories of Human Nature ("The Story")

Although a fully collaborative society has not been around for a very long time, if ever[38], I can easily envision such a society, and a large portion of this book is dedicated to describing such a vision in as much detail as I could muster.

To lay forth what I believe is the fundamental story of human life that would underlie a collaboration-based society requires a degree of faith that transcends and sees through much of what exists around me, to uncover, excavate, and reclaim pieces of humanity that have been submerged, subjugated, or negated for a very long time. I hold everything I say in this segment with great humility: it is what I am working towards, along with many others across the generations, well before me, and likely after me.

---

[38] It is not entirely clear whether there has ever been full collaboration between men and women, or between adults and children, even when other forms of stratification were essentially non-existent. It is even less clear whether any complex society has ever been collaborative. Riane Eisler, in her classic *The Chalice and the Blade*, argues that such societies existed, and has convinced me. Still, hers is not a majority position, and ultimately we have no way of knowing the extent of collaboration in any society that doesn't have extensive written and explicit documentation of itself. As far as I know, all societies that have written records have been authority-based to a larger or smaller degree.

The fundamental assumption that stands at the core of any needs-based approach to life is that the core motivation of human beings is to attend to needs, and that human needs are common to all of us even though the strategies we employ to attend to our needs are as varied as we are across individual variation and cultural differences.

Other elements of this worldview could be:

- People have the capacity for compassion just as much as the capacity for harm.
- People enjoy giving when they have choice.
- People need each other in order to attend to their needs.
- People can resolve their differences through mutually empathic dialogue.

The net result of this radically different story is that authority is not needed, and that human beings can self-govern collaboratively, share resources with care and wisdom, and steward the planet with grace and love.

Social Institutions

The ramifications of these assumptions on how institutions can function are radical and far-reaching. Everything from the purpose of collaborative institutions to how they are managed could not be more different from what we know and what so many of us assume is the only thing possible.

In essence, the function of institutions, all institutions, in a collaboration-based society, is to serve needs. No longer is profit or power per se a goal; serving needs, whether of humans or other life forms, is the only purpose for any institution to exist.

Leadership is also reconceived, shifting from controlling and telling others what to do, to being servants or stewards of the whole. Such a shift can only occur when organizations are structured in such a way that people work out of the joy of serving life rather than for the purpose of amassing wealth or for the purpose of surviving day by day.

When the goal is to serve needs, then it is only natural that those who are affected by decisions would be involved in making them. The process itself would be based on naming and taking shared ownership of all the relevant needs, and collaborating on finding the most effective strategies to attend to all the known needs. In other words, decisions are made in as close to consensual a process as possible for that structure.[39] Moreover, the fundamental decision about how decisions are made involves all those who are part of the institution, organization, or group.

In short, the fundamental use of power shifts within a collaborative social order. Rather than being power-over, power is used with others towards the goal of supporting as many needs as possible with the least coercion imaginable.

There always have been, and likely always will be, people who possess enough integrity, courage, skill, and other qualities that allow them to steward their power for the benefit of all. Part of the significance of embedding collaboration within institutions and social structures means that collaborative leadership will no longer require such exceptional individuals. If the systems remain authority-based, the possibility of using power over others is too easy, and positive shifts are not sustainable. When the systems are collaboration-based, then ordinary leaders would find support and sustenance within the existing structures to use their power with others, for the common good. In either case it takes exceptional people to counteract the flow of the system: only exceptional people manage to cooperate in our system today, and only the exceptional will manage to exert their power over others in a cooperative system tomorrow.

Education & Socialization

If the overall purpose is to be as responsive to needs as possible, that would, by necessity, include the children. Parenting is just as transformed as institutions. Parents and others are still the major holders of the task of socialization, or preparing the young for life in their society. However, since the fundamental structure of society is collaboration, there is absolutely no need to coerce or encourage obedience.

In order to prepare children to take their place as empowered, loving beings in a network of collaborative functioning, they are, instead, raised with empathy and dialogue as the primary tools for making things happen and for resolving conflicts. Force is used only

---

[39] The obvious question of what to do when the number of people in a system is larger than what can fit in a room is most clearly taken up in the schematic description of the governance system in Part Two of this book.

to protect, not to punish, and therefore is the exception rather than the norm in a child's experience. The entire environment nurtures the capacity for compassion, empathy, and generosity through daily modeling. More than anything, children, and all other members of a society, know in an ongoing and fundamental way that they are part of a whole, and that their needs matter. This experience of mattering, the freedom that accompanies it, and the persistent modeling of adults about how to respond to situations where things aren't naturally flowing, are the key building blocks of the capacity to collaborate even under stress, which is essential for the functioning of a collaboration-based social order.

Human Development

In my work over the years with many thousands of individuals, I have noticed that most people find it really hard to imagine *all the way* the degree of freedom that such upbringing would leave intact in people. Our experience is so tainted by the pervasiveness of restraint, obedience, and coercion that full freedom is either inconceivable, or seen as dangerous (a residual belief in the authority-based story), or even both.

Describing what people would be like and how we would act in such an environment is, indeed, a feat of imagination. Still, part of the privilege of doing the kind of work I do over so many years, and approaching people – in many cultures and contexts within those cultures – with the unwavering faith I bring to the work, is that I have a vivid and repeated experience of what happens when trust in our fundamental mattering is rebuilt. What I have seen, time and again, even if not always, is that even a small amount goes a very long way. People move, spontaneously and smoothly, towards greater capacity in three different areas at once: choice and inner freedom; willingness to care about the effects their actions have on others; and resilience for handling the effect that others' actions have on them. Dialogue, the primary communication mode that accompanies collaboration, becomes ever more possible, allowing more and more seemingly intractable conflicts to be resolved or transcended.

The Challenge of Transformation

The dominant story of our current liberal, capitalist world order maintains that the overthrowing of feudal social relations has created more freedom, possibilities, and prosperity for all, and that further movement on this trajectory will continue this trend.

On a certain level, this is incontrovertible. Just in the last 150 years, so many people have been emancipated from systems that limit their potential. The examples abound. Women now have the vote and more possibilities for autonomous decision-making than in millennia. The European welfare state, although imperfect, has liberated millions from conditions of great poverty, which by necessity would have made participation in governance, for example, nearly impossible. Popular education in Latin America, and the entire Freirian tradition, have been so successful that authority-based regimes both on the right and on the orthodox left have at times seen it as a threat. More recently, open-source endeavors are opening new forms of collaboration online that could never have even been imagined, let alone implemented, even a few decades ago. Similarly, the growing presence of worker-owned cooperatives is creating a de facto path to collaboration that is on the rise.

At the same time, over the course of the last several hundred years, there are fewer and fewer separate "worlds" in which humans live. In our ancient past, it is estimated that there may have been thousands, if not more, groupings of humans that didn't know anything about the possible existence of other human groups. Even as recently as the conquest of the Americas, the Aztecs and the Incas had barely any knowledge of each other's existence.[40] By then, the number of separate worlds had diminished considerably. At this point in time, there are hardly any groups that manage to sustain an existence that is not in ongoing interaction with global capital, more often than not entirely subsumed by it. This one world, by many accounts, is ruled by corporations representing the direct interests and perspectives of a progressively narrowing proportion of the world's population – the unimaginably wealthy[41] – and supported by a global middle class eager to consume products and services at a fast

---

[40] A fact of dire consequence for the Incas, who might otherwise have been warned by the Aztecs about the conquest methods of the Spaniards.

[41] Who are, despite the popularity of the 1% frame, far, far fewer than 1%, especially if we look at the global human population.

growing rate.[42] For the vast majority of people this world continues to spell extreme poverty and little say about the circumstances of their lives.[43] Even for those of us in industrialized countries with liberal democracies, much of our cherished choice is more and more focused on patterns of individual consumption and the right to vote in elections that are less and less trusted, instead of the capacity to shape and participate in designing the conditions of our living and the way our communities function.

This is, ultimately, why I make the claim that in the past several thousand years more and more of the world's people have been living in societies that are, in essence, authority-based systems. As further illustration, I can point to the many egalitarian, consensus-based forest peoples that have ended up becoming more divided and patriarchal. I can point to a loss of the hinterlands, places where people continued to self-organize until fairly recently. And, while one of the places where experiments with collaboration abound is within corporations themselves, they generally are set up in such a way that they neither lead to changes in the fundamental way that corporations operate, nor to wider collaboration beyond the corporation.

I want those of us who are passionate about creating a collaborative future to take heed of the difficulties this presents for the possibility of moving in that direction. Any social order tends to reproduce itself – directly through socialization efforts,[44] and indirectly through the intertwining of the various elements that are represented in the diagram above. Because of that, change would need to happen on all those levels.

The diagram at the top of this piece, along with the more detailed explanation of the various elements at work in any social order, make it evident that if we want change to happen, we can begin anywhere in the system we are part of. At the same time, the intertwining of these circles also helps explain why personal change without structural change, or structural change without personal change, are ultimately likely to fail to create the deeper transformation so many

---

[42] UNEP is estimating global consumption of resources to triple by 2050. Where those resources would come from is, clearly, an entirely separate question given the state of our planetary life support systems.
[43] By the World Bank's own admission, in 2005 more than three billion people lived on less than $2.50 a day, and 44% of them survived, in ways that probably none of us in industrialized countries can begin to grasp, on less than $1.25 a day.
[44] See *Spinning Threads of Radical Aliveness* for a much more detailed examination of how we are socialized in our current societies and what each of us *as an individual* can do to transcend those limitations.

of us long for. If we liberate ourselves, for example, and don't change our parenting, our children are likely to grow up with similar challenges to the ones we have. Our own capacity to create change is also limited by the options available to us in whichever society we happen to be part of and by the tendency of the social order, especially in authority-based societies, to punish any deviation from the norm.

At the same time, as history amply shows, creating structural changes without attending to the individual dimension is unsustainable. Even in the Kibbutz movement in Israel, where structural change happened by choice and not through revolution or a coup, there were no mechanisms in place for attending to the internalized versions of authority-based elements that individual members carried within them, nor were there mechanisms put in place for knowing how to respond to dissent, or to the needs of subsequent generations that were not part of the original enthusiasm of creating the new institutions. Ultimately, the Kibbutz movement was embedded in a market economy which created intense pressures and affected decisions with critical long-term effects.[45] These challenges, along with a host of unforeseen events that happened over time[46], eventually eroded the delicately placed institutions of collaboration and resource sharing that were the fundamental building blocks of that experiment.

This complexity is a big part of why I set out to write this book. I wanted to offer tools for reflection and action that would attend to the way social change was attempted so as to incorporate inner change in how we work for change. This means, amongst other things, that we learn to direct efforts to change how we act as individuals, how we engage in groups, how we make decisions, and how we model collaborative leadership and loving intention towards all, including our current or former enemies.

---

[45] See "Lessons from the Israeli Kibbutz Movement" on page 214.
[46] Among them: the appearance of the television after 1968, which created lifestyle pressures, and the influx of Holocaust reparation money from Germany, which went to individuals rather than the collectivity, and strained the economic equality that had been established and protected for years.

Working with Others in Community

Time and again I continue to discover that even when we undergo considerable personal transformation, we continue to create groups and organizations that reflect the current social structures rather than the vision that inspires us. The consciousness doesn't jump to a next level of functioning by itself. Once again, if we want to see different results we need to apply different practices.

Since social change cannot be done by individuals alone, and requires organizing with others to achieve results, the questions that we face are of deep significance in these times of such high stakes for our future mixed with extraordinary uncertainty. What can help us work better together?

Every attempt to create structural change entails being in relationship and dialogue with other people. Even when focusing solely on organizing people for concrete projects, the capacity to work with people of divergent views and approaches is essential to moving forward anywhere. Even when people have fundamental agreement about their worldview there are still endless differences about how to get where we're going.

This is why working with others to create change means learning to collaborate across different understandings of how to create change; across differences of working styles and personalities; and across differences such as class and race.

We also need concrete steps for putting into practice our understanding of and commitment to interdependence, so as to transcend the deeply ingrained habits of operating as collections of individuals instead of communities of mutual support and effective feedback loops. In addition, we need facilitation and decision-making tools to contribute to effective functioning of the groups and organizations in which we participate.

Why Is Collaboration Challenging?

One of the core paradoxes facing us when we attempt to organize for social change is that we end up aiming to create alternatives to the existing models we have inherited while having neither external examples for what we want to create nor tools for overcoming the obstacles that our internalized version of the existing social order presents. Given these conditions, I am not surprised at all that so many movements get mired in conflict, distracted by mistrust, or end up looking frightfully similar to the structures they seek to transform. Nonetheless, I continue to believe that many tools and practices exist that are relevant and applicable right now, even before the transformation that would make them the norm has happened. Not only that, we can actually use those very tools in order to make our work for this transformation more effective.

Collaboration, like empathy, is something we hear about more and more as a general abstract good, and yet we are given so little by way of the how. What happens as a result is that we try to collaborate without knowing how, or we don't even try because we are too consumed with fear, overwhelm, or outright judgment.

Collaboration is a very exacting discipline, and rests on only one uncompromising commitment: to attend to everyone's needs. This commitment challenges our habits of separation and scarcity, and thus requires conscious choice at every turn. Put differently, collaboration is the purest antidote to either/or thinking because it rests on the faith that, in addition to a solution that works for all involved being possible, it is also potentially better. The biggest obstacle we encounter is our habit, often deeply entrenched, of seeing our own needs as separate or even opposed to what someone else wants, even if we philosophically believe in collaboration.

There is no question in my mind that the willingness to risk an outcome that's different from what we want is essential for the possibility of collaboration, despite the potential consequences. It's not about giving up on what we want; it's only about the willingness to consider a different outcome. That willingness is what allows us to open up to hear others, to see their point of view, to consider other possibilities, to shift at times, and to speak about what we want without insisting on it happening. All of these are fundamental building blocks of the process of collaboration.

Perhaps counter-intuitively, in order to collaborate well we need to learn how to engage in conflict in a productive way. Sometimes when we are uncomfortable with conflict, rather than face the discomfort directly we end up acting indirectly, which may result in more pain and discomfort for others, sometimes even for ourselves.

Why is collaboration so difficult and tenuous for so many people? Since we are so clearly social animals, wouldn't we naturally know how to collaborate? I'd like to believe that before separation set in (see the section "How We Got Here" in my book *Spinning Threads of Radical Aliveness*) we used to know how to collaborate, and with the advent of a consciousness of separation, we lost that capacity. I have heard so often from people about their collaboration challenges, and so many different kinds of such difficulties, that I have come to believe that in today's world effective collaboration is an accomplishment rather than a given. Here are some snippets from my work with people about their collaboration challenges, with some tips we can all use to increase our chances of collaborating successfully.

Full Responsibility

I often hear from people something to the effect that they can't collaborate with someone because of that person's actions, choices, or communication. For myself, I hold that if I want to collaborate with someone, the responsibility is on me to make that collaboration work. In tough moments I remind myself that I am the one who wants to collaborate, and therefore I want to take the responsibility for making it happen. The less willingness another person has, the more presence, skill, and commitment are required from me. Expecting fairness interferes with the possibility of collaboration. Instead of thinking about what's fair, I think about what's possible in any situation given the level of skill and interest of all the players. Sometimes this may be more than I want to do, in which case I may choose not to collaborate. I still know that it's my choice, and not the other person's limitations, that ends the collaboration. This orientation has helped me tremendously, to the point of carrying no resentment to speak of, even in situations that break down.

Making Use of Input

A senior program officer in a high-profile non-profit organization attended one of my workshops and talked about dreading the experience of bringing her ideas to her team. The reason? They usually don't like what she says, then she sits and endures their input despite the pain, without saying anything to them, and finally she thanks them for the input and makes whatever decision she makes.

One way of transforming such a challenge is to be proactive about the kind of input that we want. For example, when she proposes a plan, she can start by saying that she wants to hear a few people express only what they like about the proposal. Providing specific positive comments supports her in relaxing, and supports the others in connecting more with the reason the proposal is there in the first place. Then she can ask the team to name those areas that they don't like and for which they have concrete suggestions for improvement. This builds a sense of movement and possibility. Finally, she can ask for any additional concerns for which people may not have a solution. By then, enough goodwill gets generated that the group can look at those concerns together and brainstorm suggestions with her. She is then not alone and overwhelmed with so much input without solutions. And everyone has the experience that their input is valued. In that way she leads them to collaborate.

Telling the Truth with Care

In another workshop I worked with the founder of a start-up company who brought up the challenge he had about having a sales person whose judgment calls he doesn't always trust. What can he do to move towards a collaborative experience with this employee?

Sometimes the most important thing about collaborating is truth telling. Often enough we avoid telling the truth because of fear of hurting other people. This is because we've been trained to believe that truth and care are mutually exclusive. Instead, I aim for truth *with* care. In order to find a way to shift the dynamics with the employee, I invited everyone at the workshop to imagine themselves being that employee, and what they would want to hear from the founder in such a situation. Within moments we came up with several ways to present the truth. One example: "I have some concerns about how you respond to some situations. I want us to work together well, and

I want to support you in being successful in this job. Are you open to reviewing a few situations together so we can get more alignment around our priorities?"

More generally, whenever we have a difficult message to deliver, we can imagine being the other person, really and truly stepping into their proverbial shoes. From within that perspective we can often feel directly what would register as care, what's necessary to say or highlight to make room for the truth to be digestible. It's never about compromising the truth; it's only about framing it in a context of collaboration.

Sameness and Difference: Creating Communities of Struggle

None of us can walk the path to radical consciousness on our own. Wherever it is that we are in the social order, we are complicit with the existing social order. This may look like accepting the goals that are defined as worthwhile, or it may look like not standing up to the oppression of others, or it may look like just living our own individual lives, consuming and discarding products. To become conscious of this complicity, to open our hearts to the consequences of our actions, whatever their intention is, often requires the presence of others. That's one of the major differences between this path and that of therapy, whose goal is inherently individual. Why do we need others? They can hold our feet to the fire, remind us of what's true of us when we forget and succumb to fear of stepping out of role or obedience, or to the messages we have internalized from our life – that we are powerless, or inadequate. The people we engage with as we emerge into freedom help us gain and confirm insight, they share the pain and struggle with us, and remind us, by their very presence, that we are not alone.

Because of the deep internalization of separateness, even within groups and communities that come together to create change on the basis of shared understanding and vision, breakdowns in mutuality continue to occur. A commitment to social transformation entails, and is strengthened by, facing such breakdowns head on, and viewing them as yet another opportunity to reflect on the depths of our participation in structures of domination.

The example of the women's movement can serve to illustrate the dynamics of sameness and difference. The earlier wave of the women's movement in the late 60s and early 70s took the form of consciousness raising groups, at least within white culture. Individual women came to such groups in order to gain in strength. They were able to question their prior existence, identify thoughts and feelings that were unnamed before, and change their relationships with themselves and others. Within and outside of that process much feminist theorizing was born. Emotional engagement preceded the change in consciousness, as well as being enhanced and deepened with new understandings.

The movement started with a period of joy and enthusiasm, with images of "sisterhood" and joint strength. But the sense of comfort women initially found in each other's company could not live up to the differences between them. Sisterhood was a narrowly defined concept, forcing identity and sameness that were not there, and making the realization of differences threatening.

Within this climate Audre Lorde urged women to change their perspective: "Difference must be not merely tolerated, but seen as a fund of necessary polarities between which our creativity can spark like a dialectic. Only then does the necessity for interdependency become unthreatening." Lorde presented a major challenge both to white and Black women[47]. Since both white and Black women engaged in this complicated relationship with differences, both needed to address it. Among the white feminists, the complexity often shows up in the form of pretense of unity even while actual exclusions and separation are maintained, albeit unintentionally. In the Black community, it takes the form of a need for unity, mistakenly assumed to mean homogeneity.

Lorde's challenge is at the heart of the paradox of mutuality. She calls women to task on our handling of differences between us, and invites us to use differences as an opportunity for learning that can lead to deeper connection. There is no way to hold on to any comforting conception of nature, reality, unity, without thereby giving in to the tradition of domination. A search for an essential identity as the fundamental unifying force is more likely to create more separation and splintering than to achieve unity.

However challenging, unity and coming together are critical at this time in history. For a growing number of people worldwide survival is not an academic issue, nor a future threat, but an everyday reality. And so we keep trying. However, for as long as we try to achieve unity through sameness, we still haven't transcended the legacy of fear of difference.

In the absence of a great deal of mindful practices about how to be in community, the combination of the *need* for others and the *fear* of others may easily result, for those of us who are accustomed to privilege, in an attempt to impose our ways on others. It's only by

---

[47] Audre Lorde and many other writers working to dismantle racism have capitalized Black but not white. E.g. see Lorde's *Sister Outsider: Essays and Speeches*, Berkeley, 1984. For an explanation see dcentric.wamu.org/2011/10/when-to-capatalize-black-and-white/index.html.

recognizing otherness *and* meeting it with connection that we can forge communities robust enough to withstand the pressures of standing up to the dominant culture and structures.

Similarly, waiting for those with more privilege to change before we can work with them may keep us waiting for a long time, however understandable that longing is. The legacy of oppression often results in considering the act of "understanding the oppressor" a sign of weakness and of continued participation in structures of domination – be it women in relation to men, people of color in relation to white people, gay people in relation to straight, or others.

Individuals alone cannot effect social change, no matter how much personal work they have done: they need to come together. Communities, on the other hand, remain largely ineffective for as long as the separations between individuals are maintained. This dynamic within communities is one of the key places where empathy for the oppressor becomes a vital tool. With enough willingness to face our differences with love, we can forge alliances that allow us to continue to do the work of transforming our consciousness and transcending social cleavages within our communities even as we face larger structures we work on changing.

Balancing Process and Action

Although coming to terms with differences within groups coming together for social change work is a sine qua non for being able to work together for change without recreating structures of domination, we also need to do the work itself. Sorting out conflicts, building new ways of relating within community, is no substitute for taking action in the world. One challenge that many groups face is that the work of forging trust and relationships within the group can spill over into the business of the group.

A related challenge arises when people learn the principles of Nonviolent Communication (NVC) and try to bring them into their communities and social change groups. One principle, in particular, presents early practitioners with enormous challenges: attending to the quality of connection before focusing on outcome. Some people, in learning this practice, develop a tendency to focus on connection almost to the exclusion of outcome.

With or without learning NVC, many groups expend inordinate amounts of energy on struggles about how much process to have in their meetings. The people who, by inclination or habit, are drawn to being in process, to working out conflicts all the way to the bottom, to reaching robust consensus on everything, and to focusing on the relationships within the group, are pitted against the people who, by inclination or habit, are drawn to creating tangible results, to moving towards clear goals, to staying on track with intended agenda, and to focusing on the stated purpose of the group in terms of action in the world. The tragedy of this particular kind of conflict is that the conversation often ends up being about whether or not to be in process rather than the process itself, which satisfies neither "camp" in the struggle.

Key to shifting this kind of dynamic is learning to adapt to different circumstances. Attending to connection within a high-paced, decision-making meeting would be different from attending to connection during a debriefing meeting when we focus on learning from what happened, and different again from a mutual support group.

This adaptation takes two forms. One is about creating all the different contexts so that there is ample room for connection, mutual support, trust building, working out conflicts, and all the other process tasks necessary and vital for ongoing thriving of any group. Those of us working for change could all benefit, for example, from having times set aside deliberately to provide support for the trauma of witnessing the suffering we see around us and in the world at large. As history shows, whenever groups become effective enough, their encounters with existing structures can become more and more brutal. We need to work out our despair and anger regularly in order to be able to maintain the uncompromising love that is the absolute baseline of nonviolent social change. If we don't set time aside to provide this mutual support, the trauma is likely to erupt in disruptive behavior, unloving arguments, and other familiar behaviors that have been known to derail groups trying to achieve transformational goals. During such times set aside for support and empathy, connection is the only goal. The unrushed atmosphere of not having an agenda is vital to creating lasting healing and increasing our effectiveness as agents of change.

The other form of adaptation necessary is to match our process with the context. The principle, as I understand it, is to provide sufficient connection in the moment to be able to restore presence in the moment with the purpose at hand. Even in the midst of time-pressured decision-making, I know I want to have sufficient room in my heart to notice when someone is upset beyond their capacity to function effectively, and to provide just enough empathy so this person can resume their active participation without cost to their heart and soul. Too little space for connection, and we lose the person as well as the trust in the room. Too much space for connection, and we lose sight of why we are together in the first place. The paradox I have seen is that the more tension we bring to those moments, the longer they last. Any attempt to rush the connection tends to result in a longer amount of time before the focus can resume. With enough trust in the process, on the other hand, such connection dips can usually be achieved within a surprisingly short amount of time, sometimes only seconds of just acknowledging what happened. Ultimately, everyone in the room wants the group's purpose to be achieved, and wants to be mobilized and present to participate. Key to allowing that commitment to flourish is operating in a way that reassures everyone that their needs matter. This is one of the ways in which we model ways of organizing that mimic the vision of the world we want to create.

Maximizing Willingness
for Efficiency and Sustainability

Two challenges that people face when coming together to organize and work for change are how to function together efficiently in the face of different opinions and wishes, and how to sustain the energy over time. Focusing on willingness as an organizing principle of group functioning addresses both of these challenges.

Willingness is distinguished from preference, on the one hand, and from any notion of what should happen, on the other hand. Willingness is also distinct from resignation, apathy, or even "going along." Willingness, as I understand it, is a true movement from within that is wholehearted and clear. I am willing because I know to what my actions are contributing, and those purposes are significant to me even if they are not my preference. I am truly choosing, as opposed to having no clue what else I would do and therefore, essentially, giving up on participating fully (e.g. in the face of one person who is pushing for his or her ideas strongly).

Overall Group Functioning

In truth, I don't know of any groups or organizations that are operating *fully* in line with the principles I am outlining in this book. Even BayNVC, the organization I co-founded, has had periods of immense challenges during parts of its history, while much of the time, and now again, I have felt moved by and celebrated the extent to which this organization approximates that level of alignment, and mostly functions smoothly and without endless meetings because of a high level of trust.

If we want to create groups or organizations that do function in line with these principles, I would want to apply them from the get go. Marshall Rosenberg, the creator of Nonviolent Communication, suggests that the most important decision to make collaboratively is the decision about the process of making decisions. This is the highest level at which to apply these principles. If all agree that certain decisions are made by one person, then that person is likely empowered and entrusted. If, however, that one person decides to make those decisions, and others don't have a say, they will likely experience the same behavior as imposition or domination. I suspect that many groups and organizations have implicit agreements about decision-making rather than explicit ones, and that can interfere dramatically with the experience of trust in working together. At BayNVC, we have looked at these questions several times, and from time to time have reviewed who makes what decisions. I don't think we have a perfect solution. I do have a sense that most people within the organization trust that their needs and perspectives are valued in arriving at decisions that affect them and the organization.

Assigning Tasks

One of the sources of burnout in many communities and groups rests on the way that tasks get assigned or taken on. Instead of focusing on what each person is willing to do to contribute to the business of the group, the discussion more often than not is focused on what "should" be done, and who is the "right" person to do it. Or people take on a task or project because "it's important" and/or "no one else will do it, so I have to," and not because they are drawn or even truly willing to do it without resentment.

I am more and more able to accept having things not happen rather than having them done without true willingness, so that whatever does happen can be sustained over time without stress. I think of it as a deep discipline to be willing to let go of whatever no one is willing to do. I was inspired in that growing commitment by the words of Thomas Merton: "To allow oneself to be carried away by a multitude of conflicting concerns, to surrender to too many demands, to commit oneself to too many projects, to want to help everyone in everything is to succumb to violence."

I have often seen startled looks when I have worked with various groups and suggested adopting the guideline of letting things not happen rather than having someone do them based on an inner or outside pressure. The ethos of overriding our bodies and souls in order to get the work done is so pervasive, that it takes effort to transcend it.

This principle is a natural application of the core intention to transcend domination in any form. It works for a number of reasons:

- Doing only what we're willing to do reduces or eliminates resentment and burnout.

- Finding out whether or not people are willing to do something provides a more accurate feedback loop about what resources are truly available to attend to tasks.

- When we know we won't be forced to do something, not even in subtle forms, we are more likely to find our generosity and goodwill, and to feel empowered to contribute all we have.

- When true willingness guides our choices, the quality of work we accomplish increases.

- Adhering to this principle creates honesty and more predictability, as fewer of us are likely to say "yes" to something and proceed to not do it or even sabotage others' actions.

- Meetings become more efficient when discussions, even arguments, about what a group should do or what are good ideas are replaced with clarity about who is willing to take on action.

- Solutions often tend to be more creative when people only stick to what they are willing to do, because the tried and true approaches often require work no one wants to do nor even knows for sure why it gets done.

- The overall level of self-care within the group increases as people begin to identify and stand up for the limits of their willingness

Lastly, my vision and dream, and complete conviction, is that we can make the entire world work by willingness alone. There have been so many times when I have seen, on a small scale, evidence of this fundamental goodwill and capacity for stretching once the guilt and fear factors are removed. The solutions are often more creative and piecemeal: one person will take the notes, and another will type them up, for example. We learn to work together and do what we can without harming ourselves and others.

Working with Willingness in Decision-making

Attempting to reach decisions that everyone is happy with is likely to result in more meeting time in groups than most people can tolerate, and is one of the obstacles many people experience to wanting to go to meetings and commit to working with a group. Even with time and heated discussions, often fatigue and resignation result in some decision being arrived at rather than a fully chosen decision that is acceptable to all. At other times, it seems no one is willing to shift, and the polarization itself takes a toll on everyone.

Some decisions involve content, such as which action a group wants to take or what response to a condemning article the group wants to adopt. Some of them are about what happens in the group as content is discussed: Who will speak next? How will the group know when a topic is complete? How will the ultimate decision be made? What will happen to those who are unhappy with a decision?

Facilitators who are skillful in this art create trust by handling these and the many other small questions that arise in the moment skillfully, such that movement is prioritized at the same time as everyone's voice and needs are held with care. Such trust allows for willingness to be experienced within a context of everyone mattering, which makes all the difference in the world when the hard decisions arrive.

In my experience, to reach collaborative decisions we need only focus on what people can accept with true willingness and distinguish it from what would be their most desired outcome. With sufficient facilitation skill and attention, many decisions can be arrived at with surprisingly little tension and within a timeframe and level of engagement that are much easier for people to experience. The essential tools are the capacity to identify and create collective ownership of needs, and the skillful application of a search for willingness rather than preference. The underlying principle is the unwavering commitment to having everyone matter, holding everyone's needs with care. Both the commitment and the skills are necessary to be able to maintain togetherness in the face of differences. Time and again I have seen the power of persisting in inviting a group to find a solution rather than re-polarize into initial fixed positions about an issue. In my experience, that kind of insistent and yet relaxed faith has always yielded a creative, previously unimagined solution to what could appear as an inherent and unsolvable conflict.[48]

Like every deep practice, mastering the art of facilitating groups on the basis of the principle of willingness takes effort over time.

---

[48] See pages 383-4 for an example from my work in supporting an attempt at collaborative law-making in Minnesota.

Below are a few pointers for anyone who wants to begin learning and experimenting with this principle.

Reflect Everything That Everyone Says

This practice provides several benefits. First, it allows each person to have an experience of being heard, which contributes to a sense of inclusion, as well as to peace and calm, which are very useful resources when facilitating a group. In addition, this provides information for the facilitator about what's important to different people, which is essential for creating a solution that works for everyone or close to that. Lastly, reflection also slows down the conversation and makes it more mindful.

Identify and Record What's Important in What People Say

Especially in polarized situations, this one key skill is particularly helpful – the ability to hear the dream, vision, value, need, or goal that is hidden behind the different opinions. For example, let's say that we are in a meeting to evaluate two different software platforms, and someone says: "This product sucks. They haven't been supporting it for years." What I hear is that what's important to this person is reliability in terms of tech support. Or if someone says: "It's so boring, there's nothing to it," I hear that they want a product that's innovative or has complex functionality. Why is this capacity important? Because moving towards something has more potential for getting people together than arguing about what's not working.

This practice, which is an application of the distinction between strategy and need, is an irreducible foundation of the process. All conflicts happen at the level of strategy. It's hard to sustain a conflict once the underlying needs, values, and aspirations of all parties are heard by all. Hearing the needs and recording them begins the process of de-polarizing. For example, in a simulated city council meeting I conducted, one of the participants who was opposed to a proposal to build affordable housing in the center of town raised the issue of loss of property value. What we identified as the essential core of this concern was a wish for security for homeowners. Everyone in the room could line up around wanting security for homeowners, even though some people didn't resonate with preserving property values. Recording each item also deepens the sense of being heard.

Create a Shared Ownership of the Criteria for Resolution

Once we verify with each person that we got clearly what's important to them, the next step is to generate one list with all that's important. This, then, becomes the list of criteria to use to evaluate the product in this case, or to evaluate any proposal that's on the table more generally. Key to the success of this approach is to create one list with the core qualities that are sought, without any reference to the specific action, direction, strategy, or product that's being discussed. What then happens is that the group can move to shared ownership of the list, an act that gradually de-polarizes the group and shifts it into an orientation of finding, together, a solution that meets as many of the criteria as possible. In that way we support collaboration even in a charged context.

Although this may seem small, having one shared list of what's important to people in terms of criteria/qualities/needs for the proposal makes a huge difference. If two lists are maintained, the polarity gets reinforced. With one list everyone is invited into a space of shared responsibility for the well-being of all. The idea that any solution would need to address as many of these needs as possible can become a refrain, an ongoing reminder to people to transcend their own self-interest and embrace the whole.

Invite People to Only Say What Hasn't Been Said Before

Everyone needs to be heard. Not everyone needs to speak. Once a particular position has been heard in full, there is no need for anyone else to say it again. One of the reasons for recording all the needs is precisely to avoid repetition and create efficiency in hearing everything only once.

As facilitator, I make a point of asking specifically for only new pieces to add to the puzzle. From a certain moment on, when I already have confidence that the shared ownership is taking place, it no longer matters who has which position, and there isn't even a need to ask for position. People grasp the concept easily, and can add directly to the list of needs/criteria.

Track People and Honor Transitions

To increase everyone's trust that their voice and presence matter, it's vitally important to track who has something they haven't yet said, and also to explicitly acknowledge and get agreement from people before moving to speak with another person. This could look like: "I know you have more to say, and I would love to hear it. At this point I am worried about staying with you because so-and-so hasn't spoken yet at all and wants to. Are you comfortable with me switching to so-and-so and coming back to you later?" Or, in a different context, "I see that your hand is up. Are you OK waiting another couple of minutes until I finish hearing from so-and-so?"

I have found this kind of practice to be incredibly calming for everyone, even those who are not directly affected. I have heard from people that those moments support them in trusting that their needs and well-being matter through seeing how everyone's well-being is tracked and held.

Transcend Either/Or Proposals

Although sometimes the group may not have a say in the matter, whenever possible leave room for taking things back to the drawing board for re-doing a proposed decision. The more criteria and needs we include, the more flexible and creative the solution. Such flexibility usually transcends a "yes" or "no" to a fixed proposal.

My favorite example of this happened when two colleagues of mine flew to Pakistan a number of years ago and trained Afghani leaders in a refugee camp. By the third day some of the people were so excited about the training that they invited my colleagues to come to the mosque with them. Others immediately expressed upset about how anyone could possibly ask people from the US to come into the mosque. Within minutes they were actively fighting about this, going back and forth in the familiar polarized ways. My colleagues seized the opportunity to use all the principles they had brought to the training. They slowed the process down and identified all the needs for both positions, and then invited the group to come up with solutions to the dilemma. In the end, a complex hybrid solution arose. They came up with some arrangement that allowed my colleagues entry into the mosque in a way that would not offend those who didn't want them to come in. At the end, one of those present reflected, with sadness, that if they had had these tools in earlier years they wouldn't have needed to go to war.

Observe and Challenge Patterns of Over-Extending

Often enough groups include members who have much more capacity to access willingness than others, and therefore run the danger of doing it again and again until they reach overwhelm, exhaustion, and finally burnout. As a leader in a group, a commitment to nonviolence includes keeping track of who is willing at any point in time. If such patterns emerge, embodying the principle of true willingness means sometimes challenging people's "yes" and engaging them in fuller dialogue to see what their needs really are. Such explorations can then uncover additional needs that may be useful for others to hear anyway, and can allow for solutions that address more needs, including those of the person who is over-extending.

Structure, Process, and Facilitation

It's important to remember that having group members with personal skill does not necessarily make for effective group or organizational functioning. Several variables interact to affect the functioning of a group. Personal skill is only one of them. Others are the presence or absence of a skilled facilitator, and the structure of the process available. Many processes for group functioning exist that are very structured, and do not require a facilitator or any specific skill on the part of the people who participate in the group. Others require a high degree of personal skill and/or a facilitator. The process of decision-making that I have worked with and developed tends to require a facilitator, and requires a significant degree of skill. There is no need for everyone in the group to be skilled if a facilitator or leader is sufficiently committed to using this process and to holding everyone's needs with care.

Facilitating from the Sidelines

For a participant in a group who is not a designated leader, the depth of commitment to nonviolence means speaking the truth with courage, integrity, and care for others. It doesn't mean allowing everything to happen. The latter is the essence of passivity, which Gandhi was, in moments, more concerned about than violence itself.

A quiet person who sees patterns from the side, someone who is not ready to speak up boldly and publicly, could begin the slow, complex process of connecting with the person who has the drive, and with the people who are "going along" to bring about more connection. I don't know of shortcuts. The only power available to someone who is not the designated leader is the power of heart and mind to listen, to love, to create connection, and to empower people.

Business Not as Usual

Sometimes I think that some people have no idea how simple and easy it could be to function in groups in a way that works for everyone. I want to offer, perhaps, some way of imagining what it could be like by describing some of the history and the functioning of the Consciousness Transformation Community I created in 2010, which operated for two years.

The biggest surprise of the first few months of this community was the delightful collapse of the very elaborate structure I initially attempted to put in place. I found it so liberating that a simple and organic structure I couldn't possibly have thought of on my own replaced my original complex one through an emergent and dialogic process. After some months, any member of the community had full access to contributing anything they wanted within a collaborative, co-creative, spontaneous, and voluntary structure. Anyone was invited to take responsibility for the functioning of the community and to participate in decision-making.

From the start, this community was an experiment in doing things differently. As part of that, I created a gift economy structure, so that people who joined were invited to contribute and were not in any way "required" or even subtly "expected" to contribute, either financially or otherwise. I had a very large vision for what we could create over time, and I was ecstatic to see the initial response.

Although vision comes easy to me, sometimes staying patient during implementation doesn't. I confess to getting discouraged rather easily at times, which I am sad about because of the toll it takes on others around me. With that community, too, as the first few months unfolded and I didn't see the self-organizing happening, I became overwhelmed and worried that unless I did everything (which I was clear I wouldn't do), the community just wouldn't happen. As part of my own path of living the commitments that formed the basis of this community[49] I chose to share, in full, with the community what my experience was. I was deeply moved and amazed by how I was received. This initial reception turned into a

---

[49] The commitments are described, in detail, in *Spinning Threads of Radical Aliveness*. For a list of the commitments, see baynvc.blogspot.com/p/core-commitments_24.html.

structure that was more aligned with my original vision than the one I initially created. The most compelling part of it was the process by which it came to be. In addition to my own coming forth, other people stepped forward and empowered themselves to make requests, offer themselves to the community, and express their longings, dreams, and concerns about the initial design. The new structure emerged from our collective engagement with all that was put on the table.

One of the elements of the new structure was the establishment of monthly, open meetings for attending to community business. Anyone who was holding any responsibility for anything in the community (whether offering groups, doing administrative support, welcoming new members, or any other function, all of which were voluntary) was welcome to participate. In fact, anyone, even if not holding responsibility, was welcome to participate or submit agenda items. Our intention was to have these meetings, themselves, be conducted in accordance with the commitments we had all embraced.

In addition to this group, another decision-making process was adopted by the community after significant discussion. Any member of the community could initiate this process, which was a multi-layered effort to engage, in a distributed, asynchronous, and virtual manner the same kind of shared holding of needs at the heart of the in-person process I described earlier.

Sample Meeting

To make this vivid, I want to describe what happened in one particular meeting that had a number of agenda items. The one that engaged us for most of our time was the process for accepting new members to the community. At one point all but one of us were comfortable with the process as it had been previously. For a moment there seemed to be an impasse, because this person wanted something I was very much non-negotiable about. One of the commitments was primary in guiding our conversation: "Openness to Dialogue." We engaged fully with attempting to understand the needs behind what this one person wanted. I was in awe at the care, the openness, and the presence. One by one the needs and their related strategies became known, until everything was heard. The result was a deeper understanding on all of our parts, which led to a process of accepting new members that *all* of us liked better than what was proposed previous to hearing this person. Along the way we discovered that one member was challenged at an earlier moment in the conversation and had lost trust, and we turned our attention to her. From this bit of conversation emerged more clarity about our process for deliberation and decision-making.

I have been advocating that connection and effectiveness can go hand in hand and that full collaboration and inclusion do not necessarily mean loss of efficiency. Here, in that meeting, I experienced it in full. Granted, we were not producing anything on which anyone's life depends. And yet experiments like this can pave the way and show what's possible.[50]

---

[50] If you're curious why this community only lasted two years, go to pages 167-72 to see important lessons I learned about conscious choice of unilateral force.

Celebration as Fuel

In 2004, when the organization I co-founded, Bay Area Nonviolent Communication (BayNVC) was very young, Kit Miller joined us as a managing director. Kit brought with her many practices and skills that we didn't previously have, many of which we have not been able to replace since her departure in 2009. It is from her that I learned the extraordinary power of dedicating significant resources to celebration even while being engaged in attending to business. In our staff meetings about a third of our time together was focused on celebrating what we are doing. It's a practice I offer to clients as part of my training about how to run meetings. Even though as an individual I have fully integrated the practice of gratitude into my orientation to life, I still find it challenging to integrate celebration into a group or meeting given how different it is from our habits. I am committed to continue on this path, because I see it as enormously powerful for several interrelated reasons.

What convinced us to give this practice a try when Kit first introduced it was her statement that she wanted to change our habit of focusing on what's not working. This is a very well-honed habit. So many of us can easily detect problems and issues and get mobilized to fix them. It's an entirely different orientation to look at what is working, to keep noticing it, to have a sense that the efforts we make are meaningful. I remember many times when I came to a staff meeting without much enthusiasm, and as the celebrations proceeded I found myself energized by the sheer pleasure of hearing what is already working. The overall task became less daunting.

None of us can continue to do things indefinitely without knowing what they are contributing to. At least we can't do them with true willingness, rather than just to keep a job or out of some sense of obligation. To have active satisfaction in what we do, being the meaning-seeking creatures that we are, we want to know why we are doing what we are doing. Celebrations satisfy that hunger in a particularly powerful way: they remind us, at one and the same time, why we do what we do and that we are, at least some of the time, successful at doing it. I have learned, in particular, how much the people who are not doing the service work directly – such as the administrative people who make everything possible behind the scenes — are deeply fed by knowing what the work creates in the world.

For these and other reasons, the practice of celebrating in a group nurtures our energy for doing the work. Especially if we are committed to creating transformation in the structures that keep the world not working for so many people, we will need energy for a long time to come, to work against obstacles, when the obstacles are so immense. Sitting together and sharing our successes, both internal and external, is a deeply bonding activity that in a tangible way gives us fuel to keep going when so much around us and sometimes inside us spells despair and resignation.

If you are part of a group working for a project or a cause, I hope these notes will inspire you to try. I am confident you will not regret it, even though initially you may find some joking or cynicism in the group. Keep doing it. In the end, as we experienced, having someone who's a champion for celebrations eventually inspires everyone and results in much more joy and energy for all.

Power and Leadership

The questions surrounding power and leadership are integral to our ability to work together as we form groups, communities, and organizations. I am separating them out only because I see them as so significant that I wanted to explore them in more depth.

Learning to recognize and accept that power is a core human need takes significant effort for many because of how deeply power is associated with control and abuse. What I want to accomplish is nothing short of redefining power and leadership in ways that are completely congruent with the deepest consciousness of nonviolence, and especially with the radical principles of holding everyone's needs with care and of complete non-coercion.

To move toward a radically different future we need clear guidance and ongoing practice of new forms of power and leadership, without which many individuals committed to a vision of care, inclusion, and distributed power form and run organizations based on command and control practices, and others are unable to stand up to their leaders with love and clarity.

I have personally been grappling with the complexity of issues of power for some years, and see it as an urgent necessity to learn how to come to a place where we can truly build servant leadership, not only talk about it; where we can both yield power and know when to stand up for our needs despite opposition; where we can listen to the wisdom of anti-authoritarian sentiments without thereby losing sight of how vitally leadership is needed; and where we can assert leadership without falling back into models of authoritarian control. We have extremely little by way of robust models of communities and organizations that are effective, supportive of their members, and able to sustain their commitment and integrity over time.

My dream in this area is that we provide a radically different legacy and understanding of power and collaboration to future generations than what we have received. In this legacy power can be increased and shared, those in power can be loved and supported and share their power with others without fear, those with less power can find more power to lovingly engage with those in power, and all of us can embrace the uncompromising commitment to make things work for all.

Coming to Terms with Power

One of the challenges I see for people organizing to create change is what I see as an aversion to power and authority. After experiencing the ways that power can be used to create so much harm, many are understandably challenged to see a useful role for the exercise of power, and prefer to create leaderless groups in which everyone participates equally and fully in all decisions. Although many smaller groups function for years on the basis of fully participatory consensus for all decisions, there are also many instances, especially in the absence of skillful facilitation, in which consensus devolves into conflict, inefficiency, lack of decisive action, or, ironically, into premature suppression of minority views.

I know this is a controversial topic. I also know we have no real way of knowing whether or not leadership is truly necessary. I must take a stand without knowing. My stand is this: if we are to succeed in organizing large masses of people to create a world that works for more and more people in more and more ways, we will need to figure out how to offer effective leadership rather than no leadership at all. I envision structures that empower people to take leadership and responsibility. I also see a vital need for figuring out ongoing support and feedback to those who lead. Instead of abdicating power as a way to ensure we don't recreate structures of domination, I long to see a transformation in how power is conceived of and used, so that power can be put to the service of attending to everyone's needs. The challenges are both immense and surmountable.

What *Is* Power?[51]

I have made many references to power in this book. Because I am now discussing it directly, I want to start by offering a simple and neutral definition for power: *the capacity to mobilize resources to attend to needs*. While the attempt to attend to needs may or may not result in actually meeting them, having resources increases the likelihood of needs being met. Power is an essential need that everyone has, because without it no other needs can be met, and the human being

---

[51] The material for this sub-section was developed jointly with Inbal Kashtan.

will die. What power does an infant have? A baby needs sufficient resources to get its caregivers to take action to care for its needs. The key options that a baby has are crying and smiling, both known to tap into adults' care for infants.

Anything that can be used to meet needs is a resource, be it strategies, ideas, behaviors, things, or other people. Some resources are external, such as tools, seeds, money, social networks, or education, and some resources are internal, such as beliefs about our entitlement to resources, self-connection, or awareness of choice.

The less access we have to external resources, the more we need internal resources in order to have power. This is especially true when we are interacting with people who have structural power in relation to us, such as bosses, parents, or police.

One of the aspects of the tragedy I experience in the world is that limited access to external resources also results in people having more challenge in cultivating internal resources. One reason is that so often cultivating internal resources requires external resources (such as money, access to special social networks, etc.). In addition, lack of access to external resources exposes people to ongoing struggles for survival as well as basic human dignity. Such struggles mean, often, that more healing and inner work would be needed to reach full inner empowerment to meet people with power and successfully engage in dialogue with them.[52]

For some years now one of my biggest longings has been to find ways of offering internal resources to people who lack external resources. Ironically, my own and my organization's lack of sustainable access to external resources has been one of the obstacles to a widespread program along those lines.

Use of Power

Whatever amount of access to resources we have, and every single one of us has access to some, we face the deep question of how we

---

[52] These questions are deep and complex, and I am somewhat challenged to speak about them in a way that neither romanticizes nor pathologizes the people who don't have access to external resources. Perhaps more accurate would be that in a society riddled with separation and domination, cultivating inner resources is elusive for everyone, and different inner resources are available to different groupings. For example, the inner resources of generosity and the capacity to share resources and live interdependently are much more prevalent in lower income communities in response to need, while the inner resources of advocating for oneself and going for dreams are more accessible to people who grow up in more privileged circumstances.

use our power. *Having* power and *using* power are not the same, because our use of power involves choice. The fundamental choice we make with regard to our power is whose needs we are going to serve with our resources, and how much of a say others will have about our own choices.

The amount of say that others have lies on a spectrum. Some of us, at least some of the time, give away our power entirely, and make choices purely on the basis of others' wishes. This can be done in response to threats and pressure, or in response to training to obey, or in response to being raised to attend to others' needs (as many women often are). On the other end of the spectrum is acting in a way that leaves others essentially with little or no say. This is what we usually refer to as power-over: getting our way, even if intending to benefit others, without including in our decision others who are affected by it. It is this way of using power that I believe is responsible for so much aversion to power in social change movements.

Only others	Everyone affected	Only person with power

Abdication of power	Power With	Power Over

Somewhere along that spectrum we can find the use of power that involves all who are affected by our choices. This is the heart of a conscious practice of interdependence. It is also key to our capacity to create a world that works for all life, rather than simply replacing a world that possibly works for some and not for us by a world that possibly works for us and not for others, as many revolutions and coups have done. The capacity to reach decisions with others instead of alone, at their or our expense, is what is known as power-with.

Whatever resources we have, it is our choice which of these forms of power we end up using. While this is a choice that we can make as individuals, in each moment of life in which we find ourselves making decisions about our actions, such choices are shaped, in large part, by the social context into which we are born.

Many indigenous cultures view resources as belonging to the whole. In such cultures each of us is seen as charged with stewarding those resources that were given to us on behalf of the whole, oftentimes including the next seven generations. Such cultures are often inclusive in their use of power. In particular, people are included in processes that involve listening to everyone before reaching decisions. The talking stick circle process, in which an object is passed around in a circle and each person speaks while everyone else is listening is an example of such depth of listening and concern. As Oren Lyons, faithkeeper of the Turtle Clan of the Onandaga Iroquois, said of his tribal council tradition: "We just keep talking until there's nothing left but the obvious truth."

Some cultures view resources as belonging to God, or the State, or certain special families or individuals, and some individuals are entrusted with making decisions about use of resources in the service of such entities. Such cultures are often authoritarian and overtly coercive in their use of power. There is no illusion that others participate in any way. The hand-picked individuals, who are often members of certain families or social castes, are the ones that make all the decisions.[53]

In the North American culture within which I live and work, the prevalent view is that resources belong to whoever happens to own them. This is a culture that values autonomy to a very high degree, and has made our material possessions one of its most sacrosanct institutions. By virtue of owning something, we are given the right to dispose of those resources as we see fit. The idea that we can make this choice without consulting with anyone else is part of the core allure of the modern commodity-based economy, despite all the hardships so many of us experience. We have the carrot of believing that if we accumulate enough resources then no one can tell us what to do or not do. Use of power in such a culture is conflictual, with everyone and every institution fending for their own needs and desires. As I see it, we have a collective illusion of participation in shaping decisions while, in reality, decisions are made by the collection of individuals and groups that have the lion's share of resources.

---

[53] Exceptional individuals have been known to solicit input from those they rule. Harun al-Rashid, the 8th century Caliph, is reputed to have gone out at night in the streets of Baghdad dressed as a common citizen to collect information about his subjects that later informed his rule by day. Nothing structural, however, required him to do so, so his successors did not continue in this practice.

It is no small task within this culture, with its commitment to this form of autonomy as the consolation prize for the separation, scarcity, and powerlessness that we experience so often, to cultivate the capacity to use power with others. When we have few resources, it's hard to imagine that we can truly have a say. More often than not we give up without even trying. At other times we stand up defiant and forget about the humanity of others, thereby losing power with them. When we do have access to resources, it's hard to imagine letting go of the option of making all the decisions about our own actions, and it's often hard to maintain a sense of true care for and interest in others who may not have as many resources.

In addition to these challenges, most of us didn't experience true power-with in our upbringing, and lack models for what exactly it looks like to use our power with others. Including others appears more like asking for permission than anything that could possibly benefit us.

Lastly, those of us who are consciously thinking about power and its use often are not aware of the depth of thinking and modeling that's happened in the world in terms of using power with others, and thus eschew power altogether in order to ensure that everyone is included.

Conscious Use of Power

In order to be able to use power effectively in the service of creating a world that works for everyone, we need to know how to use power with others, and we need to have facility in choosing when to use power with others and when it might make the most sense to use power over others. One clear example is the use of our greater resources in order to protect life. As an obvious example, if a child runs into the street and is about to be run over by a car, we are not going to involve the child in the decision to jump and pick her up and bring her to safety. Protective force is used for the minimum amount of time necessary to achieve safety and return to exercising power with others.

In the example of bringing the child to safety, awareness of power dynamics will support us in knowing that this choice has significant consequences for the child, and we can then be with her in recovering from the shock to her system of being overpowered. While this may seem fantastic to many, since children are overpowered routinely, and such practices are endorsed by so many institutions, changing the overall paradigm of power extends all the way to children, or else we will need to re-learn each generation anew.

The other conscious form of using power over others is simply about using our greater access to resources to effect the outcome we want without including other people's autonomous choice, simply because we do not have the internal or external resources to make the choice to share power. This can happen in myriad ways every day. It can look like a boss telling an employee what to do rather than asking the employee if they are willing, or it can look like taking a child to school so that the parent can make it to work on time. This is unilateral, or functional force, which is not designed to punish or impose, although its effect may appear to others punitive or coercive. The motivation is simply to meet needs such as movement, ease, resolution, etc., which we don't see another way of meeting.

My experience is that when we first learn about use of power, we recognize many instances in which we resort to unilateral force, like telling our children what to do, or making decisions alone even though they affect others. Over time, as we develop greater internal resources, we have more and more capacity to imagine ways of working with complex situations and including others' needs, and are therefore more and more likely to choose to use our power with others in more circumstances.

The key, for me, is about making conscious choices. There is no question that because of habit, stress, social modeling, and many other reasons, we are very likely to have many moments in which we use our greater access to resources habitually, without awareness and conscious choice about this fact. It's hard to imagine that a time could come when everyone, all the time, would be attending to everyone's needs and attempting to make sure everything works for everyone. The issue is more about what happens when we become aware of new information, such as the effect of our actions on others. Do we then open up to dialogue and the willingness to change our strategies and approach in order to include the needs we were not aware of before? For example, as a workshop leader, I often set up a schedule ahead of time without awareness of how it affects people and without consulting with them. What happens when the workshop starts and I learn of circumstances that make the schedule

I set up difficult? For example, I might set up an evening session at a residential retreat without knowing that a group of local people are commuting, and want to leave in the evening to be with their children. *What do I do then?* is the true question about use of power.

Power without Corruption

In blunt terms, having structural power means having the *option* of attending to my needs without including others' needs. Structural power means access to resources based on my position within a structure, not based on relationship or personal resources. Here are some personal examples:

- As a boss (which I mostly am not), I can fire someone. They cannot fire me.
- As a program leader, I can choose not to give someone access to the program. They cannot restrict my access in the same way.
- When I sit in a room and speak, people listen to me and are likely to go along with what I want much more often than when someone else, who is not a "designated" leader, speaks in the same group.

I find it extraordinarily challenging to know this and to have any clarity about how to operate in integrity. I am so committed to moving forward in a way that honors everyone's integrity, dignity, and autonomy that I sometimes act with less than my full *personal* power in certain moments as a way to avoid imposing anything on anyone. On one level I know that what I am trying to learn how to do is to err on the side of asserting my power more, and the movement is slow, because I am so aware of the challenges and temptations.

I am full of questions, with few answers. Can we transform power dynamics so that the statement that "power corrupts" no longer appears so completely like a truism? Another way of asking this question: What does it take for any of us to become "incorruptible," meaning being so strong in our inner practice that we can withstand the allure of power? I want to believe that we can operate in a way that diminishes and eventually makes obsolete the responses of submission and rebellion.

I am a relatively small fish in the large order of things. I have fewer than 800 subscribers to my blog, for example. The team that supports me at work consists of about four employees, all but me part-time, and I have at most a few hundred former and current students who look to me actively as their teacher. Nonetheless, I am quite aware of at least some of the dynamics of power within which I operate, and have intimate knowledge, even on the small scale at which I work, of the dilemmas and complexities that come with power.

The Temptation

I hold a very large vision for the world, and my life is completely mobilized for the foreseeable future to do all I know to do to increase the likelihood of a livable future. This is a lot of work, a huge amount of effort. I teach, I write, I am a key leader in the organization I cofounded[54], I am part of several collaborations, and I receive a steady stream of requests from former students, colleagues, and others. That in itself could easily be more than a full life.

When I was grappling with these issues, my sister, Inbal, whom I love beyond words, was living with cancer. I was a major and active part of her support and care network. This was a journey full of uncertainty and immense beauty, as my two sisters have been the biggest joy of my life for so many years.[55] Hard as it was, the clarity of the priority to dedicate myself to her support, even if it had been for many more years, was unequivocal.

If that's not enough, I myself had cancer in 1997 and want to do all I can to minimize the risk of having another one (cancer runs deeply in my family, on both sides). I am very committed to attending to my own body and self-care, and to do things that nourish me.

Between these three primary commitments, my life was essentially unmanageable for years.[56] The metaphor of a blanket that's too short seems very apt to me. And, on top of that, I am a person with many sensitivities – physical, emotional, and social – and I find daily living often challenging.

I crave ease in the midst of so many commitments and challenges.

---

[54] Bay Area Nonviolent Communication, baynvc.org.
[55] Inbal died after seven years of living with ovarian cancer on September 6, 2014. I wrote about my experience of this transition on my blog: thefearlessheart.org/loss-empty-space-and-community-2/
[56] The editing of this book is being completed within weeks of her death, and the restructuring of my life that I am thrust into following this immense loss has only begun.

I know I am far from the only one who is challenged by life. Many, many people are craving ease in the midst of challenging lives, all over the world. Most of them will never have enough ease and relief. I can't *not* be aware of that truth. I also know that I do have enough power to arrange for some ease in my life if I want to use my power in this way.

Because I am so mobilized and putting so much of my energy towards service, I can easily "justify" using my power to create ease for myself. I feel that pull. I also know, and trust this insight, that it's not going to serve the world for me to resist the pull and do nothing to create ease in my life, because it would result in my being less effective. At the same time, I want to steer clear of slipping into more and more ways of creating ease that are less and less aligned with my values. Like many, this is a very complex line to walk.

For example, I like the outcome of my own decisions and how I do things better than I like the ways most others do things most of the time. Full ease would mean making all the decisions and telling other people what to do to support me. That is going too far, is too similar to old models, and in that way ultimately does not serve my vision. It's also not doable for me emotionally, because I have a visceral aversion to imposing my will on others. I am still learning about when and how to involve other people in decisions and, while doing so, to maximize effectiveness, connection, collaboration, and empowerment for all of us. Like many things, this is a tall order.

Full ease would also mean working only with people who are fully empowered in their relationship with me, able to transcend the submit/rebel paradigm and make choices based on their full sense of inner power, and are easily aligned with my vision and direction. This would mean people who can say "no" to me when I ask them to do something, who would give me divergent opinions when I offer mine, and who would be relaxed and comfortable shifting through dialogue with me. It would mean people who can speak clearly and articulate what's important to them even when there is tension, as well as be able to hear me and open their hearts to me without much effort. That's *a lot* to ask for. If I don't have it with someone, then I am at a loss about how to tend to the relationship with integrity, how to use my power *with* others, when it could consume so much effort and eliminate a number of open spaces in my schedule to do so. How can I do it? How can I not?

I don't have answers. All I know is to keep asking the questions, to keep opening my eyes and ears and heart to more and more input, and to keep taking the next step, whatever it is, knowing full well I don't know how.

Finitude

Perhaps the most pressing question for me remains the question of the limits of my resources. What does it really mean to care for everyone's needs, to really care, and also hold clarity about finitude of my resources? When I fully let myself feel the weight of this, I could scream, because I care not only about the people with whom I happen to come in contact. Although in some ways impersonal, my care for all people living on this planet, and for the unspeakable horrors so many experience on a daily basis, is large and the level of pain I am in about it is often beyond my capacity to tolerate. How do I match that up with my limits?

I derive some solace from a poem written by a friend, Ted Sexauer, who is a Vietnam vet:

> I am not responsible
> for the movement of the earth
> only what I can handle
> what I can take in
> is the right amount

I find it easier to know my limits with regards to people I don't know than with regard to those I do. When someone is in front of me, on my path, someone I interact with, whose life is affected directly by my choices, I struggle mightily with knowing when and how to extricate myself. I do it. I am just never sure whether I am truly holding the other person's needs as I do it, or essentially succumbing to my lack of imagination and closing off, however slightly.

This is a complex issue for anyone with anyone. It gets even more entangled for me when I am the one in a position of power. Honoring my limitations then borders too closely for my comfort with an assertion of my power over others: for example, I am exhausted after a long trying day, and my assistant approaches me with a bunch of questions about something that doesn't feel urgent *to me* and does *to her.* Do I engage in dialogue to reach agreement, or do I just decide that her questions can wait? I don't know what it means to use my power with others when I am reaching the limits, when there are more people with whom to be in communication about more things and more often than I can possibly handle.

Feedback

One of the lesser known aspects of Communist parties is the practice known as "criticism/self-criticism." What I like about it based on my readings is the intention to provide feedback, including to self, to keep learning, and to support learning for others. I am particularly delighted to see that the process was intended to be applied to people in leadership positions alongside others within the party.

From what I read, I have quite a bit of trust in the intention that led people to set up this process. In particular, I was relieved to see an instruction put out to stay away from personal attack, and to criticize political and organizational mistakes rather than character. Nonetheless, I still find the prospect of this process horrifying. I want people in power to receive feedback, not criticism. The two are dramatically different, even if some of what gets looked at can be incorporated into both. Feedback supports learning, while criticism tends to stir up shame.

For myself, I am still learning through feedback more than any other way. I so much want to know how to train or encourage people to stand up to me and tell me of their experience of me when I am in a position of power. For example, I know I need to learn something about why it is that with all of my profound commitment to power-sharing, learning, transparency, and vulnerability, I still hear regularly that people feel disempowered in relation to me. Is there something for me to change, or is it part and parcel of living in our culture that some people will not find their voice and power even when I am open to sharing it? What can I do to minimize the risk? Is there a different invitation I can issue?

Embracing Power

The more I look at power, the more I find fascinating and endless challenges to explore, grapple with, and continue. As soon as we drop the two positions of authoritarian power and abdication of power, we are on our own, figuring it out, without clear role models. The way through, as so often, is not by returning to previous models of authority but by finding new forms of authority that engage differently with power.

For example, I know that I, and others, can get caught in what I sometimes affectionately call the "tyranny of inclusion." I believe it's another of the issues that stops those of us working for change from being effective. I see it as based in fear of making decisive moves and offending others. I am learning. Balancing unabashed power with complete humility is such a new territory for us to explore. I feel myself on a learning edge, sometimes alone, sometimes discouraged, and mostly curious and excited.

One clue I hold on to is knowing that power with love is the heart of collaboration. Power differences, from either end, make it harder for us to hold on with clarity to the deep knowledge that everyone matters and we can always aim for a solution that works for all. Collaboration remains a possibility even in moments of great challenge.

Dilemmas of Leadership

When I read that the Civil Rights movement was heavily centralized in its leadership style, I found that fact disturbing, fascinating, complex, and provocative. Specifically, I find a generative tension in juxtaposing the effectiveness of the Civil Rights movement in its form of leadership with the anti-authoritarian ethos that came to prevail in many subsequent social change movements and lives in me in the form of this aversion to imposing.

At about the same time I watched a rare documentary about Gandhi made in the early 1950s, and discovered a similar leadership style. In the conversation that ensued, in which several nonviolence experts were present, I raised the question that by then was already burning in me: Is top-down centralized leadership of the kind that both Gandhi and Martin Luther King apparently used absolutely necessary to have an effective movement to create significant change in society?

The conversation that ensued raised even more questions for me, and resolved hardly any. What does it really take for a group to function effectively in service to a complex task? Are emergent, self-organizing groups able to meet such challenges as mobilizing large numbers of people to create structural change using nonviolent methods? If strong leadership is indeed necessary (even Gandhi with all his charisma and willingness to sacrifice everything wasn't ultimately able to prevent violence from erupting), where is the line between authority and authoritarianism? What can keep people empowered enough so they can entrust decision-making to leaders rather than submit or rebel? What can leaders do to avoid the abuses of power that stem from their own and others' habits? Is there a way to preserve the efficiency of functional hierarchies for making things happen while cultivating systemic collaboration around fundamental decision-making structures? And what does all this mean in terms of our collective capacity to contribute to transformation on a significant scale, and to do it with love, courage, and creativity?

Precisely because I am so committed to transcending and transforming the deeply ingrained models of living and leading that we have inherited, I want to keep asking these questions. I want to think about them deeply, to learn more from what has happened before, to engage with others about them, and to experiment in my own small-scale leadership. I have small-scale evidence that efficiency is possible without compromising collaboration and empowerment. I feel completely humble about not knowing what's really possible or necessary. This doesn't stop me from cultivating the faith that collaborative, empowering, effective, and transparent leadership is scalable, and we can collectively meet the challenges of our time provided we have clarity of purpose, a deep commitment to nonviolence on all levels, and a rigorous personal practice. That is part of how I understand Gandhi's legacy: an invitation to see means and ends as one, so we can live every moment, personally and as leaders, in courageous pursuit of love and truth.

Myths of Power-with

The terms power-over and power-with were coined in 1924 by a woman who has mostly been forgotten – Mary Parker Follett – while writing and lecturing about management theory and practice. Her approach, which centered on human relations and collaboration between management and workers, stood in stark contrast to the mainstream management practices of her day, which were rooted in what was then called scientific management, pioneered by Frederick Taylor.

I don't know, nor do I imagine it easy to trace, how these terms migrated far away from management theory into the realm of social justice movements. Along the way, they have acquired iconic status. Power-over has become a symbol of domination, is equated with hierarchy, and tends to be seen as "bad." Power-with is promoted as the be-all and end-all of "good" practices, and is often equated with an absence of leadership. This has been a huge issue in the Occupy movement: its "leaderlessness" has been the source of both admiration and condemnation by its participants and those who wish it well but don't join in.

I am embarking on writing this piece and sharing my thoughts about this topic with a fair amount of trepidation, the kind that comes from fear of upsetting people. Here is my dilemma: I am profoundly committed to using power with other people and not over other people. In fact, I am temperamentally averse to imposing anything on anyone. Nonetheless, over years working with groups, both within organizations and in community settings, I have come to believe that a certain rigidity surrounds these terms and results in loss of effectiveness for groups and causes I dearly want to see thrive.

I've been collecting what I am referring to here as "myths" of power-with for some time. Learning to identify and counter some of these has been a personal journey of significant magnitude. I've had to stretch within myself, to transcend my aversion to exercising unilateral decision-making, in order to arrive at a much humbler and more nuanced understanding of how use of power can support the elusive project of attending, as best we can, to everyone's needs in any given situation. This humility includes, in part, an acceptance of our human limitations. It's been painful, sad, and sobering. At times, it's also been inspiring and uplifting to recognize and think of ways of going beyond blocks to compassionate effectiveness.

My fear about writing all of this is none other than being seen as betraying the ideal and vision of holding everyone's needs dear, of losing my heart, of giving up on the dream and becoming "one of them," whoever "they" might be. I am well aware that this fear means that I haven't fully completed the inner process of self-acceptance about my thinking and practice. I have waited for many months, and I want to wait no longer before offering these insights in the hope that they may contribute to others' efforts at navigating the old and the new and finding a path that truly honors our humanity as we move, haltingly, and learn about creating a livable future.

I have identified, so far, six different misconceptions.

Myth #1: Everyone Can Be Included

I've been thinking about inclusion ever since a wise friend pointed out to me some fifteen years ago that total inclusion is impossible, because the explicit inclusion of all so often leads to the implicit exclusion of those who cannot bear the behaviors of some. During the months that the Occupy movement was operating in the streets, for example, many insisted on having all the meetings be open. I had so much admiration for the endless willingness of some people to weather the intensity, the wildness, the difficulty in maintaining any sense of continuity, the fighting, and the lack of movement, in order to maintain that principle of openness. Others, on the other hand, left the movement in part because they couldn't tolerate these experiences and lost hope that the movement would move anything anywhere.

The question, as I see it, is not about whether we can create a space where everyone is included. I am quite confident that we cannot; at least not under present conditions in the world in which so many have been so starved for being heard, for their basic human dignity to be recognized, for their presence to matter, that they either cannot participate in a collaborative manner, or cannot tolerate others' difficulties in collaborating.

So what do we do?

I've been pondering these questions for years, and have yet to reach anything that feels robust enough to serve as foolproof guidelines. Still, I've seen too many groups flounder and disintegrate because of too much inclusion, and the heartache I have about this is large enough that I am willing to offer my unfinished thoughts because they may spark more conversation and more clarity for many.

The direction I've been pursuing in exploring this rests on learning to accept our limitations. As organizers, leaders, and members of groups, we can come to terms with our limited resources. To come back to the example of Occupy, there simply wasn't enough capacity within the encampments to handle the overwhelming needs of people who had been living on the streets, who had been having addictive relationships with substances, who had a different relationship with reality than most, or who suffered from severe trauma. As much as it may seem like abandoning the dream to decide to keep some people out, it seems to me that it's more honest to recognize that sometimes we simply don't have enough love and attention to provide to those in serious need. The art form, what makes this tragic awareness humanly bearable to me, is to maintain the true humble understanding that it's our own limitations that make it necessary to exclude someone, not any fault of that person.

I want to believe that someday we will catapult ourselves into a way of living in which there simply aren't individuals with so much trauma and anguish that they challenge all around them. I want to believe that we can find ways to surround people with enough love that we can move forward with everyone intact. For now, I don't see it quite happening. My heart aches, and I am willing to accept this tragedy in order to support groups in continuing to exist as groups.

Individual difficulties are not the only challenge facing groups. Another core issue is the question of shared values and shared strategy. This, too, came up in powerful ways within the Occupy movement. At least in Oakland, and I believe in some other cities as well, the struggles around whether or not to adopt nonviolence as a key principle became overwhelming for many. Once again, I suspect that quite a number of people stopped participating because they couldn't bear the repeating discussions that didn't ever result in a resolution everyone could support. Might it not have worked better to amicably depart? Then, perhaps, those who were dedicated to nonviolent protest, non-cooperation and the creation of alternative power structures could pursue their strategy for gaining popular support for their cause. This is a case where what appears on the surface as exclusion might have given the movement a real chance to grow in popularity and draw in many more people that were turned off by the presence of those who wanted to include confrontational, even violent strategies, within the range of options they would consider.

The question of how a coherent strategy might be formed in a large leaderless movement remains open and unresolved. At some future point in this mini-series or elsewhere, I want to return to this topic, because I tend to believe that the anti-authoritarianism that exists in many progressive movements can get so extreme as to prevent forward movement. I am still digesting and pondering the reality that the large nonviolent movements of the 20th century, both Gandhi's and Martin Luther King's, were based on strict adherence to rules and precepts that were set by a very strong leadership. Nothing like what we see now. I am by far not advocating that model. I am just humble enough to recognize that something is sorely missing in the total rejection of leadership.

Back to the question of inclusion, I know that based on my own and Occupy's experience, I have shifted. In practical terms, in the groups I help start myself, I am now willing to set conditions for membership instead of keeping everything open, and to accept that sometimes a group will need to ask someone to leave rather than lose itself as a group. How to do all of this with love and care remains an open question for me.

Myth #2: The Either/Or of Decision-Making

Recently, I was at Rainbow Grocery, a local worker-owned coop where I do a lot of my shopping. Rainbow has been around since the 1970s, and is one of not so many such places that have survived the test of time and are still thriving. As I was looking for a particular bulk spice (for those who care, their bulk section is what I most often go all the way to San Francisco for), I overheard a worker explain to a customer an oddity in the way that the spices were organized. I heard weariness in her voice, so I turned to her afterwards and said something to the effect that this oddity could be fixed. She looked at me with what I saw as an odd mixture of commitment and resignation, and said: "Change is very slow when you run a democracy."

To me this sentence sums up the crux of the issue I am exploring today. This response assumes something I myself question: Why would change have to be slow in a democracy? I know the answer, because I think I know what she and others mean by a democracy. I think they mean a certain version of participatory democracy in which everyone participates in all decisions. I used to share the belief that this was the only possible path. In this understanding, we either compromise on the possibility of making things happen, or we compromise on the ideal of power-with, the value at the heart of this version of democracy: no one has anything imposed on them in any way, shape, or form.

Although this dilemma overlaps with the issue I named in Myth #1, I see a significant distinction between the two. When writing about the first myth, that everyone can be included, I was focusing more on the complexity of *membership*, which is about who gets to be part of a group or organization in the first place. Membership, then, involves a host of privileges and responsibilities, of which decision-making is only one. Here, in writing about Myth #2, I am focusing on the process of *decision-making* within a group or organization whose membership is already clear.

Because I am deeply committed to doing all I can to contribute to creating a world where *everyone's* needs matter, I am a natural candidate for believing in the necessity of participation at all levels. The standard version of decision-making we have created within our existing models of democracy have lost the initial appeal they had when I was in my teens and learned the history of such forms of government. I no longer believe that representative democracy, the electoral process, or majority voting more generally are strong enough tools to enable us to make wise decisions that can work for all or the vast majority of people. I also know that even in relatively small groups, involving everyone in all decisions and aiming for consensus in its usual form are either entirely unfeasible or endlessly exhausting and impractical. I want methods, processes, and forms that are responsive to human needs at all levels, that are scalable, and that are efficient enough for production environments. Of course this is a tall order, and I nonetheless have plenty of reasons, not just faith, to believe it's possible.

Mattering and Needs

One key to making sense of the solutions I see is understanding a fundamental human reality I have learned over the years: when we trust that our needs matter, we are much more flexible not only about *how* they are going to be met, we are also more flexible about *whether* they will be met. Think about it: if I know and trust that you care about my needs and you go ahead and take action that doesn't work for me, I am way more likely to be fine with it than if you do the same action and I think you don't care about my needs.

This has led me to believe that in order to solve the decision-making dilemma, it would be important to create structures and processes that institutionalize the experience of mattering. That is the path that can lead to collaborative decision-making that doesn't by necessity require everyone to participate.

At the level of personal relationships, the direct connection, and tending to it well, is all it takes. When we get into groups, the context is dramatically different, and more is needed. This is a rich field, about which many have written, and in which countless experiments and innovations have taken place. I do not pretend to know more than a little about all that's been happening in the world. I do know enough to know that the tools are there. I don't believe, though, that the specific lens of human needs, and therefore the specific focus on mattering, are already out there.

Small Groups: Deciding Together Who Decides

Even in the context of two people, it's never the case that everyone participates in all the decisions. If two of us are raising one child, and only one of us is with the child, only one of us will decide how to respond to an unexpected, challenging behavior. As the number of people increases, it's progressively more important to have systems in place for how decisions will be made in order to make it possible for things to flow smoothly and efficiently while attending to everyone's needs.

I am indebted to Marshall Rosenberg, inventor of NVC, for the profound insight that the most important decision to be made collaboratively is the decision about who makes which decisions. One other insight I've had in my years of working with groups is that most people will form an opinion about something if asked for one. At the same time, we don't necessarily *want* to form opinions about everything. To go back to the example of Rainbow, it's quite likely that many of the workers would engage in a possibly heated discussion about how they want the spices to be ordered. At the same time, I am confident that most of those same workers wouldn't even notice if the spice order was rearranged to fix the problem if they weren't told.

What could be done, then, to create movement and still hold everyone with care, is to make it possible for everyone who wants to to participate in the type of discussions that are of interest to them, and to accept others' decisions about other issues. For example, everyone who is interested in how the shelves are organized and what the store looks like would be part of the group that makes those decisions. Others would know they could, and therefore would be just as happy not to.

How the decision itself is made once we know who makes it is an entirely different topic I am not addressing here. I have written on my blog about the collaborative decisions-making process that I myself created[57]. For now, what I want to emphasize is that it's entirely possible to reach a collaborative decision efficiently, precisely because we can uncouple the core needs we have from the millions of strategies and opinions that we create to meet them, as well as separate the needs from the people who happen to have them, and therefore we can come up with a coherent list of criteria for a decision that doesn't depend on everyone continually defending their position. Of course, my own process is by far not the only one that has been created for collaboration. If anyone is particularly interested in this part of the topic, I would urge you to familiarize yourself with two resources. One is a particular process called Dynamic Facilitation, invented by Jim Rough, and the other is a website full of resources about groups, decision-making, collaboration, democracy, wisdom, and much, much more: The Co-Intelligence Institute, Tom Atlee's organization, about whom I speak more shortly.

---

[57] See references in the blog post from which this sub-section was taken: baynvc.blogspot.com/2012/12/myths-of-power-with-2-eitheror-of.html

Scaling Up: Alternatives to Representation and Voting

Even when the feasibility of collaborative processes for small groups is accepted, most people still resign themselves to the inefficiency, corruption, and alienation of large scale human institutions, which range from seemingly democratic institutions that don't function democratically, to those, like the overwhelming majority of organizations, that don't even pretend to be democracies. Alternatively, many others, especially those who advocate for the democratic forms of strict participatory democracy, believe that we simply cannot form large scale institutions that have any hope of serving the needs of those that comprise them, and therefore call for the dismantling of anything but small, local, free associations of people who would, again, participate in all decisions that affect their lives.

Once again, I know that more has already been shown to be possible, and believe that even much more is possible if we, collectively, find a way to make it a priority. Again, the tools and know-how are there, and ideas, practices, and methods abound. The question of why we don't use them, to my mind, is one of political will and worldviews more than actual possibility.

Tom Atlee, just mentioned in the previous section, recently published his third book called *Empowering Public Wisdom: A Practical Vision for Citizen-Led Politics*, where he discusses hundreds of actual situations where randomly selected groups of individuals that represent a cross-section of the population were facilitated using dozens of processes to reach an informed consensus about topics or issues, including those that polarized the population from which they were selected.

Using the lens of needs that I discussed earlier, I can see why this would work. A randomly selected group of people coming together, as individuals and *not* as representatives, through effective facilitation in a collaborative process, embodies the variety of needs that underlie the diverse opinions and viewpoints of the larger population. Tom calls these *Citizen Deliberative Councils*. Especially if their process of coming together can be shared by the larger population, their deliberation can be a way for people who are not involved to see themselves mirrored in this small group, and to trust that their own needs matter, especially if they are named.

In the next section of this book, "Wisdom Tales from the Future," (page 281), I envision an elaborate system of governance in which decisions are made in small circles built as concentric groups; representatives known to all in a circle are selected to participate in a higher-level circle, and so on up to the highest level. People in a higher-level circle are also members of the lower-level circles from which they were selected and to which they are directly and personally accountable, all the way down to neighborhood-based circles. In a system such as this, in combination with periodic and repeated randomly selected citizen deliberative councils, I have more faith that we can truly institutionalize the trust that each of our needs are carried forward all the way in all decisions made, even to the highest-level global circle I imagine we will one day have (if we survive our current crises) when we coordinate the vast interdependent processes that affect all of us in consideration of all life on the planet.

I know we are quite far from such an eventuality. I also see small signs that keep reminding me that my faith is not unfounded. Because I work with people at so many different levels within organizations, I know, for a fact, that the people at the top, more often than not, care about the needs of those at the bottom, more than is evident to the latter. Often, they act counter to their care because they lack imagination, vision, or knowledge about how to do things differently, not because they don't want to. When I offer them the option of acting collaboratively without a loss in effectiveness and results, many take the offer with relief. Therein lies my hope.

Myth #3: The Maligning of Hierarchy

Like many people I know, I used to think of hierarchy as entirely synonymous with power-over, and of both as fundamentally wrong. It still takes conscious, mindful practice to remember that I no longer see it this way. Because it's not fully integrated in me, I am delighted to be writing about this particular myth, imagining that my own faltering understanding might improve as a result, and that it will also make it easier for others to follow my thinking, as I am less likely to speak from the other side of a piece of personal evolution.

What Is Power?

Given how difficult it is to tease apart hierarchy from power-over, I want to explore this topic further, beyond my earlier discussion (page 130, "Coming to Terms with Power"). Defining power, simply, as the capacity to mobilize resources to attend to needs, makes it neutral, in addition to being necessary. This definition separates power from how it's being used: despite our general use of language, power-over is not something we *have*; it's something we *do* – it's our choices about how we use the power we have.

I have found these distinctions exceptionally helpful in understanding our behaviors, because it serves as a reminder that the urge to use power *over* others is independent of the actual ability to do so. In other words, it's not so much that power corrupts; it's that power provides the possibility of carrying out urges that we might have anyway, regardless of our access to power.[58]

Power-over and Power-with

Using our power over others is about taking actions that allow us to attend to our own needs regardless of whether that works or doesn't work for others. Having certain forms of power shields us from engaging with what others want. Specifically, I am referring here to structural power as that which gives us the *option* to use power over other people, because of access to more resources. With structural power, we have the possibility of limiting others people's access to resources, of narrowing their options, and of making choice difficult for them to exercise because of possible consequences we may deliver. That is what structural power gives us. Having such power doesn't force us to use it over other people; it only makes it possible. It's still our choice what we do with our power and how we use it. Unless we change our relationship with power internally, we are then likely to use it over others, often not even realizing that we are. Because others bring habitual fear of consequences into every relationship of power difference, it can be invisible to us that we are getting our needs met at their expense. We get our needs met, others don't, and we can simply make things happen for us, regardless. If people don't do what we want, we can deliver consequences to their

---

[58] More on this below, in "The Powerless Are Not Necessarily Pure," page 173.

actions that tend to leave them more motivated, based on fear, to do what we want.

Using power with others is difficult to define or describe in part because our linguistic models of power are completely steeped with the power-over model of power as quasi-synonymous with power itself. The key feature of that model of power that makes it so challenging to present something else as power is the zero-sum aspect: if one person has power, another doesn't; the more power I have, the less power someone else has. The very notion that it's possible for more people to have more power all at once challenges our habitual ways of thinking.

The notion of human needs, and the question of whose needs are attended to by any action we take or decision we make, has helped me immensely in being able to grasp in full what using power with others can mean once we transcend the framework we have inherited. Using power with others, for me, is about attending to more needs of more people, thereby adding both to their power (their capacity to mobilize resources to meet their own needs) and to the whole – time and time again I am astonished by seeing that bringing in more needs results in solutions that tend to be more creative and more robust. I mourn how many people live and die without having this magical experience, because explaining it takes the life out of it, and because I find it so nourishing and trust that many others would, too, if they could only accept the apparent initial loss of control (which we never have in any event).

The Two Meanings of Hierarchy

The etymological meaning of the word hierarchy is "the rule of the sacred." It had, initially, nothing whatsoever to do with human ranking, status, or power. I suspect it came to have these associations through the history of the Christian church, a topic about which I know rather little. The Oxford English Dictionary says, "The earliest sense was 'system of orders of angels and heavenly beings'; the other senses date from the 17th century." By now, after whatever history affected the meaning of the word, this word is seen as describing a power-over system.

Nonetheless, even within this context, a different meaning has emerged, again from history I don't know, which is "a series of ordered groupings of people or things within a system," the most notable examples of which are the classification of animals and plants, as well as linguistic or mathematical systems such as databases that are organized as a series of nodes that are connected to each other, very similar to the familiar picture of an organization chart.

The key difference between those examples and an organization chart is that such systems and orderings are not representing or implying any notion of power, authority, or influence. Sometimes they imply an ordering of importance, sometimes not even that. There is nothing that says that an ant is more or less important than a microbe or an armadillo, for example.

This is exactly the point of entry for understanding how hierarchies don't by necessity mean power-over. For me that "aha" happened when I learned about Sociocracy, which is a system of governance invented in the Netherlands and now in use in a growing number of organizations and communities in the US as well. In my understanding, Sociocracy includes a governance system as well as a very specific decision-making process, and only the former is relevant to this discussion. A sociocratic governance structure is based on functional hierarchies that are designed in such a way that the functional leaders do not have the structural power that would allow them to exercise power over others. The mechanism by which this is done is quite technical and detailed, and I am leaving it out (I am also not a big authority on the topic). The important piece for me is the principle: combining the potential efficiencies that arise from the expertise and authority of functional leaders with the wisdom and emergent qualities of sharing power. Because of how extraordinarily difficult it is for any individual leader to single-handedly overcome the collective legacy of what power means and how we use it, sociocratic structures have built-in mechanisms for subverting the possibility of power-over. Such mechanisms are designed to ensure that even people at the far end nodes of the functional hierarchy have a say in the core decisions that affect the functioning of an organization and their own lives within it.

I don't imagine that a sociocratic system is the only way to accomplish the complex task of separating the functional from the structural aspects of hierarchy. I only know that I am excited to know that at least some people sorted out this issue and have *a* solution. Prior to hearing about it, I had some vague inklings that the hermetically negative view of hierarchy was missing something, and I couldn't put my finger on it, because I was still personally so embroiled in the moral evaluation of hierarchies as bad.

Hierarchies that Serve a Purpose

I want to illustrate this difficult point with two examples. The first was one of the moments that changed my visceral response to hierarchy. It happened some years ago, when I was involved in a massive training project in Nonviolent Communication for an international organization that puts together many large scale events every year. When we reached the part of the training that was about systemic and organizational elements, and especially decision-making, they shared with me their process of putting together their events. For each event, a team gets created with a point person that heads the team. While they are committed to collaboration for the creation of the events, for the last few days of preparation the head of the team becomes a temporary "dictator" – it is understood that even if someone has a better idea and is convinced of it, the team leader makes all the decisions so as to maintain the efficiency and movement, and to keep their very high standards for esthetics and logistics. As soon as the event is over and done with, the team does an extensive and collaborative debrief, so that all the lessons can be learned, documented, and passed on to the next team for the next event. By having different people holding different events, by having a collaborative debrief in which everyone gets to participate, and by making the learning available to future groups, the wisdom is generated and everyone's voice is respected, even though for a few days everyone is asked to put their wisdom on hold. The resulting events, some of which I have seen, are stunning in their elegance and flow. I have since viewed this system as a powerful example of flexibility.

The usefulness of a hierarchical order can be apparent. Unfortunately, more often than I would like, such systems don't operate with the grace and wisdom of the above example. For one such example, I know that I get comfort and relief from knowing that if I were to undergo an operation, there would be one person that would be holding primary responsibility for what happens, even if they choose to consult with others. At the same time, hospitals rarely if ever institutionalize a feedback structure in which the surgeons have the opportunity to learn from the nurses. In our current structures, the nurses end up holding their tongues even if they see ways of improving outcomes. Not all hierarchies are born equal…

Conditions for Power-with Hierarchies

In order for a hierarchical organization to function in line with power-with principles, direct and careful attention would need to be given to how the structural elements are supporting the use of power. I am grateful to my friend and colleague, Greg Kendrick, for conversations that led to this understanding of mine. This list is far from complete.

Accountability: having everyone in a circle or team accountable to a shared purpose that they all participate in articulating, rather than to an individual. This changes the working relationships and supports increasing collaboration.

Feedback: creating processes and structures for everyone to give everyone feedback on the quality of their work and on the relationships and how everyone is supporting everyone else. This allows partnership and reduces the possibility of power being used over others. This is because full flow of feedback would reduce the kind of fear associated with feedback coming from only one source to everyone else.

Decision-making: distinguishing between operational decisions, which each person makes for their own functions, and larger, less frequent decisions, which are about goal setting, policies, relationships, compensation, and the like, which are made by the entire team. This allows the efficient flow of daily actions that the hierarchy makes possible, while protecting people from negative consequences that can come their way if all decisions are made by one person.

The goal of all these elements is to remove the whim of the individual, so that it's not up to the functional leader to decide how power will be used. Instead, the structures themselves are set up in such a way that using power over others is next to impossible. A big extension of these small experiments appears in a form I am cautiously heartened by called a B corporation (B for Benefit), which exists in a growing number of states. Intention alone is not enough as long as the structures that keep power-over practices remain in place. I'd like to believe that we can create many new structural forms that support the intentions and move us closer to the dream of making our organizations places where we can all live and thrive.

Myth #4: When Connection Trumps Everything

In my discussion of Myth #3, I made a connection between power and needs, suggesting that the quintessential flavor of power-with approaches rests on attending to ever more needs of ever more people. I said then, and will say as often as I can remember, that the repeated experience of magic that arises from engaging in this way has sold me on it forever. I have facilitated so many groups and teams to reach decisions that are based on this approach, and the results often astonish everyone who participates.

Nonetheless, I have a huge caveat about how to apply this approach within groups. I became familiar with this issue in communities of practitioners of Nonviolent Communication (NVC), especially when people gather in an attempt to make things happen, rather than for the purpose of healing. Often enough, people experience immense frustration with how such groups function, and are discouraged to see how challenging it can be to make any decisions about anything. I suspect that this issue shows up in a variety of forms in any number of groups and contexts where inclusion and power-with are important to participants in a group. Nonetheless, because I have experienced it primarily in the NVC context, this is the main context in which I talk about it here.

Although I had experienced the challenge soon after I became part of the fledgling community that has since grown considerably worldwide, I didn't have a framework for understanding the issue until a particular conversation I had with my late colleague and co-founder of BayNVC, Julie Greene, in 2001. The way Julie characterized the problem was that people didn't make a clear enough distinction between what she referred to as empathy circles and action circles. The difference between the two is a difference in purpose, not in who is present – the same group of people can sometimes come together as an empathy circle and sometimes as an action circle. In fact, that was one of her clear recommendations to people gathering to make things happen – to have some meetings that are purely designed for relationship-building and empathy.

I have thought about this challenge many times in the intervening years, and now have some hope that I can support NVC groups, and likely others, in finding more effective ways to manage the difficulty.

Understanding the Role of Purpose

In North America, where I live and work, most people learn NVC in a workshop or a study group. This means that they are exposed to NVC in the context of learning, healing, and personal growth. The level of transformation that many people experience is such that they become excited about the potential of NVC to contribute – in their own lives, to the lives of others, and beyond, to schools, organizations, or wherever else their passion takes them. And so they come together, enthusiastic about the potential, eager to make a difference, and full of energy. Without knowing it, more often than not, they bring with them the memory of the sweet, magical intimacy of the workshops and retreats they have attended, and the expectation of having those same experiences while they work together to initiate a project.

When the purpose of a group coming together is to be an empathy circle, maximizing connection makes complete sense, because it is through the connection that the healing and intimacy happen. However, when people come together to start a project or run an organization, the purpose is different: the purpose is to make things happen in the world. This means doing design, engaging in strategic thinking, making operational decisions, and attending to logistical details. Mixing up the kind of connection that supports healing with the kind of connection that supports trust and effectiveness is likely to lead to disillusionment – with people, with groups, with decision-making, or with NVC.

Instead, what I see as the path of possibility rests on understanding two key elements. One is about matching the kind of connection to the purpose at hand. The other is about choosing the range of needs, beyond connection per se, that a group or leader attend to as part of the commitment to conscious power sharing. It is my deep faith that mastering the capacity to flexibly attend to multiple needs in multiple ways can result in groups that function effectively and collaboratively, without resorting to power-over strategies or getting mired in endless discussions that lead nowhere.

The most frequent example of what can derail groups is the very common experience of someone becoming upset during a meeting. Because of the commitment to authenticity, empathy, and power-with strategies, people are no longer willing to accept masking the upset and pretending all is well, nor are they happy with overt anger, power struggles, or behind-the-scenes political maneuvering, which are so common in traditional groups. Instead, what I have often seen people do is stop the flow of a meeting and shift, automatically, to focusing primary attention on the upset person, in an attempt to create full resolution. Sooner or later, someone else gets upset, usually at the loss of momentum, not getting to the agenda, or the amount of attention one person is getting. From there, things can easily cascade.

This example illustrates both strands of the challenge. What I see as key to a different kind of functioning rests on keeping an eye on the purpose of the meeting, and making conscious choices, relative to the purpose, about how to attend to the upset. A group that is meeting as an "action circle," to use Julie's term, which means that it has tasks to accomplish, would attend to an upset differently from a group that is meeting for the purpose of mutual support and attending to relationships. In the former case, I would want those who are leading the group to attend to the upset with care and empathy as briefly as possible: just enough to re-establish trust and presence or choose consciously to shift focus.

Within that brief time, one of three things can happen. One possibility is that the upset person may settle fully and come back to full presence and alignment with the intention of the meeting. Another possibility is that the upset person will settle *enough*, though not *fully*. In that case, the issue can be placed on the agenda of the same group for when they meet as an empathy circle. If that name is odd, think of it as a time to attend to the relationships and functioning of the group, without specific operational agenda items. The third possibility is that the upset person doesn't settle within the short amount of time that is consistent with the intended purpose of the meeting. That's a time to either send someone out with the person to support them in recovering and coming back, or a time to make a conscious and fully-informed choice about shifting the purpose of the meeting into a healing session or embarking on a mediation with whoever's action preceded the upset.

I have sometimes done this when, as a facilitator, I sense that the level of upset or the nature of the issue are such that the group cannot resume its task without growing loss to its ability to function. These are delicate moments for a facilitator or a group to navigate, moments in which nothing is perfect, and we are looking for the optimal way to balance many needs: for effectiveness in utilizing group resources; integrity in how people are held and power is used; care for everyone present; and learning for the group, to name only a few that may be present.

All these choices, if done deliberately and with awareness of all the ramifications, are entirely consistent both with the importance of connection and with the commitment to power-with strategies. Still, such decisions are challenging to make for people who have become used to following healing potential all the way through to resolution. As I said, I don't believe this is singular to NVC groups. Indeed, a new manager I have talked with recently, who was promoted from a clinical position, expressed confusion about how to shift from a therapeutic model to a management model, and how to do so without compromising his sense of who he is, which is about caring for everyone and seeing the potential for healing in every interaction. It bears repeating: which needs we attend to, and to what depth, has to do with what the purpose at hand is, and what we – collectively as a group, or as facilitators of a group – decide is consistent with that purpose.

Power and Group Purpose

This is exactly where the confusion around power comes in, too. Often enough those who may be leading a group would shy away from making those choices for fear of being seen – by others or themselves – as compromising on the ideal of power-with leadership. Others, frustrated with what's happening and helpless to change it, might be clamoring for decisiveness and "moving on" without realizing the cost, effectively recreating the power-over models. In many such groups people balk at being facilitators, or minimize the role of facilitator to a very narrow procedural part so as to eliminate the need to make such decisions in the first place. The either/or frame gets reinforced: we either accomplish things without sharing power, or we share power without accomplishing things.

What is the alternative, then? Is there a way for a group of people to share power, care for each other, and still accomplish what they set out to do? Clearly I think so, or I would not be writing this piece. Here are some of the building blocks I see:

Establish Clear Purpose for Each Meeting: Whether the group as a whole, using whatever decision-making process they use, decides, or a facilitator guides the group in deciding, I see it as indispensable for any group to have clear agreements about when it meets as an action circle to attend to tasks, and when it meets as an empathy circle to attend to people and relationships. It's just as challenging for a group when someone insists on taking action when the group is meeting for connection as it is for the opposite. At different times in its existence a group may have more or fewer meetings for connection, depending on circumstances and needs as they are expressed. For example, transition times and times of conflict would generally require more empathy meetings, and times of urgency with regard to certain actions would generally require more action meetings. Both are always needed. Even the US military has concluded that any group needs, on average, about 20% of its time to be used for relationship building and process (I sadly lost the reference for this research).

Develop Clear Agreements about Group Functioning: There is no one-size-fits-all for groups to be able to function. Some groups end up working better with rotating, minimal leadership, especially when there is a clear process and structure that hold the group together, and clear personal commitment to the group on the part of members. Other groups function better with a clearly designated leader, especially in the context of an organization with clear goals. Whichever path a group takes, for its functioning to be consistent with a power-with model means that people in the group have a say about how the group functions and participate in deciding how decisions are made.

Prioritize Sufficient Connection for the Purpose at Hand: If we want to operate in a power-with model, which means that everyone's needs matter, the glue and lubricant is connection. Without connection, we lose trust and goodwill very rapidly. Whenever something happens in a group, at a minimum people need to be heard about their experience to be able to function productively in a meeting. This basic truth about how we operate as humans is often ignored in business settings, resulting in people checking out and in degradation of function that everyone comes to accept as inevitable when a remarkably small amount of listening can dramatically improve the functioning. Those who come from a business frame will need to stretch to accept some connection, which tends to appear to them as "touchy-feely." Those who come from an NVC or a therapeutic setting will need to stretch to accept less connection than they would most prefer in order to keep the focus on the purpose, which tends to appear to them as "power-over."

Adopting these three guidelines takes a lot more than an overall conceptual understanding – there is quite a bit of personal development and facilitation skills that are needed. I believe it's a process over time. I still have some hope that having the clarity about what can support groups in functioning effectively without resorting to power-over strategies can increase the chances that those of us who are committed to creating a caring future can also move in that direction instead of just dreaming about it.

Myth #5: All of Everyone's Needs Are Equal

One of the core principles that shows up in just about everything I write is the commitment to holding everyone's needs with care. This, with a specific focus on holding with care everyone's needs for meaningful choice, is the core guideline I use for understanding how to apply the power I have. For as long as those in my circle or organization with less power than me have access to choice, I am satisfied with my use of power.

That said, I've always been uncomfortable with the addition of the word "equal," which changes the principle to "holding everyone's needs with *equal* care." Aside from the philosophical uncertainty about how equality of care can even be measured, I don't see it as either possible or even desirable in all situations to hold all of everyone's needs equally. In fact, I believe that the insistence on equality of this kind can compromise both the effectiveness and integrity of movements and groups.

This is why I have replaced the word "equal" or "equally" with "full" or "fully." I can say, with far greater ease, that I can hold everyone's needs with full care even when I don't hold them with equal care.

As I see it, power-with means finding the path that, relative to the purpose at hand, supports maximal empowerment and participation on the part of all. That doesn't necessarily mean equality, though often it would. Here are two concrete examples of when I see a difference.

Compensating for Lack of Power

When I facilitate groups, I make a point of holding in my awareness the power relations present within the group. This can be formal power relations, as in an organizational power hierarchy, or social-structural power differences as in, for example, racial groups. Whether in a teaching context, when facilitating a business meeting, and even in a two-person mediation, if my commitment is to holding everyone with full care and to maximize choice and participation, then I will in some ways prioritize the needs of the person with less power even while holding those with more power, also, with full care.

Sometimes this means inviting someone to speak before another even if they raised their hand after, because of knowing that having less access to power makes it harder to participate. Sometimes it means lingering longer with some people while keeping an eye out for others to make sure it's not at cost to them. Sometimes it's a willingness to have some people feel some discomfort in order to find a place at the table for those who previously didn't get included.

The form may be different and adapted to the context. The principle is clear to me: I use my own power as a facilitator to support people with less power to have more choice and voice than they might otherwise. I don't mean I support them in having more than others, just more than they and the circumstances would allow them without my intervention.

In the context of race relations, for example, this is one small thing that I can do, as a person with access to white privilege, to destabilize the invisibility of power differences in a group, to actually increase the chances that everyone's needs *are* held with care. In this way I act as a steward of, and hence *use* my privilege for the benefit of all, rather than try to deny or hide it out of guilt or embarrassment.

The Needs of People in Support Roles

A few years ago I had a very difficult interaction with an assistant trainer. The details are now gone from my memory and are not so important. What stayed with me was that the person in question wanted me to change something in my plan for teaching because it didn't totally make sense to her. Being generally open to feedback and loving thinking collaboratively, I invited her to tell me her concerns or objections. After hearing them, I knew I still wanted to keep my plan without change, and I asked her to set aside her disagreement so that I could complete the agenda of a meeting and be prepared for the next session. At that moment, she expressed intense dismay, and wondered out loud how my action squared with the commitment to hold everyone's needs equally. Later, she said that she saw my request of her as an example of power-over.

From my perspective, something completely different was going on, which I saw as lack of alignment between us about what it means to be in a support role. As I see it, when I enter a support role, I am willingly accepting that some of my needs will not be a priority as decisions are made. Supporting someone else means going along with their vision and direction, offering my perspective when it seems relevant, and accepting the other person's choice about where to go, even if it wouldn't be my own. The most intense example of being in a support role that I have is supporting my sister's journey with cancer. It's always understood that she is the one who makes the final decision about treatment options even though she values and seeks my opinion. I still experience complete collaboration, even in moments when her choice is not what I would do in her shoes. It wouldn't occur to me to ask her to keep engaging with me until one of us shifts.

As another example, Dave, who edits most everything I write, makes a clear distinction between helping me say what I am saying more clearly and trying to get me to agree to say something different from what I am saying. The former is the kind of collaboration of a support person; the latter the collaboration of a co-author.

Precisely because of this deep understanding that I have about what it means to be in a support role, I know that it wouldn't be easy for me to be a support person for someone (though it's super easy for me, joyful and enriching, to do with my sister). I have opinions about everything, usually strong, and I don't have the most ease carrying out something that is not of my own choosing.

That said, collaborating with a person in a support role does not confer the license to ask the person to do anything. I do hold immense care for and hold with reverence the well-being of people who work to support my vision, whether they are paid staff, volunteers, or friends. Primarily, this means that I am always willing for the person to say "no" to a request of mine. The balance is delicate – if the "no" is frequent, this person may not be a fit to work with me; still, in each instance of asking, I want to freshly be open to the "no."

Sadly, my own willingness to hear "no" doesn't necessarily translate into the other person knowing that they are free to say "no." I still find myself, with regularity, compensating for the other person's lack of power by questioning a "yes" that may not sound fully on board, or by asking more lightly to make it easier to say "no." It has not always been successful. In part, this is because my way of expressing myself is passionate and forceful, which some people find challenging, especially those who generally find it hard to say "no" to someone in a position of power. This is work in progress.

In this, as in the previous example, I am looking at the question of power-with from the perspective of the choices made by the person with access to power. When I am in a position of power, I want to be the one to do the work of using my power *with* the people with less power, the more so the less willingly they are there. That is, in a nutshell, the challenge of shifting how power is used in the world.

Myth #6: Unilateral Choice is Always Negative

Along with the beliefs that hierarchies were fundamentally power-over structures, and hence irredeemable (see myth #4), I equally fervently didn't see any role for the use of anything unilateral. Again, unilateral choice or unilateral force became synonymous with power-over, and I was committed to never imposing anything on anyone, for as far back as I can remember. When I first heard from Marshall Rosenberg about the protective use of force (page 199), I was quite uncomfortable.

It's been quite a journey since those days to have arrived at the conclusion that I want to learn to overcome my aversion so as to be able to consciously choose to make unilateral choices, even to use unilateral force, when I believe that choice would attend to the maximum needs possible under the circumstances in which I find myself.

The first of these is the protective use of force, both individually and collectively. I consider the entire project of nonviolent resistance to be an extension of the protective use of force as applied to structural situations. Just as in the case of stopping an individual from inflicting harm, nonviolent resistance uses the force of a collectivity of people to create conditions that would allow harm to stop, all the while remaining open to dialogue.

In addition, I want to illustrate the challenges of this myth using two more examples, each of which illustrates another aspect of what the choices might be about that would lead us to unilateral actions that affect others directly.

Facilitation

Facilitation, at its best, is an art of supporting empowerment and participation in a group, especially when it comes to decision-making. This commitment, nonetheless, requires facilitators, often, to make, sometimes even enforce, unilateral choices. As soon as I was able to see this clearly through the fog of my aversion to imposition, I almost immediately realized that most of what a facilitator does is done unilaterally, even if there are strong group norms about sharing power.

The facilitator is the one who decides which decisions are made as part of the flow – sometimes even something as simple as "Let's take a break for ten minutes now" – and which decisions are brought to the group to make. The very reason a facilitator exists is so that they can support the process. No amount of agreements eliminates the choice about which agreement to use when and how.

This is so much the case, that facilitators who are unwilling to exercise this kind of power are, generally speaking, doing a disservice to the group rather than supporting empowerment and participation. I know, because before integrating this insight, I used to involve groups in more decisions than made sense for what we were trying to do, and I still remember the discomfort and unrest this created at times. Decisiveness on the part of a facilitator is an asset to the group. It provides clarity and smooth functioning, and allows people to focus on what's most important instead of being asked for opinions and involved in a decision-making process about matters that are not germane to the purpose of the group.

This kind of choice on the part of the facilitator is fundamentally about matters of process, not about the content of the group's actions. Facilitators can hopefully decide, and easily, how long a break will be; who speaks next; or, sometimes, what process will be used for making a decision about a piece of content. That's where it ends. I wouldn't want to decide for a co-housing community what color the walls of the common room will be painted, as a contrasting example.

Maintaining Community Integrity

In "Business Not as Usual" (page 123) I described the functioning of a virtual community I created. As I wrote there, I was at first really satisfied with what had transpired, how the community came together, and how we developed a structure that allowed for collaborative leadership. A little over a year later, the only way I could see moving forward was to leave the community, because the balance of needs for me had tipped so heavily into the "unmet" zone. I had hoped that the community was robust enough that it would find a way to continue without me. That didn't happen, which, in retrospect, doesn't surprise me, both because, as the founder and main leader of the community, I was a big draw for most, and because the issues that I didn't find a way to handle continued to challenge the rest of the community.

Of all the experiences I've had in the last many years, the events that led to this decision were the most significant lesson I've had about power, and especially how to use it in the context of a model of collaborative leadership and of my own profound commitment, as the leader, to power sharing. Now, more than a year after the community disintegrated, I feel able to write about what happened and what I learned from it.

Attending to Conflict: Any group, community, or organization functions better in the long run when clear agreements are in place about how to handle conflicts when (not if) they arise. When I created the initial set of agreements, the draft of how the community would function that I used to invite people into it, I had in place a particular structure for handling conflicts. When a group of people didn't think that structure was sufficient, and came together for a series of meetings to address the question, I was delighted. This was just my hope: that people would spontaneously organize themselves to attend to the needs and functions within the community. What I didn't anticipate was that a conflict within that group would rapidly tear it apart, and those people who were involved in the conflict would not accept the repeated offers of mediation, nor the invitation to avail themselves of the structure that I had put in place for attending to conflicts.

In retrospect, that would have been the first moment I would have chosen to take action. I knew full well at the time that the situation called for my attention, and yet I didn't do anything. In part, it was because I didn't have enough information and was challenged to learn more within the context of people choosing not to speak about what had happened. In part, it was because I felt helpless to intervene, because I wasn't asked and I wasn't sure I was trusted. In part, it was because all through that time my sister's situation with cancer, and an ongoing challenge within my organization, were consuming so much of my attention that I didn't have enough presence of mind to recognize how critical the situation was until months later.

Responding to Criticism: For the following number of months, a few people, one in particular, were expressing more and more dissatisfaction with the community while not attending calls set up specifically to provide feedback about community functioning. Eventually, that person began sending extensive messages within the private social networking platform of the community. These messages became more and more critical, especially, though not only, of me, with increased intensity of language and interpretation, and longer, sometimes stretching to several pages. My choice as to how to respond was as consistent as I could possibly imagine with the commitments that formed the foundation of the community. I did all the work I needed to do internally to make use of what was written as a form of feedback. I focused my attention on expanding my heart to receive that person empathically, at least within myself, and to find love for her despite her very challenging actions. And I made efforts to dialogue up to a point, provided others were there in support. As the pace and intensity of the messages intensified, and as more and more of my energy was consumed with attending to all the ramifications of this and other actions that this individual took, I became less and less joyful about my involvement in this community. Eventually, as I said above, the balance tipped so strongly that leaving was the action that made the most sense to me.

Meanwhile, even before I left, more and more people were choosing to leave the community, for reasons few of them expressed. I can only imagine that they became overwhelmed with tracking or tending to the various conflicts within the community, and, probably disillusioned with why it was all happening when we were all trying to live by the commitments.

This is an important aspect of the dilemma of leadership I was facing. Now, looking back, it would have been my signal to take decisive action, most likely in the form of asking that person to leave weeks before it came to me seeing no choice except for me to leave. I considered this, I wanted it, I was desperate for it, in fact, and yet I didn't ever do it because of my misguided idea that it would have been an act of power-over and, therefore, by necessity something I would want to avoid as a person committed to living a nonviolent life.

Exclusion with Love

In describing Myth #1, I was already talking about how a group might choose to exclude some people under certain circumstances. This is, without a doubt, what I would have chosen to do with this individual.

Writing now and looking back, I see that at that time I couldn't uncouple exclusion from judgment and retribution. What I learned is that as a leader of a group or a movement, I would on some occasions, mostly super rare, be called upon to ask someone to leave a group. What the commitment to nonviolence and power sharing means, in those circumstances, is about making sure that I do not, as much as I can, fall into the trap of thinking that I am excluding the person because of a problem they have. Instead, I want to be able to keep extending love and acceptance towards the person and to remember that the issue is my own inability to find a way to handle the situation rather than any deficiency on the part of the person being asked to leave. "Not being able to handle" doesn't even mean, solely, that I am suffering. I can imagine taking on the suffering willingly if the only effect of the difficulty is between the one person and myself. What I mean by "not being able to handle" is about not knowing how to respond in a way that also serves the group, the other people who are part of the unfolding without having much of a say, in general. It means that I cannot protect the group from the effects of one person's actions.

In this particular case, for example, this stringent requirement (that the leader take full responsibility for her inability to handle the situation, without blaming anyone else) would have been in place. Throughout the entire episode, which lasted many months, I was able to maintain a soft tenderness towards this person, recognizing the suffering and understanding, at least in part, though never fully, what the experience actually was on her end. There were only momentary exceptions, spikes of shock when a new message arrived that took my breath away with the dramatic intensity of metaphors or interpretations. It wasn't even exactly that it was about me; just seeing the power of the expressions was enough to affect me with its intensity. So it took some time to recover. Even then, I re-found my care almost immediately. It was the care for this person that muddled my clarity. It would have been care for the group that would have led me to make that courageous and extraordinarily difficult step of letting this person know that I had lost my ability to be an effective leader to the group, and therefore I wanted her to leave.

This would not have been easy for her, or for the group. Intention and effect are not the same, as every case of nonviolent resistance shows. Those who find themselves prevented from doing what they want to do experience those of us who lovingly stop them as exercising immense force and power-over, regardless of how much love we may extend in their direction. Still, the love matters. At the very least, in this case, the love might have been clear to other members, and in that way might have supported the group in surviving the ordeal. I cannot know. What I do know is that I now feel prepared to exercise choice. Not with ease, certainly with a heavy heart, and still with a sense of total integrity with my overall intention not to impose outcomes on people.

The Powerless Are Not Necessarily Pure

I mentioned earlier that I am not so keen on the idea that power corrupts. My difficulty with this framing is multiple. For one thing, this saying maintains the pervasive belief that power is bad in and of itself, a belief that can only result in perpetuating itself, since it will keep many people away from taking power lest they oppress others.

As I see it, coming into power does not create the fundamental desire to have things be our way; it only provides access to resources that make it possible to do so. In the process, extraordinary harm can be done to others, sometimes millions of others. Whatever our sphere of influence, and whatever our vision or personal goals, our power gives us access to extra resources, and thus can multiply both our benefit and our harm. There is no substitute for meticulous attention to the effects of our actions. I see it as an enormous challenge to come into power and live its attendant responsibility without creating harm. I am concerned, in part, that less of this work will happen for as long as we continue to believe that the issue is power rather than what we do with it.

Another difficulty that I see stemming from associating power with badness is the corollary move of associating powerlessness with purity. I cannot imagine finding a way to say it any clearer than Dr. King:

> One of the greatest problems of history is that the concepts of love and power are usually contrasted as polar opposites. Love is identified with a resignation of power and power with a denial of love.... What is needed is a realization that power without love is reckless and abusive and that love without power is sentimental and anemic. Power at its best is love implementing the demands of justice. Justice at its best is love correcting everything that stands against love.[59]

If powerlessness is associated with purity, then those without power are, by necessity, better in some sense. This absence of

---

[59] "Where We Go from Here?" 1967 speech.

humility is one of the reasons I see for why when previously oppressed people come into power they often recreate what was done to them. In fact, we don't have to go very far. Every parent was once a child with their own parents who, most likely, didn't leave them very much power. As research seems to indicate, and many, myself included, believe is deeply true, every time a parent mistreats a child, we can assume they were previously mistreated. Not engaging with the effects of being powerless, and, especially, denying the effects of internalized powerlessness on our ability to make choices that take the effects of our actions into consideration, can have serious and harmful effects.[60]

The most painful example for me is what happened to my own people, the Jews, after many centuries of oppression and lack of sovereignty in particular. When political independence suddenly gave us the state of Israel, with it came the possibility of oppressing others. Right in the wake of the Holocaust, my parents' generation participated in a mass expulsion of hundreds of thousands of Palestinians from their homes, sometimes after many centuries of living there. My own generation and beyond engage in an occupation that deprives the Palestinians of livelihood, political independence, oftentimes of survival, and almost always of dignity. I have yet to be able to breathe fully enough when I contemplate this turn of events. I feel a tremendous urge to pull away and distance myself, a big factor that went into my choosing exile for all these years. I keep choosing, as much as I can, to manage, internally, my appreciation for some aspects of my culture while holding in the same awareness the other aspects of that same culture that are so painful for me to know about. To whatever extent I do this, I expand my human capacity within myself – to hold complexity, to hold everyone with tenderness, to have empathy for many forms of being human. This is not an easy task.

My high point of a training I once did for a group of union organizers was the moment when they were able to see and acknowledge that if they had power, they would treat management as poorly as management was treating them. This example is key to me for illustrating why we need to do the work of transforming our judgments and continuing to see the humanity of everyone, including

---

[60] See *Power Under: Trauma and Nonviolent Social Change*, by Steve Wineman, unpublished manuscript available freely on the web.

those whose actions we most deeply deplore. Unless we are able to do that along with healing from the effects of our own traumas of powerlessness, nothing will protect us strongly enough from becoming oppressors if we come into power.

Leadership 101

Is leadership the same as power? Is leadership something given to us, or something we enter into, or something else? Is leadership only significant when it's formal, or can we usefully refer to certain acts of people without any formal authority as exemplifying leadership? Is leadership a function, an attitude, or a perception?

Each of these questions folds within it some other questions. For example, disentangling leadership from power includes attending to the tricky issue of whether having leaders is necessary or desirable. Of course, what we believe that leaders do or how they do it is intimately interlinked with whether or not we would want there to be some form of leadership, and what we could imagine alternatives would be.

Still, this piece is entitled Leadership 101, and I want to aim for keeping it simple.

The dictionary definitions I looked up were no help, defining the concept of leadership either by using a verb (lead), or by using another noun (leader). When I followed those leads (pun so very intended), I still didn't find anything that provided a description of what it means to lead or to be a leader.

Leadership as Influence

And so I turned to some articles I found on the web. The references I found speak of leadership as influence[61], which helped me understand more fully some of the reluctance about leadership that I hear from so many people, and why so many groups are opting to explore functioning without leaders. The capacity to have influence itself can be seen as a form of power, which helps me understand how the deep-seated fear and mistrust about power that so many people have would prevent them from stepping into leadership in any form (yes, I know I haven't yet provided my own definition). When so many people shy away from leadership, only those who are comfortable with exerting power would occupy positions of leadership. This state of affairs is one of the features of our current

---

[61] I was not attempting to be exhaustive in my search. I read the Wikipedia entry on leadership, as well as two articles: leadershipnow.com/minute0005.html and
forbes.com/sites/kevinkruse/2013/04/09/what-is-leadership/.

human life that I am eager to transform. In the way that I see leadership, I would be so fantastically happy if everyone in the world stepped into leadership in one form or another. To understand what I mean by that, it may be necessary to conceive of leadership in a different way.

Leadership as Orientation to Holding the Whole

One of the definitions I found already has a hint of what I have in mind here. An article at Leadership Now (see footnote) ends by stating: "Leadership is intentional influence." The hint I found here is the word "intentional." This definition leaves out the core question of the purpose of influencing others – towards what ends? At what cost? It also leaves me in some discomfort, because I can see so many acts that I would recognize as leadership that include no specific attempt to influence others.

Starting with purpose, I see leadership in an entirely different way. I see it as taking responsibility, in a most personal way, for the well-being and goals of the whole. The form of leadership that is about influencing others, the one most widely recognized, could then be re-written: leadership is intentional influence in support of the whole, or in support of a common goal. While it may seem as if what I am speaking about is desirable leadership, I still see this as the essence of all leadership. As hard as the example might be, I see Adolf Hitler as more of a leader than people who are in charge of large-scale organizations or even countries and exert their power for their own personal gain. As much horror as we have about Hitler's actions, there is no doubt in my mind that he was seeing himself as serving a larger whole, a big vision of the well-being of his people. It is not the nature of the goal that makes something an act of leadership; it's only that it is done with the intention of being a service to a larger whole.[62] Of course, a major caveat is that things are rarely in neat, conceptual purity in the world. People would usually be somewhere on the spectrum, having some personal gain that they may or may not be aware is affecting their choices, alongside an intention to serve the whole. It's always a matter of interpretation, and outside perspective is notoriously skewed. If we like the

---

[62] This example, and my knowledge, in addition, that Hitler was chosen by people and supported by them for a long time, is sobering for me. I want to grapple with it, so as to come up with methods for preventing such harm from arising again rather than simply seeing it as some sort of an aberration.

outcome, we are more likely to attribute "noble" intention to the person in charge. If we don't, we are more likely to conceive of the person in power as doing things for their own personal gain, or to pathologize them in some form. Despite these considerations, I still believe that the distinction itself is helpful to understand our own behavior, if nothing else, and to help in choosing where we direct our attention.

If leadership is not just about "influencing others," then what actions count as exhibiting leadership? Speaking up, for example, when others are nervously noticing something going on and saying nothing, can be a form of leadership. It's not designed to influence anyone in any particular way, yet it's motivated by caring for the whole. Perhaps the key to understanding the difference is that if we are committed to the whole, we are fully open to being influenced, not only to influencing others. When we take on a leadership stance, we act with the intention to serve the whole, and whatever that means – even if it means changing our own preferences or desired outcomes – is what we choose to do.

Stepping into Leadership

Having thought about leadership and trained people to become leaders for so many years, I see a particular move that anyone can practice internally which moves us into the perspective of leadership, from which we can then choose what we want to do. In the simplest terms, this entails shifting from making choices based on my own personal preferences to making choices based on what I see as benefiting the whole. An example can illustrate this, and I have a particularly dramatic one to offer.

I was sitting with a group of five executives in an organization, and supporting them in reaching a decision about an issue they were facing. At first I asked them to each state what they wanted to see as the outcome. That was when each of them was speaking from within their own position, and expressing their preferences. What they said couldn't have been more divergent. They looked at each other, partly helpless, partly amused. I could see this was not a first.

Then I asked them to take some time in silence to reflect on all the responses they had heard, and to come up with a proposal that would attend to the entirety of what they heard, in service of the entire group and the organization. I waited until they all were ready with an answer before hearing from any of them, so that they could truly form their own opinion of this new angle. Then I asked each of them to say what their current proposal was, and all of us were in awe of what happened. Within two minutes they settled the one remaining difference, and all agreed on the path forward.

What changed? They shifted from advocating for their own position to attending to the whole. Although they are all in positions of authority within their organization, they weren't doing it before I directed them to think in that way. It is this kind of thinking that invited them into leadership, and the results were stunning to them.

Leadership within Groups

Unless we make the conscious choice to think about the whole, we are habituated to live within our own perspective and preferences. Given that we all were raised in the world of either/or, how we habitually respond to differences in preferences, especially in the context of a group, rarely leads to outcomes that we are happy with.

Either/or thinking results in believing, usually implicitly and without reflection, that we can either give up on our preferences and adapt or push for our preferences at the expense of others. We either serve ourselves, even at the expense of others, or choose to be of service to others, often in a self-sacrificing way.

Having worked with many hundreds of groups, both those that form for the purpose of learning (short or long term), and those that form for the purpose of accomplishing specific tasks, I have seen this either/or habit result in one of several responses that repeat themselves time and again when people have preferences that they believe are at odds with others' preferences in the group. I want to list some of the common ones I have observed.

Giving Up: this can take various forms, such as being silent despite discomfort or agreeing to decisions that don't really work for the person.

Calling Attention to Self: this often takes the form of persistence in speaking up for a position or an experience without evident awareness of the effect this has on others.

Leaving: this is often the result of a prolonged experience of either of the above. The inner experience of this, to the extent I have heard about it from people, is often summed up as "this is not the right group for me."

All of them have a common root: the belief that the group exists independently of the participation of a specific individual, and the lack of faith that it's possible to work it out in a way that supports everyone in some way.

Instead, I see a path – in precisely those moments when our preferences don't line up with what appear to be others' preferences – that allows us to care for the whole. When I work with groups over time, especially groups that are together for the purpose of learning about stepping into more leadership, I invite everyone, myself included, to consider the whole. If, for example, something is happening in a group that isn't working for any of us, what can be a way to hold the whole?

The answer is quite similar to what the executives did. If a group has adopted a policy, made an agreement, or engages in activities that I don't like, I can ask myself the same question as the one I posed to the executives: what proposal can I make to the group that will improve the outcome? This means that I search for a solution that attends to the needs the existing policy, agreement, or activity addresses as well as to the things that matter to me that are not addressed by the current way things are done. This is stepping outside either/or thinking into what Mary Parker Follett referred to as "integration."

This internal move is what I see as the core practice we can engage in to bring us more and more into a place of leadership.

Leadership and Power

Intuitively, I believe that so much of the definition of leadership revolves around influence because the people who write about leadership are immersed in the organizational world, which is mostly organized with one person on top leading the rest, mostly in the form of making all or most of the decisions that affect the whole.

I don't have any faith that this model is going to take us into a future that works. I am committed to doing all I can, taking my own form of leadership, in support of the possibility of a livable, vibrant future. I see the way forward to be many more of us taking on the active, empowered stance of leading, wherever we are, and whatever our official position may be.

While power can be assigned to someone, especially within an organization or some other kind of social grouping, leadership cannot. People in positions of power sometimes act as leaders and sometimes not; they are sometimes perceived as leaders and sometimes not. In fact, part of the danger of the model that currently exists is that it is so vulnerable to the possibility of people using their structural power to further their own preferences without regard for their effect or for the whole.

In a similar manner, it is possible to inhabit an intentionality of leadership without having power. The famous (though entirely fictional) story about the Dutch boy who put his finger in the dyke, held it there for a whole day until others came, thereby preventing a flood and saving the entire country is, to me, an example of leadership. There is no question this was not this boy's personal preference of how to pass his time that day. It was him taking responsibility for the whole.[63]

Leadership, while not synonymous with power or influence, does create both. Without any guarantees, it is still the case that the choice to step into leadership is often noticed by others, and provides an invitation to others to join, to participate.

Leadership from a position of power interacts with leadership from a position without power. An empowered person who holds the whole would more likely follow someone in power only to the extent that the person in power is exhibiting leadership.

In short, people who feel empowered know they are agents, not pawns. When people take on an orientation of leadership, it becomes near impossible to oppress them. Stepping into leadership, by all of us, then, can become an inoculation against submission and passivity, paving the way for a collaborative future.

---

[63] In a novel by American author Mary Mapes Dodge, published in 1865, a boy on his way to school saw a small leak in a dyke. Knowing it could swiftly grow and inundate the community, he stemmed the flow with his finger and stayed, risking punishment for being late to school, until a passer by saw him and raised the alarm. He saved the community. This story is apparently better known in America than in the Netherlands.

Leadership from Below: On Becoming a Change Agent

So far I have primarily looked at the challenge of understanding and moving toward shared power when we are the ones in the position of power and leadership. For most of us, most of the time, the challenge is different.

On a daily basis we all find things we want to change. We watch the news, go to our workplace, interact with family, friends, and the community at large, and often encounter events or behaviors that we would like to see change. Maybe a landlord who raised our rent; maybe our neighbors who have late night parties; maybe relationships in our workplace that are strained; or maybe it's a government action that we believe is harmful.

Again, if we manage a department within an organization, we usually have the resources to change policies or procedures. It is entirely up to us whether or not we will engage others in the process. If we are the landlord, we can evict a tenant. It is entirely up to us whether or not we will try to work things out with the tenant. If we are the parent, we can move our children to another school. It is entirely up to us whether or not we will consult with them about which school they want to attend.

But what if we are the employee, the tenant, or the child? What are our options when we lack access to power?

Suffer: We can stay put and suffer, which can look like complaining, taking drugs, playing small, becoming numb or cynical, or simply experiencing pain and active helplessness.

Exit: We can quit our job, end our relationship, or move to a different town if things become unbearable. But how often can we do that, and in how many spheres? How much can we tolerate experiencing a sense of power only through leaving?

Fight: We can fight with the people who are in positions of structural power. What happens then? By definition, someone who is in a position of power can easily mobilize resources to prevent the change from happening. And even if we win, we may lose. So often individuals and groups who successfully challenged people in power repeated the same practices they initially started the fight to change.

Collaborate for Change: Is there any other way of engaging with the existing power structure? Can we overcome the fear, discouragement, and tendency to see others as enemies or threats to the success of change, and work together to create an outcome that works for all?

We all have examples of successful collaborations: citizens working with developers to create plans that work for more people; employees engaging effectively with their bosses on proposals that support everyone; teenagers opening up conversations that transform family relationships; and the path of nonviolence, from Gandhi onwards, is full of examples of political changes that were created by appealing to the humanity of people in power.[64]

Leadership from below, like nonviolence more generally, focuses on cultivating internal resources to make up for the absence of structural power.

Acceptance: Collaborating for change without forcing our way or giving up presupposes staying open and accepting the reality of what *is*, and being motivated by clear vision rather than desperate energy to create change because what *is* is not bearable to us.

Courage: Collaborating for change leans heavily on the inner power that comes from the willingness to lose everything and still be at peace.

Stewardship of the Whole: Collaborating for change points to a vision of leadership as stewardship of the whole. Even when people are opposed to our proposed changes, we maintain a commitment to include their needs in the mix of what we are trying to create.

Fruitful dialogue with people in power can be hard work, and benefits tremendously from concrete skills in addition to an inclusive attitude.

Empathic Listening: If we lack structural power, those who have it are likely to only want to listen to us because of the quality of connection. Connection thrives on empathic listening, no matter how much we disagree, no matter how people express themselves, in order to hear what's behind the words and actions. Empathic

---

[64] Although often the *method* utilized in nonviolent resistance – mass mobilizations that put political pressure on those in power – appears to be a fight, the *intentionality* is dramatically and essentially different from what I categorized as "fight" before. It is an intention to create collaboration, to work toward everyone's benefit, and the use of force emerges as the only path that can bring about the conditions that allow dialogue and collaboration to occur.

listening is also vital to being able to integrate objections so that we can propose solutions more likely to work for everyone.

Concrete Proposals Grounded in Needs and Observations: Our power to create change increases to the extent that we focus on: 1) specific strategies instead of oppositional critique or vague abstractions; 2) the needs and vision behind our proposal, including what we know is important to the people we are talking with; and 3) specific observations to support our proposal instead of generalizations and evaluative statements. The combination of these elements can support the people we are talking with in knowing what we want and why it matters, and in having enough clear, honest, and fearless information to understand what we are responding to.

Focus on What We Want: Our habit and training is to focus on what is wrong around us (or within us). Collaborating for change relies on inspiring others by focusing instead on where we want to go – our vision, our values, and a picture of what's possible.

Making Requests for Connection: Engaging with those in power to create mutually beneficial change calls upon us to nurture the sense of connection even, and especially, when obstacles arise and we need to find trust and mutual understanding. Making frequent requests to establish connection conveys to the people with whom we are talking that we are not so focused on getting our way that we ignore them. Everyone wants to matter, whether or not they have structural power.

When everyone matters and we cultivate skills for leadership regardless of structural power, not only do we create possibilities for new outcomes, we also lay the foundation for a new way of living together. As Martin Luther King, Jr., said: "The way of acquiescence leads to moral and spiritual suicide. The way of violence leads to bitterness in the survivors and brutality in the destroyers. But, the way of non-violence leads to redemption and the creation of the beloved community."

Invisible Power and Privilege

In an earlier section I wrote about what I see as the root causes of attachment to privilege. Here I want to look at again at privilege with three different aims. First, I want to shed some light on the way privilege operates on a societal level, and how it comes to be so invisible. Second, I want to speak about the challenges of invisible power relations as they play out within groups. Lastly, I want to describe some basic tools that groups and leaders can use to begin to open up conversations about taboo topics such as race and class. I am confident that such conversations and the collective actions that might arise from them are an essential ingredient for creating the level of togetherness and active interdependence necessary to bring about a social order that transcends separation while making room for differences, and where people matter regardless of how their humanity manifests.

Understanding Privilege[65]

Privilege is a form of invisible power. Sometimes privilege also provides us with structural power in direct relationship with another. In the past, this form of privilege was legalized and prevalent. For example, until not that long ago, men had the legal right to have sex with their wives, and consent was not legally necessary. Many forms of formal privilege based on race, gender, bodily abilities etc. have now been removed, though notable ones remain, like the privileges of shareholders, parents, and the married (still denied to same sex couples in most states and many countries outside the US).

Ironically, the reductions in legal discrimination in recent decades mean that the structural nature of privilege is now much more invisible and indirect, and hence sometimes more insidious.[66] As a person with fairly light skin, for example, I have access to untold number of privileges that are mine to enjoy and which are not

[65] This discussion is almost hopelessly cursory. Anyone interested in learning more about privilege and its invisibility could get started by reading "White Privilege: Unpacking the Invisible Knapsack" by Peggy McIntosh, which is posted widely on the internet, and by watching *The Color of Fear* directed by Lee Mun Wah.

[66] I have often read about how the blatant form of racism that exists in certain parts of the South is sometimes easier for Black people than the invisible forms they encounter in the North and West of the US.

available to people with darker skin. I can, as a very simple example, go in and out of stores without having security officers look at my movements. If I break the law, I am likely to get a lighter sentence than a person who belongs to other groups.

Those of us with privilege are often unaware of the legal or social norms that give us access to such resources simply by virtue of being members of a certain group, without any particular action or even awareness on our part. It's easy to assume that everyone would have the same access, or to not even think about it at all. Even when our privilege provides us direct individual advantage at the direct expense of another individual, the direct relationship may be hidden under socially sanctioned norms such as individual merit, which replace the more explicit forms of the past. A particularly acute example of such relationships occurs both in the educational system and in the workplace.

And so it is that these forms of privilege are largely invisible to those of us who have them unless we take proactive action to learn about them. Those without such access, on the other hand, are usually acutely aware of their lack of access. This creates a gap in experience that is usually excruciating for members of both groups.

Privilege and Group Dynamics

Considering how invisible privilege can be to those who have it, and yet how apparent to those who don't, it is no surprise that creating truly diverse groups and organizations is the exception rather than the norm.

Here's one classic form this struggle takes. Whenever I am in any group in which the question of diversity arises there will almost invariably be a well-meaning white person who will express some version of "Why can't we all just get along and forget our differences? We're all human, after all, aren't we?" The gap between this experience and the pervasive, acute, and unending barrage of discrimination, lack of access to material resources, and negative, frightening, or even fatal encounters with the authorities takes more effort to bridge than most people can muster, especially those who are already worn out by such ongoing challenges of just making it through the day every day. Even if nothing gets said, the gap in experience remains enormous, all the while being known to one group and not to the other.

In addition to the gap in experience in terms of understanding what happens, the different training that different groups receive – itself part of the gap in access to resources – recreates societal dynamics within the group. White people, men, and people with class privilege are more likely to speak in groups and to have their opinions taken seriously than people of color, women, or lower class people, respectively. As one particularly painful example, when a jury is selected, the likeliest person to be chosen as foreman, and I use that word in this way deliberately, is the white male with the highest education in the room. We clearly don't mean to dominate or take away from others' access to power, to choice, to participation in decisions, to shaping the vision and direction of a group. And yet we do, without knowing we do it.

Different access to resources makes for different life experiences, which makes for different perspectives, sometimes even about reality or the nature of life. This is part of why the conversation can get so hard. In many situations the differences in perspective are so deep that we see and hear completely different realities, even before the inevitable process of interpretation and assigning meaning to what we observe begins. When the gap is so large, both people want to be heard at the same time, and both, simultaneously, have trouble hearing the other.

How do we address these historical and present challenges? What can we do, especially if we are people with privilege, to transform these conditions? Guilt and shame, though prevalent, too, are not likely to contribute, because they maintain separation. What I believe is needed is a way to face the excruciating pain and grief together, and forge ways together. The issues are structural and societal, not individual. Ultimately, the solutions will be, also. In the meantime, however, whoever is in the room, that particular collection of individuals, can learn to face the intensity using every tool available and more, so that they can learn to work together, and in the process put a drop in the bucket of showing that diverse groups can, indeed, work together.

However challenging these kinds of situations are, and whatever our position, we can move towards more inclusivity by learning and doing significant inner and outer work. To begin with, we can develop our understanding of the dynamics of power even when there are no explicit power-over or structural power experiences. If we are in a position of privilege, we can learn to trust what we hear from others, so we can learn to discern what happens that was previously opaque to us.

In addition, rather than waiting for people of color and/or working class people to join white- and/or middle-class-led organizations, those of us with privilege can join people-of-color-led or working-class-led organizations and learn to follow the lead of others. One of the ways that privilege works is that we are accustomed to knowing the answers and leading the way, and we continue to act in those ways. Without intending harm, just following our habit and what's familiar, we create conditions that reinforce the power dynamics that are invisible to us and intolerable to others. By learning to follow others' lead, we change the dynamics and learn to work together.

Learning about Privilege in the Moment

Every group, including any group that attempts to have conversations about power dynamics and privilege, contains diversity and power differences, whether visible or invisible. In US culture, race and class tend to be particularly charged topics, and the tendency to avoid them can be particularly high, sometimes by both white people and people of color. What can make such conversations possible given the level of pain and mistrust?

I have led or participated in many such conversations. Some were successful, some less so. The more I learn about dialogue across differences, the more I want to focus, first and foremost, on learning, mutual understanding, connection, and healing. Only after establishing some modicum of trust can actual collaboration toward concrete goals become possible. I have found the tools of Nonviolent Communication (NVC) to be especially helpful in forging a path in the midst of difficulty. More than anything, the particular form of empathic reflection that focuses on understanding what matters most to a person when they speak tends to diffuse misunderstanding and support everyone – those who listen as well as those being listened to – in moving toward shared holding of the astonishingly complex dilemmas of race, class, or other cleavages in society.

My most successful experience took place some years ago, when I was invited to a national gathering of a political movement, and asked to provide training about diversity. I was told all the people in the room would be white.

I started by engaging the entire group in responding empathically to one woman's situation that was not about the topic, because I wanted to provide them with some tools before going into deeper waters. I asked people to reflect and check with that woman their understanding of what was at the heart of the experience for her, what she most wanted, or what was most important. After this modeling, which the group completely managed, and after additional similar work in pairs, I felt confident in embarking on exploring issues of diversity together.

I then supported the group in hearing from only a few people, and hearing them fully.

The questions I asked were as follows:

- What are you afraid to look at?
- What are you afraid to say?
- What are you afraid to hear?
- What does it mean to you to be white? (This question was subsequently changed after I learned that despite what I was told initially, not everyone in the group was white).

Once we went into the answering of the questions, we continued with the same practice of whatever was said being received with full empathy until the person completely reached a sense of being fully heard. One such piece of work that particularly touched me and many others was when we accompanied a white man in his thirties in moving from a place of feeling tremendous guilt and holding harsh judgments of himself and other whites into pure and clean and deep grief about what has happened in the USA.

On another occasion I facilitated a conversation in a group where a few people of color expressed their outrage at what they perceived as racism in the group, and subsequently several of the white people expressed complete bafflement about that assertion, with some amount of defensiveness, and wanted the people of color to explain it to them. Some of the white people who *did* understand what had been happening were concerned about putting the people of color through one more instance of having to explain their experience and not be believed. And so we came up with a different strategy: the white people who had the clarity used an NVC tool to convey to the others their understanding of the experience of racism that the people of color named. What we did, which was slow and appeared painstaking, was to find concrete and specific observations for each of the elements of the moments of unaware exercise of invisible privilege by white people instead of generalizations or evaluations. I am sad to say that although that particular conversation brought clarity to the white people, and for some of them a first-time understanding, the overall dynamics of the group didn't shift and the people of color left with considerable upset.

In both instances a key element of what made the conversation possible was slowing down and truly listening to what was being said, however uncomfortable that may have been. What makes such listening and such slowing down possible? What do we need to learn, as individuals and as leaders of groups, in order to support more such conversations?

Becoming a Resource to Others

Beyond the obvious, which is to keep learning about these issues and how they affect everyone's lives, I believe there are some specific capacities that we can cultivate, whether we have privilege along certain dimensions or not. First and foremost is receiving enough support, and doing enough inner work so that we can have a relaxed and spacious attitude and less susceptibility to being triggered. Working with our own intense emotions is one way to increase our capacity to remain open and calm in contexts of intense emotion and disagreement (see the section "Strategic Discomfort" in my book *Spinning Threads of Radical Aliveness*). As we increase our capacity to differentiate between our experience of reality and the actual observations about what's happening we become more of a reliable resource to others.

Our general training in nonviolence can always help, especially the deepest and repeated re-commitment to connection before outcome, to everyone's humanity no matter their actions or positions, and to doing the inner work necessary to show up for these dialogues with our full humanity.

Along the way we acquire more ease in noticing our inner experience and softening it, so we can open our hearts, and reopen them when they close, so that when we get triggered we know it's an opportunity for learning about ourselves rather than an indication of a problem with the other person, and we learn to recognize that agreement with our position, however "factual" our position appears to us, is not our goal; connection is our goal.

Nonviolence includes the commitment to move beyond right/wrong thinking, which means moving beyond right thinking as well as wrong thinking. This means that when we agree with someone's version of reality, we still look for the underlying needs and offer empathy rather than our heart's resonance with their story. Resonating and affirming an experience may well be a key and important aspect of healing from isolation and may also support other elements of healing. Ultimately, however, empathic listening supports a deeper kind of healing that leads to full inner freedom that is not dependent on agreement from outside ourselves.

Part of what helps us get to the place of being such a resource includes loosening our own hold on reality, so that we can stay present when there are intense agreements or disagreements because we are open to the possibility that reality as we know it is not a full description of reality, and that other people's reality can live alongside ours. This also helps us open our hearts to others' experience even if our group, or even we ourselves, are implicated in their experience.

The more honest we are with ourselves and others about where we are now, and are able to acknowledge the gap between where we are and where we might want to be, including in particular being honest about our prejudices and invisible privileges, the more present and real we can be for these difficult conversations.

Section 3

Concrete Actions for Change

Actions for the Future

Working on our consciousness and tools, even if we do it at all levels, is still working on process, and is not affecting the structures that affect our lives. I want to know how we do the latter.

Without making any decisions about what actions to take, what I am doing in this section is to look at strategic questions that arise in the context of aiming to create change from within the perspective and principles I've been advocating all along.

This part of the book is the only section that speaks to action in the world. The reason is twofold and paradoxical. First, I feel extremely humble about what actions would take us there, because so many efforts are continually being made by people far more experienced and focused than I am on the work itself, and still I haven't seen any sweeping success. Even Gandhi, the epitome of nonviolence as I understand it, ultimately failed to create a nonviolent alternative even as he succeeded in leading India to independence. As I mentioned earlier, the India of today is not what Gandhi ever dreamed of. I believe that my own contribution lies much more in the *how* and the *why* than in the *what*, and, a lot is already available for those who are interested in terms of learning about and plugging into nonviolent social change movements.

That said, I still want to address the questions of nonviolence itself when it comes to action, the relationship between nonviolent resistance and dialogue, and the lesser known role of what Gandhi called Constructive Program in the possibility of creating a future world that works for all.

To create order in the vast array of options and possibilities that we can engage in when we want to work for change, I rely on the work of Joanna Macy, who has been urging us for some time now to operate simultaneously in three directions to move towards a sustainable future:[67]

- "Holding actions" in defense of life on Earth: actions to slow the damage to Earth and its beings;

---

[67] See Joanna Macy with Molly Young Brown, *Coming Back to Life: Practices to Reconnect Our Lives, Our World*, pp. 17-24

- Creation of alternative institutions: analysis of structural causes and creation of structural alternatives;
- Shift in perceptions of reality, both cognitively and spiritually: a fundamental shift in worldview and values.

Each of these directions can be done in a manner fully consistent with principled nonviolence, the Gandhian approach. In the rest of this section, I look at each of these in more detail.

Combining Love with Force: The Power of Nonviolent Resistance

It is not nonviolence if we merely love those that love us. It is nonviolence only when we love those that hate us.

– Gandhi

As much as I would wish for it to be different, power structures don't tend to be dismantled through collaborative dialogue designed to attend to everyone's needs. It is the rare exception that people in a position of power release it voluntarily purely through a change of heart.

Here, then, is the challenge of nonviolence at its most extreme: Since nonviolent resistance is a form of force, how do we ensure that our actions are not going to fall into the trap of recreating the past? Put differently: What is nonviolent about nonviolent resistance, and how does the language of love fit in with it?

Throughout this book, so far, I have mostly been talking about nonviolence as it applies to those parts of life where dialogue is possible. I have stressed my vision of a non-coercive approach to life, collaboration to attend to everyone's needs, and use of power that is consistent with those principles.

Now it's time to take on the challenge of the apparent contradiction between these principles and my wholehearted support of nonviolent resistance, the direct legacy of Gandhi and King.

For one thing, the experience of those who are on the receiving end of nonviolent resistance movements is that they are being "forced" to give up their power and make changes they don't want to make. How does this square with the non-coercive path I have been painting?

As another example, while I am speaking of a future without winners and losers, and a path of making things work for everyone, Gandhi used the language of winning as well as other military metaphors, actively opposed policies and people, and explicitly made demands of the British. How can the commitment to attend to everyone's needs align with such actions?

These are some of the questions I plan to attend to here in Section Three.

When Dialogue Breaks Down

Because this book emerged from my engagement with Nonviolent Communication, which emphasizes dialogue as the primary tool for creating change and, in general, eschews force and imposition of any kind, I want to dedicate some space now to exploring the link between the approach of NVC and the more familiar forms of nonviolent resistance. In particular, I want to examine the difficult questions surrounding the very practice of nonviolent resistance: Isn't it, fundamentally, a coercive practice, albeit coercion done with love?

A more open-ended way of approaching this difficult territory is this: What do we do when the stakes are high and we are facing active or potential harm? Can dialogue always be used, or are there times when force is absolutely necessary in order to protect life?

Protective Use of Force

Marshall Rosenberg was deeply aware of the challenge of placing dialogue at the center of an approach, knowing full well that the option of dialogue isn't always available. As part of his explorations that led to the creation of the practice of NVC, Rosenberg set out to investigate such extreme situations, and to consider under which conditions the use of force is consistent with a nonviolent stance.

My understanding of these conditions as they apply to engaging with specific individuals is as follows:

Imminent Risk of Harm

It takes great discipline when we are worried about potential harm to remain calm enough to discern when the risk is truly imminent or unavoidable if not attended to immediately, and when dialogue remains an option to continue to explore. Some classic examples include a child running into the street; a company about to begin logging in an endangered area; a person with repeated episodes of violent behavior.

Options for Dialogue Have Been Exhausted

This condition is quite exacting. It's only about the other party's willingness to engage in dialogue. Even when danger is imminent, if dialogue is still an option, we would prefer to approach the other party collaboratively rather than through force. Maintaining our commitment to nonviolence means a readiness to show up for dialogue for as long as the other party is willing. (Exploring how to address those moments in which we are beyond our own capacity and resources is beyond the scope of this particular piece.)

Pure Intention to Protect

It takes a deep spiritual practice to attain a state in which we can exercise force and remain entirely connected to another's humanity, so that there is no ounce of subtle punitive energy behind the action. At times the clarity of focus on protecting rather than punishing may result in different forms of force being used, or more minimal force, only what's absolutely necessary to protect. At other times the specific use of force may be identical, and the only difference is the intent behind the action. The most challenging example of this is when the force used is legal, as when we appeal to laws that may have been enacted in response to nonviolent resistance in order to protect people and the environment. It's challenging because those appeals predictably result in specifically punitive action against those causing the harm in the first place. How to take action that will for sure result in someone being punished, and do that with love, boggles my own imagination. At the very least, a likely component would be having true sadness *for the person being punished as a result of our actions* alongside the joy and relief of being successful in the protective measure. If the *intention* to punish is not there, the action could still be purely protective. For example, I trust that the people who were pressing for the Voting Rights Act[68] had as their only intention to protect the ability of people of color to vote. The *mechanism* to get there was to rely on the threat of legal punishment, not the *intention*. Knowing that the white people in power had not actually come to embrace inclusion of people of color meant that dialogue alone would not have gotten them the necessary protection. I'd like to believe, though

---

[68] So ironic to invoke this image of iconic success of the Civil Rights movement just as the supreme court knocked a major part of it out.

I have no way of knowing, that everyone would have preferred the outcome to be reached without the threat of punishment, and that is the exact criterion I am using here. I contrast this with the example of capital punishment, where some people press for keeping it precisely in order to *punish* those who kill, independently of how effective that act is in protecting others from harm.

That intention – to use only the force necessary to protect – supports the possibility of maintaining human connection with the person against whom we use the force. It is that connection, which at times can only be inside our own hearts, which makes those actions nonviolent.

Force, Resources, and Nonviolence

Using force in these situations goes beyond preventing harm. If our hearts remain open, we continue to aim for sufficient connection to arrive at a solution that works for everyone. We are more likely to get there if we are successful at maintaining a clear, unwavering commitment to upholding the dignity and humanity of those against whom we are using force, even if we never see them again, even if they will continue to hate us for the actions we took. This is the essence of the link between protective force and nonviolence.

Through this lens, Gandhi's noncooperation can be seen as a form of protective use of force and may well have been the inspiration for Marshall Rosenberg's understanding.

The question of the relationship between force and nonviolence is not easily resolved. For example, Gandhi said: "I can only teach you not to bow your heads before any one even at the cost of your life." Clearly he was willing to die for what he was working towards. Does this mean he wouldn't put up an arm to shield himself from a blow if personally attacked? Does force ever cross over into violence even when used to protect? It seems to me that these are questions to continue to grapple with rather than try to resolve once and for all. It is my belief that Gandhi himself continued to wrestle with questions about nonviolence throughout his life and work.

As I sketch out a framework for looking at these questions, I want to start by naming what is so dear to me: nonviolence is ineffable. It cannot be defined; there is no language that can describe nonviolence with simple words. I honor the wisdom that says that nonviolence can only be described as what it is not. For me, as I said, it's a combination of love, truth, and courage. Force is simply not what nonviolence is about, not by fundamental design. It becomes the material outcome of what we do when we stand, courageously and lovingly, for what is true for us. This is how I understand Gandhi's term "truth-force" – as his way of trying to differentiate between "regular" force and what he was doing.

One of the difficulties we face is that nonviolent resistance with love is something so entirely unfamiliar, so different, that it's hard to put it in juxtaposition with familiar categories. The power of the love that infuses Gandhi's and King's work results in use of force that is entirely different from what we are familiar with. Although the person on the receiving end may experience it as force, it is not intended to vanquish. It's intended to create a wholesome outcome that, ultimately, *will* work for everyone. This commitment is beyond what the word "intention" can capture, although it is of that ilk: it is unwavering, uncompromising, and always holding out the conviction that the outcome will serve everyone, as Gandhi himself stated in exactly such words (see pages 41-2 above).

Did Gandhi use force to work towards his goals? Force looks different depending on how much power we have in a situation. If I am in a position of official power, the question of protective force is meaningful for me as an individual: What actions can I take to protect, and at what cost to others?

Gandhi didn't have a lot of political power in relation to the British, and could not directly "force" them to do anything. Knowing this, Gandhi opted for different forms of power based on different resources. He cultivated a level of personal power, already apparent by the late 1920s, through the incredible personal appeal he had, to both sides. He also mobilized a mass of people willing to endure anything. I see a group of people with that level of commitment as an enormously powerful force. Gandhi had two sources of power, at least: his internal resources, and the access he had to a large group of people ready to act. Used strategically, these resources did dictate outcomes without physically harming the British rulers.

When dialogue is not an option, and individuals don't have the resources to dictate or even influence an outcome as individuals, the capacity to exercise force only comes from collective action. This is precisely what nonviolent resistance amounts to: a collection of individuals attempting to exercise protective force.

The Spectrum of Force

Having love at the center means, to some extent, that the failure of dialogue is a loss. This loss is not only internal. Every time we have no other path except the strategic force of mass mobilization on the large scale or other protective measures in the smaller spheres (e.g. a restraining order issued to prevent harm to self or children), we have lost some of our capacity to reach an outcome that truly works for everyone, regardless of how much we aim for one.

As much as Gandhi engaged in civil disobedience and nonviolent resistance for the bulk of his life, he actually maintained (see "Constructive Program" page 220) that if enough cooperation exists in a nation, they would not be necessary. I take that to mean that, in some ways, engaging in these acts was a concession for him, operating with less than the fullness of what he saw as possible.

This is so not because of what our hearts and intentions are. It's so simply because of how others experience us. This is why Gandhi was so adamant about not humiliating the British after successfully driving them to leave India. Once we mobilize force rather than dialogue, the other party will experience our actions as coercive even if we don't intend them this way. The very fact of losing the power to rule a group of people can, in and of itself, amount to such deep threat to those who are used to being in charge, that our intention simply doesn't matter to them. I see this as part of the reason why Gandhi devoted so much energy to cultivating positive relationships and maintaining dialogue with the British officials throughout his campaign. One way of seeing nonviolent resistance is as an attempt to create the conditions that will make dialogue possible when otherwise those in power refuse to engage.

When we can achieve our aims through dialogue and connection, there is less of a chance that the other party will harbor resentment and look for the first opportunity to reassert its control. The possibility of a future that works for all is enhanced the more voluntary the change.

This is also why I take issue with the language of making demands, even though Gandhi used that language in working to achieve independence. Demands give us the illusion of power. Do they necessarily create change? Part of what I want to bring to any work or project that I take on is the humility of knowing that nothing we can do is certain to achieve results. As soon as we use the language of demands, we increase the chances that the other party will experience us as trying to force a solution on them.

Given that use of force lies on a spectrum, the commitment to nonviolence means, in part, always using the least amount of force possible while keeping the doors always open to dialogue and offering an open heart and open arms for people, leaving them room to have a change of heart without losing face. We want to focus internally on not using force, without losing action and without losing love. Perhaps naïvely, I have some faith that the ongoing commitment to love and honoring the dignity of others does change their experience and it becomes less abhorrent to them, less of an experience of force. I don't, however, know.

I see those of us who are committed to nonviolent social change as being called to engage in these questions, to wrestle with our commitment to love, to grapple with what makes it so, so difficult for us to reach those in power to create fruitful dialogue. There is no way anyone can decide for us how far we will go. So long as we keep our commitment to love at the center, so long as we keep questioning ourselves, so long as we continue to seek feedback from others, so long as we put in place ways for us to know when we have crossed over a non-existent line and have become violent, I want to trust that, collectively, we will find a way to uphold the commitment and move forward effectively.

The Effects of Force and the Role of Love

Whenever possible, Gandhi was aiming for what he called conversion: an experience for those in power that results in an actual change of belief, coming around to agree internally with what is being asked of them. The best known example of this effect is when upper caste Hindus opened up temples for the Dalits after many months of nonviolent resistance.

George Lakey, longtime nonviolence theorist, organizer and activist, points out, sadly, that this kind of conversion is the exception.[69] Eventually, Gandhi gave up on the possibility of getting the British to embrace Indian independence, and accepted that the British would only leave when coerced to do so through the loss of cooperation of the Indian. That is, indeed, what happened. Still, even

---

[69] See wagingnonviolence.org/feature/should-we-bother-trying-to-change-our-opponents-hearts/ for much more detail.

when coercion is the only means possible, what distinguishes it from violence is not only the absence of certain tactics. Rather, I see the role of love as core and central to the possibility of the results being sustainable. However few of the British left India because they were converted to the cause, they were able to leave with their dignity intact because their humanity was seen and honored by Gandhi and the movement throughout the campaign. At all times, Gandhi maintained cordial relationships with them, continued to be available for dialogue even when imprisoned, and ended up building friendships with some of his former opponents. To me, this is not an incidental part of the victory that Gandhi achieved.

As Lakey points out based on his extensive research, both outright coercion and complete conversion are less likely outcomes. Most often, in his understanding, the effect of the force of nonviolent resistance on those in power is that they choose to agree neither because they are coerced nor because they change their mind. Instead, they come to a strategic realization that the cost of continuing with their policies and practices, even if they continue to believe in them, is higher than the cost of agreeing to the changes being fought for. As Lakey puts it, the movement succeeds when "there is no longer the willingness to keep the machinery of punishment going that's needed to continue the injustice."[70] There can be more or less acceptance of the actual changes; it seems to me to be more on a spectrum than a yes/no division. For example, in some instances there can be some initial seeds of doubt being sewn by the actions of the resistors, even if it is never acknowledged publicly.

As I reflect on the examples Lakey uses and other historical situations, I wonder what a disciplined practice of love that is widespread within the population of those engaged in nonviolent resistance can accomplish in terms of moving the response of the powerful closer on the spectrum to acceptance of the changes sought.

Lakey uses an example in which the suffragists referred to Woodrow Wilson as "Kaiser Wilson" as part of their continued campaign through World War I. Initially, a strong reaction to this

---

[70] This quote is taken from the same article. Lakey makes a further distinction between persuasion and a larger category of accommodation, and introduces a fourth category of disintegration. From the perspective I hold here, focusing on the role of love in nonviolent resistance, these further refinements are less crucial.

took place, both politically (repression) and socially (loss of support). Lakey believes that "polarization can close doors in the short run and open them for the longer run," and, indeed, in this case it did. As stories about the brutalization of the women circulated, the familiar pattern of nonviolent resistance surfaced: the sight of repression against peaceful resistors is often a powerful image that sways many to shift their allegiance.

Nonetheless, I am left with a question that I obviously cannot answer. In my mind, the sign that says "Kaiser Wilson" is not expressing love. I can imagine the women doing everything they did, continuing their pressure on the government and the press, even engaging in civil disobedience if needed, while continuing to hold an open heart to Wilson, inviting him to the table while resisting his policies, unmasking the injustice done to them without making a monster out of him. I imagine they would still have been brutalized, and could have had the experience of opening doors in response without the initial loss of support. I'd like to believe that love is powerful, that with more concerted efforts to keep imagining and advocating for outcomes that are truly workable for everyone a movement can win over more people. I don't know that I will ever know. I am acutely aware of how, even with love, even with persistence and ongoing dialogue, the distance is larger than can sometimes be crossed without force.

Why Reaching the Powerful Is Challenging

When I enter into dialogue with anyone, the fundamental premise of it is that through connection we can reach a state in which we both care about both of our needs, thereby forming a shared commitment to a solution that works for both of us. This frame depends on a profound kind of trust: that the other person is human like me.

Several times in recent years I failed to find a way to reach people in power even when I was able to approach them openheartedly. Especially in relation to one particular person, I was confident that she would be wholeheartedly committed to creating change once she truly understood the effect of her choices on those who worked in her company. I completely underestimated the extent of her commitment to having things go her way. I gradually learned that the experience of rarely hearing "no," the quintessential characteristic of being in a position of power, was a source of comfort and ease:

having power meant she didn't have to negotiate, to show her vulnerability, to ask for what she needed and be in dialogue with others about it. She could just say it, and it would happen. I can see the seductive appeal, both in terms of this very personal level, and in terms of the ease of getting things done. I can see how the cost of others' "yes" becomes conveniently invisible.

Much has been written about what *New York Magazine* calls "The Money-Empathy Gap" – the phenomenon of people with wealth showing less capacity for empathy, compassion, and even ethical behavior, and a higher preoccupation with their own well-being in disregard of others'. My own "aha" about this phenomenon came when I realized that rising up the ladder, even inheriting money and retaining it, require a willingness, at least to some degree, to get needs met at the expense of others. Sometimes this relationship is direct, as in the case of CEOs whose salaries are orders of magnitude higher than their employees, while at other times the relationship is indirect, even hidden, as in the overall willingness of all of us in affluent countries to get goods produced by devastatingly poor people in faraway countries.

More than once, in my efforts to connect with people in power, and even though I knew all of this information, I continued to anticipate and trust they would act "like me" and was repeatedly shocked to hear and see behavior that I could only interpret as lack of care. I am still unclear, even after many months of considering this fundamental failure on my part, what I can do differently. What would be required in order to cross over the barrier I experience in relation to that loss of interest in others that seems to accompany, as both cause and effect, the acquisition of power and wealth?

The Path of Empathy

One of the possible paths is the path of empathy. This approach would be based on the premise that when people feel fully heard, when they know they matter, they are more likely to be open to hearing from others. This makes some sense to me, even as I think of the specific individuals in question. What I don't know is how much empathy would be sufficient to make room for offering the necessary feedback for people to learn about the effects of their actions. I am frightened to imagine that there may be people whose emotional needs are so high, whose concern with their own safety and well-being so consuming, and whose lack of trust so extreme that no amount of empathy would be sufficient to open their hearts. Is this fear my own lack of faith, or is it an accurate perception of the level of dysfunction in our money-driven society characterized by a class of CEOs, and especially those at the very top of the largest corporations, who are no longer able to connect empathically with others? If it is the latter, what hope would there be for anyone's attempts to create connection and dialogue across power differences?

Part of the irony of this situation, as I see it, is that whenever someone "buys" their needs through others' compliance based on fear or reward, they are bound to know, somewhere deep within, that they are outside the web of interdependence and love: those who serve them do not do it because of care. If this conjecture is accurate, then external power doesn't necessarily *feel* powerful, which can reinforce the uncaring behavior on the part of those in power. That's a lot to bridge through love and empathy, and most of us don't have enough staying power, faith, or even capacity to create and sustain the relationships to create transformation in this way.

To close the loop, the other reason why we cannot bank on the kind of voluntary change of heart as the foundation of significant social change is that the amount of harm being done – to individuals, to our fellow creatures, to the carrying capacity of the earth, and to our very biosphere – is such that the conditions calling for protective use of force are already in place. There simply aren't enough of us around who can muster sufficient love and faith to engage in sufficient dialogue with sufficient people to make it happen. This is, in essence, why nonviolent resistance, despite being, in some ways, a loss and a compromise, remains absolutely necessary. It doesn't reflect less love, just less reliance on it alone.

Nonviolent Resistance
Done with Love

Nonviolent resistance can be seen as an escalation of dialogue just as much as war can be seen as an escalation of diplomatic fear-based negotiations. In nonviolent resistance we bring to bear resources to increase engagement, to make visible our plight, including unmasking the methods and practices of power, to appeal to the humanity of those whose actions we want to change, or simply to reduce their ability to keep doing their actions without cost so as to invite more consideration of other options. Nonviolent resistance was the quintessential method of Gandhi and King, and continues to be the mainstay method of many movements, including some of the recent ones in the Arab world.[71]

Nonviolent resistance in the form of acts of civil disobedience has been a mainstay of nonviolent social change movements for a long time. In my understanding of how Gandhi and King in particular used civil disobedience, at least three factors need to be in place to make the action effective:

- Those taking the action must be willing to disobey the law and suffer the consequences in an entirely peaceful manner. This may include imprisonment, physical harm to self, or even death.

- The action needs to be strategically placed and go beyond symbolic protest. As I mentioned earlier (see pages 43-5 "From Opposition to Vision") Shariff Abdullah maintains that purely symbolic protest actions did not have anywhere near as much effect in Gandhi's or King's campaigns, and only those that exemplified what he calls *vision implementation* were fully successful. Vision implementation means that the action itself prefigures the envisioned world.

---

[71] For Erica Chenoweth and Maria J. Stephan's analysis of nonviolent movements during and since the Arab Spring see their article "Drop Your Weapons: When and Why Civil Resistance Works" in *Foreign Affairs*, July/August 2014.

- Those taking the action must be committed to ending the harm done while maintaining love and respect for the people they are opposing.

I see these conditions as very exacting and rarely followed fully. I long to see campaigns that manage to train enough people in the art of courageous, loving willingness to stand up to what they see as harm or injustice, while finding avenues to do so that are visionary and inspiring to all.

Denmark Rising

Until I read Michael Nagler's *The Search for a Nonviolent Future*, I had no idea that some efforts to respond to Hitler nonviolently did take place, let alone that by and large such efforts were successful. The most notable of them is partially known to many: the successful effort on the part of Danes to save virtually all their Jews and smuggle them to Sweden. What is usually less known is the progressive and widespread nonviolent resistance to German occupation that Danes mounted as the war dragged on.

Author Barry Clemson used these facts of history as the foundation for a literary project the likes of which I had never seen: a what-if novel about a full-on nonviolent resistance on the part of Danes right from the first moment of occupation. Barry didn't veer significantly from the historical record. Almost all the characters in the novel are real-life people, albeit with some embellishment and added circumstances. In addition, many of the specific acts described in the book took place, sometimes by fewer people than described, sometimes in more circumscribed circumstances or later dates than appear in the novel. The fundamental difference lies in the novel's premise: whereas real-life Danish resistance started from the bottom up and built over time, the novel's context is an already established upfront plan of action designed from the top and encompassing the overwhelming majority of the population.

The result is *Denmark Rising*,[72] a document that defines an entirely different flavor of heroism from the popular image of the person who kills the "bad guys." The people populating this novel, from

---

[72] The book can be ordered through the author's website – barryclemson.net/store. The site also contains many historical details and an explanation of the relatively small difference between the reality and the novel.

Danish King Christian to the workers in a factory who risk flogging to delay and prevent the construction of a submarine for use by the German navy, all exhibit the double courage that defines the passage into nonviolence: the courage to overcome internal habits of reaction, and the courage to face the potential consequences that arise from standing up to those in power, especially when they are fully committed to subjugation of the resisters.

I found this book hard to put down, because the story and the characters were so compelling, and the effect so profoundly inspiring. I had already seen and read enough prior to reading *Denmark Rising* to know that ordinary citizens do and can rise up to extraordinary circumstances. What this book provides, in addition, is a level of detail that makes the vision of massive nonviolent resistance utterly believable. I definitely have a wish that, somewhere, someone with enough influence will read this, become inspired, and mount such a principled and comprehensive program. My own intuitive conviction that even war can be met with nonviolence now has a vivid story to back it up.

Creating Alternatives

At whatever scale possible, freeing ourselves from the legacy of systems and practices that prioritize anything other than meeting the needs of humans and of nature (e.g. profit, control, or mechanical efficiency) will require some people engaging in and showing the rest of us what is truly possible. There are already groups, organizations, and magazines dedicated to documenting and making known to all who wish to know the numerous examples of such experiments and options. These kinds of experiments fall into the second of Joanna Macy's three paths towards the future.

In fact, some claim that all the technology and human processes necessary to shift to a carbon-free caring society are available and have been tried somewhere.[73] Stories abound about individuals finding ways to effect significant change, too many to document. In addition, more and more local areas are moving closer to collaborative living. There are even many communities around the world that, in their own small ways, are standing up to the power of globalization and the exchange economy. If we look, we can find places like Curitiba in Brazil and Gaviotas in Columbia, which are

---

[73] For starters, you may want to get a subscription to *YES!* Magazine (yesmagazine.org), or search a library for old issues of *Hope* Magazine (defunct since 2000), to begin to learn about human ingenuity and to become inspired about what's possible.

operating in remarkably sustainable ways. We can find regions with a high proportion of cooperative functioning such as Mondragon in Spain. We can find companies that function in dramatically different ways from the mold in terms of use of power and levels of involvement, such as Semco in Brazil.

In this segment of the book, I look briefly at what we need to know in order to create true alternatives; what lessons we can learn from an almost-successful-and-tragically-failed attempt to create an alternative; what we can learn from current attempts to reclaim and revive the long history of the commons; and what Gandhi's legacy can offer us in terms of what nonviolence means when we are creating directly rather than through opposing what exists.

Because explicit and clear vision of the details of operation are so important to the possibility of success, I have dedicated an entire section of this book to envisioning in some detail what the world of the future can look like – it's called "Wisdom Tales from the Future," and follows this section. Even in the smaller scale experiments we may be involved in today, I see it as essential that we have explicit agreements at least about key aspects of life.

Lessons from the Israeli Kibbutz Movement

If we are going to create alternative institutions, cities, organizations, or locales, integrating nonviolence and interdependence will point us to include some explicit agreements about aspects of functioning that are essential for creating transformative results.

In the absence of an explicit system for handling these aspects of human functioning, we are simply too likely to recreate old habits of separation and scarcity, such as mistrust, command and control structures, or punitive approaches to conflict. Alternatively, we may also rebel against such habits and operate in chaotic ways without leadership, order, care, or effectiveness. Sometimes we will do both at once.

For me, the saddest example of such a recreation of old habits happened in the Kibbutz movement in Israel. Whatever else can be said about this movement, I believe it was an extraordinary social experiment that lasted about ninety years before losing its focus completely. The founders of the Kibbutz movement were passionately committed to both economic and sexual equality. However, they only made explicit agreements to institutionalize economic equality, and none about sexual equality, other than declarations of commitment. The economic agreements lasted decades until the arrival of television in the early 1970s and of payments for Holocaust survivors at about the same time. Both of these were significant challenges that the founders could not have anticipated and thus they didn't put in place any provisions for addressing them. Television brought the enticements of the consumer economy and catapulted many individuals out of the cocoon of simplicity and a "pioneer" mentality of disdain for material possessions. Holocaust reparations payments made some individuals wealthier than others, without there being any system in place for attending to the complexity of factors present in considering whether such payments would be shared with the whole kibbutz or not.

Even with the new challenges arising, I can still imagine the possibility of robust mechanisms for attending to changes, conflicts, or unforeseen circumstances. Why did this not happen? My intuitive sense is that the later generations didn't have sufficient visionary zeal to address these challenges within the framework they had inherited. And so those institutions began to crumble some fifty years after being put in place. Although I see this, ultimately, as a "failure," I also am in awe at the success of a small movement (at no point did the movement comprise more than about 3% of the Israeli Jewish population) to act as an island of different values within a society that was continually moving in a different direction and with different economic models.

In contrast to the economic institutions that were created, when it came to sexual equality, nothing was put in place to transform habitual and familiar gender relationships and to establish *structures* that would support people in shifting their deeply embedded habits. As a result, as soon as children were born, there was no discussion to speak of about who was going to take care of them, or how. It was automatically given to the women to do. Initially, there could have been a way to still have women fully integrated into the productive aspects of the economy by focusing on growing vegetables and similar activities that would have allowed women to participate and still be close to their children for breastfeeding. However, because ultimately the kibbutz operated as a collective entrepreneur within a market economy, those sectors were not profitable enough. Many of the early kibbutzim chose to cultivate large fields and orchards, which were further from the hub, making it progressively more difficult for women with small children to participate. In addition, no encouragement was ever given to men to participate in women's traditional activities. The result was a recreation of traditional gender roles within less than a generation, despite the early commitment to full sexual equality. As I see it, they never took the idea of sexual equality to its fullest extent, which always would have to mean allowing and inviting men to take on women's roles just as much as allowing and inviting women to enter men's roles.

Necessary Agreements

Based on this lesson and other reflections I have made over the years, I have come to believe that if we want to approximate the longed-for image of walking our talk, we will be called to engage in and make agreements about a number of key functions, so that we can create structures that will support us as we continue to make the inner transformation to a new way of being. Without them, I don't have sufficient confidence that we will find a way forward that won't gradually devolve into recreating the past.

Especially when attempting to create and demonstrate alternative ways of functioning, being able to demonstrate different relationships and structures can go a long way toward overcoming the habitual cynicism that so many people carry to protect themselves from experiencing the heartbreak associated with seeing where the world is. We need to inspire ourselves, those who work with us, and even those who oppose us, by "being the change" on a larger scale than individually.

This, in a nutshell, is what I see as the bare necessities:

Decision-making: I want us to be able to show that we can have decision-making processes, at all levels, which are collaborative and use resources effectively.

Feedback Loops: I want us to be able to put in place feedback loops, both material and relational, that will allow us to learn, individually and collectively, the effect that our actions and choices have on others and beyond, and continually grow in our ability to live our values and be effective in what we do at the same time.

Conflict Resolution: I want us to be able to show that restorative approaches can handle conflicts at all levels in all kinds of situations and systems with an ever diminishing role for punitive responses.

Resource Allocation: I want us to be able to show that an interdependent and voluntary use of resources can be scaled up to workable and effective models. This is, perhaps, the most radical of all changes that we can model in our work.

Self Care: I want us to show that we can treat each life with complete reverence, including our own; that we can find ways of supporting each other, and holding each other accountable for recognizing our finitude, and still work effectively towards our goals.

Reclaiming the Commons

Prior to the large scale enclosures of the early capitalist era in Europe, and in parts of the world still to this day, traditional village structures defy our modern notions of private property. Although each family has its own living quarters and small plot of land for growing food, the larger area beyond is held in common. This tends to include grazing and the collection of wild plants, firewood, and other items used for the subsistence of the villagers.

Because of centuries or millennia of ongoing use and tending to such resources, there is a deep bond between the villagers and the land: they belong to it and it belongs to them. The land feeds them and they steward it, collaboratively. Collaboratively doesn't mean without conflict; it only means having time-tested methods for attending to the conflict and managing the resources sustainably. At the same time, no matter how deep the bond is, it was never a legal form of private property. In the days prior to capitalism and centralized states, this was not an issue. In fact, only a fraction of the land in the UK was privately owned, and the rest of it was held as a commons. Tragically, though, the absence of a document stating legal ownership was the entryway through which states encroached on the commons, seizing and literally enclosing it with fences, leaving the villagers completely unable to maintain their livelihood in the absence of access to the land on which they had previously grazed their animals and collected nature's bounty. The result was the creation both of land for the capitalists to build factories and mansions on and of a desperate new workforce, compelled to work in those factories to supplement and later supplant the earlier ways of subsisting.

Other types of commons exist, too. One striking example is the *acequias*, a system of irrigation that's been in operation in parts of Spain and in previously colonized areas of the USA, especially the arid Southwest. This is an elaborate system of ditches and canals that spreads over hundreds of miles and is governed by a collaborative and complex arrangement explicitly at odds with norms of private property. For example, private property approaches to water management rest on the doctrine of "prior appropriation" which "considers water to be a commodity owned by private individuals while acequia systems treat water as a community resource that irrigators have a shared right to use, manage, and protect."[74] The system includes methods for dispute resolution for those rare occasions when the collaboratively maintained agreements are not sufficient. In addition, this system has been an improvement to the natural terrain and has been preventing erosion and depletion of resources. Considering the fact that disputes over water have often been causes for war, the fact that a collaborative, environmentally-friendly, and sustainable system for managing water in a semi-desert area has been in continuous operation for hundreds of years challenges many of our assumed notions about optimal resource management.[75]

The existence of the commons, by virtue of its fundamentally different premises and norms, is an ongoing threat to the taken-for-granted framework of private property and the unlimited accumulation of wealth.

Because of its challenge to corporate domination, its essentially communal and interdependent nature, and its proven and ongoing capacity to lead to sufficiency for its users alongside sustainability in resource management, reclaiming and reviving the commons is a rich and fertile area of work for those of us who seek to create a future that is collaborative, attentive to needs, and sustainable.

This work challenges us, as individuals engaged in it, to tap more deeply into our atrophied collaboration muscles and to transform our consciousness regarding the primacy of private property and individual freedom. The level of experimentation in the commons around the world is increasing, along with a growing awareness of the continued, uninterrupted existence of some commons. New commons are being created – both the virtual ones such as Wikipedia and others, as well as physical commons, especially in Europe.[76] This makes the commons a unique ground for experimenting that acts as a real-life laboratory for collaborative processes.

The commons then becomes an aspect of constructive program, an ongoing alternative both to the individualistic norms and to

---

[74] See en.wikipedia.org/wiki/Acequia for more details about the ways in which the acequia norms stand at variance with more modern notions of governance and private property.

[75] See Randall Amster's article "From the Headwaters to the Grassroots: Cooperative Resource Management as a Paradigm of Nonviolence" in the edited collection *Exploring the Power of Nonviolence*.

[76] Because land held in commons is virtually non-existent in modern states, establishing physical commons nowadays requires novel arrangements with governments to create sufficient communal autonomy in managing those resources, akin to the true original commons. If interested in concrete examples, the *Wealth of the Commons* volume describes a number of them in some detail.

massive, impersonal, large-scale institutions that dominate our lives. And, at the same time, those involved with reclaiming the commons continually stand in substantive opposition to both the market and the state, aiming to keep or restore access to resources at the level of the communities that use those resources while corporations continue to push for more and more enclosures and privatization of resources previously available to all. Those who work for the commons, whether aware of being part of a global and ongoing struggle or not, engage in serious resistance to such attempts. One such arena is the internet, where many groups and activists are continually vigilant about maintaining free and open access for all. Another is water, where many communities around the world, most famously in Bolivia, risk livelihoods and sometimes even life in order to maintain local access to their water and protect it from corporate privatization.

Despite these levels of complexity that situate the work of reclaiming and sustaining the commons in all three areas of actions for the future, I chose to place this chapter in this section because it lends itself to people engaging in this work locally, on a small scale that doesn't *have* to engage in opposition to large-scale institutions.

The commons also serves as a lens through which we can examine actions and resources. Through this lens, the growth of the co-housing movement partakes of this ongoing effort. Most communities have some areas that are, de facto, managed as a commons, thus requiring facility in collaborative decision-making, one of the singular gifts of the commons to our continued existence on the planet.

Constructive Program

I already mentioned the role of the constructive program in Gandhi's work. I find it tragic that so little is commonly known about this aspect of his work despite the importance that he himself assigned to the constructive side of the work towards independence. He maintained, in fact,

> "… that Civil Disobedience is not absolutely necessary to win freedom through purely non-violent effort, if the co-operation of the whole nation is secured in the Constructive Programme. But such good luck rarely favours nations or individuals. Therefore, it is necessary to know the place of Civil Disobedience in a nation-wide non-violent effort." (Gandhi, *Constructive Programme: Its Meaning and Place*, 1941)[77]

Because I am so deeply inspired by Gandhi and his work, and want to learn how to apply it in our time and place, I am in ongoing conversations with whoever will have them with me about what could possibly be the constructive program aspect of current nonviolent movements for social change.

Creating a full constructive program would be a monumental effort. Gandhi's program, as I already mentioned, had eighteen different elements in it. Here I want to look specifically at only the centerpiece of such a program, which would be today's version of the role that spinning had in Gandhi's efforts.[78]

As far as I have learned so far, we are looking for an activity that can be done as part of everyday living and has concrete material results. It's like the difference between daily meditation and a seasonal ritual, or a grand event with a big buildup. It would be an activity that can, in principle, be undertaken by anyone and everyone. Such an activity must be proactive and responsive to a need in the community, without asking others to do anything for the community, thereby fostering self-reliance. Ideally, such an activity challenges the

---

[77] See also a fuller description in
gandhi-manibhavan.org/gandhiphilosophy/philosophy_consprogrammes_bookwritten.htm
[78] Michael Nagler and the Metta Institute have been developing one version of a full program along similar lines as Gandhi's, with spokes and a center: mettacenter.org/roadmap/what-is-roadmap/

ongoing source of the problem that the constructive program is designed to transform.

Part of the genius of Gandhi is that he found an activity that met all these criteria. He even found a way to make spinning portable, and was thus able to engage in his political activities and campaigns while spinning, thereby continuing to demonstrate his commitment to being one with the people even when working for independence.

In my conversations so far I have encountered two major candidates put forth and explored by nonviolence advocates: human relations and food. As I see it, neither of these candidates fits the criteria perfectly.

Transforming the way we relate to each other is most definitely a daily activity. Like spinning, it can be done anywhere and everywhere, and anyone can choose to participate at all times. However, I don't see that it has concrete material results, though indirectly changing human relations would change everything. I am also impressed by how deeply such a transformation can attend to the core of the problems we are facing as a species, since I see the consciousness of separation that permeates our world as being at the root of so much. Most significantly, our human relations are so frayed that putting collective and massive attention on them would clearly be a response to a deep need felt by so many.

The food revolution has a different profile. If confined only to growing food, I doubt that it would "take." While it is an activity that can, in principle, be done by anyone, the conditions for making it possible are difficult. So many people experience overwhelm in their life already, and to allocate resources to growing food would simply be beyond most people's capacity. On top of that, since so many people now live in urban centers, changes in the infrastructure would be necessary to allow for large scale urban farming. That said, in the United States more and more people are growing at least some small amounts of food, and even more are changing their purchasing habits. The organic sector is the fastest growing sector in agriculture, and farmers' markets have been exploding all over the United States as well as other countries. In that broader sense, changing our relationship to food appears more practical and would have profound consequences if adopted. Food growing, Community Supported Agriculture, and farmers markets are all challenges to the centuries-long diminishment of our capacity to shape and affect the source of our food. This would be a way to take it back from large corporations both in terms of the food growing itself as well as the channels of distribution and retail. In addition, these developments in food have the potential to lower the amount of stress we put on the biosphere. On the other hand, again, unlike the focus on human relations, this direction lacks the simplicity and ease of access in areas that are not already established, and requires larger initiative on the part of some for the benefit of many (e.g. working to establish a farmers market in a new city).

Which way to go? It's not for me to decide. Until a large scale movement emerges, each of us can choose either, both, or other activities to engage in on a daily basis as part of preparing.

Consciousness Transformation

All over the world thousands of approaches based on love, oneness, and fearlessness are being taught and practiced, and are available often at low or no cost. This is the point where the distinction between personal growth and social transformation loops back on itself. Ultimately, personal growth in the form of consciousness transformation is indeed an essential part of social change work, so long as clarity remains that social change is not *all* personal growth.

This path is the last of the three that Joanna Macy outlined as necessary for turning the tide, alongside stopping the worst of the harms and creating alternative structures, organizations, and other experiments that point the way forward.

A word of caution remains. Perhaps two.

One is that I want to keep remembering that most people who engage in personal growth do not emerge from that work with a commitment to social transformation. As painful as it is for me and others, I want to recognize that this is how it is: only a minority of us choose to engage on behalf of the whole.

The other is that the overwhelming majority of personal growth work that is offered is apolitical and partakes in the illusion of a context-less individual mastery, without inviting people to become conscious of the conditions that have created their suffering, and without regard to the immense degree of privilege that allows some people to engage in personal growth while others, billions of others, barely manage to put food on the table for their children, if they even have a table. An ahistorical "mind" is often the culprit, without any regard to what puts the ideas and thought structures in our minds in the first place. As a result, some personal growth can only be helpful as an investment in the future, hoping that people who open up to certain ways of seeing life might end up raising generations of children that are more alive and open, or engaging more collaboratively within their workplaces. I am not sure that always happens.

Freeing My Consciousness

I would like to illustrate the difficulty with an example from my own life. Since I learned of Nonviolent Communication, I have been working steadily to free up my consciousness from the traps I have inherited. I relentlessly make the effort to remove from my language words that point to certain ways of thinking such as "should," "can't," "have to," "I don't have time," and all war metaphors. I make deliberate choices that are at odds with the addiction to convenience, an addiction whose pull I recognize within myself. I consciously choose to interact with people I don't know so as to challenge the notion that anyone is a "stranger." I reveal in public and even in writing aspects of my experience that I would have felt far too vulnerable to share earlier in my life, but which I do happily now in part in order to affirm my continuity with others. I continually challenge myself to question anything that appears like accepting others' deference to me because of the position of partial power in which I find myself. I regularly make a conscious attempt to understand people whose actions are incomprehensible to me to increase my capacity for empathy and my ability to hold needs with care. I walk directly towards emotional discomfort again and again so as to create true freedom in myself to live as I want.

Is this an act of social change? Absolutely not, in and of itself. I continue to engage in these and dozens of other practices, large and small, because it's the only way I know to have some trust that another way is possible, not because it is an act of social change. Rather than waiting for some miraculous victory to begin to create some mysterious world whose contours I haven't imagined, I want to know that I have done all I can, truly all I can, to move in the direction of my dreams in each and every moment, internally, and, with others, in the world. In that sense, then, although my inner work does not amount to social change, it makes it easier for me to aim for social transformation in a way that feels aligned with my values, with the vision, and with manageability.

Because I have another book, *Spinning Threads of Radical Aliveness*, in which I talk at great length about the kind of consciousness transformation that I see as possible and want to support, in this small segment of the book I only provide some reflections about what makes change possible even though the conditions that create it are so often masked. I also offer some clues about how we can support others in waking up alongside our own path of liberation.

What Makes Change Possible

Why is it that with so much suffering we don't see massive movements for social change? What are the conditions that make change possible? This is what I want to explore, briefly, in this final segment of this section.

It is not enough for people to know and experience suffering. Several conditions must be in place before a person or a group will become more likely to overcome feelings of powerlessness and despair, imagine a different reality, and discover how such a shift can catapult them into action, sometimes even when a "rational" assessment would show them otherwise.

Understanding the Existing Conditions

Many who attempt to bring about change through education are astonished to see that students often reject what the teachers believe are facts about discrimination or systems of oppression. When it comes to the level of suffering in the world, the pervasive myth is that people bring their suffering upon themselves. The older versions focus on sin or character flaws. The more recent versions focus on negative thoughts. There is no essential difference between these different ideas. They all serve the same function: to keep the focus on individual failure.

Even when the subtle blame is removed, the focus is still on the individual. We may be told it's genetic predisposition, or a medical condition, or childhood trauma. For as long as we keep looking at individual causes to our problems, we block off a mechanism of social feedback: if more and more people are suffering, then we have created a system that doesn't work for people.

Ironically, the very institution of therapy is itself a social product. We didn't use to have therapists at all. When in trouble, people went to family members, neighbors, or spiritual leaders, all of whom were interwoven into the communal fabric of life. What changed in human social arrangements and in our thinking about ourselves that makes room for this new institution of therapy? Collectively we have shifted from community- and family-based living to being atomized individuals fending for ourselves with less and less support from family and community. In parallel, we have shifted more and more of our activities from the informal, relationship-based economy to the exchange, formal, money-based economy. Consequently, when we are in need, we find ourselves directed towards paying professionals for support rather than to our disintegrating communities. Lastly, we have created conditions of progressively more individualized living, and therefore theories that explain life that are more individually based.

If people are to mobilize to create change, they would first need to believe that the suffering they endure and witness is caused, at least in part, by social and historical forces that are beyond individual choice, be it moral or spiritual. While individual choice has some connection with individual outcome, that connection is limited. Moreover, without changing the structural conditions of zero-sum systems, not everyone can get to have well-paying jobs. If one person advances in the social ladder, others will step down. There simply aren't enough jobs, houses, or other coveted resources, to provide for all the people at the levels of consumption deemed comfortable.

Seeing an Alternative Reality

Even when people understand the forces that operate to maintain a social order that is at cost to their well-being, in order to entertain the possibility of action, it's essential to have a vision of what else is possible. This is probably why, intuitively, the World Social Forum slogan is "Another world is possible."

It is no surprise that many times in the course of history revolutions took place when conditions started to improve, and people could see that a better life was possible.

Trusting the Possibility of Change

Even when a vision of another world exists, people will not rise up unless they trust they can mobilize the resources to do so. What is it that makes people rise up in a certain moment in history? How does it happen that, seemingly overnight, millions of people shift their internal story of apathy, despair, and personal endurance and protection into one of hope, inspiration, and willingness to face consequences?

I remember when I was studying sociology a running joke was that sociology is great at predicting the past. We can always look at a particular uprising, revolution, or mass social movement and find, retroactively, the conditions that made it possible. I don't believe we can ever learn enough from the past in order to be able to predict the likely eruption of change on a large scale. Ultimately, I don't believe we can eliminate the inherent mystery of what makes change possible.

Inciting Change in Others

I still see it as a mystery that any of us recovers the ability to see what remains so carefully hidden. Once we have recovered our radical consciousness, I ultimately don't know what we can do to support others in unveiling their own eyes and ears and opening their hearts to new possibilities. I do have some sense of the obstacles and offer some small clues as to what may make transformation possible.

By now it may come as no surprise that the main obstacle to learning about the hidden costs of the system we have all inherited tends to be a failure in empathy, mostly in the form of complacency and minimizing others' pain. A particularly poignant example of this kind of obstacle is the story told by Ann Berlak, a university professor, who recounts her efforts to reach her students, many of whom are of African descent, with information about discrimination, which they reject. One of her Black students told her that "if Blacks are disproportionately poor it's because they don't work hard enough." Some other Black students rejected statistics she presented to them of discrimination against Black people, and insisted that they were untrue. This is what the legacy of separation can create.[79]

Another obstacle is an inability to see a different possible society, mixed with lack of hope or faith that anything could be done about what's going on. One of the most tragic consequences of that failure in vision is people's preference for allying themselves with the more powerful groups, just to protect themselves in what they see as a harsh, zero-sum world. It takes effort to overcome the attachment to the rewards of the system we are being asked to question. This is how the belief in scarcity, handed down for millennia, takes away our sense of power and possibility.

A major part of the difficulty in inviting others to change is the invisibility of both the oppression that creates complicity in the first place, as well as the acts of resistance against the oppression, both in our own personal history, and in the history of our various groups, especially oppressed groups. Without recovering the possibility of resistance from personal or social history, it would be difficult for

---

[79] Ann Berlak, "Teaching for Outrage and Empathy in the Liberal Arts," Educational Foundations, 3(2): 69-93, Summer 1989.

any of us to believe in our efficacy in a culture that fosters a sense of inevitability and helplessness.

Empathy for Creating Change

Aside from the obstacles that are based on inherited beliefs and attitudes, another major obstacle is that we are not habituated to bringing love to people who hold beliefs we consider dangerous or stupid. We are more used to explaining, arguing, and dismissing. We do this even though we know better. It is nearly impossible to push through another's defensive anger, no matter what strategy we use. If anything could dissolve anger and defensiveness, it is only love and empathy (and even then there is no guarantee).

I would like to illustrate this unique possibility with examples. The first is a ten-year action research project conducted in England by Patricia Dannahy, who used unorthodox methods, including the regular expression of verbal empathy of the kind I am describing in this book, while teaching math education to prospective teachers. Dannahy discovered that not only were her methods more conducive to students' ability to learn mathematics, but that her students changed in other ways as well. Her students became more willing to trust their own judgments, and to express their feelings with other tutors. Such a practice in and of itself is a form of radical consciousness, as expressions of feelings are greatly discouraged in teaching contexts, especially when teaching math. Students developed more willingness to work together and to expend time and energy in sorting out conflicts. To some extent, even their political awareness changed in the process, although that was not even directly the subject matter (as compared with Ann Berlak's students whose awareness at times didn't change even though the curriculum included items directly relevant to political questions).

The second example is the amazing story of a Jewish cantor who was able to reach and transform the consciousness of a Klansman through his and his family's offers of love. Larry Trapp, a hardened and bitter Klansman, was able to recover his full humanity through the love extended to him by Michael Weisser and his family. Trapp subsequently apologized to the victims of his actions, and has since spoken out actively against racism and bigotry.

Another example is a story told by Helen Caldicott, a physician, founder of Physicians for Social Responsibility, and a leader in the arms freeze struggle, in a radio interview in 1994. Caldicott described her willingness to really listen openly to a Los Alamos nuclear scientist, which resulted in an incredible transformation in his responses to her. The scientist started his conversation with her with a prideful boasting of the achievements of nuclear energy, and ended with revealing to her, within the same conversation, his deep anguish and anxiety, his nightmares and episodes of waking up in cold sweat at 4 a.m. wondering what he is doing. Such listening as she exhibited requires a tremendous courage in which we are rarely instructed: the courage to stay truly open to others even when our values are deeply violated by their actions.

A final example took place in San Francisco during a two-day workshop given to high school students. Here is the story as told by the trainer, Catherine Cadden:[80]

> Sixteen-year-old Zeke was an active member of the Ku Klux Klan. During a game, when it was revealed that a Jewish girl's older sister would be having a wedding ceremony the following summer to marry another woman, he did not hesitate to voice out loud what was happening in his mind, "That's just wrong!"
>
> "Are you uncomfortable because there are people in here you are not used to connecting with?" I asked.
>
> Zeke replied with reasoning to explain his beliefs about why certain people are just "born inferior." After a monologue that stimulated agitation in several people throughout the room, he added, "Well, you know I hate these people. Don't get me wrong. I'm not a violent person. I wouldn't want harm to come to them. It's just I hate certain people."
>
> "Well, now I'm confused because you're saying you hate these people yet you don't want any harm to come to them. I am guessing you might even have some confusion about your feelings towards these people because you say you don't want to be violent yet you speak of hate." Zeke continued to listen with his arms folded across his chest, his eyes fixed on mine. "I'm still confused about your choice to be a member of the KKK. From what I've known they have created an amazing amount of violence against the folks you say you hate. Can you tell me why you joined? What was your primary motivation to join?"

---

[80] See zenvc.org

Zeke looked right into me, "My dad is a member of the KKK!"

The room bristled with comments. One student, Terrance, chimed in, "Ah man, just cause your dad's a hater doesn't mean you gotta be one too!"

Nodding to that profound statement, I added, looking as intensely into Zeke's eyes as he had into mine, "I'm actually hearing how much you'd like to connect to your dad. I am also hearing that maybe you feel conflicted about being a member of an organization that tries to create connection through violence and hating others." Leaning toward Zeke, trying to tangibly soften the room with my presence, "Has this really met your need to connect with your father?"

Zeke's eyes swelled with water but he was not going to cry, not in front of this group. "Yeah," Zeke paused to take a full inhale and exhale audible to the room, maybe a bit from the gravity of the realization and a bit to stop the tears. "I guess I joined cuz I wanted to connect to my dad. I just wanna get along with him."

He walked up to me after the workshop, "You know, that was the first time I felt fear begin to leave my body. I'm actually relieved."

With his new clarity he began to assess the effectiveness of his choice and decided that hating others was not truly his path, not an expression of his authentic presence. He was able to get past the enemy images his mind had created and the fixed ideas he had about himself to see what he needed. Zeke quit the KKK, developed all sorts of friends, and continued to work on various strategies to find connection with his dad.

Section 4

The Next Generation

Transforming the Lives of Children[81]

In my earlier book, *Spinning Threads of Radical Aliveness*, I wrote extensively about how the process of socialization is a key lynchpin that maintains and perpetuates any social order and prepares the young for accepting the constraints of adult life. Unless we close the loop in terms of how we treat our children, I don't see how our efforts could be sustainable, as each generation will have to reclaim themselves from the effects of a process of socialization that takes away our authenticity, autonomy, self-trust, and power. Accordingly, even though relating to the young is not traditionally seen as part of social transformation, I am including it in this book as an insurance policy. It is also a frontier in terms of radical consciousness, as the overwhelming majority of people have not considered the possibility of sharing power, fully, with children of all ages.

While we are painfully far from having full equality and respect along many other dimensions of social life, such as gender, race, or sexual preference, the established norm is one of equal rights under the law.[82] When it comes to children, however, there isn't even a lip service commitment to equality. Children are still fully "owned" by their parents, and it's acceptable and customary to restrict their movement, punish them at will, including physically, and make decisions that affect them dramatically without consulting with them first.

Not only that, the reasoning and justification of such treatment uses the same kind of arguments that in the past were used to justify the mistreatment of women and people of color: they can't think for themselves, they are too close to nature, they cannot be counted on to be responsible, they have evil tendencies that must be controlled, and similar such ideas.

I simply don't buy this.

For one thing, I have been blessed (or cursed?) by vivid memory of what life was like as a child. I cannot believe for a moment that by evolutionary design we must suffer for years before we are allowed to live as we want. Even more tragically, the way we are brought up, by the time we have the official freedom, we mostly have lost our direct

---

[81] The title of this segment is taken from an organization by that name: the Association for Transforming the Lives of Children.
[82] Not so fully for sexual preference in all places.

knowledge of what we want and how to go about fulfilling our needs. I often ask people in workshops if they were ever asked what their needs were. With extremely rare exceptions, the answer is always no. We end up needing years of therapy to recover what was ours to begin with when we were born.

When everything is structured around the needs and convenience of the adults, we learn that we don't matter. When we are told what we should do to be helpful, for example, we learn not to trust own impulses and lose contact with our genuine generosity. When we are directed about how to behave, we learn that our authenticity is dangerous.

Children, who are seen as closer to their bodies and to the "state of nature," represent the aspects of being human that have been ignored, downplayed, or banished. Their spontaneity, intense and unrestrained feelings, honesty, and imagination, are incompatible with the Western ideals of what it means to be human, especially with the modern ideal of rationality. Within this widespread view, children must be tamed, even punished, to ensure that they grow up to become the right kind of people. This ideology makes the mistreatment of children both endemic and invisible.

Another way is possible.

It is based on offering children the same fundamental understanding we offer each other at our best: an empathic attempt to understand, a genuine effort to attend to the child's needs, and authentic expression of the parents' needs. Like language, empathy is an innate human capacity that needs modeling to be acquired and integrated. I am confident that children who are raised with empathy will more likely develop their own empathic capabilities. Similarly, when respected and trusted, they will more likely trust themselves and others. Without cruelty and shaming, the chances of violence diminish drastically.

In fact, empathy is such a powerful tool that, even when absent at home, its presence elsewhere in a child's life can have a profound impact on the outcome of the child's experiences. Even seriously abused children can grow up to have meaningful and satisfying lives if they have an adult outside their family who provides understanding, support, and recognition to the growing child.

The Challenges of Parenting

Because images of mainstream child-rearing practices are projected everywhere, it is a tall order for any family to embark on raising a child differently. The media and most advice books will offer conventional "wisdom," and well-meaning family members and friends, and sometimes even strangers, may often be critical of our efforts. In addition, raising a child, with or without empathy, is an enormously taxing experience, especially under the conditions of intense isolation that are prevalent in contemporary US life.

Children's actions and wishes are very often in conflict with their parents' immediate wishes or goals: the parent wants to go off to work, and the child responds with cries of anguish; the child wants to keep playing, and the parent wants the child to go to sleep; the child does not want to eat what's presented on the table; the child wants to make noise that's intolerable to the adult at a given moment. The examples are endless, and become progressively more complex as the child grows. Without a deep commitment to placing needs, emotions, and empathy at the center, parents are not likely to respond to their children with empathy in such times, not even when the child is exhibiting what would look like obvious distress to a bystander.

Instead, one common response is to register their child's actions as manipulative, willful, out of control, testing, or even to imagine that the child is "asking for punishment," and that punishment will provide relief for the child. Many see controlling the child as a major part of their task of parenting. Another common response is to minimize the significance of the child's suffering, an act which enables many parents to let their children cry alone for extended periods of time, or to send them, later on in life, to their rooms to be by themselves. Even parents who are otherwise absolutely committed to caring responsiveness to their children often support such practices. Yet another response is to react to crying by immediately acquiescing to what the child wants. This kind of reaction is not motivated by empathy. Instead, the parent appears to want to stop the child's distress as an attempt to stop the parents' own pain.

Empathic Parenting

Empathy, and the dialogue attendant upon it, require a simple quality of presence with the child, an attentiveness to the child's emotions and needs, including an active attempt to understand what they might be even when not described or articulated directly, and an abiding faith both that the child's needs are benign, and that dialogue focused on creating connection will likely shift either the child's or the parents' attachment to their conflicting strategies for meeting needs.

Based on the experience of my sister Inbal, her partner Kathy, and their son Yannai, who is sixteen as this book is moving to production, many of my intuitive ideas about relating to children have been reinforced and deepened.

Yannai has been able to actively and consciously reflect on and respond to others' needs since before he was three, since before he was three. I tell a story in my previous book (*Spinning*, page 349) about a time when Inbal asked three-year-old Yannai if he would be willing to stop banging on the floor, which she worried would disturb their houseguests. He said "I don't want to, but I'm willing." When asked why, he explained it wasn't waking *him* up, and that he was willing because he did "want to consider you." The incident ended without anger, resentment, or power struggle. This and other, earlier incidents illustrate how well a small child can respond to others' needs when asked without compulsion.

Inbal and Kathy never questioned Yannai's intentions and were always able to reflect to him, implicitly or explicitly, an understanding of his being, which assumes the benign nature of his wishes and actions. They never tried to control or suppress his spontaneity and being.[83]

While empathy is more and more recognized as important in child-rearing, the unique feature of Kathy and Inbal's approach is that the empathic stance towards Yannai was their guiding philosophy for all their interactions, for the very way they conceived of him, even if on any given occasion they were unable to act on it. No other principle overruled this commitment, only fatigue or stress on occasion might have. As a result, they enjoyed a level of trust in their family that I have never seen anywhere else. Moreover, even in his teen years, their interactions have been free of power struggles. On a core and fundamental level, they always made decisions together. Even at a young age, Yannai sometimes came up with

---

[83] Since Inbal died in September, 2014, Kathy and Yannai's relationship continues to operate on the same principles.

creative solutions that neither Inbal nor Kathy had thought about before being in dialogue.

While being with Yannai in his early life, Inbal developed an approach to parenting based on Nonviolent Communication (NVC) principles.[84] As part of this approach, she rethought the notion of limits which is so intrinsic to current parenting practices. Instead of external limits, which are arbitrary and outside the relationship, she conceived of natural limits, which are organically emerging through the parents honoring their own needs in relation to the child. By making limits relational rather than arbitrary and external, the child learns core lessons about dialogue and about holding everyone's needs with care. In a very real sense the child gets feedback *from life* that her needs are not all there is in life, instead of being told.

When everyone's needs in the family are part of the equation, the child grows up in a different world from ours already. In choosing how we relate to children we can take real steps to transform the legacy of separation, scarcity, and powerlessness. We can show children that even in times of opposing wishes we can remain connected. We can show them that with enough care and dialogue we can find solutions that work for everyone; that there is no scarcity of workable solutions. Lastly, we can show children that they have power as participants in decision-making and that they can share their power and still have their needs matter. Exactly the world I want them to co-create with us.

---

[84] Inbal Kashtan's CD and booklet are available at baynvc.org/connected_parenting_cd.php.

Parenting for Peace
by Inbal Kashtan[85]

As the United States stands again on the brink of war, I seek ways to contribute to our collective ability to resolve conflicts nonviolently. What resources and skills do we need, as a society, to sustain peace? How can parents contribute to society's transition to nonviolence? What can we teach our children that will really make the world different for their generation?

Some time ago my son, nearly four years old at the time, asked me to read a book about castles that he had picked up at the library. He picked the book because he loved the Eyewitness series and was methodically going through as many of those books as we could find, irrespective of their subject matter. I didn't like this one. It depicted not only castles but also knights, armor and weapons of all kinds used in battles in centuries past.

I am not ready for weapons. One of the things I enjoy about my son not going to preschool and not watching TV is that his exposure to violence has been extremely limited. He has never said the word "gun" or played pretend violent games – yet. He doesn't know about war and people purposely hurting one another – yet. But here was the castle book, and he wanted to read it.

I am not trying to shield my son from the reality of violence and suffering in the world – but I am in a (privileged) position to choose, often, how and when these realities enter our lives. I read him some of the book, with numerous editorials. But when he asked to read the book again a few days later, I found myself saying that I'd rather not. When he asked why, I told him that I feel a lot of sadness about people being violent with one another because I believe human beings can find peaceful ways to solve their conflicts.

Questions, of course, ensued. In response to one of his questions, I shared with him that my sadness was related not only to the past, when there were knights and castles, but to the present as well; that people in the area where I grew up, Israelis and Palestinians, are also fighting. "Why are they fighting?" he asked. "Because they both want the same piece of land and they haven't

---

[85] This article was written by Inbal Kashtan in 2002, and is reprinted with permission.

figured out how to talk about it," I replied. "I'll teach them!" he volunteered. "What will you teach them?" I asked. "I'll teach them that they can each have some of the land, they can share," he replied easily. "The only problem," he continued, "is that I don't know how to find them."

I felt a mixture of joy and grief at his words. How wondrous to hear from my son — and from so many children — a desire to contribute to the world and a trust in the possibility of solving conflicts peacefully. Yet how apt his words were — "I don't know where to find them." How *do* we find the hearts of "enemies" so we can reach them with a message of peace? How do we find our *own* hearts and open them to those whose actions we object to profoundly?

This search for our own and others' hearts is at the core of my hope for peace and has been the greatest influence on my parenting. It has also led me to teach a process called Nonviolent Communication (developed by Dr. Marshall Rosenberg and taught around the world). I lead workshops for parents, couples, teachers, social change activists, and others who want to connect more deeply with themselves and with others and who want to contribute more effectively to mutual understanding, safety, and peace in families, schools, organizations, and in the wider world.

My experience convinces me that what happens in our families both mirrors and contributes to what happens in our societies. Just as "enemies" fail to see each other's humanity, so we, too, at times fail to relate with others, even loved ones, with compassion. Probably the primary challenge most parents tell me about is that though they yearn for peace and harmony at home, they find themselves getting angry with their children more often and more quickly than they would like. Because the problem-solving model we follow so often relies on threat of consequences or promise of reward, it's almost guaranteed that anger will crop up regularly. What children learn from this model is not cooperation, harmony, and mutual respect; it's more often the hard lesson of domination: that whoever has more power gets to have his or her way, and that those who have less power can only submit or rebel. And so we continue the cycle of domination that is leading human beings close to self-destruction.

What alternative do we have? As parents, we have a remarkable opportunity to empower our children with life skills for connecting with others, resolving conflicts, and contributing to peace. Our conception of what human beings are like is key to learning these skills. Nonviolent Communication teaches that all human beings have the same deep needs, and that people can connect with one another when they understand and empathize with each other's needs. Our conflicts arise not because we have different needs but because we have different strategies for how to meet them. It is on the strategy level that we argue, fight, or go to war, especially when we deem someone else's strategy a block to our own ability to meet our needs. Yet Nonviolent Communication suggests that behind *every* strategy, however ineffective, tragic, violent or abhorrent to us, is an attempt to meet a need. This notion turns on its head the dichotomy of "good guys" and "bad guys" and focuses our attention on the human being behind every action. When we understand the needs that motivate our own and others' behavior, we have no enemies. With our tremendous resources and creativity, we can and – I hope – we *will* find new strategies for meeting all our needs.

We can teach our children about making peace by understanding, reflecting, and nurturing their ability to meet their needs while we also understand, express, and attend to our own. One of the needs human beings have is for autonomy, for the ability to make decisions about things that affect us. This leads us on a path of self-interest and a search for confidence and power. Yet if we nurture this need in our children to the exclusion of others, it can be difficult for us to get our own needs met. Thankfully, our need for autonomy is balanced by another shared human need, for contribution to others. This need leads us on a path of consideration, care and generosity to others. Nonviolent Communication enables us to look at both needs (and many others) and find a way to balance them so that we recognize our need to give, to consider others and contribute to them, *as an autonomous choice*. When we give freely, out of mutual care and respect, it does not conflict with autonomy and choice but rather complements them.

From this perspective, parents may find that we don't need punishments or rewards in parenting our children – we can instead invite our children to contribute to meeting our needs just as we invite ourselves to contribute to meeting theirs, with joy and willingness instead of guilt, shame, obligation, fear of punishment or desire for reward. This is not permissive parenting – it is parenting deeply committed to meeting the needs of parents and children through focusing on connection and mutual respect.

Transforming parenting is hugely challenging in the context of the daily, overwhelming reality of parenting. Yet this transformation enables a profound depth of connection and trust among family members. Perhaps more poignantly for me, choosing to parent this way gives me hope for peace for our world – perhaps for our children's generation, perhaps for future generations, when human beings have learned to speak the language of compassion.

As the world enters our home and my son's exposure to life's realities grows, I hope he will sustain these lessons and carry them into his own life. I hope he will know that the path to peace is most effectively followed not by rewarding the "good" guys and punishing the "bad" ones, but by striving to find strategies that will meet people's needs – not just our own, but everyone's. I hope he will have the confidence and trust in his own peaceful resources and in human beings' capacity for peace. I hope he remembers that we can find other people's hearts by seeing their humanity.

Section 5

Case Studies

Why Case Studies

I am including case studies in this book for two reasons. One is simply because of the power of real examples to bring to life principles I have previously discussed. Exploring the selected few specific campaigns and programs below provides an opportunity to see at least some of the ideas in operation, to get more understanding of what some concepts mean, and to fertilize our imagination about what's possible.

The other reason for including case studies is because I want to learn about effectiveness. I chose the specific examples I did because I believe there is a lot we can learn from them about what works and what doesn't. I aimed for diversity of location and context, choosing one example from the US and two examples from India. I chose them, also, because they illustrate different aspects of the lessons of working for a new future, especially in terms of the role of nonviolence in effectiveness. Also, I picked the examples in India because they clearly are successful, and the Occupy Movement because of its ambiguity with regards to success.

It is my great hope that the pages that follow indeed provide an opportunity for deepening understanding, and for the depth of inspiration I have felt regarding these movements to come across and perhaps kindle a fire somewhere.

Taking on Wall Street: Reflections on the Occupy Movement

Did the Occupy Movement succeed, fail, neither, or both? It's the biggest experiment that has taken place in the US in many years, and I see immense potential to learn from what has happened as we continue to discover and explore the possibilities of nonviolent social transformation.

I want to start this exploration with what attracted me to this movement, what I saw as the potential to create significant change. Especially early on, as the encampments began, and even despite the demolition and the significant issues I have with what unfolded, this movement did something. For some people, something different happened that was changing their lives. They saw themselves and others create something that was thought impossible only weeks before. At least for a while there was no going back. There was some magic happening, something I don't understand, something I wanted to support.

This movement showed more and more people that "we cannot fix our crises isolated from one another." Separation, the very foundation of what makes our current system possible, was being challenged, and the future, for that window of time, felt open again in the midst of the difficulty. Although it didn't last, the words of an anonymous writer persist in my memory: "you can't evict an idea whose time has come."

Creating a Parallel Existence

As critical as I was and continue to be about many aspects of Occupy that I articulate below, I am overall impressed and humbled by what happened, regardless of how short-lived the experiment was. The movement was ingenious in its capacity to act without visible and destroyable leadership, which made the repression significantly more challenging to accomplish.

As difficult as the decision-making processes were, this was a large-scale experiment in participatory democracy that was at least partially successful. It was a time of solidarity across the globe in a variety of ways. And the occupiers exhibited, to my mind, a lot of creativity and sophistication in the form of organization, a willingness to keep learning and adapting, including in response to critiques from people of color, and quite a bit of tenacity and resilience. I can't imagine a movement succeeding without these qualities.

More than anything, however, my main admiration for the movement stems from the experience of being in one of the encampments and seeing how it operated, knowing that this was duplicated across the country in similar ways. Simply put, the group of people that took possession of the Frank Ogawa Plaza in Oakland created a small-scale experiment in living without relying on large institutions. Anyone could join, anyone could contribute, anyone could challenge, and anyone could talk.

In their own small way, and however imperfectly, they were creating the world in which they want to live. There was free food being served 24/7, there were supplies of all kinds, energy created by people pedaling a bike, and everyone appeared to be part of an incessant conversation.

Barring the repression, this was a form of action and a movement without a clear end point. There was nothing someone else could have done in any immediate way that would have given the people gathered at the park in Oakland what they were already creating for themselves. I don't believe that anything could have happened, nor can I imagine a set of actions on the part of anyone, that would have led people to say "Now we are done and we can go home to our daily living." They didn't seem particularly interested in the form of daily living that has become the norm in this country. It is, in fact, that very form of daily living that this movement was challenging.

The vision that wasn't being articulated was fully lived, as best the occupiers knew how. For me, what they created served as a small example and precursor to the vision of a world based on caring for human needs. It was a magical snapshot of possibility. For a while, Occupy captured the imagination of most people,[86] because it tapped into the depth of longing that so many people had.

Still, over time, support kept decreasing, despite the astonishing beginning. What contributed to this decline?

---

[86] At the height of support, more than 80% of the population expressed support for the goals of Occupy.

In *Why Civil Resistance Works: The Strategic Logic of Nonviolent Conflict*, which draws on research covering over 300 violent and nonviolent campaigns, scholars Erica Chenoweth and Maria J. Stephan write that the key to a successful campaign is the ability "to recruit a robust, diverse, and broad-based membership that can erode the power base of the adversary and maintain resilience in the face of opposition." This is the key reason they see for why nonviolent movements succeed more than violent ones: they have more capacity to mobilize and retain people. This is the exact piece that didn't happen for Occupy.

Was it simply that Occupy didn't have a clear commitment to nonviolence? Was it the relentless repression? The internal dynamics of a movement without clear leadership and vision?

I am sure many will continue to examine and study the movement, and perhaps it's too soon and I know too little to be able to answer these questions with any authority. What I offer below is simply what I myself have learned in reflecting on this movement, as an individual deeply committed to a nonviolent path and future. From that perspective, what I see is that in many ways Occupy failed to create the conditions that would sustain mass popular support.

Us/Them

Right from the start, Occupy was based on galvanizing masses of people through creating a divide. The famous slogan that catapulted so many people into action is based on separation: "We are the 99%" implies the existence of a 1% that is the source of the problem. While I was impressed with the ingenuity of a simple line that captures so deeply the reality of power differentials, it gradually became about the people rather than about the system. When the specific people become the issue, then the struggle becomes about ousting those people, which makes it exceedingly difficult to maintain a loving stance. The desire for wealth is widespread even if wealth itself is concentrated. I would so much rather that the slogan and the actions focused, instead, on how to transform the system that created the conditions that made it possible for some individuals to amass such enormous wealth.

Nonviolence is based on love, not on separation, even in moments of intense struggle. This is not a sentimental love. This is love in action, designed to bring about concrete and material results.

The point of this love is to ensure that our actions are free of violence, hatred, and separation, so that we don't end up where so many revolutions have in the past: recreating the very conditions that the revolution was seeking to change.

When I imagine that the Occupy movement, or some other movement like it, were to succeed in replacing existing governments with some other form of governance, I am not so confident that the outcome will be what I most long for: a world that truly works for everyone.

I am fearful that the people who are now the 1% would be mistreated, shamed, incarcerated, or even executed. I am fearful that women would still have an equally challenging time having physical safety, full inclusion in decision-making, and the possibility of affecting the ways that decisions are made. I am fearful that racial and ethnic divides would continue to plague us, and that some people would continue to suffer poverty and human indignities. I am fearful that consumption would continue rampant and the march towards depletion of the earth's resources would go on. I am even fearful that a new 1% will emerge, sooner or later, and what might be gained would be lost.

I know and understand that it's not easy to extend love to everyone. I have been engaging with this effort for years, and it's still sometimes challenging. It means loving the ones who are nonviolent, the ones who aren't, and the ones calling themselves nonviolent and maligning the ones who aren't. It means finding love for the mayor of Oakland and the police officers who destroyed the encampments all over the country. And it means, ultimately, finding love for the 1% or the 0.001% who are truly in power. Everyone. No exceptions. That's no small task. And it's the only way I know, ultimately, to end the millennia-old cycle of violence, hatred, suffering, and separation in which we live.

One of the ways that nonviolent movements have traditionally worked is by undermining the sources of support of existing regimes, including by encouraging and nurturing defections. When the police or army can no longer be counted on by a regime, its final legitimacy is finished. This is the kind of situation that leads dictators to abdicate their power. This is an avenue that was forestalled in the way that Occupy functioned at its peak. With the police being demonized and, in some locales, physically challenged, only a handful of police officers could find the courage to create alternatives to the grueling and difficult situation in which they found themselves. None were offered them by the movement.

The biggest transformation I aim for is to transcend either/or categories of any kind, any shred of any idea that some of us have to lose in order for things to work for some others, whether it's 1%, 99%, or even 0.01% who lose.[87] It's entirely possible for 100% of us to work together for the benefit of 100% of us. It is only together that we can partake of and steward the bounty of life and our precious planet.

The Irreducible Significance of Vision

Throughout its large-scale existence, I knew much more about what organizers and participants in Occupy didn't want than about what they did want. Where was the loving vision that would win people over? Where were the clear goals that could galvanize mass popular support for the movement?

One area where Occupy exhibited immense creativity and courage was the encampments themselves, which makes it so clear to me why they became the target of such systematic repression. The encampments were a microcosm of a different possible reality, one in which human needs, everyone's needs who came through, were front and center. Still, the vision remained implicit. Once the encampments were destroyed, it was difficult to keep the momentum going. A movement cannot continue indefinitely when all that unites people is what they are against.

Lack of Avenues for Participation

Because so much of Occupy centered on the encampments, many people who supported the implicit vision of Occupy, including people who identified with the deep protest and challenge to the rule of corporations, could not find a way to participate, ultimately losing their interest in the movement.

---

[87] As is always true in nonviolent movements, the point is to hold the intention for everyone to benefit in the end, though, as was the case with Gandhi, the British clearly didn't have a sense that they were benefitting, nor would many of the holders of extreme wealth experience a sense of benefit if and when we transition into a system that makes such accumulation impossible. It still is the case that the rest of us can hold that intention and faith that it can work for the 0.01% even if it's not their experience; that there isn't a *desire* for them to lose.

Visionary nonviolence goes way beyond acts of protest and paves the road to the future by utilizing creative actions that are, in Shariff Abdullah's words, highly illegal and highly moral. When the level of support was high, breaking the law peacefully could be capitalized on. What was needed, beyond the encampments, were actions that people could take outside the encampments, acts that would take the vision into the wider population and could increase support for the movement at the same time. Such options didn't emerge from the movement until much after the encampments were destroyed.

Decision-Making Challenges

Despite the extraordinary patience of hundreds of people in the many sites of Occupy at its peak, the movement never developed a successful decision-making process to handle disagreements. Most especially, I didn't see any mechanism in place for anything I would call dialogue or collaborative decision-making. People had the space to speak, and yet there was nothing set up for them to be heard. How would anything emerge in such a context that would allow creative solutions to take place? How could people ever come together on a divided issue?

Despite its appeal, the consensus process that Occupy had adopted encountered serious obstacles because of the issues that arise around blocking[88], because it can take such a long time, and because random people that show up can interfere with reaching decisions. Over time, consensus was modified in many places to a super-majority, and still people gradually gave up, because the fundamental challenges didn't get addressed.

I am longing, instead, for what I described in an earlier section (pages 116-22) – a process of decision-making in which what's important to everyone can be heard and they can truly affect the outcome. I want those working to create change to have access to the plethora of ingenious methods that exist to support groups in converging, learning together, and integrating divergent opinions. I want movements for change, especially large-scale movements like

---

[88] In a pure consensus form, one person can block an entire group from agreeing to something. This is so by design, and in groups that are intact and consistent over time, often works well to invite deep reflection before any decision is made. In this context of a continually changing group, including people who are only there randomly, the commitment to shared purpose, values, and relationship that consensus processes often rely on was not there, and many more issues arose. Longer discussions of these issues can be found on the internet and are beyond the scope of this section.

Occupy was, to have this as part of what gets modeled: the possibility of transforming conflict and disagreement into a solution that works for everyone.

From the vantage point of the process I have created, and especially with the transformative power of dialogue that aims to bring people together, expressing a dissenting view gets depolarized through the finding of shared human needs that everyone subsequently owns. I have found people willing to express their concerns, and others willing to hear them, when a facilitator can maintain a relaxed attitude of trust in the process. In fact, the process of surfacing the concerns, issues, and underlying needs is one of the key building blocks towards a decision that is attentive to more and more needs and is therefore more likely to lead to robust agreements that are kept by everyone, because they know they matter and are part of the whole.

Is Leadership Necessary?

Rebellion against power sometimes takes the form of rejecting the whole idea of leadership and power. This was the context in which I had a conversation, in the first weeks of Occupy, with one of the core organizers in NYC, a young man who had applied himself seriously to the study of Nonviolent Communication. I was struck by the astonishing challenge of continuing to make decisions on the basis of full consensus with everyone present as the number of people participating kept increasing, while more and more of the participants were transient members. As I offered him some tips about facilitation and decision-making to address some of these issues, he told me that even though he loved the ideas, he didn't see a way to implement them. He was deeply concerned that anything that looked like active facilitation would be viewed as taking power and leadership, and would be challenged because of the intense ethos of operating in full shared power and in a leaderless manner.

Once again, this was either/or thinking: the only alternative to dictatorial power-over was seen as operating in a permanent state of full, inclusive participation. This anti-authoritarian ethos was one of the reasons why the Occupy movement ultimately didn't manage to catapult larger segments of the population into significant nonviolent resistance, even though at one point the positions of the movement reached an unprecedented degree of support within the entire population of the US.

Absence of Commitment to Nonviolence

The more I learn about nonviolence, the more I discover that movements tend to choose nonviolence because of their belief in its strategic value, not necessarily because of a principled disavowal of the use of violence in certain circumstances. It's a pragmatic choice, not a values-based choice.

Full commitment to nonviolence on the basis of values, whether spiritual or secular, means maintaining a nonviolent stance even if it doesn't seem to work, even if the goals never materialize, even if the movement is crushed by force. This is an extremely challenging position to take. I cannot imagine asking this of anyone whose life has been affected by trauma, severe deprivation, pervasive discrimination, police brutality, poverty, or any other kind of structural ongoing violence. Those are the classic conditions that breed violent uprisings, terrorist activity, or, in less extreme situations, anger or even hatred. The level of internal resources necessary for a full commitment to nonviolence, especially in the face of potential or actual repression, cannot easily be available under such conditions, because those conditions erode the human spirit.

The primary reasons for the success of any movement, whether violent or nonviolent, is popular support and the ability to undermine the sources of support of the existing regime. No matter how repressive any regime is, coercion alone is never enough to maintain the status quo unless the armed forces remain supportive and the population remains fragmented and disengaged. As the case of Egypt in 2011 demonstrates, when the population rescinds its implicit willingness to go along with the regime, and when the armed forces shift loyalty, even a very established repressive regime crumbles.

If sympathy for the movement and delegitimation of the regime are essential conditions for success, that provides clear understanding of why nonviolent movements fare better, and especially why their response to repression adds to their relative success. A movement that manages to maintain a nonviolent stance in response to repression is much more likely to achieve both of these conditions. It's harder for most people to support a regime that cracks down on nonviolent resistors than a regime that appears to be responding to violence initiated by a movement.

I find it sad and tragic that in the vehement discussions that took place in Occupy between those committed to nonviolence and those who advocated for "diversity of tactics" (which typically meant including the option of violence), so little information was shared about the actual and known effectiveness of nonviolent movements. As Erica Chenoweth and Maria Stephan showed through their study, of 323 violent and nonviolent movements that they analyzed between 1900 and 2006, 53% of the nonviolent ones succeeded as compared to only 26% of the violent ones. What's even more telling is that when the movements were repressed, the nonviolent movements were six times more likely to succeed. Especially because there was so much repression against the Occupy movement, I keep wondering what would have happened had the commitment to nonviolence taken hold of the movement as a whole.

The Lost Art of Interdependence

When we rebel, we still operate under the terms of those in power. True autonomy, real freedom, involves making choices from within rather than in reaction to what happens outside of us. Just being on a spree of doing what we want because no one can tell us what to do is not the same as knowing what we really want and finding ways of going for it that are proactive and interdependent. Without deep engagement with self, without knowing what they wanted, without having sufficient calm to interact with others even in the face of differences and challenges, it was more and more difficult to maintain the delicate balance of peace within the encampments. When exhausted people who've been at it for weeks at a time need to make decisions that are attentive to everyone and to interact with and even collaborate with people who are on drugs, or have sexually assaulted others or are displaying extreme levels of rage, their capacity to choose from within and in line with their values is a vital asset.

When we wake up to our human needs and to our power to take actions to meet them without an awareness of and practice in engaging with our interdependence, we are then most likely to advocate for our needs rather than take on the complex art of balancing our needs with those of others. Simply put, our collaboration skills have been stunted by centuries of focusing on competition and individualism. As a result, for many of us waking up to our needs means increased conflict in our lives. In the context of a group, this means more challenge in navigating group decision-making and flow. This is precisely what happened in Occupy. More and more energy on the part of some people was consumed with managing the stream of challenges within the encampments while still trying to maintain some forward movement. It wasn't sustainable.

The Means and the Ends

In all the ways I have described, I see Occupy as having fallen into the trap of separating means and ends, a logic I have never under-stood. Most significantly, I am challenged to understand the people who kept advocating for diversity of tactics, which leaves room for the possibility of using violent means in certain instances. If people are willing to use violence in order to bring about peace, how would they suddenly, after victory is achieved, know to shift into peaceful modes of operating? If women were still sexually assaulted in the encampments, how would victory create a situation in which all would be safe? If decision-making is fraught with challenges and highly inefficient, what would happen if, suddenly, the movement succeeded and large-scale problems had to be addressed? What kind of collaborative decision-making would they have to offer that would prevent either chaos or the re-establishment of authoritarian leadership styles? As women know all too well, they have often been asked by men in national liberation movements to set their needs aside until victory is achieved, only to see them never come to the foreground then, either. Although I don't pretend to know everything that's ever happened on this planet, I don't know of any examples of a victory magically creating such changes.

I have much more trust in aligning the means and the ends. If we begin to live now the values we seek to bring about, and if we create, now, the relationships that we want to see everywhere, I have more trust that there will be a natural continuity into the world of our dreams, where everyone's dignity and needs are valued, including those who have done harm. I like this image much more than the prospect of a victory over some enemy or another.

In the Face of Repression

Is it possible that, despite all of the challenges that Occupy faced, it might have managed to mature, learn from its experiments, and come to a new phase? Might the movement have developed emergent leadership and structures of coordination and decision-making able to withstand the pressures of transience and the many other complexities? Could clearer visions and goals have been articulated over time if the encampments continued and settled?

Ultimately, no one can answer these questions. What we know, which when I learned it was shocking though not surprising, is that the efforts to repress the movement began even before the movement started. Documents that were released to The Partnership for Civil Justice Fund[89] show clearly that the repression of the movement was a concerted effort on the part of the FBI in tandem with the major banks. Indeed, the crackdowns happened in waves, across the nation.

Just as much as we can ask what might have happened if the movement had not been repressed, we can also wonder what would have happened if the response to the repression was 100% nonviolent. According to the study of nonviolent movements I have been citing, it is quite possible, even likely, that under such conditions the repression would have escalated rather than destroyed the movement, since in the face of repression nonviolent movements are six times as likely to succeed as those that aren't.

This is why any bit of violence, even minimal property destruction, is capitalized on by the mainstream media, and makes it so much easier to justify the repression. Towards the end of the encampment in Oakland, after a minority from Occupy had smashed store windows and thrown rocks at police during difficult clashes, more and more people directed increasing amounts of anger at the occupation, claiming it was destroying the fledgling efforts to revive Oakland's downtown and maintain local businesses, arguing that Oakland is a city of the 99%, that even the local business owners are part of the 99%.

At the same time, I want to acknowledge the serious and caring thinkers who maintain that it simply isn't possible to be nonviolent in

---

[89] See "FBI Documents Reveal Secret Nationwide Occupy Monitoring," December 22, 2012, at: justiceonline.org/commentary/fbi-files-ows.html.

our culture, where so much ongoing violence is done in our name all the time, whether we know it or not, choose it or not.

Is there still room in this culture, with its intense structural violence that disproportionately affects certain groups of people, to make the choice not to add more violence by inflicting it personally?

The repression of the movement managed to destroy the encampments. It removed the issues from public awareness, without solving them. Soon it seemed to be business as usual again, the same business as usual that allows massive and growing numbers of people to suffer daily indignities, poverty, lack of access to resources, and marginalization. In the absence of making it impossible for business as usual to continue, what would otherwise provide the energy for making change?

Too Creative to Fail

For a while after the final dismantling of the encampments around the country, I believed, along with many others, that the whole Occupy movement died with the encampments. Then I learned of two offshoots in New York City that continued to demonstrate the spirit of the movement, the creative act of taking charge of core needs without waiting for large institutions to care for people.

Occupy Sandy

After hurricane Sandy, a group of former occupiers capitalized on what they learned during the encampments about providing services to large numbers of people, and set up Occupy Sandy, designed to support those affected by the hurricane. Occupy Sandy proved beyond a shred of doubt that citizen-led efforts, without government or corporate intervention or coordination, are more than adequate to address conditions of extreme need, given the right conditions.

Indeed, Occupy Sandy's efforts were so much more successful than the Red Cross', that there was a de-facto collaboration between Occupy and the local government. My heart delights at this possibility of setting aside former or even possibly current enmity and working together on a task of alleviating suffering. This is precisely the kind of collaboration I hope will become, one day, the new normal.

Debt Forgiveness with a Twist

Some statements, even those I consider to be an expression of wisdom, are so often heard, that it's hard to even think what they mean in practical terms. One such statement is the idea that "problems cannot be solved by the same level of thinking that created them" (which is attributed to Einstein, apparently incorrectly). After being apparently dead, another offshoot of Occupy has offered a clear example of how this operates.

The problem: runaway debt.

The direction for solution: mobilizing masses to buy and forgive debt.

The idea is dramatically simple, and it's called Rolling Jubilee. This group solicits donations, large and small, and then uses the funds to buy debts from those who "own" them – a practice favored by many corporate entities, with the going rate being as low as 5 cents on the dollar. So far, this may sound like nothing unusual, until you learn what the group does after buying debts. Simply put, any debt purchased is then forgiven instead of collected. As of January, 2013, the group had bought and forgiven more than $1.2 million of medical debts and forgiven 1,100 people. It has enough resources, currently, to abolish about another $10 million.

As far as anyone knows, this is 100% legal, and, if I may add, 100% subversive. In their own words: "Think of it as a bailout of the 99% by the 99%."

I love human ingenuity. I am inspired by people coming together to alter the course of events beyond the power of any one of them to change. And I appreciate the willingness of so many of us to support these efforts on behalf of people we will never know. Because debts are bought and sold in blocks, it is anonymous people who benefit from this new practice. It will continue to be anonymous people until and unless this initiative catches enough fire that millions of US citizens or others all contribute and all debts are forgiven. Rolling Jubilee is, still, a drop in a bucket in terms of altering the power games. I am so enamored by it because of the potential.

In addition to being so successful, this activity "qualifies" as constructive in the strict Gandhian sense, in the way I discussed earlier in this book (page 220), because of the following factors.

- It produces concrete material results.
- In principle, *anyone* can undertake it.
- It can be done alongside daily living (rather than a campaign or a one-time event).
- It is responsive to a need in the community.
- It fosters self-reliance instead of implicitly or explicitly asking larger entities for support.
- It challenges the ongoing source of the problem that it is designed to transform and thereby creates a more desirable future.

I know I want to live in a world where debt has been eliminated. My ancestors, the ancient Hebrews, saw the disastrous consequences of debts, which is why they instituted the laws of debt relief and jubilee. Seeing the creative genius of this group of people, another indirect offshoot of Occupy, I have ever so slightly more hope that we can find ways into a more collaborative and responsive future.

Walking in Gandhi's Footsteps: Reflections on Visionary Programs in India

One of the hallmarks of nonviolent campaigns is how those in power are engaged with it. Most essentially, seeing and appealing to the humanity of those whose actions we oppose, and maintaining the willingness to engage in dialogue even through intense struggles, are core and central to the philosophy and practice of nonviolence.

While I have known this for years, it wasn't until a visit to India in 2012 that I learned in full just how far this principle goes. I visited two programs that consider themselves Gandhian. They gave me much reason to reflect about what could be done in North America, where I live, that would even begin to approximate the work they do. One is an unusual school created for the poor called Barefoot College, and the other is Navdanya, an organization that has seed sovereignty as its core mission.

Pushing the powerful into a moral corner

Based in the rural desert area of Rajasthan, one of the poorest parts of India, Barefoot College aims "to work with marginalized, exploited and impoverished rural poor, living on less than $1 a day, and lift them over the poverty line with dignity and self respect." The bulk of what the Barefoot College does is direct empowerment of communities through training poor, rural people in critical skills that contribute immeasurably to their lives and counteract the massive conversion of self-reliant rural people into unskilled urban laborers. Barefoot College has a collection of programs and projects that include training mostly illiterate rural women from around the world in solar engineering; running night schools staffed by "barefoot teachers" for poor children who need to support their families during the day; making medical lab services available at a fraction of the cost anywhere else; and perhaps a dozen others. Rural communities evaluate the relevance and applicability of projects to their specific conditions, participate in design, provide labor and skills, and form community management teams for all projects.

As people become empowered, many learn about their legal rights. They are supported and encouraged by Barefoot College staff or alumni to engage with the government, as individuals or as groups, to ensure that laws are actually applied. The results are at times astounding, ranging from getting water pumps installed in villages in locations accessible to the poor, to changes in how minimum wage laws are applied. Despite repeated experiences of Barefoot activists putting enormous pressure on local and sometimes national government to uphold laws, the state of Rajasthan provides a significant portion of the college's budget. Clearly, the campaigns are not alienating the government.

The similarity with Gandhi's commitment to and remarkable success at maintaining good relationships with the British despite vehement opposition to their practices, and even to the Raj itself, became immediately apparent.

Gandhi often spoke of the significance of the intimate knowledge of British culture he acquired while living in London. Knowing the British meant, in part, understanding their values and modes of operating. This made the appeal to their humanity much more tangible. Not knowing the British culture as well as Gandhi did, I can only guess what those were: a gentlemanly attitude, being civilized and reasonable, being seen as decent. By both being treated with dignity and being assumed to care about dignity, the British were pushed into a moral corner in relation to their own values and invited into living in integrity with such values.

Barefoot College's struggles also engage with a government's moral legitimacy, in its own eyes as well as the citizens' – a legitimacy based in this case mainly on its claims to beneficence and to supporting the rule of law. As I understand it, India has many laws on its books that, if enforced, would create immense benefit for ordinary people. In a manner similar to Gandhi's approach with the British, Barefoot College inspires and supports people in pushing the government or its agents into a moral corner in relation to practicing their own laws.

How might this deep principle and practice be applied to current conditions in North America? We live in a place where laws for the people are lacking, and where a professed commitment to support poor and marginalized people paints us in suspect political colors. We cannot create a moral corner for those in power by appealing to the values of care, generosity, or interdependence, since these are not among their primary professed values. The entire practice relies on the fundamental assumption that everyone would want to act in integrity with their own professed values.

In this way, the Barefoot College has created a modern version of Gandhi's spinning wheel, empowering village economies by training women (and some men) to be solar engineers who then built and installed solar units in 10,000 households in 574 villages. The Barefoot College has also updated Gandhi's policies towards the British Raj by holding Indian governments to their own stated purposes. We can look to their example so we can learn how to adapt and translate Gandhi's principles and practices to our own very different conditions.

For one thing, we can learn to use the moral language of the people in power, not just that of our own constituencies. Then, when we engage in nonviolent resistance campaigns, we can be in dialogue with the people in power about what practices, institutions, social structures, and overall social arrangements can truly align with their core values as well as ours, for everyone's benefit.

If we only see those in power through the lens of greed and desire for control, we lose our ability to have power with them to create change, and we fall back into the win-lose, either-or paradigm. When we recall powerful people to their own deep values, we offer them a gift in return for their giving up significant elements of their power: the gift of their own full humanity in the form of their own ethical and spiritual consistency.

What are the values that are deeply rooted in US culture that would be recognized as such by the most powerful people in North America, values that they could be called on in order to act according to their own sense of integrity? The candidates that come to my mind immediately are independence, the freedom to act, self-responsibility, and fairness. I'd like to believe that our movements for change could become that much more powerful if we strategize together about how to mobilize our resources to create a moral corner for the US power elites around precisely those kinds of values.

Constructive Program

Although Gandhi's "constructive program" is the less well-known aspect of his work, I know that people all over the world are continually reflecting on how its principles can be applied in today's circumstances. In the global North, the differences with Gandhi's India are radical enough that the application of these principles would require a combination of great ingenuity, creative imagination, and strategic thinking (see the Roadmap project of the Metta Center for Nonviolence Education for an entryway into that conversation). In India, on the other hand, some of the conditions present in Gandhi's time remain, leaving room for more to happen.

Gandhi's constructive program was designed to create the material and social infrastructure on which the future society could be built. Gandhi understood that in the absence of such a program, political independence would not amount to much. The program consisted of eighteen different parts, only one of which is widely known: spinning. Spinning was an act that both materially and symbolically freed Indians from relying on the British Empire for their clothing. Spinning was an activity with material results, that was essential for creating the future, and that *anyone* could undertake on a daily basis. This allowed everyone to participate, including and especially the rural poor, who were a pillar of Gandhi's vision of the future.

While nonviolent resistance struggles have proliferated since Gandhi's times, concerted efforts to create a constructive program have been far fewer and less known. For example, the Black Panthers are far more famous for their militant resistance to authority than for the network of parallel institutions they created to empower and free people from having to rely on state power for their needs. These days, small, local projects exist aiming to create alternative structures, such as the cooperative workplaces of Mondragon in Spain, the city of Gaviotas in Colombia, and countless others around the world.

What I have not been aware of are efforts that involve large numbers of people taking specific actions, along the lines of spinning in Gandhi's time, that create economic independence from large institutions or government for many individuals, and that are integrated into larger coordinated strategies to create social change. This is precisely what the Barefoot College and Navdanya organize.

Planting Seeds for the Future: Navdanya Stands up to Giants

For many people in the environmental and sustainability movements, Vandana Shiva has become an icon of courage, determination, and creativity. She has opposed oppressive multinational companies with significant success, as in her campaign to nullify the patent W.R. Grace and the USDA took out on products of the Neem tree, an ancient and free source of medicinals and other benefits for Indian villagers. This was only one of many campaigns she has contributed to organizing, mobilizing hundreds of thousands of farmers and others to oppose the practices of companies like seed giant Monsanto, which she argues have been a major contributor to the ever- expanding cycle of debt that has caused over 250,000 suicides of Indian farmers since 1995.

To respond to this human crisis, Vandana Shiva and the many who joined her also developed a constructive program, using Gandhian terms. They are supporting farmers in shifting back to time-tested methods of organic farming, seed saving, and prioritizing feeding one's own family before raising any cash crops. In 111 locations around India the organization created seed banks, preserving and restoring some of the phenomenal seed diversity that existed in India prior to the corporate takeover of agriculture. Massive educational campaigns, often relying on farmers passing on knowledge to each other within villages, and an ingenious support program are making a small and growing dent in India's farming life. Over five million farmers have been trained in these methods throughout India.

Although each farmer that joins the program is minuscule in comparison to the progression of agricultural corporations into India, the collective effect – on the farmers, their communities, the Indian government and the corporation – is more and more visible each year. The small act of saving seeds for next year's planting is just as symbolic and tangible as spinning was during Gandhi's campaign.

Navdanya also engages in nonviolent resistance campaigns, and the two are very intertwined. Seed saving is being criminalized in India through patent laws. Given this corporate landscape, the very act of saving seeds is subversive, in some cases even illegal. In addition, over the years Navdanya has mounted dozens of specific campaigns, many of them successful.

Puppet Shows that Change the World: Gandhi and Paolo Freire Meet at Barefoot College

I decided to visit Barefoot College after watching Bunker Roy's Ted talk about it[90]. What I saw and heard deepened my understanding of Gandhi's methods in unexpected ways. In addition to the aspects of nonviolent resistance I wrote about above, I learned how a constructive program can be designed to adapt to different conditions from those that Gandhi encountered.

Unlike Navdanya, where all programs and campaigns revolve around one core activity, the version of constructive program operating at Barefoot College centers on a core principle applied to many types of activities. Since its founding by Bunker Roy in 1970, this principle has been that "what the poor thought was important would be reflected in the college."[91] Indeed, the poor and marginalized are the driving force of the organization and its direct beneficiaries. The college has served three million of this population, mostly from India, and some from around the world.

Bunker Roy's approach is to support the existence of "self-contained, self-sufficient villages that don't depend on any expertise from the outside." Getting there involved a radical departure from much of our modern, urban set of assumptions. It meant letting go of any notion of illiteracy as a barrier to acquiring necessary expertise. It meant letting "ideas come from the community" and learning to "listen to the poor people." It continues to mean "demystifying technology and decentralizing the control of it." The level of trust in the fundamental wisdom, resilience, and skill of the villagers is uncompromising. Most of the effort is about "confidence building, not capacity building." Priorities and even methods keep shifting as villagers express their needs and resources are uncovered.

Just as Paolo Freire, Brazilian radical literacy educator and author of *The Pedagogy of the Oppressed*, listened to villagers and developed a literacy curriculum to fit their circumstances and life experiences, the Barefoot College approach is to engage the poor in identifying what they need and in recognizing what skills and capacities they already have, what resources are available to them, and what support they need to activate those resources. Just as Freire used drawings based

---

[90] See barefootcollege.org.
[91] All interviews are widely available on the internet. See, for example, youtube.com/watch?v=qLVSl6L27BQ.

on farmers' life experiences to teach literacy and political awareness at the same time, Barefoot College uses puppet shows to engage villagers in empowering conversations. Ramniwas, the puppeteer and radio person at Barefoot College, told for example of a time when the main puppet asked a crowd of hundreds of villagers if they had heard of minimum wage. Following the conversation that ensued, several hundred women successfully negotiated receiving that minimum wage from their employers. Puppets, like clowns and court jesters, can say things that are otherwise forbidden to utter. The result is an easier access to empowerment.

Experiments in Trust

With a handful of exceptions, all people who live and work at Barefoot College have no formal education or degrees; all programs are staffed by "barefoot professionals." No one at Barefoot College gets more than $100 a month, and the top salary is less than double the lowest. Barefoot College staff work side by side across caste and religious differences. In a manner similar to how Gandhi's ashram in Ahmedabad operated, everyone who is part of the college participates in the work required to maintain it.

When I first read about these practices, I was prepared to discover holes, exceptions, and concessions to life's complexities. I was delightedly surprised. Although I was at the Barefoot College for only a couple of days, I doubt that anything was hidden from me on purpose, and what I saw left me inspired for a long time to come. The two people that took my friend and me under their wings were a young woman who grew up in the community and has become one of the core administrators without formal education, and Ramniwas, the puppeteer who created and runs the radio program. When he first joined the community, he had no skills to speak of, and was invited to learn enough accounting to become the finance person of the organization, which he did. I was also introduced to a woman who is still illiterate, which doesn't prevent her from being the librarian of the video and audio recordings of the entire operation, numbering in the many hundreds.

Working with few resources means, among other things, a requirement to innovate. The radio room, for example, is soundproofed with egg crates, and recycled World Bank reports cover some of the walls. Everywhere we turned, I saw small and significant innovations that made life work more easily without taxing resources.

Another example of the commitment to combine empowerment, innovation, and creative use of resources is the toy manufacturing, done manually, or by foot, by people who have lost limbs to the astonishingly high number of accidents in this remote, poverty stricken, rural part of Rajasthan. What they use to create the toys are discarded objects and materials.

What the experiment of Barefoot College illustrates to me, among many other things, is the dramatic power of having decision-making and hiring processes that are consistent with the projects and philosophy of the campaigns. One of the conversations I had at Barefoot was with a man who is, perhaps, the most formally educated (aside from Bunker Roy himself), and who, nonetheless, left all of it behind and joined a community that, by world standards, is operating in conditions of near poverty. He never looked back, and has joyfully given to the community all that he has learned, just like Bunker Roy himself. These two extremes coming together – the formerly rich man who now lives and works alongside illiterate people, and makes the same amount of money as they do – send a powerful message of integrity to the outside, and an internal message of inspiration to those within the community.

Barefoot College also resists growing, in at least two significant ways. With all the support that's pouring in from around the country and the world, their budget could easily be tripled, and yet they keep the organization as it is to maintain a spirit of innovation that can get squashed by too much money. Another path to growth is also explicitly prevented. Instead of expanding to create replicas in other locations, Barefoot College supports new colleges for only a limited amount of time. Although other Barefoot Colleges exist in at least thirteen other states, all of them are independent. After two years of mentoring and support, they are asked to run on their own and have their own registration and projects. This way, no college is saddled with a large administration, and the local connection, so essential to the particular way of operating, is maintained.

Applications to North America

What could a Navdanya or Barefoot College-like approach look like in the context of the radically different challenges of the urban poor in the US? I can see elements of it in many programs, such as having former gang members staff organizations that work in the inner city; carefully-planned community meetings in many locales, which engage local residents in developing programs to support them; garden projects for ex-felons; or even farmers' markets and the grow-your-own-food movement. I come back to the Occupy Movement, which combined significant civil resistance (albeit not always purely nonviolent) with clear and self-conscious attempts to provide for human basic needs in the encampments and beyond. This was done in a manner fully consistent with Gandhi's constructive program principles, whether or not those organizing knew about those principles.

I am, as often, left with more questions. How can we reach more coherence and scale up? What has already been learned about the ways current US society makes it easier or harder to engage in both constructive programs and nonviolent resistance than the Indian society of today or of Gandhi's day?

Section 6

Getting from Here to There

Unanswerable Questions

The unifying thread of all that I am advocating for in this book is the move towards collaboration, towards working with others. Just as much as we moved from pre-determined coercive structures and life (the mainstay of medieval Europe) into competition-based societies, so we can move, in response to the urgent needs of our times, towards collaborative and cooperative functioning, unleashing co-creativity in pursuit of solutions to seemingly intractable problems. It's already happening, and this is what gives me hope. The enormous pressures on all of us to continue to operate as small, insignificant individual consumers primarily preoccupied with finding the lowest prices for what we want to buy and protecting ourselves from individual collapse are not insurmountable. People, every day, in many places around the world, join forces and make things happen.

Still, as much as I hope that we all take noticeable steps towards each other, despite the attendant discomfort, until we are able to co-create the world of our dreams, none of us ultimately knows what would (will? could?) bring about significant change, beyond our experiments with alternatives, beyond a vision created in the absence of material resources, beyond the smallness of our efforts. Without pretending to know the answers, I want to address each of these challenges.

Scaling up

To inspire confidence – both for ourselves and for others – in our ability to create significant change that affects large numbers of people, we need to find a way to continue to operate in radical, visionary, uncompromising ways while scaling up. We need to find ways to break out of the conviction that we can only do radical experiments with small numbers, and that becoming more visible, increasing our numbers, and gaining power and influence are bound to bring corruption, and/or bureaucracy, and/or inefficiency, and/or all other social evils. This conviction will either keep us small and ineffective, or become a self-fulfilling prophecy.

I don't know the answer. I am convinced it exists. I will continue to look for it, and to keep imagining and encouraging everyone I know, including myself, to move towards it without fear of falling.

Who is the "we" that I have used often in my writing here? I use this word loosely to refer to everyone who is in the grips of the heartbreak about our beautiful planet being destroyed by the actions of human beings like us. After all, all of us, regardless of our beliefs and affiliations, are, ultimately, struggling to make sense of the world and attend to our own, our loved ones', and others' needs in the best ways we know how. All of us are implicated in the destruction, whether we want to be or not.

Building Alliances and Coalitions

It is possible that the next Buddha will not take the form of an individual.
The next Buddha may take the form of a community —
a community practicing understanding and loving kindness,
a community practicing mindful living.
This may be the most important thing we can do for the earth.
                    – Thich Nhat Hanh (Vietnamese Buddhist monk,
                              poet, and peace activist)

The days of one-person operations appear to be largely over. The Lubavitchers, the largest Hassidic movement, now operate without a new Lubavitcher, because the tradition held that only seven generations of leaders would be guiding this movement, and now, after the death of the seventh, no one knows what comes next. This is not about giving up leadership. This is about many more people taking leadership all around them.

Working our way out of charismatic leadership will require us to work with others who are not members of our specific movement. As we reach out to create such connections, we will encounter people who will agree with us on some bits and not on others. And we will still need to work with them. If we are to be truly effective, we will need to work with people who are far from our positions. We cannot make significant change without connecting with people who are in fundamental opposition to what we are proposing (if we even propose anything rather than simply protesting). The Department of Peace Campaign has been working hard for some years now to support the establishment of a federal level Department of Peace in the US government. As of the last time I checked, they still hadn't crossed the Democrat/Republican divide. It would be surprising if a Department of Peace, dedicated, in part, to conflict resolution, were ever created without some level of bipartisanship in the constituency that operates the campaign.

How? We need tools to dialogue, to become more present, to know how to separate strategies from needs, to see the underlying vision of opposing views, and to know that more is in common between us at the level of vision than we may be comfortable admitting. We need to learn to listen with a willingness to be changed, and take on the hard and thankless work of listening to our ideological enemies, no matter where we are, so we can learn and grow, so we can create bridges, so we can find ways of collaborating, and thereby begin, now, the work of the future. Because in that future there will still, and always, be people that disagree with us. There will always be people who will see our implementation of our vision as an absolute threat to what they hold most dear. And we will need to include and embrace their needs and wellbeing in full if we are to operate with integrity.

What to do now

Since we cannot, as the Talmudic Jews said, "press the end" (meaning force things to move faster than they do), and since acceptance of *what is* is part and parcel of our work, we cannot escape the reality that, for now, we don't know what will create change. In fact, taking seriously the fundamental uncertainty and unpredictability of life in part means that even if we plan change, we have no way of knowing that the change we seek will ever happen, nor when the moment will be there. We can only be as ready for it as we can be. Two years before the Berlin Wall was taken down no one would have predicted that outcome, even if many were secretly planning for it. And it happened. What might happen within the next two years that we cannot imagine now?

This is especially so for change at the scope and of the kind that I am speaking about, which is about replacing the entire economic and governance structures on a global scale, for everyone's benefit. It's never been done before, even though our economic structures have changed over the centuries in myriad ways. We haven't had structures, in large and complex human societies, that truly support human needs.

If we cannot predict, can barely plan, and cannot implement large-scale social change, we can only keep working to be ready for opportunities when they arise. Every once in a while (we never know when, how, or for how long), the existing order of things is put on hold, and much more is possible. At such times, many more in the world are hungry for direction, for hope, for tools, and for possibilities. I'd like to believe that we can use our small-scale efforts at obstruction, creation of alternatives, and consciousness transformation to get us all ready, so that when the window opens up, we will be available to respond to the call to lead and to offer inspiration and clarity that can make a decisive difference. I hope I am still alive when that day arrives.

It May Start Like This

All along I have been saying that I don't know and can't know how the transition could happen. While this remains completely and entirely still true, as I was approaching the end of writing, a possibility approached me. It felt almost like an answer to a prayer, except I don't have a memory of ever praying. The prayer, or the question, has been the same for some years now: What would a Gandhian movement look like that could meet the challenges of our time with love, courage, and imagination?

The idea that came to me is to take back access to basic needs that are now primarily residing in the hands of very large institutions: food, shelter, clothing, health, education.

In terms of the civil disobedience end of things, I see large numbers of people being mobilized and in the process taking on the most sacrosanct of institutions in this country: private property. In a manner similar to how Gandhi worked, I imagine a fully transparent movement, announcing its intentions and offering the possibility of full dialogue to the powerful, knowing all too well that such dialogue is extremely unlikely. Those in power, whether in large-scale corporations or in government, already know the needs of suffering people and are choosing to continue with their practices. They either are numb to the suffering, or believe that their actions are actually the best possible outcome. Either way, as many who have attempted dialogues about smaller changes (such as with logging companies) know, the possibilities are sadly limited, though, perhaps, if enough love and empathy are brought to bear something might just happen.

Along with such efforts at dialogue, the movement I am envisioning is likely to engage in some campaigns that demonstrate vision implementation – civil disobedience that at one and the same time demonstrates the future we are trying to create. I imagine, for example, a large march to the Central Valley in California, where vast areas are being cultivated by large-scale corporations. Like Gandhi's Salt March, this would not be a purely symbolic protest. Instead, what I imagine people doing once they get there is harvesting vegetables and other crops and bringing food home for themselves and others in need.

Another possibility is a large group of people taking over a corporate warehouse of medicine and distributing it to people in need.

Yet another possibility is enumerating all the abandoned buildings in a particular city, and organizing a city-wide squatting by homeless people and their allies of all of the unoccupied buildings at once.

Possibilities are endless.

Like the Civil Rights Movement, these kinds of actions would require tremendous acumen in design and implementation, and massive amounts of mobilization, trust building, and training in the core principles of nonviolence, especially love. The only way that this kind of action can lead to massive transformation would be if the marchers are able to love the people they are targeting in their actions. Harvest vegetables illegally and leave some for those who own the field. Raid a medicine warehouse and thank the people who developed the medicine that can save lives.

Without love, whatever gains are made will be short lived. Historical examples abound.

In addition to these efforts, I anticipate such a movement will have its own Constructive Program wing. This, too, could be focused on these essential five basic human needs. Gandhi instructed his followers to dedicate thirty minutes a day to spinning. In our current circumstances, what I can imagine is a movement calling its members to dedicate thirty minutes a day to identifying, learning, and executing home-based or community-based ways of owning those needs: creating home remedies, growing food, establishing learning cooperatives, making clothes, or anything else that can increase self-reliance and empowerment and undo the dependence on external institutions for those basic needs.

I live in the USA, and I am familiar with the peculiar set of challenges that this country faces in terms of organizing movements. One of them is the barriers of crossing race and class divisions. For example, white and middle class people who are committed to nonviolence tend to engage with issues of war, the military, and foreign policy on the one hand, and environmental issues on the other hand. Although poor people and people of color are profoundly affected by both sets of issues, sometimes more and sooner than others who have resources that can shelter them, the immediate survival needs that people in many disenfranchised communities face on a daily basis make it exceedingly difficult to find energy and passion for what can appear as abstract and irrelevant issues.

Organizing around basic needs, on the other hand, may create unexpected alliances. For one thing, everyone's interests are united. The poor may not have enough to eat while the rich don't have a say in what's available to eat, not even at the upscale chain called Whole Foods[92]. Either way they are largely at the mercy of larger forces.

Such organizing, especially with the willingness to break the law, can provide long-time activists with avenues to use their skills, experience, and willingness to be arrested in ways that can directly contribute to struggling communities. At the same time, people who are otherwise vulnerable can be supported without having to risk arrests, which for them would have far different consequences than for richer, whiter people.

I have no illusion that this idea, as is, would be implemented. I rather imagine this writing to be the launch of a conversation, of finding partners in thinking and envisioning, of finding people with willingness and skill in organizing. If any massive plan of this scope and nature is to succeed, everything I have written about collaboration and leadership would need to be assimilated so as to create a movement that is also at the same time a caring community that inspires and models the world we are trying to create. Nothing short of that will work.

---

[92] Although this may seem inconceivable given the astonishing array on offer at Whole Foods, I have been noticing that over time Whole Foods has fewer organic vegetables, more pre-packaged and less bulk items, more of their own brand and less of local varieties, more plastic packaging on everything and fewer recyclable containers, and overall more and more processed food and less fresh and whole foods, despite all that has been learned in all these areas.

Getting from Here to There: Deepening the Vision

Throughout this book I have been alluding regularly to the vision that has been inspiring me to dedicate my life energy as fully as I can to doing and inspiring others to do work for transformation – the vision of a world that works for all, where everyone matters, and where all institutions and social structures are designed to attend to needs.

Now that this book has completed the arc of the known, or at least the knowable, taking us to what we can do together to begin a process of transformation, it's time to present this vision in more detail. At this point, hopefully you have sufficient understanding of what I mean by human needs and why I see them as central to the project of making the world work. You know enough about how I see the intricacies of human relationships and institutions to have an appreciation of the challenges of creating a world that truly works for all. Perhaps, you are now in a frame of mind of openness to see possibilities, and have enough context for making sense of what I am trying to do.

Vision is essential, as I outlined earlier in this book ("From Opposition to Vision," page 43). It is no accident that one of Dr. King's most remembered speeches is the "I Have a Dream" speech. Vision, like human needs, is charged with energy, shows us where we want to go, and in the very act of being articulated already makes itself more possible than any long list of injustices and dysfunctions. With vision, we already walk towards rather than away from something and without knowing where we want to end.

Before placing before you a vision of a world to come, which is, by necessity, based on fiction, I want to note the big absence of a blueprint for the path of getting there. Lest you fantasized otherwise, I don't know any more than anyone else a guaranteed path to getting anywhere different from where we are. This is why I focused on the specifics of the *how* to get there, knowing full well that everything we do now that is aligned with our vision and values will support us when we finally create a world with needs at the center. I don't, however, know how to create that world.

What I believe is true is that creating such a level of transformation requires one of two paths.

One is gaining access to the most powerful men in the world, those who rule our current institutions, and finding a way to mobilize their willingness to transform those institutions. The challenge here is that many of these people are shut down to their emotions, and especially to noticing their effect on other people and the environment. What could wake them up?

The other path is finding ways of mobilizing millions of people to stand up in massive nonviolent resistance to those in power. The challenge here is that most of the people who would need to participate are currently under the belief that things are more or less OK, or at least as good as they can get, or are entirely cynical about creating change. Either because of those beliefs or for any other reasons, most people are committed primarily to their own personal lives and families. I don't know how to get their attention sufficiently to create a mass movement. I don't believe anyone else knows, either. What would it take?

And thus it is that I turn to the next part, "Wisdom Tales from the Future," with humility and excitement both. My humility stems from that radical *not knowing*. My excitement from the hope that, as more people find out about this project and read, especially, my detailed and mundane stories about that future, the spark will, perhaps, take off.

Under conditions of modern capitalism, we act as self-interested beings, concerned only with our own personal gratification, and we assume others do the same. The result is that their wishes become limits on our own ability to express and fulfill our desires. Within this context, it takes enormous effort to imagine any other reality, and we continue to act in ways that reinforce our isolation and mistrust.

In contrast, under conditions of the future, what Marx called "the association of free producers," we can be conscious of each other's needs as much as we are of our own, and satisfy ourselves and each other simultaneously. This is the vision that I spell out in Part Two of this book.

Part Two

Wisdom Tales from the Future

An Invitation into a Possible Future

What follows is my own attempt to imagine a world in which *all of us* could thrive. This vision stands in stark contrast to all that we've been told about ourselves and what's possible for humans. Our process of socializing and everything we continue to be told – through the media, in books, and in casual conversations – makes it look impossible, naïve, or even dangerous.

Nonetheless, from where I stand and what I have seen, it seems naïve to me that anything less than this vision could transform the dire conditions in which we currently live. We have reached the limits of attempting to control ourselves, nature, and our children.

I want to invite you, the reader, into the simplicity and clarity of what I see possible. I do this in two ways, each comprising a section of this part of the book. As you read this part, you may choose to reverse the order and read the description of systems first and then come back to the stories, if that works better for you. Neither is required for the other to make sense.

I. The Stories

Instead of concepts and ideas that may engage interest but also incredulity, I am choosing to start this part of the book with stories that reveal this future in vivid detail. Stories are our ancient and reliable medium for cultural preservation and cultural transformation. They engage not only the mind, but also the heart, and it will take our hearts, too, to move toward the world that's possible for us.

Envisioning a collaborative future that works for everyone, when we have been immersed in a world of scarcity, separation, and powerlessness, invites us into what can be called social science fiction. The stories in this part illustrate the radically different social reality that's possible when we prioritize human needs instead of profit, care and interdependence instead of control, and dialogue instead of war.

They all take place *after* a transition that's already assumed to have happened in the coming years, somewhere in the gap between the previous part and this one. None of the stories address the specific challenges that arise in trying to imagine just how we could move from here to there. I consider that transition to be eminently possible and intrinsically mysterious and unpredictable.

Although these stories are, on the face of it, pure fantasy, I wish for them to be read as a form of reality, because I truly do experience them as wisdom tales from the future. While writing them, I felt entirely transported into that world, to the point of having the experience of living in it for the duration of the writing. The experience was immensely nourishing and uplifting, and I hope to offer you that possibility, too.

Each of the stories explores the way of life of the future world through a day in the life of one person. Each of the stories contains implicit and sometimes explicit references to the institutions and systems I describe later, in section two. I chose purposefully to write of these institutions and systems as though they are the most ordinary and commonplace occurrence rather than a thing of the future, because that will be the case in such a future society.

While each story illustrates how people might interact with each other under radically different conditions, my main hope is that you will receive a vivid image of what those conditions are. Although I described these conditions earlier, it bears repeating. Stretch your imagination far and wide. Remember as you read these stories that there is no money and no exchange in this future world. That everything that is done is done voluntarily and coordinated with everyone else's actions. That the resource allocation system is globally coordinated and locally owned. That there is no government as we know it, and no coercion except under conditions of imminent threat to life (one of the stories addresses this particular challenge). And that conflict exists and is an ongoing feature of life, and mechanisms for addressing it are abundant and robust.

This point bears some unpacking. In our current reality, conflict is frightening for most of us. When we are accustomed to not having our needs met, our capacity is greatly diminished to be present for conflict, to be relaxed in the face of the possibility that our needs, at least momentarily, might not be met. When we are used to the experience of scarcity, and experience ourselves as separate from others, we are challenged to trust that options exist that could work for everyone. When we feel fundamentally powerless to affect the world around us and make things work for us, we find the uncertainty of conflict unbearable, and tend to avoid conflict, withdraw from it, or explode in anger. It takes most of us extensive training and practice to keep our hearts open at a time of conflict. Not so in the society of the future.

Even now, even without transforming the entire social structure, we can create conditions in which people are fully heard, everyone's needs are included, and the focus is on a genuine search for workable solutions, without judging anyone in the process. Under such conditions conflict melts rapidly. When such conditions become the norm, I imagine conflict becoming easier for all to engage in productively.

Beyond the question of conflict per se, when I think about the many other questions and issues that would need to be addressed to make the world work on the basis of human needs, gift-giving, and willingness, I can easily get overwhelmed. Then I remember that I don't have to single-handedly answer all these questions. All I am trying to do in this collection is paint a picture of possibility. I show how at least *some* issues can be resolved, and through this picture point to a blueprint for *how* issues can be resolved. I chose to do this in the form of stories about specific individuals placed in strategic positions, and situations that bring to the foreground both a general picture of the new structures, as well as attending to a number of thorny issues that many skeptics would bring up.

I have been thinking about the relationship between structural change and personal/emotional change for years. There are those who believe that structural change will automatically create personality changes, and no specific attention to individual emotional life needs to be made. There are those who believe that structural change can only come about once enough people have had significant personal change, and then structures would change by themselves, without specific attention to the structural dimension. My own belief is that there is a complex relationship between the two dimensions, and I see both positions as contributing useful insights. These stories reflect this complexity, too. In some of them you can see individuals still struggling to integrate, emotionally and practically, the structural changes that had happened before their time.

One story ("All of it is Play") tangentially references a project started in a previous one ("Starting Life Again"). With that one exception, there is no connection between the different characters and situations.

Some of the stories contain little bits of truth from current reality. Because such information may not be known to all, I include footnotes about them.

One of my efforts in writing these stories has been to spread around the names and locations so the future reality will be less likely to be seen as purely North American and white. The different stories have names from a variety of current countries and regions of the world. In some instances I provide footnotes to explain the meaning of certain names.

II. Principles and Systems

The second section in Part Two describes more directly the systems of thought, economy, government, and justice in which these stories are set, a blueprint of what life could be like if we had the collective will to shift course and move towards sharing the bounty of the earth. If you have a preference for an orderly way of understanding information, you may want to start there and then return to the stories, once you have some understanding of how that society works.

One of the chapters of this section – "Systems Referenced in the Stories" – contains a list of the stories and provides a short paragraph situating these stories in time and naming the systems referenced and the challenges they address.

What You May Bring to Your Reading of These Stories

Some people who have read these stories see them as being all about individuals. Although these readers may notice the social systems, like the transport system in "Getting There," they see them as backdrops or landscapes behind the characters, so for them the real drama in "Getting There" is what will happen between the main character and the woman he's sweet on. They might barely notice what's happening on his computer screen.

Other readers may see each story as being about a different social system in the future, with the dramas between the individuals as lively human context for making the stories more "real" and easier to read.

From my perspective it's "both and." The social systems and the individuals struggling with their personal dramas are two sides of one coin. They are both fascinating to me, and both are critical to creating a society that is based on meeting needs, individually and collectively.

So, welcome to a future that we could have.

Section 1

The Stories

Collective Triage

"I know it's being investigated," Adimu said impatiently. "How on earth is it going to solve our problem *now*?" She stomped the floor in frustration as she paced the room. "I can't believe this is happening. I just can't believe it." She wanted it to be a bad dream. It wasn't. There were families waiting, each with a child, each with malaria. She only had enough artemisinin for ten of them. And this was not a temporary shortage. It was a global crisis. There wasn't going to be enough, not this year, not anywhere.[93]

A system breakdown had resulted in an incorrect calculation of how much would be needed. Some flaw in the projection module. And no one caught it, either, because it had never happened before, and everyone had gotten lazy. On three different occasions the alert had been ignored. Any change in materials orders from a previous period that was larger than 10% in either direction was flagged for inspection. At least three different people had seen the flag and signed off on it anyway. The growers had responded to the drastically reduced request by shifting to other crops, or taking some time off from growing and doing more community service, or engaging in other activities.

And now there she was. With enough artemisinin to treat ten of 32 children. And with the long growing season it would take almost a year to fix the problem. What a nightmare.

She almost screamed: "How am I going to decide who lives and who dies?"

Wachiru was thinking about the people who were responsible for this terrible disaster. He realized they would have to face the consequences for the rest of their lives. There would be many circles and much talk to repair the lost trust. And there would be lots to learn about how to support people in detecting changes and intervening. The growers, too, could have noticed it. Wouldn't they have been surprised to find such smaller quantities requested around the globe?

---

[93] Artemisinin is currently the key component in the most widely used treatment for malaria worldwide. It is an annual plant, and even recently fluctuations in demand have resulted in temporary shortages in many places in the world. Recent developments of a semisynthetic alternative may make the specificity of this particular example moot in the future. I am merely using it as a plausible scenario of actual scarcity.

"We need to go out there and talk to them," he said gently. "I'll help."

Adimu hadn't settled yet. "It's easy for you to say," she was still agitated. "You're not their doctor; you're just a supply liaison. Do you even know what it's like to tell someone you don't have the medicine that could save their child's life?" She was breathing heavily, then sat down, panting, and covered her face with her hands. When she looked at him again he could see her tears. "How are we going to make these horrible, impossible, awful decisions?"

"Together," he said, almost inaudibly. "There's no other way. None of us can decide for anyone else." They both knew about the old days, where money, or connections, or status, would make the decision. She nodded, horrified at the thought. There was no alternative to telling them all the truth, involving everyone in figuring this out. "OK," she said, "I'm ready. As ready as I'll ever be."

"Wait a minute," Wachiru said as she was approaching the door to their office. "Don't go out before you get some support. Please, sit down." She did. He took her hand. They'd been good friends for years. Sometimes there was even a little spark of sexual energy between them, not enough to make a relationship. The friendship was too precious. He made sure to stay on this side of the line as he stroked her hand, touched her face, and pulled her closer to him.

"With a name like mine," Adimu said, "I never, ever, ever wanted to be in any situation that involved scarcity.[94] It's too cruel for me, I'm just too sensitive. I sometimes don't even know how I survive treating sick and injured people all the time."

Wachiru smiled. He knew what she meant, and chose not to speak about his own name.[95] The ironies were too strong. Instead, he said: "What touches me most is how much you care about people, that even with your sensitivities you chose to dedicate your life to healing the sick and the injured. That means a lot to me. I am inspired to see your courage." He could feel her breathing deepen, and she was silent for a while, just breathing.

"It's true," she said dreamily. "It has to be true, or I am simply a masochist, which I know I'm not. I'm rare, but not *that* rare." She laughed a little. "Thanks, pal." She paused, unsure if she was really ready to face them. He could sense her hesitance. "I know it's hard

---

[94] Adimu is a female Kenyan name that means unique, rare, or scarce.
[95] Wachiru is a male Kenyan name that means son of a judge.

for you to take the time for yourself, especially knowing the people are out there waiting, desperate. Please stay. It could make a huge difference in what happens next." She accepted. "It's going to be rough, I know," she continued, more confident. "And I know that we're together and you'll help. And the families will help, too."

Ten minutes later she opened the door, walked into the hallway with Wachiru just behind her, and stood, preparing to talk. The noise was intense, with healthy children running around and everyone else singing or moaning, as the case may be. Then they saw her, and one by one the voices dropped, and a silence descended on the room.

"Let's sit in a circle," she offered. "We have some decisions to make together. This is not going to be simple." Several people started speaking at once, raising their voices to be heard. Their children's lives were at stake; of course they would be agitated. Still, she couldn't hear a single word. She motioned them to be quiet, which didn't help. She pulled out a whistle and blew it. The silence resumed.

"Thank you, all. I'm grateful for your presence. I can't imagine how hard it is to have to come here for medicine you previously could get locally, knowing there isn't enough for everyone." The noise erupted again, and the whistle brought them back again. "We definitely want to hear from people, just not quite yet. Please do all you can to maintain your silence." Maybe this time they will stick with it, she thought, not totally confident. "Wachiru here and I have talked about the situation, and all we know is this: there isn't enough for everyone, and no more is coming this year. We want to make the decision about how to distribute what we have together." She could see small signs of gratitude on some people's faces, pained gratitude, for knowing the truth and being held with care. Mostly she saw panic. "I know you're afraid for your child. All of you are. I am, too. I am afraid for every single one of these precious little beings." Her voice was quivering when she said those last few words, and some of the mothers, in particular, looked at her more closely. She was glad for the extra time she took with Wachiru, for connecting with her own grief about losing a sister when she was younger. She felt present, despite the immense challenge.

"So, here's the situation," she sounded much more matter-of-fact than she felt. "There's only enough for ten families, and there are 32 here." Once again the voices rose, alarmed. This time she let them be for a moment before hushing them again. This was real human suffering, and she knew it had to be expressed. "I can't think of any way that anyone can make these decisions for anyone else, so we will all need to do this together. I know every single one of you wants your child to survive this disease, and so do I." She paused to survey the room. Everyone looked so anxious. Where to begin?

Wachiru stepped in next. "Let's figure out the criteria first, and then apply them," he said. He was always so sensible and clear; she admired him for that. Whenever there was any issue in the hospital, everyone asked him to come, even when it wasn't his direct responsibility. "I have one to propose, and then I want to see who else has anything to offer. Anyone willing to take notes?" A girl, about 10, the older sister of a young boy who was clearly ill, raised her hand quickly. He smiled at her. "Thank you. What's your name?" She smiled broadly, despite the dire circumstances. "I am Kanika," she said. "Great. Here's a pad of paper and a pen. Please write down all the ideas. Let me know if we're going too fast for you." He waited for her to get organized, and went on. The attention in the room was focused. "I would like to suggest that we give the medicine to those who are least likely to make it without it. Kanika, would you write this down?"

Immediately several people spoke. One said, "That doesn't make sense. We need to support the strongest kids to make sure that at least some of the children survive. If we only give it to the weakest ones, then we might lose them all." That man's child was doing well despite the disease, and Wachiru wondered why he even came to get the medicine. And another: "Let's do a lottery." Adimu winced. Wachiru looked at her and blinked on purpose, slowly, so she would know he saw, and that he wanted her to remember to give room to all the ideas. She smiled, grateful. He then looked at Kanika to make sure she wrote lottery, too, even though it wasn't a criterion.

Then an older woman got up and looked around. Everyone sensed her power. A few whispers and hushed questions floated around until everyone convinced themselves they knew enough about her. She stood like an elemental force of nature. Everyone was looking at her. Wachiru figured she must have come with a grandchild, as she was older than most. Later he and Adimu learned that she had no children, no one involved with malaria, and that she was going from place to place to be of help. She had short hair, evenly spread around her face, graying near her temples. Her hands had brought many little ones into the world. Her body spelled love. "This is for all of us, together," she said. "Not each family apart. We can do this. Let's let this man support us. We may be able to save everyone. I still know the old ways, passed down from generations, of supporting children and families to work with malaria. There are no guarantees. Not even with artemisinin, as you all know. I'm inviting anyone here to work with me. It's a tough disease, but it's not an automatic death sentence. Not even for the very young ones." She stopped to breathe longer. It was the first moment Adimu could see she was aging. "I set up a healing place outside for those who are willing. I will work with everyone in the family. I know I can save many." She looked around the circle, and said softly: "Let's sing together." Everyone joined, including Adimu and Wachiru. They sang together for a few minutes, still not knowing what would happen. When the song was over, the woman walked slowly through the circle, stood by the door, and looked back one more time: "I invite all to come. This is my sacred act." And she walked out.

No one raised their voice again. People whispered to each other, and one by one several families went outside. A baby started crying, and someone comforted him. Those who remained seated bowed to those who left. Yes, it was a sacred act, thought Adimu. How she loved the people. When the commotion of people leaving ended, she counted again. Ten families went with the woman. Twelve more were not going to get the artemisinin. It was still far from done.

Kanika raised her hand. Wachiru called on her. "I don't know what to write down. It didn't sound like criteria to me. What shall I do?" Everyone smiled, and she laughed, still unclear.

"There was only one more thing to write after the one I named," he said to her.

He was talking a little slower than usual, and she immediately jumped in. "You don't need to speak slowly, I understand everything you're saying." She sounded irritated, and he let it go. They were all still learning how to treat children with full respect. He wanted her to lead the way. "I think I know what it was, thank you," She said. "Carry on, I'm good."

And then the list of suggestions for criteria followed. Those who are older, who are able to contribute right away. Those who are younger, who need the most care from others. Families with many children, where the loss might be mitigated, would not get it. Families with fewer children, where fewer will suffer the loss would not. Girls first. Boys first. Kanika was keeping up. Wachiru wasn't, and Adimu was looking smaller and smaller over time. Would this group ever come together? From time to time they stopped and sang again, gathering strength together.

Then Kanika raised her hand. Wachiru called on her. "I think I have an idea," she said cautiously. "I even calculated it. If we give one dose to the oldest girl, and one to the youngest boy, and one to the largest family, and one to the smallest family, and one to the sickest child, and one to the strongest child, that's six. And we then have four more, and we divide them equally among all the remaining families. Every child will get a quarter dose. Maybe it will help, and some will make it." And then she choked up. She couldn't say anything for a moment, and everyone waited. "I want my brother to live," she finally was able to utter. "I want him to get a full dose, and he won't, not if we accept my idea." She put her pen down, and wept. Many cried with her. No one said a word, as is common after truth is spoken.

It's Water Again

The alarm went off, and Jasmine woke up and pushed the snooze button. Once again in a strange room. Where was she? Oh, yeah. She was in the Owens Valley. Far, far away from her home in Sri Lanka. She had just finished two weeks of offering master classes to mediators, which she loved. And now, in a few hours she would be sitting with a bunch of angry people she didn't even know. This often happened at the tail end of a teaching tour. She was very talented in approaching difficult inter-regional conflicts, and had a very high rate of success, so she was often invited to handle tough local situations, even though local resources for mediation abounded in all regions.

In this moment she only felt the weight of that responsibility, not the joy of her mastery. She stretched and yawned. No point continuing if she was losing her willingness. Maybe it was time to switch jobs. Or maybe she could learn better how to say "no" when invited, and only go if she could really go willingly. She felt a familiar bitterness arise in her. She was just old enough to have still grown up before willingness was accepted as a key organizing principle, and so she absorbed her share of "should" and "have to" as a child. If only she had been born ten years later. She was envious of her younger colleagues who just didn't have that weight to carry around.

What would she do if she let go of doing high-stakes global mediations? She was suddenly awash in gratitude. Despite her rough start, she was, now, living in the post-coercion world. She didn't *have* to work. She could take time off. She could just focus on nurturing herself after several decades of intensive work. There was so much she wanted to learn and experience. She could decide not to work forever, and she would still get food and shelter. One of her closest friends back home had not worked in any capacity for over two years, and the people at the food distribution center didn't even blink. Of course they didn't know. Why would they know, or care, anyway? They, too, could choose not to be where they were. Forty years after the transition it was still hard to grasp that the old days were really over.

The alarm went off again. Now it was time to get up and get ready. The guest house was still quiet. She liked to get up early to do her morning routine. She picked her intention for the day, which was to trust the people who would come together to address the conflict. Especially when people were angry and didn't trust each other, she knew it would be important for her to trust them. She sat in silence with this intention, allowing memories, doubts, insights, to arise to the surface, then subside. Her earlier grumpiness dissipated as she connected with her love of supporting people. Maybe she wasn't quite ready to let go, after all.

Next she went for a stroll around the building. It was high desert country, and yet the garden was in full bloom. The lessons learned from experiments in permaculture[96] in the extreme deserts of the Middle East were bearing fruit, in the most literal sense. She walked around, listening to species of birds that had not been seen in those areas for decades, enjoying the lush green and the sweet smell of pomegranates, knowing what she was about to eat was mainly grown within this garden.

She used her netter[97] to type her transportation request. She knew the questions and didn't mind providing all these details. Yes, the day was clear and warm, and she could walk a little to be picked up at a more central location. No, she didn't have flexibility about arrival time. Yes, she was happy to be picked up a little earlier. From having mediated a conflict about inter-regional transportation she knew how each bit of clarity and flexibility she could provide would support the coordination.

Two hours later, at 9:35, she entered the room where representatives from both regions and a regional mediator would soon arrive. She always liked to be the first in the room, to get comfortable and fully connect with herself before anyone entered, so she could face what came later. She loved greeting everyone who came and getting to know them just a little bit before starting the formal proceedings. As angry as she knew some of these people would be, this was far better than the killings of the 1930s.[98] When

---

[96] Permaculture experiments in the Middle East have indeed happened successfully, and are slowly spreading across Jordan, as several youtube videos illustrate. The project is called "Greening the Desert" and was started by the Permaculture Research Institute of Australia. Information about permaculture is widely available on the web and in books.

[97] An invented name for a solar-powered handheld device that extends beyond our current 4G technology and is assumed to be universally available and non-toxic in production and operation. By and large, the main focus of these stories is on social systems and human interactions, not on technology.

[98] The problem that this story addresses is based on a historical water dispute that, at its height in the 1930s, bordered on active war between LA county and Owens Valley. LA has been diverting water from that valley since then, and the landscape and options in the valley have been altered dramatically.

she was reading up on the issues in preparation for this meeting, and when she talked with people from both sides, she was amazed how much of the original resentment was still ready to kindle right under the surface, so long afterwards.

She was glad the Greater Los Angeles council agreed to come to Owens Valley for this conference. She had a lot of compassion for their struggle. Fifteen years after the transition, when the global population was finally able to choose zero growth and consumption within means, that region had some of the toughest conversions to make. Scientists from around the world were invited to work with the local population to come up with an energy descent plan[99] that would be livable, manageable, and responsive enough to meet the global challenges. Water was one of the biggest issues. How could they reduce consumption fast enough without any coercive measures? What would make conservation attractive enough to people used to some of the highest standards of living in the world? Now, twenty-five years later, they had only managed to reduce 75% of what they had committed to. The paradox of success and failure in that picture was deeply moving to her.

She also easily understood the residents of the High Desert region. They had extended goodwill towards the LA folks for a long time, and they were losing their patience. The LA region had originally been using close to three times the amount of water it could supply for itself, so now, despite all their efforts, the LA folks were still living beyond their water means by 45%, and that meant water from Owens Valley was still being diverted. They wanted access to their own resources, the capacity to live in dignity within their means. They still had pictures hanging on walls of the time before the great diversions started, when Owens Valley was wet and flourishing. Hard to believe!

That's why the High Desert people wanted the LA folks to come, and why they chose this location. The locals wanted to show the visitors exactly what was happening, so they would grasp the effect of their lack of compliance with their own commitment on the Owens Valley population. The local population was stretching too much, and Jasmine was worried there wouldn't be enough willingness left to move forward. They were managing, especially with the breakthroughs that came about with permaculture being widely

---

[99] The concept of an energy descent plan is closely linked to the Transition Town movement.

applied. But they wanted to have more ease, and it was hard for them to agree, voluntarily, to continue to make sacrifices because, in their words, "a bunch of high-consumption LA residents still wouldn't budge on their swimming pools." It was true that, like everywhere else on the planet, people who were used to high resource consumption were the last to recognize the joy of living within their local means and in community with others.

One by one the representatives came in. Jasmine was friendly, and showed them each to their seats. There would be fourteen people in the room including herself. Her first and most important task was to reach a place of shared ownership of needs. Having them sit intermixed with each other would help, she knew that from years of experience. The youth in the room would likely have no difficulty with shared ownership. It's only those, like herself, who grew up under scarcity mentality, who would be challenged. If not for the historical buildup, this could be a no-brainer. With her level of skill, getting from everyone's expressed positions down to their underlying needs usually took her no more than an hour or two. This time she figured it would take at least three, if not four. It wasn't the issues that were complex. It was the lack of trust that would make things difficult.

She was right on target. Once everyone was in the room and seated with their drink, it was already 10:15. That was fine. She started them with an initial go round where each person would speak their heart as they were coming together, and express their hopes for the process they were undertaking. A couple of times she stepped in to ensure they would focus their hopes on the process itself without sneaking in any wishes for a particular outcome. Knowing how important it is for everyone to know they are taken seriously, she wrote on the board the key hopes she gleaned from each person. The hopes were almost always the same anywhere in the world she went. Everyone wanted respect, to make sure that what they wanted was taken into consideration, and that the outcome would work for everyone. At the end of the circle, it was 10:35.

The toughest part was next. With the level of intensity in the room, she knew it would be hard for people to hear each other. She invited them to go around the room again and for each person to speak and focus on what was most essential for them that the other side would hear. Then she asked for a volunteer from the other group who was willing to reflect back a summary of what was of most importance to the person who spoke.

For the first hour she had to work hard to ensure that people wouldn't yell at each other, especially the older ones. If it were only youth, she thought, we could get this done so quickly. The older generation, they still had that old habit of believing their needs didn't matter to anyone, and would get agitated easily.

A particularly challenging moment happened when Robert, one of the people from Owens Valley, spoke passionately about how they just couldn't do it any more, they had waited far too long for the LA people to comply with the agreements they had made. Before Jasmine managed to ask for a volunteer from the LA group, Sarah, a woman from LA, raised her voice and said: "Why are you on our case? Can't you see that we are doing all we can? Why do we even have to have this stupid meeting? You know we can't reduce consumption further." Seeing several people from the High Desert region almost jump to their feet, Jasmine immediately stepped in to the circle, and stood between the two people. She wanted to catch these words before their incendiary potential ignited the others. "Before anyone says anything," she started, "I want to make sure that at least I understand what's important to you." She paused to look around. Some people were still on the edge of their seat, waiting to see if she could handle the tension. Every word counted now. "What most stands out to me from what you said," she continued, "is how much you wish there were a way to reduce the consumption further." Sarah nodded her head. Jasmine knew that her words, her way of reflecting what Sarah had said, was far from the meaning that others had assumed was intended. This was so often the case – the choice of words could create polarization when the underlying intention could produce connection. "I am touched hearing this," Jasmine went on, not leaving too many pauses for anyone else to step in. "I bet anything that you just want to be trusted about your intentions." Sarah nodded again. "Exactly," she said. "It's not like we have some magical powers and we deliberately stall. We have such a mess on our hands, and it's not going to happen overnight." The blame was dissolving, and Jasmine had some confidence the High Desert people could now hear Sarah and know what needs she was speaking for. And sure enough, someone chimed in: "Is it that you want consideration for the complexity of the situation?" Sarah took a deep breath, and they could continue, all together. With her softest possible voice, Jasmine turned to Sarah again and said: "Now that you've been heard, can you tell us all what you heard Robert say?"

Sarah was getting ready to argue again. "But…" was all she managed to say before Jasmine stepped in again. "Sarah," she said gently, "please stay with Robert. I want him to be heard, too. Can you focus on him now? If not, I can ask someone else." Then she waited. If Sarah could find her way to Robert, the power of holding both perspectives together would immediately happen. Sarah's body relented, and her shoulders dropped a bit. "I think you are saying that it's hard for you to wait for us for so long… that you want to see action or something… But…" "Thank you, Sarah," Jasmine interrupted her before she could bring polarized energy into the room again. "Please, let's just stay with this for a moment before you say anything else. Can you appreciate how difficult it is for Robert?" Sarah's features became contorted as she struggled to take the emotions in. One more time she came up with a "but" and one more time Jasmine caught her. Sarah was clearly uncomfortable, and yet she persevered and shook her head when Jasmine asked her again if she wanted someone else to do it. Finally, her voice shaking, and her hands clutching the handle of her chair, she said: "Yes, I can see how difficult it is for you, Robert. It would be for me, too, if I were living here in this… desert … that we … created … for you." Each word came with effort. Jasmine beamed at her. "Thank you, Sarah," she said, "I am really grateful for your effort."

Whenever they got to the bottom of what someone was expressing, and could capture their underlying needs in a few simple words, she wrote the phrase on the board. She was constructing the needs list that would later serve as the basis for finding a solution. She made a point of putting everything in one list, undifferentiated. Her goal was shared ownership, so there wouldn't be "LA needs vs. High Desert needs." A solution could only arise from everyone holding all the needs together. That was key to the success of the conference. It didn't matter how long it took to get there.

She still was needed, that was so clear now. She had a true ability to hear each person, to give them a sense of full compassion and love, and to get to the bottom of what mattered to them. She knew they trusted her, so there would be no posturing, no power play, only raw human expression. She knew how to work with that. She didn't want to lose the tendril of goodwill that was building up, so she asked people to come and go as needed without a formal break. By 11:45 the difference was palpable. Everyone was breathing more openly. People were laughing at her jokes and talking directly to each other. At 11:55 she felt confident enough to announce a break. She suggested people stay within their respective groups, and talk about other matters. Things still felt precarious to her.

At 1:10, when she proposed a lunch break, they were about half-way done. A local group had volunteered to cook for everyone, using mostly local ingredients. They ate outside in the cool air of late autumn. The conversation was animated. The anger was gone, at least for now. She knew some of the passion would come back when they worked on an action plan. If nothing else, how would the locals trust the LA folks to follow through on any commitment they made?

At 2:15 the van arrived with their expert guide, and they went on a tour of the valley. The only voice heard was their guide's, and he was being as observational as possible, pointing to this or that area and naming the challenges of producing enough food without access to the expected level of water. She could see that the visitors were uncomfortable. Seeing the effects of one's actions is a quick and difficult way to learn. She knew they would need support later, so that they could face this discomfort without guilt or shame and let it inform their choices when it came to crafting an agreement.

They came back to their conference room by 3:30, and took another break. This would be a long day, she thought. By now she was in full gear, excited, and completely hopeful. By 4:15 they were done generating the initial list of needs. She read the whole list out loud, and asked for any additions from either side. A couple more items were called out to the room. She could feel the clarity descend on the group almost by itself, but thought it would still be better if she named the truth out loud: the only solution that would work would be one that addressed all these needs in some fashion. They all knew they had tried to work this out through compromises in the past, and it was time to work together, beyond compromise, to full mutual care. She didn't even need to ask them to take ownership all of the needs; she could see that they all already did.

Now it was just a matter of time. She looked again at the list they had put together. Some needs showed up on almost every list she was part of constructing, such as care, flexibility, and authentic choice. Others were more specific to the situation. Trust was a big one here, for both parties. The toughest balancing act was generating movement while maintaining the commitment to no coercion. How were they going to do that? She was curious, open. It wasn't her job to find the solutions, only to guide the process.

At 4:40 she divided them into small groups of four, two from each region. Their task was to brainstorm solutions without losing track of all the needs. She and the regional mediator would float between the groups and support them as needed. As she suspected, the anger resurfaced in a couple of the groups, at which point she or the regional mediator intervened, listened, and found more needs that the anger revealed that had not yet been named or added to the list. Those were then disseminated to the other groups.

At 6:00 it was time to break for dinner. There was no breakthrough solution yet. She was disappointed with the lack of creativity. Why can't they let loose? What's holding them back? She then asked each person to go take a 15 minute walk by themselves to think about the challenges the other group was facing, and how best to address them to enable a shared outcome. Then it was time for dinner. No one had volunteered to make it for them, so she figured they would all go to a restaurant. She suggested they reconfigure the groups. This way the small groups could cross-fertilize. Maybe that would allow something new to emerge.

At 8:55, after they came back and reconfigured yet again, she was getting discouraged. Their mandate was to stay together until they came up with a solution. That would mean one more day away from home. She really didn't want that. And yet she knew she had to trust the process and give them all the time needed. Solutions cannot be made up on a timetable, not if they were to be effective, long lasting, and voluntary. She reconnected to her intention from the morning. Someone in the room would find the solution, someone affected by everything.

At 9:35, just as she was ready to call it a day, one of the groups announced that they had a solution. It was the youngest member of the group who came up with the idea. That part didn't surprise her; it often happened, because they were the least burdened with past habits. It was a stroke of genius that she herself hadn't thought of. All the groups were essentially going back and forth with variations on the same theme. It was either asking the LA region yet again to agree to reduce consumption more than was really feasible, or asking the High Desert folks yet again to be patient and stretch. The young man changed the terms. Since it wasn't *really* about water, he said, and since the most important needs were about care, he suggested that the LA region support the High Desert region by sending people every summer to support local production of food, as well as scientists who would research and propose more innovative approaches to regional sufficiency that would allow local residents a higher standard of living while remaining within their reduced means. This would not be instead of reducing consumption. The commitment was clear as day; it was just a matter of maintaining the overarching integrity with the non-coercive principles. They simply couldn't reduce consumption enough without coercion, and he wanted to have another way to care for the locals. As a rep from LA, he was confident in his ability to mobilize hundreds of youth. He trusted that many youth would find tremendous meaning in coming to Owens Valley, a way to put their passion for justice into place, and channel their own frustration with the older generation that was still attached to the old ways. The locals were moved by his passion and the clear commitment to find a workable way to care for their needs. The LA folks were inspired to see a way out of the either-or. Everyone agreed, wholeheartedly. This was no longer a compromise; no one had to give up anything. It was partnership, for the first time. Now it was time for the implementers to hammer out the fine details of the agreement.

At 10:15 they finished their celebration. Tomorrow Jasmine could go home, to her mango trees and the beauty of her own garden.

Getting Somewhere

Unani poured himself a big cup of coffee and sat for a moment to read the newsfeed. He was old enough to remember what the paper used to be like in the past. What a difference! Now, many of the articles were first-person accounts. He flipped through the pages on the screen, and paused on conflict reports. One rookie conflict mediator wrote a detailed account of his first mediation. It was between two families in a small town in Europe. Both of them had wanted the same structure to live in, one family claiming historical ties and the other insisting on easy access to a distribution center for a disabled member. He flipped on, somewhat mindless, through pages of recipes, then scientific discoveries. He paused again on decision reports to see if anything would affect his work routine. Nothing. Next a report on a recent earthquake that resulted in 20 deaths. He was so glad to see multiple perspectives on what caused the deaths. No finger pointing, just concerted effort to learn for the future. What a relief.

Suzanne walked in. He had a crush on her, which he still hadn't decided whether he wanted to act on, and which made him slightly self-conscious when she was around. He gulped the rest of his coffee, got up and went into his office. He was ready to get some work done.

He walked into the computer room to replace Jalila. He liked working after her. He could almost smell the order she left behind, without ever any mess to clean up, even if she inherited one. She was that good, and a former student to boot, from his teaching days. He felt a wave of appreciation and warmth. Jalila was exceptional, and he was sad she only came rarely, for community service. He was still hoping he could talk her into becoming a permanent, like him.

His first task every day was to ensure that public transit systems were operating at full speed. Someone had recently designed a new application that showed everything happening in real-time, anywhere. He could zoom in on any section, anywhere in the world, and see a simulation based on real signals sent by people. Despite the concern about residual surveillance trauma, there was a 95% participation level. Almost everyone wanted to support the increased flexibility available to the system from knowing ahead of time the level of traffic. He enjoyed watching the little simulated people who were waiting for buses, moving, or standing. It was a nice break from the previous way of only looking at columns of data.

The system was constantly self-correcting, calculating averages for every hour of the day, every day of the week and month, the season. Small buses were doing short routes through the little streets, connecting with double-deckers running on major arteries. If anyone ever waited for more than four minutes, an entire review process would be put in motion. Part of his job was to do all he could to prevent that kind of wait from happening.

During the transition, which Unani remembered vividly, providing reliable transportation that people wouldn't have to walk many blocks to find was a key commitment by the conversion enthusiasts. Initially, they worked really hard to accommodate all the complicated and confusing requests. People, used to the convenience of having their own car, were slow to recognize the benefits of not having to drive everywhere. By now, few skeptics remained, especially since the option of asking for personal transportation was available to anyone in need. One solid evidence of the robustness of the system was how rare such requests had come to be.

Walking and biking were widespread, though not part of his job to monitor. They were on their own, little dots on his map. There was something immensely satisfying about seeing everyone get to their destination without frustration, without conflict, and without taxing the environment so much. He never wanted to do anything else, even though a job like his could easily be rotated. He and his colleagues could easily choose to do this job from home, and they almost invariably chose to come to the office, to have company, human contact.

Next it was time to look at the more personalized segments of the monitoring system – people with unusual itineraries, and goods. The automatic dispatch orders had gone out smoothly. Everything entered by midnight was sorted and assigned without any human intervention. He pulled up a list of them, and clicked on a few to check. All seemed in order. Although creating routes is inherently impossible to optimize completely, they were getting better and better at creating workable algorithms.[100] Sometimes this would result in routes that were slightly longer than a human eye would make. The

---

[100] This is a real-life mathematical limitation, since the possibilities grow exponentially, and no computer program could be built to address an exponential set of options.

overall savings in resources were immense. Everything seemed in order today.

Next he pulled up the live requests screen. Most of them were immediately being picked up by drivers, flickering on the screen for a moment and then disappearing into the archive. The system tracked where everyone was and only those within a certain radius got notice of each request.

A wave of satisfaction brought a grin to his face. One of the design principles of the system they were using was having as little human intervention needed as possible. No one had to approve or moderate anything. Everyone entered their own requests, unless they had some physical or emotional challenge, in which case someone would do it for them.

A couple of requests were still in the queue. He clicked one open. No wonder no one picked it up. It was at the far range of his district, a rural community with very few residents, far enough and sparse enough that it wouldn't show up on anyone's screen. He dialed a few numbers, and got one of the drivers on the phone. Yes, she could make the detour and pick up the velvet chair for delivery.

His computer started beeping, two signals going off at once. A truck carrying vegetables to the hospital had a mechanical failure and needed to be replaced ASAP, and a woman in labor urgently requested a driver. He hated triaging.

"Suzanne," he called out, "can you help me out? I've got two emergencies at once."

"Sure thing, Unani," her voice was friendly. He liked working with her. They were responsible for two different parts of the region, and stepped in to help each other often during their shift. "Which one do you want me to handle?"

"I have a woman in labor needing an urgent driver. I'll re-assign it to you," he said, relieved. He looked at her leaning toward her computer. "Thanks," he added, "I hope it's not too much trouble." She smiled.

He turned back to solve his other problem. What a mess, a whole truck to replace. Lunch for hospital patients, can't be delayed too much. He sorted all travel by location and vehicle type to look for another truck. One was already 60 miles away, too far to do any good, moving into another coordinator's territory. Another was delivering milk, which couldn't be delayed either. He scratched his head going down the list. Close to the end he saw the solution. It was only three miles away from the breakdown, a delicate load, which needed attention and could easily wait a few hours: pianos.

He put in a call to a technician to attend to the broken truck, then sent a message to the piano truck driver to change routes, disconnect the cargo, connect to the other load, deliver, then come back and pick up the pianos again. Was the driver sure he could handle it? Yes, he was happy to serve.

The phone rang. His housemate alerted him that the cat just disappeared again, the fourth time this month, and asked him to pick up some veggies for dinner. While he was on the phone, Suzanne walked in to let him know the labor transportation was handled.

"You got a minute?" her voice was still friendly, as always. He sensed tension, though, and was taken aback.

"For you? Of course," he tried to sound casual.

"Thank you. I'm going to sit down now," she added, a bit awkward. She looked at him, smiled for a moment, too briefly, clearly nervous.

"What I wanted to talk with you about is very uncomfortable, and I'm not sure I can do it with enough grace." She paused and looked at him intently. He blushed a little, and wished to disappear.

"You haven't said a word to me," she continued, steady, still awkward. "But I know you are interested in me. Oh, I hope I am not mistaken. That would be so unpleasant." She laughed, a short, nervous laugh, and looked at him expectantly. Even nervous she looked great. Her eyes were brown and gentle, her hair wavy, down to her shoulders. It was her eyes, and her smile, and her way of taking care of everyone so well, that particularly appealed to him. She was a permanent, like him, and they ran into each other several times a week. She came up with the most upbeat, outrageous, and creative ways to solve problems during their weekly transportation meetings. He liked her a lot.

He nodded, just to get her out of her misery, and didn't feel up to saying anything.

"Thank you," she smiled sheepishly, somewhat relieved. "I am very flattered that you are taking an interest in me." She paused. The hard part was still ahead of her, and he could tell she wasn't having an easy time. He knew what was coming; he'd heard it before, many times. She was going to say that she liked him a lot, but not as a potential lover. He wanted to scream.

"Look," she did exactly that. "I really like you a lot..."

"But not as a potential lover, right?" he chimed in, trying his best not to sound sarcastic.

"Ouch," she said. "I get a sense that this is not the first time this has happened to you, and I imagine it's painful to hear it again and again." It was harder than he imagined, and yet he appreciated how she was handling it. "I'm wondering if part of what's so hard is that you don't know why, because everyone has been uncomfortable telling you?" No wonder he had a crush on her.

"Yes," he said. "That's exactly it. Everyone has been evasive, as if that would make it less painful. Well, it doesn't. I wish it was something I could work on, change, make sense of. I'm afraid it's just something about who I am that I can't change and I will always be alone."

"I'm open to telling you what it is for me if you want to hear," now she sounded her usual authentic self, no longer constrained by the pressure of the bad news. He appreciated her for telling it like it was.

"Yes, I would like to hear. Just be gentle." He swallowed uneasily.

"It's hard to say what it is," she proceeded. "You really are such an exceptional person, and I love our conversations. I love working with you, all of it. It's just that you seem somehow as if you don't have a body." She was uncomfortable again. "I dance a lot, and I want a lover who can move with me." It was painful to hear, of course. And it was true. He never danced because he was afraid he would look foolish. "I get a sense that you are only interested in your screens, conversation, and humor," she continued. "I don't know exactly what it would take for you to open up in this way." She paused, more present, and looked at him.

"Yes," he said, "I know what you're talking about. My body has always been sort of secondary to me. I never quite know when or how to hug people. I just didn't know it was so obvious, that others could see despite my efforts to hide it."

"So you're not mad at me for saying this?"

"Not at all, really," he said, somehow encouraged. "You've just told me what I need to do to be more available. This was the best rejection I've ever received."

They both smiled, and he added, "Maybe we could have lunch together anyway?" He was somehow hopeful. Maybe he could learn. "Sure," she said. "How about Thursday?" Maybe that was why he didn't feel humiliated. She left open some possibility for the future.

His screen started beeping again. "Now I gotta run," he said, then turned the screen so they could both see it. "You see these dots? They are actually people who want to get somewhere." He waited a moment. "Like me," he added softly, braving a smile. "I better help them go there."

Look What I Found

Guillermo had completely forgotten that he had checked the "available for extra service" box when he filled out his weekly snapshot. Emergencies around community service were rare. Still, some happened, and today was one of them. Someone couldn't show up for their primary service spot. Guillermo checked his netter. Sure enough, it was garbage collection. It would either be that or childcare.

He often chose garbage collection as his community service. He liked the orderliness of it, the support his choice gave others who were less inclined to work with garbage, and, more than anything, the complete surprise about what he would find in the piles.

Everything was sorted through. Even though each household was requested to reach the zero-waste goal, ten years after the transition many people had still not gotten used to the new arrangements, as if they couldn't assume that much awareness or responsibility. Some would discard, again and again, items that could be easily reused. So he would get to sort through all of that, and find creative uses for things. What would he find today?

David, his six-year-old son, often came with him on garbage collection days, and helped sort the piles. After a while he would drop him off in the learning center, if that's where he wanted to go, or he would stay with him the whole time if he was interested enough. Would he want to come today?

David liked to know what he would do ahead of time; he wasn't wild about last minute changes. He also loved doing garbage collection with Guillermo. Guillermo looked at his son struggling with this hard balancing act, enjoying his concentration, his capacity to make decisions, and his quirkiness. He himself was impulsive, making decisions at the drop of a hat, adapting to circumstances with ease. David weighed the decision carefully for a few minutes, silent, focused inwards. "I'm coming with you, Dad," he said with his glorious smile. "Let's go play with all that cool stuff."

They walked to the corner, to the main street, to catch the bus to the service center. Guillermo had participated in the recent redesign of the basic transportation grid. He knew where all the regular bus lines were going. There was no need to ask for individualized transportation where they were going.

Guillermo reported for duty and let the dispatcher know he had his son with him. The guy barely raised his eyes. Guillermo felt a flash of annoyance. He was here to help, everyone was here to help, so why couldn't the dispatcher treat them with respect? What was wrong with him? Why was he so surly? The annoyance didn't last. Just that last question reminded him to notice the guy and the surroundings. Everyone at the center was moving faster than he ever remembered. It must be a bad day for him. He decided to connect. He looked at his badge to know his name: Bernard.

"Is today busier than usual?" he asked.

Bernard raised his eyes and took a quick look at him. "Yeah, man, I'm scrambling," he responded. "I had four people drop out of primary this morning, and I still don't have enough coverage." Then he was friendlier. "Hi," he turned his attention to David. "What's your name? Are you going with daddy today?"

David smiled shyly, then clung to Guillermo's pants. "He's David. He's often a little shy with strangers." The tension was melting.

Guillermo got his assigned route from Bernard, along with overalls for himself and little ones for David. They put them on and laughed at each other. The driver was another permanent, and his name was sewn on his overalls, like Bernard's. He shook a firm hand with Guillermo, and then bent down to David. "Hi there," he said to him. "My name is Jonathan, and you and I and your dad will hang out together for a while. I'd love to know your name, too." David smiled. He was less shy with this guy, who was, after all, friendlier; no surprises there. "David." That's all he said for now.

The vehicle they were driving was carefully designed. During conversion time, people in each region were asked for input about their experience of garbage collection, and anything they wanted to see change in that system to work better. In most urban areas in the world the number one issue with garbage that people had was the noise of the trucks. So a call went out to all who wanted to participate in intensive design of a silent engine. The resulting vehicle was solar and hydraulic. Garbage trucks now zoomed quietly through the streets of urban centers all over the world.

Most of the sorting was done on the spot, and everything was put into different flexible-size compartments on the back of the truck. Their goal, by the end of their shift, was to have an empty "garbage" bin, and to find some use for everything that they collected. Maybe the word garbage no longer even applied, not in San Francisco, at least. Compost collection was now fully owned by neighborhoods. All organic matter could be composted within a block or two, right by one of the many urban gardens that sprouted all over town everywhere possible. After all, San Francisco was one of the world leaders in urban food growing, a movement that started in the earlier part of the century.[101] All that was being discarded was whatever non-recyclable packaging was still being used, and anything that was broken. At least that was the ideal.

They reached the first house on their assigned route. The residents of this five-unit building had left three bins out on the street: recycle, reuse, and discard. Jonathan parked the truck, and proceeded to deal with the first two. David and Guillermo, meanwhile, emptied the "discard" bin into the truck's sorting area and started their familiar game, a fake competition: who would imagine more uses for each thing they found.

There wasn't much. Most things were no longer packaged now that plastic was produced only on demand for very specific uses. Every time a collector could find something useful to do with an item, a note was left behind for the residents. Sure enough, year by year, people were getting more and more imaginative about reusing things. Guillermo loved seeing the notes people sometimes left with their "reuse" items, explaining how they thought the item could be used, sometimes leaving a phone number. It was fun to drop off all they found at the recycle and reuse unit in the service center and pass along the treasures of the day.

David found, fell in love with, and kept a discarded doll with only one leg. They also found things neither of them had ever seen. Here was a collection of old bottle caps of different sizes, which mesmerized David. Guillermo, meanwhile, was caught up in annoyance. Why would they think those couldn't be used again? Guillermo was always surprised by people, especially around computers and phones. Why can't they get that computers and phones are fully reusable even when they malfunction? Old habits die hard, he thought sadly.

---

[101] Urban food growing, in community gardens and in backyards, is already happening in San Francisco, though it's far from being a significant source of food in the city. In Havana, Cuba, more than 50% of fresh produce is grown within the city.

Next they moved to a large apartment building. They emptied the contents of the "discard" bin into the sorting area, and proceeded to look through. "Look what I found, daddy," came the ecstatic call. Guillermo looked up from the pile of entangled packaging material he had uncovered, and saw David hold up a broken children's robot. David's expression was super clear: he wanted to keep the robot in addition to the doll he had been playing with. That was the risk of taking David with him. Like most children, he wanted everything fun they found. That's why parents were asked to do what they could to spread the flow of resources, even used ones. Guillermo wasn't relishing the necessity of negotiating with David about that. For a split second he wished forcing children was still the norm. He could see the appeal, the ease of making things happen. He also knew the immense cost of coercion, at any level. So he took a long breath and said: "I can see that you really want to keep this robot, too. I would much rather not, because I want other children to have a chance to play with some of the toys we are collecting, too. I want there to be enough for everyone. How disappointed would you be if we let go of it?" David thought for a while. Guillermo loved that about him. He knew what he wanted, and took the time to find it. "How about I take it just until the next time we go garbage hunting? This way I can play with it some, and then other kids can have it." Guillermo looked at his handheld. His next scheduled garbage collection time was only three weeks away. He weighed it for a moment, and said: "That'll work, sonny. I just want to check with you if you think you can be satisfied with just these two pieces?" David nodded emphatically. The negotiation didn't turn out to be so hard. It was only the memory of his own childhood that made it seem difficult. He remembered the power struggles with his parents. Yes, that's why he was so reluctant to negotiate. He could count on only one hand the number of times David had thrown a tantrum. It made sense, too. David knew that his needs mattered. Guillermo had never trusted that. He was grateful for the parenting class he and his partner took before David was born, how it helped him make the choice to hold David's needs with such respect. That has made such a difference.

They went back to sorting things quietly, efficiently. Guillermo stopped from time to time to look at David, just to enjoy him. At six, he could take care of some things on his own already. Toys went into one bin; anything that looked even remotely useable by kids' projects, including most packaging, went into another bin; computers he had to call Guillermo to put in the right bin. "What an amazing treat," he thought, "that children, my child, get to contribute directly to making things work." David didn't even notice Guillermo looking at him. He was completely engrossed in his activities. For him, there was nothing unusual.

Cauliflower

It was time to bring his dilemma to his daughter and her family. They had made it clear they needed a significant amount of help, and André had promised he would make himself available. That would mean letting go of his farm, or at least of experimenting with unusual varieties, hard-to-grow vegetables, off-season growing, and all the things that he loved so much. It was a hard choice to make. He really enjoyed what he did, contributing as much as he did, knowing so much. Neighbors would come to him for gardening advice, and he was a regular contributor on the gardening hotline. He had been growing vegetables and herbs since before the transition. From time to time he had visitors from far away regions who came to see his amazing array of rare cultivars and heirloom varieties. He was somewhat reluctant to let go of the exotic and the challenging.

It wouldn't just be his loss. Other people depended on the food he grew. Like now: day after day, for over a week, the same few items had been showing up on the top of the request list. Everything else appeared for a few hours and was immediately picked up. The system worked. Except that these few items – all cruciferous veggies, the ones bred specifically for their cancer-fighting properties – remained on the list for so long he was getting worried there wouldn't be enough of them around, because it would be too late for planting. They were his specialty; he participated in developing those cultivars, and in years past he had been growing a significant proportion of what was requested in the region. Was there really no one else who could respond to these requests? He didn't know what would happen.

Everyone had been reminded so many times, and had reminded each other, never to do anything they weren't truly willing to do. Could it really be that after all these years there just wouldn't be enough people with enough willingness to do enough of what's needed? Maybe the skeptics were right, after all. He remembered the early days. Those who didn't believe in the concept kept issuing dire warnings that the system would collapse. The bitter struggles were still etched in his memory, the effort it took to come to where enough people were willing to give it a try. And then it worked. Region after region joined as they saw the successes. After all these years, after all the successes, everything they've done, it was painful to imagine that of all places his county would fail.

Even before the transition, he took leadership in his county, introducing permaculture, urban gardening on a significant scale, and local distribution of surplus food from each family's garden. As a result, his county, Auvergne,[102] suffered very minor disruptions and even took on providing food for surrounding areas. For an area that had been considered "an isolated region with limited industrial and economic development," that was no small accomplishment. He didn't want to lose faith, and yet....

He had been keeping this all to himself, hoping and wishing someone would pick up some of the persistent requests for the vegetables he wasn't going to grow. It was getting too late. It was time to include more people. He dreaded telling his daughter how stressed out he was at seeing these requests not attended to. It would have been so much easier if there had already been a growing season where he showed her family he really could shift priorities. They had been through such a process together. He was completely on board, despite his deep sense of loss. The twins, his grandchildren, needed more attention than anyone had imagined. At eight, they were still in diapers, making little eye contact, and with a minimal vocabulary. They were receiving exceptional care from many, and yet his daughter Claire insisted that someone from the immediate family had to be an ongoing part of the care. She and her husband Guillaume had been taking turns doing it for years and they were exhausted, his own wife had died, and there simply was no one else left but him. He knew it was still the old way of thinking. It didn't *have* to be him. The twins needed someone they could have ongoing connection with; they didn't need *him*. He also knew that he hadn't been there enough for Claire before the transition. His vegetables, and his civic action, always took precedence. He wanted to make her a priority this time, to offer her some symbolic healing, to be such a major part of supporting her.

Why on earth would no one else sign up to do the damn vegetables? He tried to imagine them, the other growers close by and around the region. This was one of his weaknesses: he found it so hard to have empathy for people he judged as not caring enough.

---

[102] Auvergne is a region in France with the correct climactic conditions (at least in the present) to grow cauliflower, though I am not aware whether or not it is actually grown there.

This wasn't just about someone wanting some fancy food item. These were vegetables for healing. He just couldn't really get into understanding what it felt like to look at someone's need and not be completely propelled to want to do something about it. Was it that they had so much else going on in their lives that it was hard to find the energy? Were they protecting something that was invisible to him? Did they somehow believe the need would go away? Or maybe they just had more faith that someone else would attend to it? That last one was what made it hardest. He wanted everyone to feel personally responsible for everything, like he did. And yet... wasn't he doing the very same now, hoping that someone else would do it so he wouldn't have to face his family's disappointment again?

He stepped outside. The rain had stopped temporarily. He looked at the mountains, the mist in the air, the fallow vegetable beds, the herb spiral, fertile, getting ready for spring. He never grew tired of the majesty of the mountains, especially when the sun painted them red. This was going to be his first season of not growing. His heart was willing, his hands were itching for the soil.

He walked over to the cottage, where his Claire's family lived. Breakfast would be ready. A new batch of cheese just ripened yesterday and they were all waiting to try it out. The twins would not be there. Their care person was helping them get dressed and ready for the day, not a small task. He was greeted by the aroma of coffee as he walked in, and Claire's smile. Guillaume was pulling freshly made rolls out of the oven, and soon they were all sitting, sipping on their coffee and chattering away. He gathered up his strength.

"I need to talk to you about something serious," he said unsteadily.

"You're not going to grow vegetables again. This is non-negotiable," Claire snapped back immediately.

"Look," he said, "I don't know what the right thing to do is. I just know that no one else is signing up." He didn't feel very hopeful.

"I don't care," she said emphatically. His own daughter was like them, she didn't care. How could his own daughter not care? "They'll figure it out," she continued. "What if you died tomorrow? You think the whole world depends on you?" He felt his entire body contract, just what he dreaded would happen.

Guillaume came to the rescue. "Claire, please let your father speak first before you jump. He knows how stressful it's been, he's agreed to be of support to us. Let him say what he needs to say."

"I came to talk with you because I want your input. I can't bear to look at that screen and imagine the people who might not have the healing food they so need. I just don't know what to do. I want your help. That's all. I'm not saying I won't be with the twins. I want to; I love them. I just want help." He was nervously repeating himself, and stopped abruptly. Claire looked at him. He wanted her to be like him, to be proud of him for caring so much. She was too drained for that. Eight years of raising the twins had taken a toll on her, despite her essentially sunny disposition.

"I'm so sad not to be able to hear you, dad," she said. "I just can't think of anything but the twins. And myself. I must have a break or I will go nuts, and you know it."

It was Guillaume again, this time talking to André. "I think she needs some reassurance, some way to trust that you're not going to back off, because she's beyond her limit." Ever since Claire married him the father-daughter relationship had improved dramatically. Without Guillaume it wouldn't have occurred to them to live in such close quarters.

André stood there, not quite sure what to do. He was still agitated, still wanted Claire to just be open to hearing him. Just then the sun came in through the window and the light made Claire look like his mother. Most of what he remembered of her was the endless fighting he witnessed. How did humanity survive so many centuries with so little trust? His father would interpret whatever his mother said in the worst possible way, then he would react sarcastically, and she would be hurt and defensive. So few people knew how to reach out, be vulnerable, or show compassion. His parents certainly didn't. They regularly spiraled out of control and into name-calling and nastiness. He would run away and hide in his room until things calmed down. He was only eight when she died, the exact age of the twins. He looked at Claire, at her worn-out face, the premature wrinkles. He didn't have to fight with his one and only daughter.

And so he took her hand, and stroked it with his big peasant hands, without saying much, and then collected her into his arms and rocked her back and forth, like he used to do when she was a little girl. She smiled feebly. "We'll figure this out together," he said gently, even though he had no idea how.

"Have you talked with any of the other local growers? You're their hero. Why wouldn't they step in to help?" This was Guillaume trying to problem solve. "You were raised before the transition, and you know you don't ask for help enough. Go to them; they'll help you." André had to admit this was true. He hadn't taken any steps to make it work. He struggled with interdependence even though he totally knew it was the only way to be. He was still trying to do everything by himself.

That afternoon, when he was done with the twins, he called Gaston, then Pierre, and then Bernadette. All of them said no. Each had their own compelling reasons, not any less significant than his. None of them had any brilliant ideas. All of them were glad he had called and encouraged him to call again if he didn't find a solution, just to talk it out. By the evening he was feeling desperate again.

Then the phone rang. The woman introduced herself as Anouk, spoke rapidly, and explained to him that she really wanted to do a vegetable apprenticeship and no one would take her because she was already in her 40s. As a last-ditch attempt she poked around the gardening hotline, and then she saw his picture. She went on and on about how she based all her decisions on intuition, and how she knew that apprenticing with him was exactly what she needed. Would he take her? He liked her immediately. But what was he going to do? He said he wasn't going to grow vegetables this year, and told her about the twins. Then she started laughing. "Well, then," she said, "that clearly settles it. I knew you were the right person." It turned out that her mother had studied with the Kaufmans[103] and trained her, and what she had been doing for years was work with children who suffered just like the twins. "You see," she concluded, "I'll help you with the twins, you'll teach me how to grow vegetables."

After he hung up the phone he walked over to the computer. He felt dazed by the way things had just worked out. He just hoped Anouk wasn't one of those people he could never fathom, the ones who think God or somebody orchestrates these things. Nothing much had changed on the screen since the morning. He clicked on cauliflower, satisfied, and entered his name.

---

[103] The Kaufmans are the founders of the Option Institute and the Son-Rise program for caring for children with a diagnosis of autism and other special needs.

What Can I Do?

Dmitri didn't even have to open the email that had just arrived to guess the content. Why would it be any different from all the others? Every single one of his friends was already plugged in, doing something they liked that contributed to the whole. He was still stuck with only community service or temporary jobs. They were OK, he turned down the ones he really didn't want. It's just that they weren't what he really wanted.

He forced himself to look at the email. Sure enough, almost word for word what the others had said. There wasn't any room in their factory for one more process flow engineer.[104] They would contact him if something opened up. Dmitri wasn't surprised. It was a desperate measure to contact factories proactively. Standard procedure was to post his availability and let the system sort things out and do the initial matching. Why did this process work for everyone else and not for him? Leon and Griselda, his buddies from the fabulous apprenticeship program they had all attended, found a placement within weeks of posting, and had been happily placed ever since, each in a very cool place. He envied them. He'd been waiting for nine months already since his last placement fell through. What was the problem?

The day was stretching ahead of him, empty. He was tired of reading and watching movies. The day before he was so fed up with it all that he showed up at a food distribution center, just to work the shift, even though they hadn't posted an opening on the community service bulletin. It was a bad move to begin with, and got worse as soon as he started commenting on improvements they could make with sorting and storing produce. This always happened. He couldn't help himself, he always saw the savings in energy. That was his training, from childhood. His mother, Anya, was one of the early pioneers of redefining process flow to include environmental and community implications.[105] What a mixed blessing to be her son. He

---

[104] When the term process flow engineering came to me, I thought I had invented it. To be sure, I did some research and discovered that it is an actual discipline that exists today, which I didn't know about. The context of this story expands the usual parameters of that work that are in place today.
[105] This is not currently part of process flow engineering.

suspected that had something to do with his difficulties in finding a placement, though he was never sure exactly how that worked.

It wasn't about survival. Thank God no one had to worry about that any more. He read history books, he knew what it was like in the olden days. Most people were working just to get a paycheck. What an archaic notion. He felt for them. During the massive changes that happened at transition time someone calculated just how many meaningless, or repetitive, and certainly energy-consuming jobs existed. The study concluded that, however well-intentioned the people holding these jobs were, more often than not their work served to ensure that only some people could have access to resources. This included people monitoring bureaucratic regulations, security guards of all kinds, health insurance staff deciding what services were available to whom, and the entire financial sector. All of that was now over. That human energy and the many resources consumed in their futile efforts were then channeled into the massive project of recovering from the severe conditions caused by climate change, while learning to live again within the means of only one planet, consuming and discarding only what could be regenerated.[106]

A new email arrived. This time it was from the support center. When it wasn't *his* life, he really appreciated the automatic reminders to people who were not fully plugged in, not participating in the community, like him, that they could always come and talk to someone. Not now. "Don't rub it in," he thought to himself.

He jumped up abruptly and opened the fridge. Nothing appealed to him. He wasn't really hungry, just restless. His room felt so stuffy. He opened the window, which allowed a little breeze to come in. Outside, people were walking and biking, a bus went by, just the usual bustle of daily living. None of them had any knowledge of his plight. He wanted to scream.

The phone rang, and Janika's smiling face showed up on his screen. He looked at the mirror before picking up, unhappy with what he saw. It couldn't be fixed fast enough. The smile left Janika's face soon after he accepted the call. "You look terrible, Dmitri." Her forehead wrinkled in concern and he wanted to hang up.

"I'm OK, I just didn't shave today," he lied.

---

[106] At present, each year we are globally consuming resources that would require the planet a year and five months to regenerate. We are consuming future generations' resources.

"Don't even try," she said, trying to smile again. An awkward silence followed. What was there to say? "Listen," she continued, "I'm not going to sit still while you're in such agony. Talk to me."

Shit, he thought, why can't she leave me alone? He came out with "there's nothing to say" instead.

"It's just a phase, it will sort itself out."

No, it won't, he thought grimly. How could he possibly tell her that? He tried to change the subject. "So, how's your mom?" he said. Part of him hoped she wouldn't fall for his trick. Another part was relieved that she did.

"She's all right, it was really just a little virus, nothing serious." He tuned her out, he wasn't really interested in her mom. "I gotta go," he blurted, finally. "Are you up for going to the movies tomorrow?" She was, they made plans, he told her he loved her, knowing he didn't mean it any more. He still couldn't bear to lose her.

The conversation ended, his stomach was finally growling. He opened the fridge again. Nothing appealed to him, still. He didn't feel like cooking. He couldn't stomach the dining hall, to feel everyone's eyes on him, and, besides, he hadn't told them he would come today. It was only the 12th, and he was, once again, close to using up his monthly allowance for restaurants, and didn't feel up to asking for more based on special circumstances. His mother's place was out of the question. She would know better than to ask him anything, and she didn't need to, he could recite her questions by heart. No good options. Some aging broccoli with scrambled eggs was where he landed, surprised by how tasty they were once made.

Out. It's time to go out. He didn't know where, just that it was time to go. He let his feet take him, lost in feeling sorry for himself. He was so good at what he did, why didn't anyone want him?

Almost as an afterthought he turned right into a small street, and bingo. There he was standing in front of the support center. Nothing to lose, he thought, as he walked in and asked to see someone for empathy. He had done community service there before, and so he knew the ropes. Sometimes the permanents were less sharp than those who were there for the day from time to time. Maybe they had too much pain to witness. Maybe they needed more support for themselves.

The walls in the waiting room were decorated with dozens and dozens of pictures of different people. Some of them had little "thank you" notes under them. Dmitri plunked himself on one of the chairs and plugged his netter in to connect with the larger screen. His fingers moved deftly on the little keyboard as he typed various searches. From time to time he liked to look up the happenings in some distant place, the little news stories, those provided by the local people. It made the world come alive for a moment when he saw that in Barranquilla, far across the ocean, a group of teenagers helped out elderly people whose homes had been destroyed in a flash flood.[107]

"Dmitri Shostakovsky?" Always a little startled to hear his name in a public place, he followed the teenage girl. She introduced herself as Dorota, and escorted him to a room. She didn't make the obligatory joke about the composer,[108] so he didn't have to tell her it was not quite the same name. A super comfortable couch and several chairs were waiting for him. "Where shall I sit?" he said. Dorota made a gesture to imply total freedom. He picked the couch, a little self-conscious, and sat down. Could he trust Dorota? He suddenly wanted to go home.

"I think no one will ever want me for work," he jumped straight to what he couldn't tell Janika, determined to use the opportunity. "I feel cursed by being my mother's son." He cleared his throat, which suddenly felt narrow and dry. "She taught me most of what I know, and she's also cast a long shadow." Dorota's eyes looked kind, soft, peaceful. "I've been looking, even actively looking, for nine months. It's not happening."

He knew the training she must have been through to be with him on her own. She must be really good, he thought, to be given an intake without a co-listener. As if she was reading his mind, she said: "Are you trying to relax into trusting me? I get a sense that you are really tired of this situation and could really use some breakthrough." He smiled in appreciation. He liked her presence, but didn't say it. Dorota broke the silence again.

"I can really imagine how much you would want to be given free rein to be yourself, and evaluated as yourself, without reference to your mother." Yes, she was, indeed, sharp. His eyes smarted, and he looked down, maybe he could make the tears go away. How

---

[107] Barranquilla is a port city in Colombia and is, indeed, a place where flash floods happen regularly.
[108] Dmitri Shostakovich is a 20th century Russian composer.

annoying. He couldn't bear to speak, knowing his voice would betray him. She waited, with more grace than he would have predicted, just breathing silently with him. His shoulders relaxed, and he rearranged himself on the couch, slouching a little less.

The wave of sadness passed, and he could look at her again. Her gaze, even though he hadn't been looking at her, was unwavering. Her eyes were so clear, and very blue. He lowered his eyes again, the intimacy of the silence embarrassing for him.

"Is there more you want to tell me, or do you want to take more time to find your equilibrium?" The tears came back, different this time, surprisingly welcome. There was such relief in letting them flow. He really didn't need to protect himself with Dorota. His eyes caught hers. This time he was ready to speak, whatever his voice was going to do.

"Yes, you got the essence of it. It's so annoying. But that's not all there is. You know, I did have two previous posts that fell apart. I think I got in the door just because of my mother. That sucks. I almost didn't want to go." Dorota remained attentive. He was grateful to her. "Maybe I shouldn't have taken that position," he added, almost as an afterthought. "But I did, and they didn't like me in the end. I don't know why, and I'm too scared to ask. And now no one wants me. I feel so lost." Now he was crying and crying, months' worth of crying, letting down all his protectiveness.

"I'm so glad you finally get to cry," she said. How on earth did she know, he wondered, and didn't let that thought stop him. "You've been holding this in for a long, long time, haven't you?" He nodded, then reached for the pile of handkerchiefs to wipe off his dripping nose, laughing awkwardly. After another while she spoke again: "Is not getting the 'why' the hardest part?"

Nope, he thought, almost satisfied that she got it wrong, for once. Out loud he said: "You're good, Dorota, but not this time. The worst of it is that I've been down on myself. I know better," he hastened to add, not liking the thought of her educating him about this, tired of knowing so much about her work. "I don't know why I let it slide so long. I wish I came sooner."

"Down on yourself for …?" Such a light touch, just to match his rawness.

"Not sure. I've been spinning… It's not making sense… Like it's my fault, somehow, that I'm my mother's son and I'm not better placed." How could he possibly make it clear? If she could only see him and his mother together for a minute she would know, he wouldn't need so many words.

"Tell me something," she said, still so gentle. "Do you ever talk with your mom about this?"

He snorted. "Are you kidding? I can't talk with her about anything. I don't need to, either, because it's all on her face. She's disappointed, and she feels guilty, and that just makes it worse."

Dorota's eyes darted for a moment, and when she came back she was clearly in a different space. "I need some guidance from you," she said, a little more serious, maybe even nervous. "Do you want to get support with your relationship with your mom, or with finding a placement for you that can work?" No judgment on her part, he was impressed. And he appreciated the focus, the clarity; it was supportive for him.

"Let's focus on work," he said, sitting up some more. "That's what I came here for, and I got enough support to know there's no way around having her and me talk."

Dorota smiled, she looked relieved. "I'm glad for that. You may be surprised. She may be waiting for you to bring it up… there may be much that she wants to say to you, too. You will do this, right?"

"Yes," he said. "I will, I promise. I see that I've never given her a chance. Now, can we talk about work? What are my options?"

She didn't follow. "Wait a minute," she said. "There's one more thing before. Don't you want to understand why this is happening?" He shrugged his shoulders and insisted that he really didn't know what was going on. She persisted, and he relented.

Slowly, bit by bit, they uncovered what was going on. It *was*, after all, about his mother, or, more accurately, about how he responded to having her as his mother. He could never trust that anyone would see him for what he was bringing, separate from her. And so he was tense, and intent on proving himself and showing everyone that he knew a lot and had good ideas, like her. Empathy did its magic. For the first time, perhaps ever, he was able to feel some compassion for himself, for what it was like to be in his mother's shadow.

Now he could also understand the people who didn't want to work with him. Being as unsure of himself as he was, he was bombarding everyone with new ideas almost incessantly, certainly faster than they could integrate them, and defensively. It all made sense.

Dorota was right there with him all the way, and they'd reached some inner destination, a place of real peace inside him. But that wasn't quite like finding a placement. The problem was still there. "OK, I know why you didn't let me go to options before. But now I'm so ready I don't even want to hear one more empathy guess. Ever." He was being a little playful and over-dramatic, and they both laughed.

She composed herself, and reviewed the possible directions.

He could just keep trying, and come for more support if he got down again. He shook his head vigorously. "I'm done with that, too depressing."

Or he could shift gears and learn something different that he could do, be productive in a different way. "I don't know that I can do that," he was hesitant, "but I wouldn't rule it out. Not entirely. Just that all my life, since as far back as I can remember, I was on this path. It's like walking for 30 miles on a road and then you reach a dead end no one told you about when the road started. I'm too far on this path. You know what I mean?" She nodded. "I totally get it," she said, because words carried more clarity than smiles. "You've invested so much, and that's how you recognize yourself as you, right?" Yes, that was it.

And so then there was the third option, which would be to seek full feedback from everyone along his path, and do the hard work of integrating it sufficiently that he could look for work again, freshly, and differently. "Shit," he said, "I don't like that one either. Now what? How can I find a path now?" He was in anguish again, nothing looked possible.

"Dmitri," Dorota started, "can you tell if process flow engineering is a true passion for you? Or is it really just an identity? I can't answer for you. This is something you have to know for yourself."

He didn't answer right away, just let the memories flood him, of going with his mother to different places and being fascinated to see what she did, from early on. "I want to think about it more. It's not so simple, I don't know quite yet how to separate out the two." He was facing something big, and didn't quite have the words for it. "Maybe it will be easier after I talk with my mother," he added softly.

"For now, I want to know what's possible in other directions, and then I'll think about it. I just don't know if I am strong enough to face the feedback... but maybe it's worth it." He looked up at Dorota, who was smiling confidently, like she'd been doing this for centuries. "Before I go, though, I want to know what's possible if I do change paths." They pored over some screens together, and came up with a few leads, people he could interview, study with, learn from about what would most serve him and be needed.

Now it was time to go. "Thank you, Dorota," he said as he got up to leave. "Whatever I end up choosing, I got a lot from talking with you. I have a bunch of things to sort out, and I will."

He walked out to the street, which looked different already. He felt lighter, hopeful, curious to know what would come next. He could even imagine calling Janika and telling her; she would be happy. Neither he nor Dorota were alive before the transition. For them this kind of exchange was just the way things were now done. The new normal.

Mounting Resentment

Kiyoko was getting to the end of her impassioned presentation. The last slide showed the calculations. They were truly impressive. The proposed new production design would cut energy use by another 3% without adding any more human effort. She turned off the screen, waited for the cheering to end, and invited everyone to sit in a circle with her.

"Now we need five volunteers to stay after hours for the next couple of weeks to test it out," she said, after explaining in detail what the new production flow would entail. It was all pretty straightforward. Sachiko was impressed with the elegance of the solutions the committee had designed. "We all know that translating from paper to real life doesn't always work," Kiyoko continued. "I know you've been covering for my absence while I participated in this committee. This will be one more push and we'll be done. Is anyone up for it?"

It took Sachiko a long moment before she raised her hand slowly. She looked around and saw another twelve hands up, way more than enough. She could have predicted every single one of these, she thought unhappily. This pattern of some people repeatedly not volunteering had been going on for many, many months, maybe for as long as she'd been working in this production facility. It was getting harder and harder to do all she could. Or, put differently, she found herself having less and less willingness to step forward and do things.

Kiyoko was oblivious to the situation. She picked five people, thankfully not Sachiko herself this time, thanked everyone for their willingness, and soon the circle dispersed and everyone went back to their posts.

Sachiko rose from her chair and walked back with them. She knew she felt resentful, she had all the telltale signs. She was especially focused on Teruo, obsessing about whether she had ever seen him volunteer for anything extra. She couldn't remember a single time. He was almost always the one to come in last and go home first, and she could swear he also took longer breaks. What was she going to do about it? And why did it even matter to her? His food didn't depend on her, there was clearly enough for everyone. She wondered if anyone else had similar feelings. In moments like this she wished they would talk more about such things. Maybe she was the only one that was even thinking about it. It was tiring to count, to monitor, to check on him. And she couldn't bring herself to stop, no matter how much she told herself not to be petty. It was time to take action, and she felt resentful about that, too. Why did it always have to be her that brought up the hard stuff no one else wanted to talk about?

She decided to talk to her father. Sachiko was four at the time of the transition, and had only dim memories of anything from before. Her most vivid memory was of sitting in her father's lap while he was stroking her, humming a soft melody, and from time to time telling her stories about how the transition was unfolding. Later, when she was old enough to understand, he told her about his own involvement in organizing efforts that led to the massive shifts. He always pointed out to her how much continuity there was with their traditional Japanese values, and how happy he was that now there was finally a way to uphold these values without ever shaming anyone. This situation with Teruo would be just perfect to discuss with him.

"Otosan,"[109] she said with a smile when his face showed up on her screen. "I need to talk with you. I want your advice." He listened to her, nodded and smiled a lot, and asked many questions. She was grateful for the clarity she was getting just from thinking more deeply about the issues.

Then he said: "You know this was one of the questions that the skeptics kept bringing up, again and again. They never tired of it. Now I think an answer wasn't really what they wanted, because we gave it to them so many times. They probably wanted to be heard, and for their concerns to really be taken seriously. Somehow as we kept explaining and explaining we didn't fully connect. How ironic." He paused, and she waited respectfully, giving him the time to reflect on his memories.

"When we thought about it back then, when designing the system…" His voice trailed off, and she smiled, anticipating a tangent. "It was so sacred, so special to be participating in the design. It was the first ever global collaborative effort. We knew it had to work for everyone, across cultural differences, so we had to respect local variations. That's part of why we designed it so that as many

---

[109] Dad in Japanese

decisions as possible are done locally. So long as there was no coercion and each locale was going to aim for living within their means...."

She smiled inside, not letting him see, holding him with respect. She'd heard those exact words so many times before. She knew he would bring the conversation back to topic.

"So, as I was saying, at the time we knew there were only two ways to go in a situation like this. Sometimes through dialogue someone like Teruo will remember to come back, to connect more. And sometimes, more often, this is just how it is, and it's his limit. There have always, always been those of us who are willing to do more than whatever it would mean to call 'our share.' Especially in our culture, we were always raised to look after the whole, the group. We are changing some of it now, so it's not at such great cost to each individual. I am optimistic. Meanwhile there will be people like Teruo. There always have been, and we always agreed to do more when they didn't do anything. Even when they did try to coerce people, there still were people who did more than others. It's just a bit more honest today." He stopped to look at her.

Yes, she knew this, she'd always known this. She felt a little lighter, and still there was something else she wanted.

"Otosan, thank you," she said. "This was such a useful reminder. Yes, if we care about everyone, we can't throw him away, or anyone else. That's so tough, though. And that's the part I still don't know how to handle. What do I do with my own resentment? I tried to talk myself out of it, and it's not working. I'm at a loss. It's getting worse every day."

He took his beard in his left hand, a gesture she loved so much. That meant he was thinking hard. She waited.

"I would have to believe that you are doing more than you are *truly* willing to do. That's the ground that breeds resentment. It's not what he does or doesn't do that creates it. It's what *you* do."

She nodded silently. It made sense.

"Examine your choices and your thoughts. If you find yourself doing something because 'someone has to,' then do the hard work of not doing it. This is your way of ensuring that you won't harbor resentment. It won't be easy. I know I didn't get enough freedom for myself to raise you with this much inner freedom, and I am truly sad about it. I did what I could. I hope you can do this now, even if not perfectly. Our hope, some of it, rests on trusting that each generation will find it easier to know their true willingness."

She accepted fully. They exchanged some pleasantries and a virtual hug, she promised to come visit as soon as there was an opportunity, and they hung up.

Three days later one of the machines broke down, and someone was needed to stay and meet with the technician to show her the problem. Sachiko was only one of three that knew enough to do it. Teruo was another, and the third person had sick parents he was taking care of and everyone knew he had to leave right on time. Sachiko sat through the whole meeting sweating with discomfort and didn't raise her hand. Kiyoko looked at her in disbelief. She didn't ask directly, and Sachiko was relieved not to have to explain. Silence occupied the entire little room, and they could all hear the clock ticking. Sachiko was getting more and more uncomfortable, and still didn't raise her hand, despite the effort it took to persist. The clock kept ticking. The tension grew.

Then, slowly, in a barely audible voice, they all heard Teruo. "I'll do it." He looked like he had been tortured. Then he went on, completely pale. "I want to tell you why I haven't ever been helpful." Teruo was a bit older than her, in his 40s, an odd mix of handsome and withdrawn. His voice was shaking as he told them about his father, who was a high-ranking officer in the Jieitai.[110] He had raised Teruo with harsh discipline, even after the transition. He had ignored the shifts, the new ways of being with children, and continued with his old practices. Teruo was ridiculed and beaten up severely for anything he did or expressed that demonstrated any individuality. He had learned to be very quiet and obedient in order to avoid further punishment. It was particularly devastating to have all of that go on when everything outside his home was changing rapidly. The contrast between home and the outside world was almost unbearable. Outside, he was free to choose so much, even as a small child, certainly as a teenager. At home, he was still being held to strict norms, like in the past. Navigating the difference was unbearable, especially keeping the secret. No one knew, not then, not until this moment, what he had suffered. He never wanted to say anything, because he didn't trust his father would make himself available to dialogue, and he didn't want to shame him back.

---

[110] The Japanese Self-Defense Forces

Now, a full twenty years after he was no longer under his rule, he still hadn't found a way to experience true freedom of choice. In his quiet and distancing way, he was still in rebellion against his father. He couldn't find genuine generosity, ever, after being told so often that he was bad and selfish. This moment, when Sachiko didn't raise her hand like she always did, was absolutely terrifying for him, because he was "forced" to make a choice.

He looked at Sachiko and then added, his voice shaking: "You may find this unbelievable. I do, too. And it's still true that I am really grateful for what you just did. Don't get me wrong. It was excruciating for me. I kept waiting for you to raise your hand. You always have in the past. I was terrified, and at the same time there was this freedom. No one told me what to do. No one was going to punish me. This was the first time I can remember making a real choice. You gave me that gift. I finally could see a need without any 'should' attached to it. I simply was moved to say yes, and this yes was coming from inside me, and without fear. It was, it is, what I wanted. We talk about feedback a lot, and I never understood until now. This feels like my first day of freedom."

Then he got up and left the room quickly. He still couldn't expose his feelings. It didn't matter. He didn't need to for Sachiko's heart to open to him, to herself. The true meaning of interdependence was one step closer to being real and clear for her.

No Easy Choices

Yara[111] would happily do three restorative circles[112] a day rather than research a red alert file and make the agonizing decision about whether the case conformed to the stringent requirements for issuing a coercive warrant. In the whole region only three people had enough experience and training to know how to do this, and a new person was now being apprenticed with Yara. All three of them agreed to be asked to review such cases, despite their shared abhorrence of the idea. And now it was her turn, and she wasn't going to say "no" even though she would have loved to do so. It was her service to the community, and she knew, when she undertook the training, that it would be a tough call.

With a sigh, she clicked on the screen. The woman's name and picture popped up, and she was asked if she knew her in any capacity before being officially assigned to the case. Nothing looked familiar, and so she proceeded.

Luiza, a 42-year old woman, had lost control of the bus she was driving. She hit a bike rider who was killed on the spot, and several other people – passengers in transport vans – suffered minor injuries. Upon examination, Luiza acknowledged having drunk significant amounts of alcohol and getting on the road drunk instead of asking for a replacement driver. Every driver knew that it was a condition for driving. This was a serious violation.

So far, it looked like standard material for a restorative circle. Painful tragedy, the likes of which she had facilitated many times over. Why would they ask her to comment on this?

Then she saw that Luiza had declined to participate in a restorative circle, saying she didn't need to, because she knew what she needed to do. She had already participated in one restorative circle three years previously, and didn't want to do it again.

This didn't make any sense to Yara. Didn't Luiza know that as a routine precaution her information would be distributed to all transportation coordination units, and she would be asked questions any time she signed up for a shift?

---

111 Yara is a name with various meanings in quite a number of languages.
112 Restorative circles are common to several methods of restorative justice, a fast growing alternative to conventional, or retributive justice. The application with which I am familiar exists in several areas in Brazil. See more details in the "Justice System" chapter from page 395..

Apparently, she did know. In the two months since the accident took place, she hadn't attempted to sign up for a driving shift anywhere. So what was she doing instead? No information was available to answer that question.

Next she pulled up the record from Luiza's previous restorative circle. That's when it started making sense. At that time Luiza was operating heavy machinery to remove dirt in a construction site, and seriously damaged some equipment. No casualties or injuries were recorded. The circle notes, as always, included only the original act and the agreed action plan. The heart of the process was never recorded. Alcohol must have been involved then, too, because Luiza had agreed to attend an intensive program to receive support for shifting her habit of drinking. The post-circle, gathered six months later, indicated satisfaction on everyone's part, including completion of the program and apparent shift in behavior noted by co-workers. The net result was erasing the precautionary system alert for Luiza's driving and providing her carte blanche to drive buses and machinery without further dialogue.

Now Yara became more engaged. Was the previous restorative circle Luiza's first? She looked again, a bit more thoroughly, and found another restorative circle from much earlier in Luiza's life, when she was thirteen. She was the receiver in that circle. Some other girl referred to her as fat to a group of kids who were laughing while Luiza was present. She would have dismissed it as entirely unrelated until she noticed that Luiza expressed lack of satisfaction with the results of the agreed action during the post-circle. No further notes were available.

She couldn't find anything else in her initial search. Going back to the current situation, she looked for any indication of dialogue with Luiza, and didn't find any. Did no one engage with her about her choice not to participate in a restorative circle? Surely she knew that whenever someone's action resulted in death an automatic review would be generated. Why would she knowingly risk the possibility of coercion? Something must be really important to her. Did anyone else look up her past? Did they see the clue she just found?

She wished more prep work had been done before she got the case, instead of getting it in this incomplete state. That was just how it was, and she took a deep breath to accept it. Very few people had any willingness to engage with the potentially coercive parts of the system. It was quite a spiritual stretch to everyone.

She sighed again, wishing this kind of case never happened, knowing there was no way around human fallibility. She waited a while until she was fully in acceptance, without a shred of resentment left, before reaching for her phone. As a courtesy to Luiza, she sent her a message first, explaining why she was calling, so she wouldn't be taken by surprise. She waited a few moments, and then called. Luiza answered immediately. Her eyes looked tired and a little scared. Yara smiled at her.

"Hi, Luiza. Thank you for answering. I can only imagine how unpleasant it is to get this call from me." She brought as much warmth into her tone as she knew how.

"It's all right. I figured someone would call." So no one called her so far, Yara confirmed for herself. How sad to leave her alone with her distress.

"Are you getting any support for yourself to deal with having killed the young man and the consequences to his family?" she tried again.

"I'm OK. Just tell me the business of your call." Yara was taken aback. There was clearly something going on here.

"Could we meet in person instead? I have some questions to ask, some things to say. I like to do that in person." Would she go for it?

"I don't think so. I want to put this behind me and just move on with my life. I'm going to do the program again, maybe this time it will stick. What else do you want? This is supposed to be a voluntary process, isn't it?" Now she heard some frustration building up. Maybe they'd get somewhere.

"Yes, it's voluntary, and I can so totally understand why you'd want it done and over with." And Yara paused for a moment, to let that sink in and see if anything else would come up for Luiza. Nothing did. She decided to try something else.

"Luiza, what happened when you were thirteen? Why weren't you satisfied with the results of that restorative circle? Is this why you are choosing not to go this time?" Luiza covered the camera on her phone, and Yara couldn't see her face.

"Wouldn't you rather continue in person?" She asked as gently as she could. Then she heard a click, and her screen turned black. Luiza had hung up.

Yara dialed again, three more times. Luiza didn't pick up. A couple of follow up messages received no answer, either. Yara called again the next day, and the next. It was time to up the level of action. She documented every step she took, aiming to preserve Luiza's dignity as much as possible.

She sent Luiza a message expressing her heavyhearted feeling, how much she wanted to work in cooperation with her, to find a way of caring for her and assuring safety for others, and alerting her that she was going to engage with her neighborhood next. This time she received a short response from Luiza. All she said was she wasn't going to do anything that would endanger others, and to please leave her alone to have her life. That was wrenching, exactly the pain she dreaded most in doing this job. And it would only get worse as she escalated. She sent a message back to Luiza letting her know that she just wasn't finding sufficient trust, sufficient reassurance that things would be different, and that Luiza's reluctance to engage in dialogue was particularly worrisome to her. She was going to go ahead and talk with neighbors unless she heard back from her with a willingness to engage in dialogue. She also said how distraught she was about not seeing a different way, and how much she understood the agony of being pressured like this. No response. What a nightmare.

And so she approached some neighbors, those who were registered as the current facilitators for the neighborhood decision circle. Both of them had been coming to meetings regularly for years, and neither of them had ever seen Luiza come in all that time. She hardly ever volunteered for any local community service, either. She mostly was home, alone, when she wasn't working or running errands.

So there was no community support, either. Not enough connection to organize a community-led action to support Luiza. The red alarm kept growing. Now it was time to look into family. She sent another note to Luiza, not expecting a response. "Please don't talk to my sister," was all she got. Luiza's parents had died, and she had one sister, a year older, who lived in another county, same region. Yara was amazed Luiza managed to lead such an isolated life within this community. It was the first time she realized how many cracks remained that someone could fall through. Despite the huge efforts, since the transition, to build an interdependent infrastructure, someone could still live so isolated, so clearly full of shame. How tragic.

When she started writing the report she was still hoping to find a collaborative solution. That's what they all lived for. She sent one more message to Luiza. "I'm so sad about how tough things appear to be for you. Please respond, I really want to work this out with you." No use. She had become the enemy. Luiza didn't respond. It was agonizing, because part of her training was about being fully transparent as a way to mitigate the enormous cost of coercion of any kind. She would be sending Luiza every single thing she wrote about her. That was one safety net to ensure dignity. She was still hoping against all odds that Luiza would relent. There was no intermediary, either, to provide support. Her heart went out to Luiza, despite everything. She appreciated the wisdom of having her be in touch only with Luiza while others were supporting the family of the bike rider who died. It would be hard to do both at once when there was so much antagonism, too.

She wrote down everything she had learned, including all her efforts to communicate with Luiza. It was now time to write her recommendation. Like everyone else, she was raised on the premise that no one would be forced to do something they weren't willing to do. That was how they organized everything. Only those things got to happen that someone was willing to do. This was as deeply ingrained in her as principles of retributive justice had been ingrained in lawyers before the transition. That's why they cross-reviewed each other's reports whenever the verdict was to let go of using protective measures. They all wanted to make sure that public safety would not be lost just because of extra care for one individual. She felt the pull to let Luiza off the hook. Maybe she would go to the program, maybe it would stick, maybe she would, finally, get enough support to overcome her shame, maybe she would open up to her community, in the end. She wanted to believe it would be true.

Then she weighed the risk. If Luiza was not going to be driving again, which she obviously wouldn't be able to do, she didn't pose a threat to public safety. She would be denied jobs, just about any job, if she applied for one, because of her record. Even if she never participated in any program, there was no reason to believe she would do any harm to anyone. It was mostly her own suffering. What a relief.

She hit enter, and the final screen appeared. "Please enter your recommendation:" She typed each letter slowly: C-i-r-c-l-e w-i-t-h s-u-b-s-t-i-t-u-t-i-o-n. Yes, they could do the circle without her. No need for an involuntary circle, which was always so painful. And she still hoped Luiza might join for the post-circle.[113]

---

[113] In the existing application in Brazil, circles with substitution exist whenever someone is unwilling to join. The rest of the people come up with an action plan that is intended to benefit the needs of the missing person, and sometimes, as the person learns of the action, they join the post-circle.

So Much Love

George had read the letter so many times, he almost knew the words by heart. Here it was, the culmination of a journey of many years of his life. He'd been up since dawn, staring at the screen, tinkering with his application. Few jobs demanded as long a commitment as this one. Was he ready to do it?

He hadn't showered or shaved in a couple of days, and he could smell the faint odor of tension on his body. The knock on the door startled him. Rick's smiling face popped in, then he walked in with a tray. "Sorry to interrupt, I know it's a big day for you. I just thought I'd bring you some dinner." Rick was like that. He put the tray down next to George, carefully avoiding the many pieces of paper. "It's basic," he said, almost apologizing. "Just a piece of salmon, the season just opened today, and asparagus. No grain, I know you don't want any." They looked at each other for a moment, George grateful, Rick playful, happy. "Bring it downstairs when you're done. And don't let it get too cold. Your application can wait." Rick closed the door gently behind him. OK, it was time to admit that he needed to stop. He hadn't eaten, or even moved, in hours.

After eating, he shoved the tray aside, not heeding Rick's request. He could deal with the tray later, maybe he would even wash dishes, or do more household chores. Later, after all this was over. He had only two hours left to make up his mind. He read the letter again, as if for the first time.

> Dear applicant,
>
> Thank you for your interest in becoming a prison guard.
>
> If you are accepted for this work, you will be committing to a life of the most challenging service, where you would willingly expose yourself, on a daily basis, to behaviors and attitudes that will require you to extend your capacity to love and challenge your beliefs about the nature of human beings and what is possible in our society.
>
> We want to ensure that those who apply for this job are absolutely aware of the level of challenge it entails, and are fully ready to make this commitment. Please review your application again and submit only if this is true for you. We make this request not only in consideration of your wellbeing, but also the

wellbeing of the people you will guard, who need to trust that you will be there for them. We are also considering our own wellbeing. We work in community, and invest extensive resources in supporting everyone who does this job, and we want to use all our resources wisely.

In gratitude,

Michelle Jackson and Ariel Rosenthal

Prison Services Coordinators, Edwards Plateau Region[114]

He was ten when he first learned about prisons, while facilitating a tough circle. Samantha, an eight-year-old from his neighborhood, had killed a dog. To this day he didn't even want to remember the details. Even more disturbing for him, she taunted the distraught friend whose dog she had killed. When he met with Samantha in the pre-circle, she talked about it with glee, as if her friend's suffering was a source of pleasure for her. It was so unfathomable to him, he knew he needed support before convening the circle. It was the first, though not the last time he made full use of the built-in mechanism that offered him, the facilitator, a pre-circle with a colleague, so he could make full connection with Samantha, and attempt to understand this extreme and bizarre behavior. For an entire week, it became a total obsession. He had to understand her, as if his life, everything he believed in, depended on it. This was beyond the normal fare of conflicts he had seen, and he was overwhelmed. Wasn't this kind of behavior the very essence of what the transition was dedicated to making a thing of the past? What could possibly have happened to Samantha that got her to this level of cruelty? And what if the circle failed, if she didn't learn? What would happen to her? What about the girl who lost her animal? And the community surrounding them? What if Samantha continued to act this way? He and his colleague talked it all over with Damian, his primary mentor, asking him many tough questions. Damian supported him in doing research, and his colleague kept offering him opportunities to confront his own emotions. He really wanted to know how to reach Samantha so she could trust him. Later he learned that his parents and Damian were alternating between worrying about him and being deeply impressed and touched. During that week he stayed up into the late hours, and got up early to continue his research. He barely

---

[114] Edwards Plateau is a bioregion that encompasses large parts of southwest Texas.

gave attention to anything else, and was consumed with learning, reading, and thinking about issues no one would think a ten-year-old would be drawn to.

His research inevitably led him to discover that prisons still existed. He was deeply shook up by the very idea of prisons. Then he learned that prisons, like everything else, were dramatically different from the past. People would only get locked up when no number of restorative circles, no amount of people ready to listen, were enough to assure safety for all. He was utterly unsurprised when he found out that prison guards had to be chosen above all for having an unusually high ability to exhibit love, so as to compensate for the unbearable restriction of liberty. The prison population had been high at transition, he learned. Then, as more and more people were loved into healing and released, and fewer and fewer people experienced the kind of trauma, abuse, and poverty that were common before the transition, there was a steady decline in the number incarcerated. It was still declining when he was doing his research, though not as fast as before.

Some people theorized that the decline would plateau, because there would always be some people with an extreme level of trauma, or possibly a genetic variation, that would render them incapable of experiencing empathy. Others were more hopeful, and imagined that a day would come when even the people who were most susceptible to empathy deficiency would receive enough love in their lives to counter any violent tendencies. His ten-year-old heart went with the latter, even though he knew nothing about data that would support that perspective. He wanted to believe that eventually there would be no prisons, that the principle of willingness, of completely voluntary participation, would always work, and everyone would attend circles willingly. He also understood that when someone's behavior posed so much risk, there might be no way to maintain safety without locking them up. His heart went out to them, those people that no one was able to reach, who were full of anger and bitterness, and so closed that all they could do was inflict harm on others. What a nightmare existence, with or without being in prison.

When he chanced on a book from before the transition that talked about the conditions that created escalating violence and imprisonment in the United States at that time, he finally understood what could be going on for Samantha. He asked Damian to talk with her mother, and the last clue fell in place when he heard back from him. Samantha's mother had been coming of age just before the transition. She had been raised in poverty, tormented by her classmates, and molested by her father. After the transition she had resolved not to have children, the only safe way she knew not to pass any of her wounds on to others. Then, in her early 40s, she got pregnant despite using birth control, and could not bring herself to have an abortion. A passionate, desperate hope filled her that maybe she could do it, maybe she could provide enough love. Maybe that would be her way to heal completely. She was strong enough to ask for help. It was enough to ensure nothing overt would be done to Samantha. She never hit Samantha, no matter how angry or overwhelmed she felt. Poverty was, in any event, a thing of the past. Despite her love and her strong will, the help wasn't enough for her to be able to accept Samantha's dependence on her. That level of vulnerability in her child was often too much for her to welcome. She kept pushing Samantha, in mostly subtle ways, to be independent, to not lean on her. She wanted Samantha to be strong and resilient, and to not have to depend on people for her wellbeing. It wasn't exactly a withdrawal of affection. It was more that she constantly judged Samantha, even ridiculed her at times, for wanting her affection and for being as sensitive as she was. Samantha would cry inconsolably in her early years, and her mother would leave her alone, or push her away when she came to her. It didn't occur to her that her responses might be as detrimental for a child as physical violence.

George understood all this. He was young enough to know from within how sweet it is to have someone bigger and stronger to lean on, to rest into. His own parents had given him all the space in the world to cry his heart out when he needed. They were always there, loving and available, and he could literally hold on to them as much as he needed. He was also mature enough to imagine what it would be like to want nurturing and protection and then be pushed away into premature independence. Just imagining it, he knew he had a window into Samantha's heart. He could totally understand the humiliation, the unbearable shame, the incapacity to see and tolerate vulnerability of any kind in anyone else, not even a dog. He immediately got why she would close her heart so fully. Who wouldn't?

He was ready to see Samantha again. Equipped with all his knowledge, he walked with her one afternoon to the learning center, where she was taking more and more advanced math classes. At one point he stopped walking, motioned her to stop as well, looked as intently into her eyes as he could, and asked: "Have you ever ever felt that you were not utterly alone in the universe, that there was at least one person you could really trust?" It wasn't child's talk, and it was what he wanted to know. He looked at her, his big brown eyes unwavering, open, relaxed, curious, accepting. She lowered her gaze, and he gently raised her face again to meet his eyes. They stood there for what seemed like an eternity and probably lasted less than a minute. A tear was forming in her eyes, and he felt it in his, too. She held his gaze through it. Then she shook her head and lowered it, the tears finally dropping. It was now time for the circle.

When Shauna was talking about her pain and crying, he saw Samantha cringe. A smile almost formed on her face. She was trying to protect herself again. He asked her what she heard Shauna say. Samantha said some words, quite accurately, except she was giggling as she said it. He turned to Shauna, expecting her to get really angry or withdraw. She did neither. She looked at Samantha and simply asked: "Did you ever lose anything that you cared about a lot?" Samantha's expression changed immediately, and he could see the pain. No one said anything for a while, letting her work her way through the discomfort. George kept his attention on Samantha, withholding the urge to prod or educate. She hesitated, then nodded, slowly. "It hurts, doesn't it?" Shauna added. Although Samantha was fighting the tears, George had a sense that she trusted him and the process because she knew he understood her. As she was still sitting uncomfortably with herself, he turned again to Shauna. "Is that what you wanted Samantha to hear?" He knew there was a story. Maybe one day Samantha would tell it. For now, they were all just sitting in silence. Shauna looked directly at Samantha, still as could be. After a few minutes, Samantha's shoulders relaxed a little and she slowly turned her head to look back at Shauna. No words were said, though the conversation clearly continued. Then Samantha shifted her gaze to him, as if to say she was ready, still afraid to speak.

From then on, the circle proceeded without any effort. Shauna went back to describing her pain, George asked Samantha again to say what she heard. He could see it was almost like climbing Mount

Everest for her, and she did it, pale and determined. It took a long moment, and it seemed like the adults were almost ready to jump in. Then, without anyone's prompting, Samantha opened and closed her mouth several times, and finally spoke. "I don't know what to say..." she looked glum, helpless. For the first time since he had seen her, she looked like an eight-year-old, not a monster. "I wish I could bring your puppy back to life," she said almost inaudibly. Then she burst out crying, something no one had ever seen her do. Shauna joined her. Everyone breathed in relief. The connection had been formed. Right then and there he decided he would be a prison guard.

Now, seventeen years later, he had finished his apprenticeship. He thought he knew enough of what he was getting into. It was time to complete the application. He clicked on each of the questions again.

"Describe a time when someone actively depended on you. What was your emotional response?"

He read some of what he had written, checking it for the nth time. He was particularly satisfied with this one segment: "I don't believe in any gods or supernatural powers. Still, I know that when this boy leaned against me and cried, it felt sacred, like this is what I was meant to do here on planet Earth." He was so glad to be alive at a time when such expressions were allowed, when love was accepted, when vulnerability was welcomed. In the past, before the transition, such words would have been considered "corny." He felt for all those people who died before seeing what was possible.

"Describe a particularly challenging incident you experienced over this past year of training. How did you work it out within yourself and with whomever else was involved? What did you learn in the process?"

There was nothing left to tweak. He had been through this incident so many times in his mind. He knew how important this was for the kind of work he was seeking. There would be difficult interactions all the time, and he absolutely needed the capacity to understand himself, to be able to be totally non-defensive and transparent, in order to work as a team with others. He would need to work through so much. He closed his eyes and reviewed this incident one more time, just to make sure he didn't leave out any important nuance. He focused especially on that one moment when his prison guard mentor for that early rotation questioned him because the prisoner he left him with complained about him. The whole thing was touchy, because it was his first rotation, and, technically speaking, his mentor was not supposed to leave him alone with a prisoner. So his mentor was a bit off balance, too. George didn't mind being questioned. That wasn't the truly painful part. It was knowing that the prisoner had zeroed in on his vulnerability in a moment of faltering, twisted it, and taken advantage of it. He learned then, again, that loving the people who've been so damaged could easily lead to subtly expecting them to be responsive, openhearted, or even honest and real. He would need to recognize this temptation and find ways to remain openhearted to them even when they broke his trust, took advantage of his vulnerability, or lied to him and about him. That was what he wrote about – how to balance the repeated experiences of crushing disappointment with the never-ending commitment to keep his heart on the reality of their suffering.

"Describe a moving moment, an experience of human intimacy with an imprisoned adult over the course of your training. What touched you about it?"

It was a tough call for this one. So many moments, every day, with so many people he met. Did he pick the right one? Maybe it really didn't matter. He remembered the day he described, the feeling at the end of that encounter like he wanted to run out and scream to everyone that it was always true, there is always a human heart if you dig deep enough, for everyone. Instead, he took a bike and rode to the forest, stood by the creek, caressed the trees he loved, then ran up a steep hill, singing at the top of his voice. The elation was almost too much. It was the second time he had been present with someone opening up for the very first time. What a privilege when that floodgate opened and the pain, the mangled anguish, the ocean of unmet needs, came tumbling out. After that hour, that person's face changed, as if he had acquired different features. His jaw, in particular – he could swear it became less set, softer. It gave him hope for this person, for all people, that such a transformation was possible.

"What are the sources of support in your own life? How do you maintain the openness of your heart over time?"

Nothing remarkable here. He mentioned the complete support he got from his family from the moment he expressed his wishes to be a prison guard. He wrote about his relationship with Damian, which continued to grow and was turning into more mutual mentoring over time. He described his forays in the woods, how nature was an anchor for him. He listed all the groups he was part of. He always made sure he went to the empathy center at least weekly. He knew what he was doing was emotionally demanding, and it was his responsibility and wish to keep it from traumatizing him. Now he added one more sentence that was missing. He wanted whoever read the form to know that there weren't extraordinary measures he was taking, because it wasn't an extraordinary challenge for him.

He looked at the clock one more time. He had an hour left. There was nothing more to look at, only his own heart. He would accompany one individual after another on the most challenging journeys known to humans, recovering their assaulted souls so they could regain access to freedom, internal first, and then freedom of movement. He would have a most intimate relationship with each of them, in a protected environment. He would sit with them and design their plan. Within the basic loss of freedom, they still had ample choice. And they used it, too. Some of his earlier connections with prisoners were when he came into prison to teach biology. Many of the prisoners wanted to learn. Others were looking for ways to do meaningful work. All prisons had large gardens tended to by prisoners. They could participate in sports. It really wasn't about punishment, it was about providing love, and care, and a way to heal.

In between one assignment and the next he would have months of unassigned time to rejuvenate, nourish his heart, restore his resilience. He could be in nature, or read books, or receive empathy – whatever he most needed to be able to continue, to take on the next prisoner. He would never be asked to do any other community service. Some journeys would last only weeks, and others, he knew, took years. On rare occasions it would be a lifetime. A few individuals would never heal enough. Could he face that? It would not be an easy life, however much he always thought that's what he wanted.

He opened the door and called out to Rick and the others. "Bring the cake," he said. "I'm ready to submit." He chuckled at the unintended pun. Within seconds, the whole bunch came in, accompanied by all his other friends. It was sort of a surprise, though not really. Everyone stood in the room with him, chattering happily, laughing. Someone hushed them, and now they all stood in silence. He read the letter to them, then pressed the button.

I Guess I'm Ready

Bill woke up with a start and found himself in his king-size bed, on sheets that hadn't been washed in over a month. His heart was still pounding. He sat up and reached for his glasses so he could see the world, blinking unhappily.

In his dream a tribunal had been trying him for crimes against humanity. It was never made clear what exactly he had done. His file, with a big BILL TAYLOR stamped on top of it, was immense, larger than he had ever seen in real life. It took two people to lift it and put it on the judge's desk. The courtroom was in an uproar the whole time, and the judge kept using the gavel to call the room to order. A long succession of witnesses he had never seen before came to testify about deeds he didn't recognize. Whenever he tried to speak his mouth would scarcely move, and unintelligible words came out. He had the sense that no one could see or hear him, let alone understand.

The judge stood up and started leafing through the file. Her pace was agonizingly slow. From time to time she showed something to the clerk and whispered in his ear. The clerk would nod and type more notes.

A screen suddenly materialized behind the judge's head on which Bill could see, in minute and vivid detail, all the costs of his actions over the years of his life. The total amount of resources consumed was astronomical. He could see the people toiling to produce his every possession. The conditions under which these people lived, the squalor and the brutality, were painful to watch. He wanted to turn his head, and couldn't, forced to observe, to take it in, to know.

The judge closed the file, satisfied with whatever investigation she had just done. She used the gavel one more time, without any apparent reason, cleared her throat, and pronounced him guilty as charged. The penalty, which he feared would be death, was instead forced labor at one of the factories he had owned in Southeast Asia.

He got out of bed, still disturbed to the core, and walked to the toilet. While peeing he wondered what on earth he had this dream for. While awake, he was mostly fine, just always angry about the transition, and by night he had nasty dreams like this over and over again. Never as detailed as this one. The vividness of the dream made him shudder. He reached for his robe. There was no one to wait on him any more. That life was over. They all left as soon as money was eliminated and they knew food would be available no matter what they did. Only Manuel stayed on, loyal as always. "I will be with you for as long as you want me, sir," he said. They had never discussed it since.

Bill's wife had died shortly before the transition. He never thought, when she died, that five years later he would consider her lucky for dying so young and never having to face the new indignities of life.

He walked down to the kitchen to make himself a cup of coffee to shake off the remnants of this dream. He didn't like any of it – not the dream, not having to make his own coffee, not the inevitable deterioration of the property despite Manuel's heroic efforts to manage five people's jobs. He knew his life had become unsustainable.

Every day Manuel came back with enough food for both of them. Bill despised the transitioners for treating him with such care. He hated the sweet talk about making it work for everyone. It wasn't working for him. He wanted the old freedom, the travel, the opportunity to meet people with refined taste like his, the specialty foods that were no longer available, the exquisite wine. He didn't like his new life.

He went back up to his room and put on his swimsuit. He was determined to use what he had. He stood by the pool, a tall slender man, preparing to dive in. He looked around the pool, where weeds were starting to grow again. It was no use. The swimming pool – the water use, in particular – had been a major item on his list of transgressions in the dream. He shuddered again. He and Manuel had figured out a way to cover the pool most of the time, and to collect rainwater to use on those rare occasions when it was necessary to add water to the pool. That was the only way he could keep the pool going.

"Manuel," he called out across the yard. Manuel, who was fixing a pipe that fed the pool, stood up and looked at him, ready for commands. "Come here for a sec. I want to talk with you."

Manuel wiped off his hands, and came over quickly. "What is it, sir?" he asked.

Bill looked at him for a while. He was about to ask him a question, to engage with him in a way he never had. He had no guidelines, no instructions for how to do this. "Why did you decide to stay?" he was finally able to ask. "You didn't have to, and everyone else left. Why are you still here?" He'd never asked him, never really thanked Manuel fully for his choice, just took it all for granted. He remembered that moment in the dream when his treatment of his servants was tallied – the number of times he was curt, or addressed his wife as if the servants were not there.

Manuel didn't immediately answer. He was clearly taken aback by the question. Something in how Bill asked made it clear that "I don't know" would not be an option.

Manuel was visibly uncomfortable, and Bill was suddenly hit by the realization that Manuel's training, everything he had ever learned up until a few years ago, was focused on pleasing the boss, the person in power. That was him, he noticed uncomfortably. With determination, he went on. "Don't tell me what you think I would want to hear. Just the truth, whatever it is."

Bill didn't know what to expect any longer. There was no script for this part. His voice was hoarse when he added: "I never told you how much it means to me that you continue to come every day when you don't have to. I wasn't raised to be grateful. I'm sorry I never thanked you before."

Manuel was now actively squirming. "It's OK, sir," he hastened to say. "You don't have to thank me, either. This is my job; it's always been my job." He remembered the day everyone left. They laughed at him, called him a coward. They didn't get it. No one got it, certainly not Bill. Manuel's wife, Sarita, understood. She always understood and supported him. "And there's something else," he tried, and then stopped again. There was no reason to be afraid, and yet he was; the old habit was still there. He remembered the training in truth-telling he received in the early months. There was so much they all had to learn so quickly. People like Bill never came. It took some courage to carve the words out against his fear. "I felt sorry for you. I couldn't bear to see you so lost with all of us gone. You're human, too, like the rest of us." Their eyes locked for a moment, and Manuel thought he could detect a flicker of actual pain, raw grief. Then it disappeared and he wasn't sure. The hard part was still ahead of him. He waited to see if Bill wanted to say anything. They stood silently for another moment.

"I also wanted to stay to help you transition, too. I care about you." He stopped to look at Bill again. They'd never talked like this before. "I didn't believe you really wanted to have your heart so totally closed to all the rest of us. I trusted you could find yourself again. I thought the day would come when you would understand. I hope this is OK to say." He felt panic after saying it, then happy for his courage. He was applying something he learned and never believed he would find a way to do.

Bill was grateful and disoriented. He wasn't raised for such conversations with people he considered common folks. He heard his father's voice speaking when he, Bill, was a young boy. "This will be all," his father would say when dismissing a servant. These words were making themselves ready in his mouth, and he resisted them. These were different times, and Manuel was doing him a huge favor. He didn't want to treat him like that, not anymore. And it was hard, because that meant he had to think about how he did want to interact, and then the resentment came up. It was so much easier before.

This was the longest conversation he had ever had with Manuel. He had never really paused to think about Manuel and his life – what his choices were, how he lived, what his wife did. He was just a worker bee. Now the only one, and Bill had lost the capacity to dictate anything to him. For a long time now he knew that Manuel was making his own decisions about priorities. He left him alone, knowing he was holding too much responsibility anyway.

"I don't know what to say," he opened. He was getting agitated. It was unseemly in his family to show any emotion. "I don't know what I would've done without you. You made life in the last five years possible for me. I don't know what to do next, and I hope you can continue to help me until I am clear. I know we can't go on like this for much longer. I just don't know what to do instead." There was no escaping the truth.

Manuel took out a piece of paper from his pocket and handed it to Bill without any words. It was a business card for Jennifer Maguire, transition coach. "Call her up. She can help. She's helped many people in your kind of situation." Bill took the card without saying a word. He didn't want to tell Manuel that he already knew about transition coaches. Many of his friends had already taken that step. He was one of the last holdouts, a position he took some pride in, until today. He felt tired, and old. There was little energy left in him for the fight. "I'll go back to do my work now, sir, if you don't mind," he heard Manuel say after a while. He nodded, still deep in thought.

He kept up with them, those who still hadn't accepted the transition. They were still getting together as some kind of support group, helping each other figure out ways to defy the system, to maintain as much of the old order as possible, at least in their personal lives. That's what Bill had been doing. They got together twice a week, had a reading club and a formal dinner. They still had their old dishes, and they could pretend all was well, at least in moments.

They all knew, though they never really spoke about it, that it was only a matter of time before the end. Every so often one of them would stop coming to the meetings, and they later learned that person took up the opportunity to meet with a transition coach. These were not fun times.

Bill put the card on a chair, and put a little rock on it to keep it in place. The chair was smooth to the touch, made of expensive ipe wood. He had had it shipped from Brazil on one of his many trips. He flashed on the dream again – the long, endlessly detailed list of all of his purchases, the extensive tally of his waste. He shuddered again, for the third time this morning.

Maybe the water would make this dream go away. He walked to the edge of the pool, stood there for a moment, feeling the air on his body, and dove elegantly into the water. He swam underwater for most of the length of the pool, still enjoying his lung capacity, making graceful motions with his long arms, savoring the coolness of the water in the hot summer day. He enjoyed the reprieve. There was no rush, nothing to worry about for that long moment of swimming.

After a while he pulled his body out of the water, lay down on a lounge chair to dry off and get the sun to warm up his skin again. The futility of his struggle in this naked moment was clear as day. When he was dry enough he picked up the business card, went inside the house to where the phone was, and dialed. His entire body was shaking when he heard her voice. "Hello, this is Jennifer Maguire. How can I help you?" Her voice was friendly and crisp. He liked her immediately. "Hi, my name is Bill Taylor. I bet you've been waiting to hear from me for some time. I guess I'm ready."

Starting Life Again

Her face didn't betray her panic. She didn't want anyone to know what was going on. She, Ayelet Shoshani, famed inventor of a breakthrough process for synthesizing customized, 100% non-toxic polymers,[115] couldn't think through the mathematical puzzle in front of her. This was the second time in three weeks. No matter how much she concentrated, one variable or another dropped out of her mental grasp.

She had gone to the doctor after the first time, where she learned she had a degenerative disease, incurable. The doctor told her it would be gradual. Initially it would only happen when she was particularly tired, or at the end of a long day. Then, slowly, she would be challenged more and more often. Her useful days as a scientist were coming to an end. Yes, she could lecture, and do other things. She didn't imagine she could continue on the creative edge she had been on for all these years.

What was she going to do? She was 74. Many people her age were shifting to being with the children. It was the standard approach to what used to be called childcare. She didn't know what she would do with children. Their interests didn't capture her imagination, and playing was not her thing. And yet she never forgot what it was like to be a child. She liked to think of herself as poorly socialized, which she didn't consider a bad thing. She still hadn't learned how to say things in the right moment. Like children, she tended to say things when they were true. This often got her in trouble, though she usually got out of it because of her stature. All in all, she had a lot of respect for children, despite her awkwardness with them. How could she not, given her history?

She had discovered chemistry when she was eleven, and it was all she did since. At thirteen she was playing with computer models of complex polymers, and writing letters begging scientists to let her work in their labs, which all but one of them politely declined. That was all she needed – one person to support her. By the time she was fifteen she made her first invention. At that time she was still in Tel-Aviv.

---

[115] Polymers are large molecules composed of repeating structural units. There are both naturally occurring polymers (such as proteins, rubber, cellulose and other very familiar substances) and synthetic polymers, most significantly plastics of all sorts.

By then, talk about the rapid disappearance of oil, and the immense costs of using oil-based chemicals in particular, was no longer confined to the environmental movement.[116] Ayelet, buoyed by her early success, secretly decided she was going to solve this problem. She didn't tell anyone at the time, not even her benefactor. She was smart enough to know that no one would take her seriously. Young and female, she proceeded on her own, grateful to have access to a lab, and for the freedom it gave her to play and experiment. Having produced something of value so early in her life, she was confident she would never have to worry about making a living.

She read Marconi's[117] biography, finding solace and inspiration in his determination as a young man to persist in his experiments despite ridicule. Like him, like all inventors, she didn't feel bound by linear logic. Everything was fair game. Nature took millions of years to convert dead organic matter to the complex substance known as oil – that rich, formerly abundant source of easy energy and the basis of so much of what humans came to take for granted as part of life, the polymers that filled every household. She held on to the obstinate conviction that there had to be a way to make that process faster, humanly manageable, and non-toxic.

If not for the transition happening, she might not have made it. She was skeptical at first, not an early adopter. She was worried about the predictable things. In retrospect, she was poignantly amused. So much unnecessary heartache. At the time, she thought the whole thing would collapse. Somehow she couldn't believe enough people would have enough willingness to do enough of the more unpleasant work that had to be done. She wasn't actively opposed to the transition, just skeptical. In fact, some of what shifted her was seeing how the strong opponents were handled. She couldn't believe so much love and patience would be given to them. Now, all these years later, she thought: How much conditioning, over how many millennia, have gone into having so little faith in people?

And then the call came out listing all the intractable problems left over from the collapsing civilization, and asking for support. Lo and

---

[116] In all the discussion about peak oil that I have seen, the focus has been on energy, and I don't hear much significant discussion about how to replace the huge amount of plastics that are used in everyday life and in commercial applications. I do believe this is a problem as serious as loss of cheap oil for energy, which goes way beyond plastic bags.

[117] The inventor of radio transmission.

behold, they listed the problem that she'd been working on – the polymer issue – as one of the key obstacles to a truly sustainable life. She had just been on the verge of giving up, because everyone she talked with dismissed her simple idea as impractical, and no one wanted to fund it. And suddenly there was opportunity. She was no longer alone. Someone understood it enough to put it on the list. If she hadn't had housemates she would probably have been dancing and screaming in delight. Instead, she just sat down and cried.

Within minutes she started writing a proposal. It was odd, because there was no request for a budget. How could that be? Instead, they wanted to know things like exactly how many people would be needed and what kind of equipment and infrastructure. That was clear and easy enough. And then they also wanted to know an estimate of the effect on communities, the carbon footprint, and a host of similar questions. It took some work. It was much harder to do than putting together a budget. As she was answering all the questions, slightly annoyed by the level of detail, the word "resources" was taking on a new, more precise meaning. Instead of thinking about how much money something cost, which in some ways was hiding the true cost, she had to really think through the ramifications of what she was proposing. She had a lot of respect for the thinking that went into working out what questions to ask.

Her proposal was accepted. She moved to Baghdad to participate in the first implementation, and the rest was history. Now, her initial version was wholly outdated. It was so perfected that anyone could write down the specs of a polymer they wanted, and with minimal investment of resources a computer program analyzed them, identified the molecular structure, and named the most likely naturally occurring substances that could be used to produce it locally. The process itself was simple enough that most requests could be handled locally, too.

How many people in the history of the world could claim they invented or discovered something that made life dramatically more livable for everyone? She remained shy and soft-spoken despite her fame, mostly avoiding social settings unless called to speak about topics about which she was passionate. She had only ever been truly comfortable with a few people, mostly a few other scientists and her partner Ilham who had just died the previous year. Ilham was the only one who had known Ayelet's passion fully, and her inner struggles. She would have been the only one to know that she was starting to fail. Now, more than forty years after her pivotal piece of work, Ayelet didn't want to be alone again. She had to talk to someone. Who could it be?

It happened to be the day of the weekly neighborhood meeting, and she had the urge to attend. She had been a few times in the early days, and couldn't stand the long-drawn-out pace. She thought, and even felt, so quickly. She understood the issues, and everyone's needs, and had solutions ready faster than people could even process the information, and it was just too painful to wait for people to catch up to her. And here she was, clear that she wanted to go, not knowing why. She only knew that in all matters in her life she trusted her intuition. She had chosen to have a lifelong relationship with Ilham within minutes, when they were both in their early 20s. That, too, was an unlikely decision. Ilham was not a scientist, though she loved listening to Ayelet's discoveries and understood everything she said, and fast enough. Her passion was practical art. She produced an infinite variety of objects of great beauty that were used by thousands of people around the world in their daily lives. The only condition of having any of Ilham's products was that one could only use it for a year, and then pass it along to another. Still, within thirty minutes of meeting Ilham, Ayelet told her that she thought they would be ideal life partners. She was even more amazed when Ilham immediately agreed. In all their years together they had had only seven fights, never the same one twice. She was bereft when Ilham died.

Knowing herself, she obeyed her instinct, and went to the meeting, despite the intense aversion and resistance she felt alongside the draw. She was super curious when she walked in. Curiosity, after all, was the main motivator in her life. The first few minutes, especially the check-in, held her interest. In all her shyness, she always found it fascinating to know what people were thinking and feeling. It didn't last, though. As the facilitator read the list of items to decide, she sank into a funk. If only they still allowed dictators, she thought wistfully. She could make all the necessary decisions, and even better ones that attended to more needs, within minutes. It took all she had to stay through the entire two hours. It was hard to be in this position of liking her own decisions better than most everyone else's. Ilham was the only one with whom she could truly think things through together. She was tired of remembering Ilham again and again. Would she ever recover from this loss before she died?

Finally the meeting was coming to an end. She thought of getting up to leave, defeated and confused, when one person asked if any new service opportunities had come up that week. That was all Ayelet needed to hear. She glued herself to the chair, even though she was ready to jump out and run, because she knew she needed to hear more. Someone objected to using meeting time for looking through things everyone could read at home. Someone else said that it was important to do, because sometimes some things just wouldn't be filled otherwise. The rotating facilitator logged in, meanwhile, and started reading out loud information about permanent community service posts with transportation and health, and temporary ones with food distribution to the sick in the neighborhood and with children. She wasn't giving him her full attention until she heard the word innovative. She was too embarrassed to ask the guy to repeat. What could be innovative about children? Then it hit her, and the loop was closed.

That night she put together a plan. The next day she let the laboratory personnel manager know that she would be phasing out. She would be doing all she could to find a replacement, although they both knew without saying a word that no one would step into her shoes. She didn't know how long it would take; it all depended on how soon her plans would fall into place. For now she was just going to leave earlier, or come later, or both. Over time, she would shift into just mentoring new scientists, or consulting.

When asked what she was planning, she mumbled something about assuming her role as an elder. The manager didn't press her, knowing how private she was. Inside, she was rejoicing. She had figured it all out. How could it have taken her so many years to understand why almost everyone, in the end, chose to be with children? It was clear as day. This was what humans always did, since time immemorial, and until some time in the twentieth century. Elders were with children, telling stories, preserving the culture, educating and nurturing the children, relieving the adults. Yes, that *was* what they had put together after the transition. She finally got it.

And she would be doing the same, in her own way. Except that her stories would be different. Not fairy tales, and not moralizing stories. She would put together a laboratory for kids. She would tell stories about science. Her plan, methodical as always, would work for children of any age. As soon as anyone knew enough and could articulate what they knew, they would be supervising others. Even younger kids could supervise older ones if they learned faster. Everyone would have something to learn, to share, to discover. She would be nurturing a new generation of scientists, right here in her neighborhood. She wouldn't be alone.

All of It Is Play

When Tom woke up, his mother, Shu, had already left the house. It was her community service day, and she was scheduled to do food delivery to the sick. Although they had talked about him accompanying her, they both knew he wouldn't be waking up early enough after a night out with his friends. Now he was a bit disappointed. As interested as he was in participating in service, he hadn't yet joined the system officially. Taking on the actual responsibility for a shift, so that others could count on them, was rare among kids his age. They were mostly still coming in as extras, doing what they knew to do and free to play with other kids at other times. Knowing no one ever really needed him meant he almost always got sidetracked, engrossed in his chemistry experiments, studying math, or playing his guitar.

Danielle, his other mother, was in the kitchen, preparing breakfast. He wasn't quite ready to join her, not until he had a handle on his options for the day. He was always ready to change plans for new adventures. He turned on his netter and looked at the new listings since last night. A study group had just formed to examine the lives of kids before the transition. It was a hot topic with five local members already in less than twelve hours. He signed up immediately to make sure he had a spot. Doreen, the girl who had initiated it, was with him in another study group, where they read utopias and did a compare and contrast with their own post-transition society. He liked how her mind worked, and the timing worked. He could be back just in time for the hike. He wouldn't miss the hike for anything, not after all the rain had finally ended and water would be running in the little streams in the hills.

A former military man in his eighties was offering a class on the history of war starting next week. No thanks. An intensive training in group facilitation drew his interest, except it was offered on a weekend when he would be at the permaculture research center doing a small apprenticeship. This was a tough call. Even though he wanted to learn facilitation skills, which were useful in so many situations, the apprenticeship was a hard one to let go of, as they weren't offered often. A daylong clay sculpture class was offered by a famous local artist, focusing on hands and feet in particular, with a live model. That would be just right for Danielle, she's always wanted to give her hands the tactile pleasure of working with clay. He made a mental note to tell her about it. There were all the how-to classes that were offered, ranging from plumbing to growing vegetables on less and less soil with less and less water and fewer and fewer disruptions to the ecosystem. Lastly, he saw a new literacy group show up. He still remembered his, fondly. He was nine at the time, older than most in his group. It took only two weeks for all of them to read. This was not unusual. Everyone learned to read exactly when they were ready and wanted to.

He clicked on the requests tab. "I am 82 years old," said the first one on the list, "and I really want to learn calculus before I die." That was touching, and so he read on. "I want the learning to happen one-on-one, because I lived enough years before the transition that I still have all this conditioning that I am stupid, that women can't really learn math." That sounded like fun. He wanted to check with his moms before volunteering. He was perfectly aware that he had a tendency to take on so much that he would barely leave himself room for all the things he did at home, with his family, or by himself.

The next one didn't grab him at all. "Anybody up for learning how to do archival research? I don't know how to do it, and I bet we can do some research together to find out who knows and how to ask them to teach us." He browsed through a few entries quickly, and the very last one caught his attention most. "I love doing chemistry experiments by myself. I've been doing them for years now. I think maybe it will be fun to get together with a few other chemistry nerds and do experiments together." That had potential, and he flagged it for later, after he saw who else would sign up.

"Tom," he heard Danielle's voice from the kitchen, "I'm about to sit down for breakfast if you want my company. Come say hi." It was time to get the day started. He entered the kitchen and chattered with Danielle while putting together a breakfast for himself. By the time he sat down she was already done. "I'm going to put in my four hours of writing now," she said while getting up. "Then I have a bunch of messages to attend to before Shu returns and we all go hiking. See you later."

Just as she was walking out the door he remembered. "Mom," he said, "I saw a class today that I think would be interesting to you." This was sensitive territory. "Please don't say 'no' right away. It's a clay sculpture class. Here." He showed her the listing. He looked at her when she thanked him, and was relieved to see there was no pain on her face. Maybe this time she would give herself a chance.

When he was done eating he took out his guitar and played for a while, then went to the lab. Ordinarily he would be there for the whole day, learning new things, helping newer people. This was a fully equipped lab, and they did real experiments, examined real problems. There were even a few inventions that came out of this lab. It was the first lab of its kind, the original kids-only lab created by Ayelet Shoshani.[118] She had died just before he started going to the lab, and he was sad to have missed meeting her. These labs, now adopted in many places around the world, were the clearest example of the blending of work, play, and learning. There was nothing that wasn't fun.

Today he only stayed at the lab for a couple of hours and went back home. Danielle took a break from writing and they had lunch together. He was trying, one more time, to tell her about a complex organic chemistry discovery he had just made. She didn't have the stamina for the details. They could still enjoy together his excitement, even though he was disappointed that she couldn't be part of everything, like she used to be when he was younger.

Danielle went back to writing, and he rode his bike to Doreen's house where the group was meeting. A whole bunch of kids were already there, way more than would fit in her house. They all gathered outside to figure out this dilemma. After a few ideas were tossed out, they decided to split into two groups. The division was clear, as some wanted to gather data, and others wanted to find old diaries and read them and learn that way. They decided to meet again as a large group in two months, after they had some information to share with each other. A lanky boy volunteered to be the liaison, exchanged contact information with Doreen, the girl who made it all happen, and off they went. Tom was hesitating between the two groups, and decided to stay. In part, he had enough number crunching going on in his science projects. In part he was curious to hear about the past from the perspective of the children. He also had to be honest with himself to notice that he simply wanted to be in Doreen's group. She had her grandmother's diary from 2001. Her grandma was fourteen at the time, and lived in New Jersey. They all knew how important 2001 was, the year in which war in the United

---

[118] This is a reference to an earlier story, "Starting Life Again."

States, the political entity that ruled the region they were living in, shifted from an occasional to an ongoing strategy. What was it like to be fourteen then? They took turns reading out loud. Her name was Marilyn, and she always signed in block letters.

Even though Tom knew how different their life was from those days, it was still astonishing to read Marilyn's entries about being in school. She didn't even protest much about having a curriculum set by others; she just talked about not liking most of her classes, with no indication that she had any idea things could be different. He felt sorry for her, for all those children. He had a hard time imagining how anyone survived childhood in those days with so much coercion. Marilyn's home was not much better. She wrote a lot about her fights with her parents who wouldn't let her read what she wanted and insisted she do her homework before going to see her friends, or they wouldn't drive her there. There was a long entry about a time when she was asked to do the dishes, said she didn't want to do it, and got punished. And another time when she was punished for getting home later than she said she would.

They had an animated discussion about punishment. Their own parents were the last generation still raised with widespread use of punishment. Despite all the support and training they received during the transition, they would still slip, some more often than others. Each time was devastating to the child, no matter their age. Tom was hoping the next generation they would all raise would grow up even freer.

The group ended before they got to read her September 11th entry, and those that came after. They were groaning. It would be tough to wait a whole week to know Marilyn's response. Doreen promised she wouldn't read on her own in between. Someone volunteered to read and summarize, and was booed by the others who insisted they wanted to read it all live, together. Although they considered briefly the option of meeting sooner, it quickly became clear that it would take a lot of coordination to find a time that all of them could make.

Shu and Danielle were working in the garden with a neighbor when he got home. Danielle greeted him and gave him a hug. Shu's hands were caked in soil, so she blew him a kiss. He joined them for a few minutes. There wasn't much to do now that all the gardens were joined and the area was in full balance with little input and output. From time to time Tom thought that Bill Mollison[119] would have been amazed to see how far his ideas had gone. Their block grew all their own vegetables, and there was room enough for chickens, two cows, and a few goats. Only one of the people on the block was full-time in the garden. Everyone else put in an hour here and there, and it all worked out. They even had surplus that they brought to the neighborhood food exchange events every week. From time to time one of the neighbors would even make cheese, a process that fascinated Tom. He still didn't know enough organic chemistry to understand cheese making.

It was early spring, and the days were still short. "Let's go already. We'll lose the light," he called out to Shu and Danielle impatiently. They looked at each other, and reluctantly put down their tools. Moments later they were all happily putting on their hiking boots and getting ready to set out for the hills.

The trail was indeed gorgeous. The leaves were still covered with little droplets of water in the shady areas, and the smell of clean air was all around. Their dog ran happily chasing pinecones, and they walked along cheerfully. And then Shu started singing. Soon Danielle joined her, and the two were singing and laughing, making up silly words to old tunes.[120] Tom was mortified. They had never done anything remotely like it before. He tried to be OK about it, and lost it as people were approaching. "Stop, Mama," he said, "I'm too embarrassed." Shu stopped in mid-breath, and Danielle finished one more nonsense verse and then stopped, too. Silence ensued, awkward. Tom thought, and didn't say, that this walk was just ruined for him. He knew it would pass, and that saying it would make things worse.

Danielle spoke first. "You say you are embarrassed, Tom," she started tenderly. "I want to understand more about that. Do you know more?" He looked at her, somewhat relieved. So often she found a way to reach him.

"It's about walking here and having people look at you when you sing like this. It's so weird, you guys are just so weird. I don't want to

---

[119] The well-known co-developer of permaculture.

[120] Although significantly altered, this initial description of the onset of the conflict matches a real-life conflict in my nephew's family. The solution to the issue is also the one they arrived at in real life. In fact, much of this story is based on his very real life experiences. He is home-schooled and has been raised, in the microcosm of his family, in remarkable alignment with the principles and practices I portray here as fantasy.

be strange like you." He walked in silence for a moment, agitated, curious. His reaction was bigger than this one minor incident, and he knew it. He really wanted to understand. It took some time before he knew. "I know what it is, mom," he was still speaking only to Danielle. "I want to belong with other people, too. Not just with us. I want our whole family to belong, to be accepted." Today it was the singing, and sometimes it was their clothes. There was often something. He felt a tear form, and shook it off, *not now, not yet*. He was still upset with them.

"Oh, sure," Shu joined the conversation. "We also want to be accepted, just as we are, by you as well as by other people. It's painful when you get embarrassed, because we want to be enjoyed. We both want acceptance, you see?"

Yes, he did, and that wasn't enough.

"Yes, I see," he said, his voice impatient. "But it doesn't tell me anything about you, nothing that can help me understand you. Everyone wants to be accepted. That goes without saying." What was missing, he wondered, still frustrated. "If you want me to shift in any way, I want to know what's really going on, why you think these silly nonsense songs are so cool. You know, that thing, the needs, I just don't get what you need, so I can't connect with you."

That's what broke the ice. From then on, they rapidly spoke their needs to each other, curious, open, loving. Within moments, they found the solution. He had been so contracted that he couldn't see the obvious at first. The silly singing was simply a true, spontaneous expression of joy and creativity, an opportunity to have fun and play. Once he got that, he completely wanted them to have this experience. He, and they – all of them – just wanted to find a solution that would not be at his expense. In the neutral, relaxed, open space that opened up as they fully connected with all the needs, they figured out a hybrid strategy. When no one else was around, Shu and Danielle would sing to their heart's content. When people approached, they stopped. He never had to face the potential looks of people who might cross their path, and they had the freedom to enjoy the unfolding of the singing. Life was good.

Section 2

Principles and Systems

Principles

Although I don't know of any large-scale system anywhere in the world that operates fully on the basis of the principles below, the building blocks for implementing these principles in real-life systems already exist in one form or another. The list of inspirations and models is simply too large to list comprehensively.[121] These principles are the ones that underlie the future world society I describe in my stories.

My most consistent model for this radical possibility is the real-life example I witnessed for so many years until my sister's death: a family, including their son, living in complete trust and shared decision-making. My second example is BayNVC, the organization I co-founded, where we consistently aim to operate in line with these principles. Given how much we, like everyone else, have internalized from our own socialization into the existing ways of being, I am amazed by how often we actually succeed.

Need Satisfaction

At the heart of how the world I envision operates is the principle of aiming for strategies that meet the most needs possible given the resources at hand. This would be an economy in which the needs of all were the driving force. Just try to imagine it; feel your way into what it would be like. No longer would we be focused on profit. Instead, we would be, collectively, prioritizing attending to everyone's needs, including those of the natural world. What if, for example, instead of investing in technologies of destruction we would invest in figuring out how to feed all of us without destroying the biosphere?

Since I have suggested all along that anything that humans and other life forms do is an attempt to meet needs, then by that insight what is happening now, including all the destruction we see, is also stemming from such an attempt. What, then, would be different?

Perhaps the simplest way to answer is to say: more needs, of more people, will be held with more awareness and more

---

[121] One key resource in this area is the Co-Intelligence Institute, co-intelligence.org, which contains numerous stories and other references to social innovations along the lines I am using here.

involvement of those affected. I want to illustrate with two intense examples.

The first is about war. It is now known that during World War II, leaders of the US and UK were approached with specific proposals for an armistice that could have saved the lives of untold numbers of Jews. In all those cases the answer was no. What's exceptional and relevant about this is that the reason given pointed to a willingness to have all those Jews killed for the purpose of having a complete and unconditional surrender.[122] There is no way that a true focus on maximizing need satisfaction could be consistent with an approach that prioritizes unconditional surrender. This is a clear example, for me, of prioritizing a particular strategy, without clear connection to *all* the needs of the people doing the prioritizing, and without holding the needs of others: in this case the millions of Jews, as well as the soldiers on both sides, the citizens of cities in Germany that were being bombed to the ground, and later the citizens of Japan, especially in the case of the atom bombs dropped on Hiroshima and Nagasaki.

The second is about profit. In the early 1970s Ford released a car called the Pinto, knowing that it had a fatal flaw that would result in a high likelihood of explosion when the car would be rear-ended. This release happened despite knowing that an $11-per-car repair was possible. The leaders of Ford did a cost-benefit analysis and concluded that what it would cost them to settle legal claims over people's known deaths would be cheaper than putting in the fix. The Pinto was rolled into the market after test crashes resulted in 100% explosions at speeds higher than 25 mph.[123] Once again, I can't imagine that anyone would have made such a decision while holding true consideration of the lives of those who ended up dying or being severely burned in the ensuing accidents. Ironically, Ford ended up paying out much more cash than in its original calculations, and eventually recalled the car, costing it yet more money. The cost-benefit analysis that was done didn't even achieve the purpose for which it was designed.

The implications of putting need satisfaction front and center are staggering. With this focus, leaders would act as servants, and

---

[122] See the article "Why I am a Pacifist: The Dangerous Myth of the Good War" by Nicholson Baker, published in *Harper's Magazine*, May 2011.

[123] For the full report on this example, you can read the classic article by Mark Dowie in the Sep-Oct 1977 issue of *Mother Jones*. motherjones.com/politics/1977/09/pinto-madness

decision-making would be based on dialogue, full willingness, and participation. What would it be like if leaders saw themselves as guiding a decision-making process rather than the ones making the decisions? Can you imagine how much more joy and willingness everyone would have to get up in the morning and go to work if everyone knew that their needs mattered, that their voice and opinions counted, and that their concerns would be taken seriously?

The rest of the principles address specific aspects of what it takes to create a system that operates on the basis of need satisfaction.

Necessary Conditions for Need Satisfaction

Placing the maximization of need satisfaction at the center would entail overcoming or redefining commonly used notions such as fairness, and focusing instead on what is possible given the known needs of all involved and the resources at hand.

A related condition is rethinking how to measure both cost (resources) and benefit in non-monetary terms. Resources can then be seen as the actual amounts of food, energy, minerals, human hours and other concrete and tangible items that are required to accomplish a task. Benefits can be measured in terms of needs that are likely to be met. This form of cost-benefit analysis immediately exposes the inherent difficulty, in that the meeting of needs and the available resources cannot be measured in the same ways. This is, of course, what makes monetary analogs so attractive: they mask the challenge. In a world designed to meet needs, only connection and decisions involving those affected will work as the path to evaluate difficult dilemmas.

Willingness

If the principle of need satisfaction translates into holding more needs or more people with more awareness and more involvement, the principle of willingness addresses most directly the involvement of others. Simply put, as a matter of principle, nothing in the world I envision is imposed on anyone, and people do only what they are willing to do. I am aware of two categories of notable exceptions: consciously chosen and necessary temporary impositions to protect imminent threat to life, and impositions resulting from limitations on human capacity and imagination, conscious or not, which serve as learning for improving the approximation of this principle.

Necessary Conditions for Willingness

Key to making it possible to have willingness be an operating principle is a level of trust in our mattering, which creates more flexibility and goodwill all around. When we know that we matter we have less of an intense mobilization to protect our own needs, and thus more willingness to stretch and meet others where they are.

Willingness also increases the more we are connected to others' needs. This particular phenomenon is the one that most nourishes my faith in the possibility of the transformation I am envisioning. This is both magic and total common sense. The magic happens when people previously at odds with each other suddenly find an interest in each other's well-being and are open to giving, once they understand the other person's needs. The common sense, for me, is that I believe us to be creatures that enjoy giving when we understand the need and feel free to give.

Willingness is a fluid spectrum, with complete abdication of power on one end that makes willingness irrelevant, and complete, joyful, and enthusiastic delight on the other. Key to making willingness work as a principle is the capacity to recognize what level of willingness is sufficient to move forward with an action or decision. I discussed this point in some detail in Part One of this book (page 114). One intuitive way of saying it is that the more important something is to me, the more likely I would be to move forward with less willingness from others.

Everyone Matters

This principle addresses the aspect of need satisfaction that relates to whose needs count. The answer is radically simple: everyone's needs matter. I remember a bumper sticker I saw soon after 9/11, when the slogan "God bless America" was omnipresent. The sticker said: "God bless everyone. No exceptions." I often think about people reading the "No exceptions" line and realizing that they had exceptions whether or not they knew about them. A world with absolutely no throw-away people, no unfortunate people sacrificed. Not for profit, not for the state, not for God, not for the revolution, and not even for the "common good." I could weep from the anguish of so many people sacrificed in the name of so many so-called larger principles.

Finding a way to make this principle concrete rests on the recognition that we can only start from where we are and keep learning and improving. There are so few systems that truly prioritize everyone's needs that we are simply not habituated to the concept or the experience. We suffer from what my sister Inbal referred to as "a crisis of imagination." Even when we are connected with the needs and with our desire to meet them, we are challenged to come up with strategies to address the needs we hold.

Necessary Conditions for Universal Mattering

Key to making it possible to include others' needs in the mix of decisions is the deep trust in the sufficiency of resources. A big premise of this project, which I talk about at length in *Spinning Threads of Radical Aliveness*, is that we lost this kind of trust long ago as part of the transition to agriculture. We have inherited a belief that we need to control nature and that there isn't enough for everyone. Transcending these habits to enable us to open our hearts to all is no small task.

Connection

This principle addresses the aspect of need satisfaction that relates to awareness about needs. It is the process by which we communicate to ourselves and others what our needs are and how we want them to be addressed.

Although I am stating it as a separate principle, it is, in fact, the fundamental process via which all the other principles can operate: connection, and especially through dialogue, is how we communicate to others what our own needs are, what our understanding of and interest in their needs is, and our struggles – when we have them – about how to come up with strategies to meet all the needs.

One of the core transformations required to reach the world I envision is shifting from exchange-based relationships to gift-based relationships. Our current model, in which we give in order to receive and expect to give when we receive, takes away the full pleasure of both. When we can cultivate the capacity for full connection, the fundamental form of sharing resources changes radically.

The principle of connection, when applied to large-scale systems, goes beyond one-on-one individual dialogue and extends outward to a full sense of connection when we give, be it the food we grow, the hours of our day in service, or the knowledge we have acquired, as the case may be. The knowledge that others will benefit and that we are doing our share to meet needs provides an extraordinary sense of satisfaction. Even in our world, with its adherence to exchange-based relationships, we have all had the experience of giving just for the joy of it. I have often asked people in workshops to describe times when they have done that, including times when the people on the receiving end didn't even know the source of the gift. I find that people simply glow when they describe such experiences.

Similarly, when we receive, be it food that others grow, others' hours of service to us, or knowledge that others have acquired and share freely, we can then relax fully into the receiving without the tension that says we have to pay for it, or owe someone something.

Necessary Conditions for Connection

Key to making it possible to connect at this level is the ability to delve underneath what are now our thinking habits. Within this I include the familiar contraction that comes with attachment to outcome, whether we fight for it or give up. I also include our habits of judging, be it ourselves or others or both, as well as our penchant for evaluating what anyone deserves, be it reward in the form of resources, love, and care, or punishment and suffering if we assess they have done a wrong. All of these and other such thought patterns take up energy inside us that makes it hard to breathe and find the simple truth of what we want underneath it all.

My faith is that this capacity arises spontaneously in a context in which our needs are mostly satisfied as we grow up, and in which we are met with empathy when our needs are not satisfied. Since the experience I describe is, in our current world, extremely rare, any one of us who wants to develop this capacity would need a significant amount of both practice and healing in order to reach a state of easy access to connection at this level. I describe a path that I and others have followed to take us there in *Spinning Threads of Radical Aliveness*.

It is also my faith that this experience can be the common one if and when we find ways of redesigning our social organization on the basis of need satisfaction. I am well aware of the apparent circularity. Social orders have always reproduced themselves, and have always been replaced with other social orders eventually. I bank my vision on the conviction that a paradoxical mutual reinforcement between changing individual experience and changing social conditions is utterly possible.

Resource Allocation

The Earth provides enough to satisfy every man's need but not for every man's greed.

— Mahatma Gandhi

If we bestow a gift or favor and expect a return for it, it is not a gift but a trade.

— Author unknown

The economic structure in the world I envision is neither purely local, nor market-based, nor centrally planned. In other words, it doesn't follow any of the existing models. Instead, I see a system that is distributed and coordinated. Whatever can be decided and handled locally is, and everything else is communicated and coordinated by matching up requests and offers at the lowest level possible. In that sense the system I envision operates on the basis of supply and demand and replaces the ruling power of money as the only mechanism available to mediate supply and demand. Instead, sophisticated systems can support resource flow from where it exists to where it's needed based on ongoing input from all who participate.

Example: Food

The story "Cauliflower" includes in it references to a possible system I see operating in this future world. One of the bottlenecks in our current internet system is that access is still restricted through system administrators. I am aware of current efforts by software visionaries to create a technological infrastructure that is entirely open to everyone's participation. Such a system would allow for real-time entering of requests for food items and updates on crops and other food availability. For the most part, such requests and offers would be immediately and automatically sorted out and matched. Whenever open threads remain, they would display on any one screen based on a one-time search or on previous patterns (e.g. a food grower would see on their screen requests for food they can grow in their region and/or have grown in the past). It's only then that the question of willingness vs. coercion comes up. As in that story, what if no one signs up to grow the food wanted?

I envision much food production happening in micro-local systems, sharing garden produce within towns or neighborhoods. Unless wildly successful solar alternatives to fuel are found, much of the extensive trade in food that exists nowadays is likely to diminish drastically to live within planetary means, with only certain classic food items traveling across the globe, such as spices, which from time immemorial have been traded across many cultures.

Example: Work

The essential system for assigning work is no different from the process of requesting, offering, and distributing food. I would like to highlight two aspects of the vision I have about how work is done in a possible future society.

One is the uncoupling of work from physical survival. I envision a society in which everyone is fed, clothed, sheltered, and offered community regardless of whether or not they are able to offer work. This is a fundamental aspect of what makes willingness possible. There is no coercion, not even in the form of incentive. Some of the consequences of this radical willingness are hinted at in the story "I Guess I am Ready," and the overall freedom from having to work is sprinkled through many of the stories.

The other aspect I want to highlight is that any job for which there aren't enough people who want to do it immediately becomes a rotational opportunity for the entire community to volunteer and take responsibility for the whole in some small way. This is done via a system of community service.

It is my assumption that hardly anyone would actively want to do certain jobs even though we would all want the result of that job being done (e.g. garbage collection, as in the story "Look what I Found"). In the event that someone does, I now refer to such people as "permanents" in a system based on rotational volunteering.

Transcending Money and Exchange

The implications of all this are far-reaching. Money can be seen as an incredibly efficient tool for managing the coordination. Unfortunately, money is extraordinarily unfit for addressing needs with care. In our current models, whoever has the money gets the goods or services whether or not their need is significant. Needs per se do not have power in our current models. This is true both in monopoly capitalism and in a pure market economy based on small producers and small consumers.[124]

While many have noticed this fundamental limit of money to address needs, none of the attempts to remedy the flaw have reached significant success. Local currencies, which are proliferating in many places in the world, are mitigating the issue by removing the overwhelming power of large corporations. It's still the case that those who have access to money are the ones that can secure goods and services. Market regulation and universal access to services, the approach used extensively in Western Europe, is not resilient enough to handle periods of shrinking economies. Central planning, the model used in Communist countries, was officially designed to provide a certain set of basic needs – food, shelter, health, and education – to all without any conditions. However, the ideal has rarely been implemented. For one thing, it has proven to be highly ineffective at forecasting and has often resulted in inefficiencies and waste even beyond what we experience in the Capitalist countries. For another, in both China and the Soviet Union, massive famines that were not attended to by the government leave some doubt as to the genuineness of the commitment. Related to this, the level of political coercion and personal lack of choice around consumption was unsustainable for enough people that it crumbled.

Ultimately, I don't see any way to focus on meeting human needs efficiently and with care without eliminating money, and even exchange-based relationships, altogether. My intuitive understanding is that the reason why a proposal for a globally coordinated and fully distributed resource allocation system hasn't come forth yet, and why money and market forces continue to be included as inevitable elements into the future, is primarily because of lack of imagination and previous lack of technological infrastructure to handle the traffic.

In fact, I don't believe that the vision I am proposing could have been fully realized before the establishment of the internet as a distributed and coordinated infrastructure. Once again I find my indebtedness to Marx's insight that our material conditions, in this case the presence of the internet, affect what we can think about and

---

[124] The latter form is the one on which Adam Smith based his theories. The conditions for effective market economy that he designed fall apart when consolidation of production happens. In other words, technically speaking, monopoly capitalism is not a market based economy. For a full discussion of this perspective look at David Korten's *The Post-Corporate World: Life after Capitalism*.

envision. I am also profoundly inspired and awed by the capacity of some thinkers to imagine a distributed and coordinated system even before the technology was invented. In particular, in *Deschooling Society* Ivan Illich proposed a model strikingly similar to what I see here, without including the governance features, as a way of transforming education from being curriculum-based to being based on what people at any age want to learn, and matching it up with resources and with people who want to share information.

Another significant implication is a transformation in key assumptions made by economic theory such that it will no longer see itself as dealing primarily with scarce resources. Clearly, when resources are perceived to be scarce, or made to be scarce, or are truly scarce, mechanisms for adjudicating who will have access to resources are necessary. If the assumption is made that resources are mostly scarce, then placing money as mediator is enormously convenient because it renders the decision impersonal. This means that everyone can preserve the illusion that there is no systematic exclusion, while the poor remain unable to support their basic needs.

For there to be a globally coordinated and distributed system for resource allocation that everyone trusts, we would need to do away with that assumption, and regain our ancient trust in the power of nature to provide. When resources become truly scarce, then need-based connection can provide a different path to making the tough choices. The story "Triage" provides one example of how such a dilemma can be resolved.

Governance

When I think of how many people are employed by government, private sector, and non-profit organizations for purposes of surveillance, protection, monitoring compliance, restricting access, regulation, and enforcement, I am filled by despair as well as a surge of optimism. I imagine what becomes possible when there is nothing to protect because no one is deprived of access to resources; nothing to monitor, inspect, or enforce because there are no rules imposed on anyone; nothing to regulate because everyone voluntarily participates in supporting themselves and the whole; and nothing to restrict because resources are allocated on the basis of need and dialogue.

One clear outcome of such a world is that functions usually associated with government become obsolete (e.g. food stamps and other aid programs on one end, and war on another), shift to being provided on a community basis (e.g. learning and conflict resolution), or are coordinated through the resource allocation system (e.g. health care and transportation).

While governments are likely to become a thing of the past in a world organized around the principles I outline here, the function of governance does not disappear. Any association of human beings, of any size, requires a method for making decisions about executing the business for which the association exists. We, a conscious species proliferating beyond the carrying capacity of our one and only planet, are not different. We need a system for making decisions about how we can conduct our business of living together. What could a non-coercive system of global governance look like?[125]

The system I describe below is one possible answer to this question. This is a schematic frame, and I don't presume to know how things will unfold in the future. It's likely that different cultures will have different arrangements, and how the entire system will be coordinated is probably beyond our current imagination, given the level of strife we currently know. Many questions remain unanswered

---

[125] A non-coercive governance system means that participants in the system truly accept the decision because they see how it serves the purpose for which it is made, not simply because they accept the rules of the game. In a majoritarian and competitive system, for example, the minority tends to accept the results of any decision-making process *only* because of accepting the premise of majority rule, not because they are wholeheartedly willing. The key element of a non-coercive system is true willingness.

in the detailed description below. Here are a few examples: Since the system I am proposing is based on willingness alone, how would overall coherence be achieved? How will people even find out about decisions that are made that might affect them? What will happen to people who don't go along with decisions made by others? As with everything else I am presenting in this vision of the future, and especially when it comes to the complexity of governing many billions of people, I hold these notes as tentative possibilities rather than a final plan. That said, having a way to do it that in principle could work was sufficient to give me both hope that a collaborative future is possible and motivation to share this vision with the world.[126] The other source of hope for me is the knowledge that, at least on small scales, we have many hundreds of years of collaboration in our history – management of resources that are part of the commons. These practices continue despite systematic efforts to dismantle the commons, starting with the enclosures of the industrial revolution and continuing to this day.[127] Carne Ross also provides several remarkable examples of people managing their affairs collaboratively, most notably during a certain period of the Spanish Civil War.[128]

One more example comes from my own work facilitating an attempt at collaborative law-making in the state of Minnesota in the area of child custody legislation. In the weeks leading up to the actual production of this book, the group I had been working with for over two years reached a unanimous agreement about a legislative package

---

[126] In the weeks leading up to the publication of the book, after the manuscript was beyond complete, I discovered a book that provided extensive details about the governance system in Cuba. Arnold August's *Cuba and Its Neighbors: Democracy in Motion* is written with such attention to specificity and thoroughness, that I can at least delude myself into believing that I now understand something about the extensive mechanisms for participatory democracy in Cuba. Had I discovered this book earlier, I trust it would have shaped my musings in this chapter. At this stage, it serves only to affirm my faith that a sophisticated and varied system for participatory, collaborative governance is entirely feasible. I learned, more than anything, that any belief to the contrary is based on a failure to imagine that people might be motivated by care for the common good instead of narrow self-interest. The entire thrust of our system of competitive elections, separation of powers, and checks and balances is that each individual, agency, or arm of the government is only motivated by a narrow perspective of its own, and the only way to create a workable whole is to constrain and restrict everyone's movement. The Cuban system, as much as the one I am delineating here, is based on the premise that human beings and even institutions can be, and want to be, mobilized for the common good.

[127] Such facility for collaboration is documented through many examples in *The Wealth of the Commons*, along with a number of accounts of the practice of enclosures. See pages 92-5 above and especially the footnote on page 94 which includes a discussion of the controversy surrounding the so-called "tragedy of the commons."

[128] See *The Leaderless Revolution*. It was the Communist Party, not the Nationalists, who destroyed this two-year experiment.

that they *all* believed was an improvement over existing legislation. This was no easy feat. There were many moments during the process that required a lot of patience, even faith, when an apparent impasse arose. Still, I kept reiterating that a solution was possible, and, invariably, someone came up with a way forward, and by far not always the same person. Considering that some members of the group previously wouldn't even talk to each other, along with the intensity and complexity of the issues involved, I see their accomplishment as an amazing proof-of-concept that effective collaboration can lead to breakthrough and transformative solutions.[129]

This possible governance system contains several components that I describe below in greater detail:

Geographic Decision Circles: This is the core system I envision for allowing all decisions to be made maximizing both efficiency and inclusion at multiple levels, starting from a block or neighborhood all the way to global decisions.

Ad Hoc Decision Circles: These come together to engage in a more in-depth exploration of a topic as the need arises, and could take place at all but the lowest level.

Wisdom Circles: These come together at regular intervals such as quarterly or annually, to take a deeper look at the issues affecting the population at the level at which they are convened.

Theme/Profession/Industry/Interest Circles: These are likely to emerge organically as needed and operate on a similar logic to the geographic ones, with significant changes based on density of population relevant to such circles.

Outside the lowest level of the geographic circles, many of the other circles may operate in a virtual manner or be based on some future technology as yet to be designed.

Geographic Decision Circles

These circles, which form the heart of the system of governance I envision, are based on the following principles. These are essentially an implementation of the general principles I described earlier:

---

[129] For more details about the Minnesota project see thefearlessheart.org/projects. The work of the group is not yet complete. The state legislators and lobbyists in the group are gearing up to pass the package through the legislature, while others are working on non-legislative aspects of the work necessary to actually implement the hoped-for changes.

1. Decisions are made on the basis of willingness and are not imposed on others.

2. Elections are open and unanimous and include discussion and dialogue about who gets elected until everyone has no significant objection to whoever is chosen.[130]

3. Decisions are made at the level at which the consequences take place with a preference for localizing decision-making.

Geographical Listing

Any of the levels below might be skipped depending on specific circumstances, so as to keep the number of people and of issues within each level on a par between the different circumstances.

All are defined by natural conditions rather than political conditions (e.g. watersheds, clear boundaries between sections of town, language communities, etc.).

Regions would probably be the same size as country or state in our current system except for being defined geographically rather than politically.

Rural: Village > area > county

Small Town: Neighborhood > town > area > county

Urban: Block > neighborhood > city > county

Metropolitan: Building > Block > neighborhood > district > city > county

Beyond: County > region > subcontinent > continent > globe

Schematic Operation

Each level, starting from building, or block, or neighborhood, makes decisions for what affects only the people within that level.[131] In

---

[130] While this way of electing representatives may seem fantastic to some, it is already in existence in any system that uses sociocracy (as well as holacracy, a related system), an organizational structure and decision-making system that has provisions for such open elections as part of its governance structure. Although I have significant critiques of sociocracy, the process of groups electing representatives in the manner described above happens routinely and successfully in many organizations and communities where sociocracy and holacracy are implemented. This aspect of sociocracy provided the inspiration for the circle structure and election system I propose here.

addition, each circle selects representatives for a next-level (district, town, county, region, etc., all the way to the global level) where decisions that affect a larger grouping of people get made. All the members of the next circle up are also members of a lower circle.

At the lowest level everyone is invited to participate (ideally 25-50 people). A representative at the next level up participates in decision-making meetings at both levels so as to be able to communicate the needs of the lower level to the higher level circle, and to be able to run proposals by the lower level if needed before they are decided at the higher level.

I imagine that each level up, except the top two, has 10-25 representatives from the level right below it. This allows for communication between levels to flow with maximum ease. I do not presume to quantify this further, since this is *only* a schematic rendition. If we are lucky enough to make it to a time when a system such as this gets implemented, I anticipate a team of people running calculations and looking at maps and statistics to establish an optimal division such that regions would be meaningful entities, for example. What's critical, from my perspective, is to recognize that the participatory and collaborative nature of this system requires that any representative to a higher level, including the top level of global coordination, is also a participant at any lower level below, which may be up to ten different circles, ten levels down, all the way to the street or village in which this person lives.

This setup is an irreducible aspect of the system in that it ensures that people at the top remain fully connected to the needs at all levels, and to their own participation as regular citizens.

---

[131] The question of who decides what affects whom is one that can be sorted out in practice over time. So long as there is trust in mattering, and learning can happen through mistakes, such decisions can be challenged without significant consequences.

Summary Numeric Representation of the System

	Min. # of circles at this level	Max. Ave. Population represented in each circle	Max. # of circles at this level	Max. Ave. Population represented in each circle	Level No.
Globe	1	7,500,000,000	1	7,812,500,000	10
Continents within the globe	5	1,500,000,000	5	1,562,500,000	9
Sub-continents within each continent	6	250,000,000	8	195,312,500	8
Regions in each sub-continent	10	25,000,000	25	19,531,250	7
Counties in each region	10	2,500,000	25	781,250	6
Cities/areas in each county	10	250,000	25	31,250	5
Districts/ towns in each city/area	10	25,000	25	1,250	4
Neighbor-hoods in each district/town	10	2,500	25	50	3
Blocks within each neighbor-hood	10	250			2
Part of a block (e.g. a high-rise building or a few smaller buildings)	10	25			1

In other words, each circle at level two has representatives from 10-25 first level circles, and so on and so forth until the top circle contains representatives from 5-10 continent circles.

Examples of Decisions and Levels

Description	Level	Comments
Growing food for immediate local consumption	Block in intensely urban locale; town in more rural setting	Doesn't affect anyone outside the immediate group
Identifying drop-off locations for food brought in	Could be district or neighborhood, depending on population size	This decision doesn't affect anyone outside those who will be picking up the food
Establishing a learning exchange center	District or town	While the resources needed may affect other levels, resource allocation is done by request and offering, and is separate from establishing the need and willingness within the community to have a new learning center
Agreements about noise levels	City or town	Could be smaller if natural borders exist and noise is less likely to travel
Building a road between two cities	The lowest level that spans the two cities	This decision affects residents of the entire level
Water management	Watershed, or possibly continent	Water is needed by everyone and water allocation can have far-reaching consequences for everyone
Upgrading communication protocols	Globe	Everyone could possibly be affected by the implementation
System for addressing conflicts	At all levels	Each level requires a mechanism for that level, and they don't all have to be the same

A visual illustration of the principles of governance, by artist
Bernadette Miller.[132]

---

[132] Drawings based on these photos, with full permission, anticlockwise from top right: Rooney, G.
(n.d.). *Hoi An, Man Carrying Food*; Molloy, K. (1976) *Maya Woman Carrying Tinaja*; Water.org (n.d.). *Women
Carrying Water From Unimproved Source in Bangladesh*.
URLs: travel-pictures.co/hybrid/data.svt?viewpage=picture_details_np.jsp&pclref=2017304
notenoughgood.com/2012/06/women-and-water/women-carrying-water-from-unimproved-source-in-
bangladesh-credit-water-org/

Most decisions are subject to review after a certain period of time. The more controversial the decision, the harder it was to achieve, the sooner the review will take place, so that those who stretched the most towards willingness can have the opportunity to be heard about their experience of living with the decision they stretched to make. Even if the time period is 30 years, this principle ensures that nothing appears unchangeable and everyone remembers that it's people who make decisions, not any document that has a decision made by others at an earlier time.

Ad Hoc Decision Circles

When, for whatever reason, the ongoing system is unable to handle a particular decision – either because of the necessity to develop expertise in a particular domain, or because of too much controversy to handle within the limited amount of time taken regularly for decision-making, or for any other reason – a circle is put together for the sole purpose of reaching a collaborative decision about the issue.

Unlike the geographic decision circles, which meet at regular intervals and for short periods of time, ad hoc decision circles are brought together for an undetermined amount of time, until a decision is reached.

Of all the elements in the system that I am proposing, this particular feature has already been used extensively in the world with great success, especially in Denmark.[133] A few essential features unite the diverse approaches that have sprung up around the world. When these features are implemented, and especially when certain kinds of expert facilitation are provided, such circles tend to converge on a decision to which they all agree.[134]

However these kinds of experiments have been carried out in the world, in the way I envision them, these circles would be making a

---

[133] See Tom Atlee, *The Tao of Democracy*, especially chapters 12 and 13, both of which are available online at co-intelligence.org. I prefer not to use the term he coined – "citizen deliberative councils" – because I find the connotation of states and government implicit in this term too confusing for the possibility of imagining a radically different social order. I also am not fond of the term "deliberative" because of the connotation of rational arguments and my hope of shifting focus to needs, which are non-rational.

[134] The experiments in facilitating such groups to a general agreement are still nascent and too complex to be able to draw too many conclusions from them. Some such groups reach such an agreement by leaving out areas of disagreement, others by keeping agreements to relatively general terms, to be given detailed form by legislatures or other such bodies. As I mentioned earlier, these notes are, by necessity, tentative. My own rather limited experience is that when the conditions for connection I named earlier (page 376) are in place, the likelihood of convergence increases.

decision that would then apply to everyone within the population level from which they were selected. These decisions are also subject to review.

Random Selection

Perhaps the most significant aspect of such circles is that they are selected at random from the entire population that is affected by the decision to be made. This randomization works to increase the likelihood that different individuals and constituencies would trust that they are represented in the circle. In addition, random selection means that people join the circle as individuals, not as representatives of this or that constituency. This distinction makes all the difference in the world. As individuals, they can shift their position, change their mind, be influenced by what others are saying, and speak their heart – including their doubts and concerns – with a freedom that they wouldn't likely exercise as representatives.

Outside Facilitation

In the world I envision, the skill of facilitation would be widely available, although I envision group process becoming significantly easier as people increasingly trust their fundamental mattering and the sufficiency and care available for all. Nonetheless, any group benefits hugely from having an outside person whose sole role is to support everyone else in understanding their needs, in hearing each other's needs, knowing what their level of willingness is, and stretching to imagine solutions that address the most number of needs sufficiently. As far as I know, the vast majority of all the experiments and applications of such circles have had expert facilitation.

Small Size

From the experiments done around the world, it appears that around two dozen is the ideal number for such circles. Anything smaller doesn't generate sufficient diversity of opinions and positions, and anything significantly larger becomes unwieldy to maneuver in terms of facilitation.

Access to Resources and Information

People who are selected to participate in such a circle are, by definition, non-experts in the topic. In order for them to make a solid decision on the matter that is entrusted to them, they need to have the option of researching the issue using all available resources, ranging from reviewing documents and books to interviewing experts on the topic. As I understand it, the very fact of learning the subject matter together supports the people in aiming for a solution that will be acceptable to all of them.

Decision by Full Willingness

As I envision these circles, they will meet for as long as it takes to reach a decision that everyone can willingly live with. This may appear daunting unless we recognize the extraordinary power of this principle to increase trust that everyone matters and nothing will be imposed on anyone.

I can imagine that much research could be done to explore what supports the tendency to converge when all the conditions are in place. For now, my experience demonstrates, repeatedly, that when explicitly asked to aim for a decision that works for everyone, people who join the circle rise to the occasion. When everything is on the table and people trust that they are part of the solution, they eventually recognize that they cannot indefinitely advocate for something that works for them and doesn't work for others. This focus on serving the whole provides an extraordinary incentive to hear, explore, and integrate input from others, as well as provide one's own perspective in a manner most relevant to the concerns and needs of others.

Wisdom Circles

Wisdom Circles are not decision-making bodies. Their purpose is to provide reflection and directions for the population, and thereby feedback for the decision-making process.

They are similar to the Ad Hoc Decision Circles in that they are randomly selected, they have a similar size, and they work together to reach consensus.

They vary from Ad Hoc Decision Circles in two key ways. First, instead of looking at a pre-defined issue, their task is to identify together a coherent set of issues for the ongoing coordinating and decision-making bodies to examine. They provide guidance, wisdom, and direction to the entire population to consider in matters of significance, so all decision circles can explore the issues raised by the Wisdom Circle at their level.

For example, such a circle can identify overuse of certain resources as a threat to the local biodiversity, resulting in circles at several levels beginning a process of identifying alternatives to the resource or more refined systems of allocating the resource so that it will be preserved. The Wisdom Circle itself will not be making such practical decisions, only identifying the issues. In that sense they act as an advisory body to the population at large.

The second difference is that participants in a Wisdom Circle are not there to become experts on an issue. They are only there to bring forth their own concerns and perspectives about the issues facing the population. It is the facilitation that pulls together all the disparate elements into a coherent voice.

In the experiments that have taken place with this form, coherence did arise, and the sense of "voice of the people" was very strong.[135] This is a way to poll the population without having to ask each person. The statement of the Wisdom Circle affects not only the formal decision-making bodies. In addition, every person is likely to be affected by the strength of a coherent and unified statement about what issues may be pressing for the population. Such an effect may be to bring more consciousness to individual choices so as to address the issue even in the absence of a formal decision to do so.

Theme/Profession/Industry/Interest Circles

In addition to the obvious way in which people who live in a similar region or locale are affected by similar events and would want to participate in decisions that affect them, people who are engaged in similar activities are likely to want to govern their activities together.

Such circles would be the alternative to guilds, professional associations, unions, and the like. They may be local or global or anything in between, and they may be decision-making circles,

---

[135] The most consistent experiment has been ongoing in Austria. See storify.com/andreagewessler/listening-circles-wisdom-councils-and-the-transfor for a description of the project and its implementation.

information sharing circles, or mutual support circles as the need arises.[136]

---

[136] The governance system that exists in Cuba contains groups that have a specific focus similar to what I am describing here. As far as I could tell from August's book, they operate on a national level and are not specifically participatory in the same way that local government is.

Justice System

No matter how the world is organized, conflict is guaranteed to happen. In particular, people are bound to act in ways that are harmful to others and the environment – what we now know as crime. If a system is to function sustainably, some mechanism is required to restore the lost trust that happens when harm is done.

In the world I envision, such a system would be founded on the basis of restorative rather than retributive justice.

Restorative Circles

In this instance a system already exists today that operates in line with the principles I have outlined for the society as a whole, and is operating with great success in Brazil. Rather than describe a "what if…" system, I want to provide information about this existing system and its operation.[137]

Historical Background[138]

Brazil's favela shanty towns are some of the most conflict-ridden and dangerous places on earth. In Rio alone, 5,000 people die every year as a result of gun crime. Dominic Barter, a self-educated restorative justice practitioner, ignored these dangers and, in the mid 1990s, walked into favelas to learn and listen, and gradually to propose a dialogue with residents, gangs, and police. His aim was not to convince them to change, but to explore whether there are ways to respond to conflict other than violence.

Initially, the only people willing to talk with him were young children on street corners. Over time, older kids, many already running errands for the drug gangs that control the communities, got involved too. They brought teenagers, and eventually adults to the

---

137 I am aware that restorative justice processes and systems are mushrooming around the world, with varying degrees of departure from punitive frames. Many of these systems involve the use of circles, and some call them restorative circles. I am choosing to describe this particular system for two primary reasons. One is that I am very familiar with it and have been trained in both its systemic frame and in how to facilitate circles. The other is that this particular system is deeply aligned with the principles I am outlining as part of my vision of a collaborative future.

138 Adapted and expanded from a report by UK's National Endowment for Science, Technology, and the Arts about what they call "radical efficiency." The full report is available at:
nesta.org.uk/publications/reports/assets/features/radical_efficiency.

conversation. Noticing that his preconceptions and desire to help often interfered with meaningful partnership and dialogue, he focused increasingly on following the requests of those he met, or the ideas that emerged from their conversations. This built trust. In response, the residents opened up about the tough issues they faced. Seeking to understand them more deeply, a process emerged – the seed of what would become Restorative Circles.

After getting initial funding from the United Nations Development Program in 2005, the Brazilian Ministry of Justice (MoJ) invited Dominic to apply Restorative Circles in pilot projects it established in Porto Alegre and Sao Paulo. In both cities, Dominic worked with teachers, judges, and youth, both in schools and in the criminal justice system.

Results

The following are some examples of uses of Restorative Circles and their effect:

- In some areas the police have been given the authority to offer Restorative Circles as an alternative to going to the police station. These districts have seen a subsequent drop in referrals to the juvenile courts by up to 50 percent.
- Schools are often reluctant to accept young ex-offenders, which increases the risks of recidivism. Use of Restorative Circles at this point has been shown to generate 28 percent more successful cases of reintegration.
- A survey of 400 Restorative Circles in Sao Paulo showed that 93 percent ended in agreed actions that were satisfying to participants.
- Another survey in the Campinas Municipal School District showed an impressive decrease in arrests following Restorative Circles. In 2008, there were 71 police visits ending in student arrest and subsequent court appearance; in 2009, after school-wide adoption of Restorative Circles, there was one such arrest, a drop of 98 percent.

Principles

At the core of the process of Restorative Circles lies an understanding of conflict as something to be engaged with and learned from, not "resolved." For Dominic, the question became how to create the conditions for conflict to "flower fully" without getting distracted by violence and blame, thereby transforming defensiveness into engagement. Here are some of the principles that make this possible:

Systemic Frame: Restorative Circles work well in part because they are an accepted solution at the system level, not just on an interpersonal level. Towards that end, Dominic engages all levels of a community as well as institutional authorities to gain acceptance for the process and validity for its results.[139]

Power Sharing: A key element is to bring all those involved together in a space of "shared power," within a community-owned agreement to generate common understanding, so that each person involved can find a willingness to explore truth.

Community Involvement: One of the key innovations of the Restorative Circles process is the inclusion of the community as a third equal "party" in the circle. This is based on the understanding that conflict affects not only those who are immediately recognized as involved. In addition, conflict affects other members of the community, who are also co-responsible for the conditions within which the actors' choices arose. Thus their participation is doubly vital to increasing the chances of a truly restorative result.

Voluntary Participation: Each person who comes into the circle does so voluntarily and in a personal capacity without any official role they carry outside the circle. They may choose to exit the circle at any time.

Relatedness: The Restorative Circles process makes visible the depth of significance that human relationships carry. Accordingly, the agreed action at the end of a circle contains both real and symbolic components. The former are reparative and the latter are restorative. After years of experience in hundreds of circles, the evidence seems compelling that when circumstances prevent participants from having an agreed action that is both restorative and reparative, they

---

[139] This is typical of many restorative justice projects around the world: they divert some people away from the existing retributive system without necessarily being openly antagonistic to it. However, such practices do challenge the system and its retributive paradigm and therefore experience stress from it.

tend to prefer solutions that are restorative and not reparative over solutions that are reparative and not restorative. This may seem counter-intuitive, and yet I find it unsurprising. The way I understand this is that, often enough, the break in trust, the ache of the heart, or the loss of faith are more painful and more in need of transformation than the material losses themselves. I don't believe that this hypothesis has been researched, nor that any other explanation has been offered.

Adaptability: Restorative Circles operate on the basis of core principles. While a clear protocol exists for facilitating the circles, adapting the form they take in each unique circumstance is a key aspect of that protocol. Thus the maximum possibility of creating a space for having conflict be worked through is created. For example, although the protocol calls for everyone to be present in the room, in actual fact sometimes participants are initially unwilling or unable to meet face-to-face. At such times, handwritten notes, text messages and any other form of communication can be used to ensure dialogue, or experienced facilitators can substitute for missing parties.

This kind of flexibility and scalability have seen the program spread to 22 different countries in the period 2008-2010, including cultures as distinct as Senegal, Pakistan, Germany and Korea.

Community Facilitators: In order to support power sharing even more, facilitators are community members and are drawn from all segments of the community, not necessarily or primarily those in positions of power. Thus, for example, in schools, Dominic puts an emphasis on training janitors, cleaners, canteen staff, and pupils to be circle facilitators. The facilitator can vary between sessions but always reflects the local community.

How the Process Works

For ease and clarity in understanding references, the word "author" refers to the person whose action triggered the pain, and the word "receiver" refers to the person who experienced the pain. These terms were coined by Dominic Barter, the originator of this system. In addition to providing clarity, these terms also support the intention of humanizing everyone involved.

Restorative Circles operate in three phases:

1. **Pre-Circles:** The facilitator meets separately with the receiver, the author, and community members to provide each of them with an experience of being heard about what the conflict means to them. In addition, the facilitator gains clarity about what the act is that the circle is about, and which parties are needed to participate to increase the chances of a restorative result. Finally, the facilitator connects with each person to ascertain that everyone arrives voluntarily.

2. **Circle:** This is the heart of the process, and includes three steps: mutual comprehension, self-responsibility, and agreed action.

   Mutual Comprehension: During this step each participant may speak to their experience at present as a result of what happened in the past. The process entails reflective listening, so speakers address each comment to the individual they most want to hear it, and that individual is asked to express the essence of what they heard until each speaker feels adequately heard.

   Self-Responsibility: During this step each participant speaks to what led them to take the action they took. It is understood that the receiver and community members also took actions in response to the action of the author.

   Experience indicates that in most cases a spontaneous expression of mourning or regret arises during this step, largely as a result of the humanizing effect of the entire process, which allows actors to experience the effect of their actions on others, and on themselves.

   Agreed Action: The individual action plans that together form the agreement describe specific, doable steps involving only resources accessible to those offering them. They seek to ground the restorative results by establishing concrete actions to repair harm where possible, restore or build relationship, and reintegrate people within their communities. Like everything else in the circle, everyone participates voluntarily in the action plan (including the facilitator, who is fundamentally a community member and not an external authority). Its goal is restoration, not retribution. Each action chosen has a specific time frame, so that its effect can be measured.

The action plan is designed to address as many of the needs identified in the earlier phases as possible. The action plan cements the connection into a sustainable shift in community relations, which can support all parties in changing the nature of their actions and relationships.

3. **Post-Circle:** Everyone who was present in the circle, plus those involved in carrying out the action plans, is invited once again to gather to explore to what degree the results of the action plans have, indeed, been restorative, and whether any changes in the action plans or subsequent steps need to take place to attend differently to needs discovered, and/or to more or different needs that have been identified since the action plans were designed.

Protective Measures

From my vantage point of the society in which I live, I find it impossible to predict whether or not having restorative processes in place would attend to all instances of real or perceived harm taking place in the world. I have complete trust in the system to support restoration when all the parties agree to use it. What I am not able to predict is the ramifications of the profound commitment to voluntary use of the system. While I wholeheartedly applaud and uphold this principle, I see instances in which it leaves the system vulnerable.

In the current applications of the system, when anyone chooses not to participate, at any stage of the process, such a person is usually replaced by a substitute, most commonly an experienced facilitator. The circle then proceeds with the substitute, going through all the phases. However, the agreed action cannot, by definition, include steps taken by the missing person, because she or he is unable to provide their agreement.[140] An even more serious limitation exists in those instances when the person who is not willing to participate, or

---

[140] At the same time, experience within the current system in Brazil indicates that while those who do not participate cannot give their consent to the agreed action plans, and thus do not affect the plans, they are, nonetheless, often affected by them. Since plans are designed for restoration, those effects are often positive. At times, people who elected not to participate in a Circle feel the difference and appear at the Post-Circle, or add their consent after the fact in some other way.

who claims not to be the author or not to have done the action that the receiver brings to the circle, poses a potential threat to others.[141]

To address the long-term safety needs of a community, some measures would likely be necessary to protect people from potential future harm. When would such measures be used, and how could they be used in a form that is the least coercive and the most caring towards all? When such measures are used, how can dialogue accompany the restriction of liberty?

One of the trickiest lines to walk is figuring out the conditions that make use of force consistent with a fundamental orientation of love and nonviolence, a topic I discussed repeatedly in Part One of this book. What seems clear to me is that some decisions would be called for in some situations, with two possible outcomes. One would be rare instances when someone would be part of a Restorative Circle without voluntarily agreeing to do so. Since this creates a massive reduction in the restorative potential of a circle, the reasons would have to be compelling enough. In addition, in the Pre-Circle much attention would likely be put into connecting with the intensity of this person's experience that leads her or him to not want to be part of the circle.

The second possible outcome is use of enough force to actually limit the physical freedom of a person in those even more rare instances when someone's freedom could mean more people getting killed, or maimed, or sexually assaulted, to cite a few obvious examples. In those instances, given the extreme harm to the person being restricted, massive efforts would go into supporting this person with empathy. A great deal of empathy would be needed for this

---

[141] As far as I know, adults who have engaged in serious harm to others, and especially those who have done so repeatedly, have not been part of a large-scale restorative justice experiment anywhere. However, the country of New Zealand has run its entire youth justice system on restorative principles for over twenty years. All young people arrested by the police go to Family Group Conferences (FGCs), not courts. In the FGCs, with the help of their families, community members, police and the people they harmed – if the latter agree to participate – the young people work out a plan to restore to all parties, including themselves. If that plan is completed, all criminal charges are dropped and they have no criminal record. In the cases where young people deny their involvement in the offense at issue, they are referred to a defended hearing, with traditional arguments before a judge. If the court concludes they were involved, the youth goes back to the FGC to develop a plan. The judge does not have to abide by that plan when passing sentence, but will listen carefully to it. Similar programs on a smaller scale are in operation in other places, including my home city of Oakland, California. These are huge steps on the way to creating restorative judicial systems.

person to even begin engaging in dialogue about how to address the safety of others.[142]

In no instance do I ever see any need for punitive measures in a world entirely based on needs and willingness. I like to believe that in such a world the need for such protective measures, which are by definition coercive, would never arise. I'd like to be prepared for the eventuality that it might. Disentangling the complexities of discernment in such instances is what I envision a new legal code would address. Some cases would be obvious, and some would be ambiguous enough to warrant legal research and exploration. In that sense, the legal code I envision would be no different from any legal code that exists: since we can never predict everything and codify it ahead of time, some human being, at some point, would always need to make a judgment call and decide how to interpret the law and what actions to take.[143] In another way, this legal code would be entirely different, as it would be a more process-based, context-sensitive guide to discernment than an outcome-based evaluation of specific actions the way current legal codes operate.

An entirely different path opens up when we truly imagine an entire system that is based on restorative principles. In such situations, a Restorative Circle with a substitute can engage in designing action plans that could include protective measures to be applied to the absent author. The details of such possibilities clearly remain to be determined by those who will create such systems in the future, ideally already liberated from our either/or, retributive practices. I can barely imagine what loving protective measures can develop into.

---

[142] The story "So Much Love" addresses this particular situation, the role of prisons and prison guards in a society based on restorative justice principles.
[143] The story "No Easy Choices" is an illustration of the enormous care needed to handle the complexity of involuntary measures.

Systems Referenced in the Stories

Below is a list of the stories and how far after the transition they are taking place, along with a brief summary of the systems they reference and the specific challenges they address.

Collective Triage   (50 years)

One of the core issues of a gift-based economy is handling scarcity, the real kind of scarcity as distinct from the manufactured scarcity in which we currently live. What emerges here is that scarcity held in community results in togetherness and creative solutions.

It's Water Again (40 years)

This is the one story that speaks directly about the systems in place for resolving conflict. It makes tangential references to the transportation and food distribution system. It also grapples with some of the issues relevant to making the transition in a voluntary manner, especially the question of reduction in consumption.

Getting Somewhere (15 years)

This story zooms in on the possibility of creating a transportation system that is coordinated and flexible, responsive to needs, mostly and not entirely automated.

Look What I Found (10 years)

The lens of this story focuses on a community service system along with a new approach to disposing of items after their originally intended use. This story also refers to new ways of parenting with full respect and participation for the young.

Cauliflower (20 years)

Here we get a snapshot of the food system, which operates like all resource systems in this society: an internet-based sophisticated matching of requests and offers, which leaves few items to manual handling, just like the transportation system. This story also addresses the core issue of how far willingness can go in a non-coercive system.

What Can I Do? (30 years)

The main feature of this story is the organization of work. More so than in any other story, I highlight here the separation of work from extrinsic motivation, and the clear absence of the latter, in a society based on voluntary participation and attending to everyone's needs. We also get a peek into the community service system that is the solution to all jobs that most people would never want to do on a permanent basis: voluntary, rotational shifts.

Mounting Resentment   (35 years)

One of the issues that people most raise in regards to a non-coercive society is what would happen to the freeloaders. This story takes a look at one possible aspect of this phenomenon.

No Easy Choices   (25 years)

This and the next story both address the core issue of how to handle individuals who present dangers to others. Navigating through the decision of when, how, and to what extent someone's freedom would be restricted could never be simple in a society based on voluntary participation.

So Much Love (45 years)

This story looks at violence from the perspective of how people can be supported in their effort to overcome whatever generated the violence in them instead of being penalized and shamed for it.

I Guess I'm Ready (5 years)

The purpose of this story is to illustrate how, once food and shelter for all are guaranteed, incentives for doing meaningless work are removed, along with fear for one's survival, and therefore the entire apparatus that holds in place the power of the rich disintegrates. And yet the experience of those who had access to resources prior to the shift is not simple; for them, they've been coerced – until they are able to choose.

Starting Life Again (55 years)

Caring for everyone's needs means everyone, including the young and the old. The solution this story hints at is the possibility of having older people and the very young be together, in stark contrast to our current system in which seniors are unbearably isolated and unable to contribute, while parents of small children are struggling to pay for childcare. Another feature of this story is a peek at how some of our sustainability issues might be addressed, although for the most part this book is focused on human systems and much less on technology and physical systems per se.

All of It Is Play (60 years)

All through this book I placed young people in significant roles where they participate in adult activities. This story has this feature of the future society as its main focus. Through this lens we also see how learning can happen in an environment in which no one is forced to learn anything, and where there is no punishment or reward.

Section 3

Final Words

Getting from Here to There – A Road with No Roadmap

Now what?

Let's imagine you are as excited as I am about the vision I painted in this book, and you now have a vivid picture of how simple life could be. What on earth can we do with it? Is it at all realistic to expect that we could ever get there? In our lifetime? Before we reach the carrying capacity of the Earth? Before we blow ourselves up? Before we run out of fuel? Before climate change makes this planet inhospitable to us?

I don't know. I make a point of digging myself deep into the crushing humility of not knowing. I am fearful of all-knowing theories of anything, including even those aspects that seep into my own thinking and writing, because of seeing the damage we have created, and believing it to be in part related to thinking that we know better than nature, better than life itself. So I want to remain in the radical uncertainty of not knowing.

That doesn't stop me from having ideas, passion, longing, and energy for action. I want to take action *while not knowing*.

No one predicted the surge of mostly nonviolent resistance uprisings that sprang up in the Middle East in 2011. No one predicted whatever terrible setbacks may happen as a result of natural disasters like the earthquake and tsunami in Japan in the spring of 2011. No one predicted the Occupy movement, and its story is far from complete. We can neither predict the opportunities nor the obstacles. This is why I consider change to be fundamentally mysterious.

From Despair to Hope – A Possible Journey

This project has been an invitation to a personal and collective journey from despair to hope, from apathy to action, from numbness to aliveness, from separation to collaboration, from inertia to new forms, from scarcity to sufficiency, and from the "real" to the possible, so we can create a livable future for all.

You might think this is a utopian dream, nice but impossible. You might even find my vision here so contrary to your understanding of human nature that you fear it may seduce naïve idealists – perhaps young people you know – into wasting their time.

Indeed, much of your response to this vision and this project as a whole depends on what your view of people is. We all have deep assumptions about people and the world, and about our own selves, that are hard to access, because we just think, "Well, that's the way the world is," "That's how people are," and "That's how I am." Such ideas are so deeply ingrained, that even when we are ready to question our assumptions *intellectually*, we can still find them hard to change *emotionally*.

This is why I also wrote another book, *Spinning Threads of Radical Aliveness*, which includes, among other things, a detailed theory of human nature that places human needs at the center and leaves behind the idea of our inherent selfishness and uncontrollable drives.

In that book I look at what happens to us that results in all of us, collectively, allowing the human fabric to continue to tear; how we transmit and pass on from generation to generation the stories and institutions that perpetuate this hell.

In that book I also share the heart of my passion, what I believe to be the seed of finding our way forward to a collaborative future. Just as our modern competitive, individualist society required a huge set of changes in the way people thought, acted, and related to each other compared to the medieval culture, so a society based on collaboration, sharing, and caring for each other will require radical changes in ourselves and the ways we treat each other. That seed is our individual ability, within the context of a supportive community, to undo the cultural conditioning we have received, so we can recover from being socialized into our culture and reclaim our full power to engage with life regardless of circumstances.

Notes about the Transition

In this book I treat the transition as a kind of magical event, something that happened quickly and completely in a short span of time. I did that so that I could paint the picture of a post-transition society with many recognizable elements and technologies from our world today, and without a great span of 21st and 22nd century history to describe.

But in reality, it might well take as long as the transition from medieval to modern. We don't know. It's likely there will be conflicts, resistance to new ideas, nonviolent enthusiasts who regress to violence in the heat of the transition, and others who model for all of us how to build collaboration without coercion. We don't know how many of the ecological disasters scientists are predicting will come down, nor on what timescale.

At some point, I hope to write a new book as I learn more, with all of you, about how we can create breakthroughs in the area of personal transformation as well as in the area of mass mobilization and system transformation. When I say "with all of you" I mean that completely. Envisioning a radically different world is something one individual can do. Envisioning how to get there is an intrinsically interdependent and co-created option. I ask for your stories. I continually get some such stories in reading publications such as YES! magazine – stories of people and communities that are changing the fundamental assumptions about competition and collaboration, for example. If you are not familiar with this magazine, you are in for a treat.

I hope over time to write stories that will inspire us. I truly hope that this project will inspire some action that is based on an awareness of human needs as a central focus of that action, something I don't currently see much evidence of happening. Then, some of the stories might well be directly based on what you tell me about what you will be doing, for in truth, the transition has already begun. It began with Mohandas Gandhi, Martin Luther King, Nelson Mandela, Aung San Suu Kyi and the nonviolent elements of the Arab Spring; with feminist consciousness raising and the LGBTQ movement; with the Recovery Movement and all modalities for reclaiming our true selves; with Rachel Carson, Jane Goodall, Wangari Maathai and the modern understanding that we are interdependent with our planetary ecology; and with the creation of the internet and current communications technology that make cooperation without coercion in complex systems so much more possible (despite how much damage can also be done with such technologies); and no doubt with other developments I don't know about yet, but that you may know about.

We are parched for vision, for a sense of possibility, to counter the cynicism, despair, and apathy of our times. I hope that the vision

I included here, along with all that came before (including in my previous book, *Spinning Threads of Radical Aliveness*), will support you to get started with your own experiments in transformation – personal and societal. All of us are needed.

Afterword: My Own Path

My mother still remembers her utter astonishment when I asked her, at five: "Why is it that we have to pay money to get our groceries? Why can't we just go into the store, get what we need, and go home? Why can't everyone just get what they need? Why do we need money?" My mother had no response that satisfied me, and neither has anyone since. I grew up bewildered by the discipline of economics. Something never computed for me, not even after I read Samuelson's infamous *Macroeconomics* – the classic textbook still used in universities – and passed an advanced placement exam with flying colors in my early 30s. I understood the equations. I could manipulate the numbers and produce the desired results. None of that presented any challenge to me. It just never made sense.

I was 40 when the lightning bolt struck and I got it. It was so simple and so painful: the field of economics as we know it is defined by scarcity. So much so, that many sources define economics as the study of the allocation of scarce resources. Scarcity is built into the field: whatever is not scarce is not included. Since I didn't share in the assumption of fundamental scarcity, everything that followed from it was puzzling to me.[144]

The dream of a moneyless society I carried as a child has never left me. I still trust that there can be enough resources for everyone's basic needs; that there can be enough willingness to do all that needs doing without coercion; that there can be enough love and understanding to resolve all conflicts; and that there can be enough creativity and goodwill to work out a global system of resource allocation and coordination that is neither market-based nor centrally planned, and is instead based on voluntary participation.

The Submerged Vision

Although my dream never left me, it went underground. For years I felt it, ticking inside of me, mute and insistent. I didn't have a name

---

[144] I am not trying to imply here an infinity, or even abundance, of resources – only sufficiency to meet needs. Again, such sufficiency relies heavily on the understanding of human needs as different from strategies, and the realization that almost always a different strategy to meet needs exists than the one that rests on a scarce resource. The question of actual physical limitations of resources (as opposed to manufactured scarcity) is one I take up in my book *Spinning Threads of Radical Aliveness*. One of the stories in this volume, Collective Triage, takes the question of scarcity head on.

or form for it other than an inner disquiet, a certain unwillingness, almost in principle, to accept that what was going on was the only human possibility. And yet I knew no other possibility, and so, despite my misgivings, I learned to share in the prevalent belief that human beings were only motivated by incentives. I didn't see the life of a kibbutz, the only other form with which I had some familiarity, as viable. Why would anyone contribute, I was happy to argue smugly, if there were no direct gain to be had from the action? I fit perfectly the old saying: "Anyone who's not a socialist at eighteen is heartless. Anyone who's still a socialist at thirty-eight is a fool."

Despite my identification with these conventional ideas, my disquiet continued and persisted for years, until feminism burst open the lid, allowing my early vision to come into the foreground again, where it has grown and blossomed for the past twenty-six years.

I know I am far from alone in having had to work hard to fully recover the dream. I recognize the look on people's faces when they find their inner vision, their original faith, pure and trusting. I have had the incredible fortune of being the catalyst for this re-finding many times over as I accompany people on their journey of reclaiming their full humanity. I recognize even more the many moments of agony for any of us who have been re-opened to life in this way when we lose, temporarily, our capacity to maintain the soft openness, the trust in others' humanity, the faith in possibility, the willingness to take risks to meet life fully. The weight of our cultural training overcomes our deepest longings and convictions time and time again. Never fully, though.

I remember a story I heard from someone who was very active in the women's liberation movement and whose mother was a heavy drinker, so much so that this person never knew whether her mother was even hearing what she was saying. She told of a time when she was expressing to her mother some of her struggles in the movement, unsure of why she was doing it, not seeing any sign of recognition on her mother's numb and absent face. Then, when she least expected it, her mother said: "Don't give up now. The last step to liberation is the hardest." This mother I will never meet symbolizes for me the mysterious drive for wholeness that pulls us to heal, to recover, to find ourselves and life again. I see the same drive in the story of Eugene De Kock, mastermind of apartheid repression. The commanding officer of a South African Police unit that kidnapped, tortured, and murdered hundreds of anti-apartheid activists from the 1980s to the early 90s,[145] De Kock asked Pumla Gobodo-Madikizela, former Truth and Reconciliation Committee member, in one of their interviews (part of the book *A Human Being Died that Night*), whether he had hurt anyone she knew. The pain and despair in his eyes, her description of his humanity, and her own complex compassion for this man who committed unspeakable atrocities, leave me deeply hopeful. Perhaps we simply never give up.

My Vision Today

I am, indeed, called naïve, idealistic, utopian.

Still, I ask: Regardless of how likely you believe a collaborative future is, or how impossible you think that such a vision is, wouldn't you rather live in such a world than the one we have?

If we truly embraced human needs as the primary organizing principle, then we would radically change the way we treat each other and our children. No one would be controlled, manipulated, coerced, shamed, or guilt-tripped. We would trust that nurturing all of our needs and supporting each other in fulfilling our dreams would lead to peaceful sharing of resources and to productive use of conflicts. All our human relationships would be based on autonomy and interdependence.

Under such conditions, human beings can grow up to be people who are able to balance their well-being with that of others and of the planet spontaneously and gracefully. Imagine what that would be like. If it were possible, wouldn't you love to live in a world where all of us embrace giving without receiving and receiving without giving? Can you imagine what it would be like to trust that there is sufficiency of resources and that we have enough collaborative and imaginative problem-solving to allow us to let go of attachment to any specific outcome? Or how much less stress we would have if we could all celebrate and mourn the mysterious and unpredictable flow of life with birth, growth, death, and decay?

Yes, I know we have been told that such a life is impossible; that our human nature is to hoard, to be suspicious, to only look out for ourselves and perhaps our immediate family and friends; that we can

---

[145] See Wikipedia article about him.

only be motivated through reward and punishment; that our needs are ultimately insatiable; and that war is inevitable.

This grim picture, resting on a fundamental despair about who we are and what life is about, has been the dominant thread for millennia in the Western world. It isn't the only picture possible. We try to protect children from reality for as many years as we can, because we know that their picture of life is not so grim and we want them to hold on to it even as we think of them as naïve. Are they? Is it possible that our children know better than adults?

And Life Goes on

I wouldn't replace my experience for one second with how it was to be me before I embarked on the journey that took me here, which I describe in *Spinning Threads of Radical Aliveness*. However much pain I am in, I feel alive, I have a sense of purpose, I have more resilience, and I know why I do and feel what I do and feel. I am so much more whole.

I sometimes believe that it's impossible to be fully alive in our world and not be in ongoing pain. At least I don't know how to imagine that possibility. I don't expect to be done, to finish, to live without anguish. I do hope that I will find more ease in embracing joy, living more lightly, and finding rest.

With the pain, I feel a deep sense of gratitude and awe about life. I am privileged in that I have a calling. My life is dedicated to practicing, living, and teaching nonviolence in word and spirit. I have been doing it for fifteen years, and don't see myself changing course for as long as I live. This provides clarity and focus, eliminates or drastically diminishes certain forms of struggle, and provides a sense of meaning and energy for action.

I have committed to following my heart, however feeble its voice may initially be. That voice has grown, and with it my trust in myself. If I have any inkling of what I want to do, I do it. When I manage to let go of outcome, I choose to take *any* action, however small.

And since I can't know the effect of my actions, large or small, I want my motivation to be, more and more, the effect that my actions have on *me*. Whether or not I create what I want in the world, I want to die knowing that I lived with the integrity of trying.

This is how it is now.

The dream of having a core community of people who are dedicated to transforming the world is still a dream. It is my biggest hope that putting this book out to the world might bring this dream closer to reality.

The experience of being at odds with the world continues. And there are still days and weeks in which life takes endless, ceaseless effort to keep going, to defy the relentless march of disintegration, decay, breakdown, death, formlessness.

I still lose my sense of something being of value to others when it's about me, or when it's very radical in terms of vision. The intensity of it is so high that often enough I literally can't tell whether or not I like what I wrote until someone else reads it.

Since I want to share what is most precious to me, my biggest visions for the world, my hope and faith in the actual practicality of creating systems based on caring for needs, this limitation feels absolutely tragic to me. I so much want people to know my vision and find their own. I so much want companionship in holding a sense of possibility. I so much want movement in that direction, for all of us.

This book is one big step.

References

Shariff Abdullah, *Creating a World That Works for All*, San Francisco: Berrett-Koehler, 1999.

Peter Ackerman and Jack DuVall, *A Force More Powerful: A Century of Non-Violent Conflict*, New York: Palgrave, 2000.

Randall Amster, "From the Headwaters to the Grassroots: Cooperative Resource Management as a Paradigm of Nonviolence" in Randall Amster and Elavie Ndura, eds., *Exploring the Power of Nonviolence*, Syracuse, NY: Syracuse University Press, 2013.

Tom Atlee, *The Tao of Democracy: Using Co-Intelligence to Create a World that Works for All*, The Writers' Collective; Revised edition 2010. See taoofdemocracy.com.

——, *Empowering Public Wisdom: A Practical Vision for Citizen-Led Politics*, Berkeley, CA: Evolver Editions, 2012

Arnold August, *Cuba and Its Neighbors: Democracy in Motion*, Halifax, Canada: Fernwood Publishing & London and NY: Zed Books, 2013.

David Bollier and Silke Helfrich (Eds.), *The Wealth of the Commons: A World Beyond Market and State*, Levellers Press, 2012

Erica Chenoweth and Maria J. Stephan, *Why Civil Resistance Works: The Strategic Logic of Nonviolent Conflict*, NY: Columbia University Press, 2011.

Barry Clemson, *Denmark Rising*, Norfolk, VA: Cybernetica Press, 2009.

Allen Cohen and Clive Matson (eds.) *An Eye for an Eye Makes the Whole World Blind: Poets on 9/11*, Berkeley, CA: Regent Press, 2002.

Riane Eisler, *The Chalice and the Blade: Our History, Our Future*, San Francisco, CA: HarperOne, 1988

Eknath Easwaran, *Gandhi the Man: How One Man Changed Himself to Change the World,* Berkeley, CA: The Blue Mountain Center of Meditation, 1978.

Paulo Freire, *Pedagogy of the Oppressed.* New York: Continuum, 2007. Published in Portuguese 1968, first English translation 1970.

Gandhi, M.K., *Young India* (weekly journal published by Gandhi between 1919 and 1932).

———, *Harijan,* (weekly journal published first by Gandhi between 1933 and 1956).

———, *Hind Swaraj or Indian Home Rule.* Navajivan Trust, 1938.

———, *Constructive Programme: Its Meaning and Place*, Ahmedabad: Navajivan Trust, 1941.

———, *Non-Violent Resistance*, New York: Schocken Books, 1951.

———, *Mahatma: A Golden Treasury of Wisdom – Thoughts & Glimpses of Life*, India Printing Works, 1995.

Gandhi Smarak Nidhi (institution), *Gandhi and Mani Bhavan 1917-1934: a short story.* Booklet from the Museum Mani Bhavan, Mumbai, India.

James Gilligan, *Violence: Our Deadly Epidemic and Its Causes*, New York, NY: G. P. Putnam's Sons, 1992.

Pumla Gobodo-Madikizela, *A Human Being Died That Night: a South African story of forgiveness.* Boston: Houghton Mifflin, 2003.

Etty Hillesum, *An Interrupted Life the Diaries, 1941-1943 and Letters from Westerbork,* Picador, 1996.

Ivan Illich, *Deschooling Society,* New York, NY: Harper & Row, 1971

Miki Kashtan, "Gandhi and the Dalit controversy: The limits of the moral force of an individual," in *Waging Nonviolence*, February 2012.

———, *Spinning Threads of Radical Aliveness: Transcending the Legacy of Separation in Our Individual Lives*, Oakland, CA: Fearless Heart Publications, 2014.

———, *The Little Book of Courageous Living*, Oakland, CA: Fearless Heart Publications, 2014.

Krishan Kripalani, *All Men Are Brothers: Life and Thoughts of Mahatma Gandhi as told in His Own Words*, Ahmedabad: Navajivan Publishing House, 1960.

———, *Gandhi's life in his own words*, Ahmedabad: Navajivan Publishing House, 1983.

Joanna Macy with Molly Young Brown, *Coming Back to Life: Practices to Reconnect Our Lives, Our World*, Gabriola Island, BC, Canada: New Society Publishers, 1998. New edition November 2014, *Coming Back to Life: The Updated Guide to the Work that Reconnects*.

Serge Marti, *Grassroots Leadership and Popular Education in Indonesia: Reflections and Suggestions from Movements for Social and Environmental Change*, Falkland, Scotland: LifeMosaic and Bogor, Indonesia: The Samdhana Institute, (forthcoming in 2015).

Mahendra Meghani, ed., *Everyman's A, B, C ... of Gandhi*. Bhavnagar: Sabarmati Ashram Preservation and Memorial Trust and Lokmilap Trust.

Alice Miller, *For Your Own Good: Hidden Cruelty in Child-Rearing and the Roots of Violence*, New York, NY: Farrar, Straus, Giroux, 1983.

Michael Nagler, *Is There No Other Way?: The Search for a Nonviolent Future*. Ed. Berkeley Hills, Berkeley, 2001.

———, *Our Spiritual Crisis: Recovering Human Wisdom in a Time of Violence*, Chicago: Open Court, 2005.

————, *The Nonviolence Handbook: A Guide for Practical Action,* San Francisco, CA: Berrett-Koehler, 2014

Pysarelal Sushila Nayar, *In Gandhijis Mirror,* New York, NY: Oxford University Press, 1991.

Sarvepalli Radhakrishnan, *Mahatma Gandhi: Essays and reflections on his life and work,* Mumbai: Jaico Publishing House 1956-1995.

Marshall B. Rosenberg, *Nonviolent Communication: A Language of Compassion,* Del Mar, CA: Puddle Dancer Press, 1999.

Carne Ross, *The Leaderless Revolution: How Ordinary People Will Take Power and Change Politics in the 21st Century,* Blue Rider Press, 2012.

Chandrashekar Shukla, *Incidents In Gandhi's Life,* Bombay: 1949.

Kathryn Watterson, *Not by the Sword: How a Cantor and His Family Transformed a Klansman,* Lincoln, NE: University of Nebraska Press, 2012.

Steven Wineman, *Power-Under: Trauma and Nonviolent Social Change,* available as free download at traumaandnonviolence.com.

Yes! Magazine, in print and online at yesmagazine.org.

Acknowledgments

Because this book was written in tandem with my first book, *Spinning Threads of Radical Aliveness*, the acknowledgments from that book also speak to this one. It took all of who I am, all of what happened in my life, to get me to write, both that book and this one.

When I think about just *this* book, its content, and the vision that inspired it, certain moments, conversations, and experiences come forth announcing their relevance.

I started graduate studies in sociology in 1990, knowing full well that I had no intention of having an academic career. It was an opportunity to immerse myself in deep research. Little did I know that graduate schools would change forever the frame through which I see the world, leading me to appreciate just how much our very individual behaviors, attitudes, and even feelings, are shaped by larger forces and systems. Fourteen years after finishing my dissertation, I continue to use in my teaching and writing the insights, ideas, frames, and even stories that I learned during my tenure at UC Berkeley. I am particularly grateful to Mike Hout, whose generosity allowed me to embark on an uncharted piece of research about international class divisions while preparing for my oral exams; Michael Burawoy, who encouraged and supported me when I chose to focus on the study of emotion during his participant observation class, and yet insisted on academic rigor and analysis that are still useful to me today; Arlie Hochschild, whose capacity to see patterns and deep structure in all matters of personal interactions inspired me to see beyond the surface and still supports me in my work and writing. More than anything, Neil Smelser, whose big spirit allowed him to push me to do the best job at what I wanted to research without ever trying to get me to do something more mainstream or easily classifiable.

One day in 1994 my then partner, Jenifer Hood, put an issue of a now defunct magazine called *In Context* on my desk. I read it, had my spirit lifted, and proceeded to order the whole set of back issues. Nothing was ever quite the same since. *In Context* no longer exists, succeeded by *YES! Magazine*. Back in 1995, though, I contacted them because I wanted to get to know others who were local readers, form a group, and do something. I didn't know quite what; it just felt imperative. I was connected with Tom Atlee, who is still an ongoing friend and colleague, and was thrust into a crash course on sustainability, group process, and the painstaking work of envisioning a future instead of just opposing what we don't like. When I was on the board of the Co-Intelligence Institute Tom founded, we engaged in what he called Imagineering, when all of us were asked to write stories about how things came to change in the world. These activities, along with all the wealth of information about technologies of sustainability, that came, directly or indirectly, from engaging with *In Context, YES!,* or Tom Atlee, were the inspiration for the stories contained in the last part of this book.

Beginning in that same year, I began studying, and then sharing with others, the deep practice of Nonviolent Communication, attending dozens of days of workshops with Marshall Rosenberg, the man who codified and developed the practice. Because words, language, and ideas have always been important to me, I continued to think about his provocative one-liners long and hard. Many pieces written in this book are the product of such reflection, expanding on the luminous and evocative statements I was graced to hear directly from him, spelling them out through the lens of my own understanding. I can't sufficiently express my gratitude and awe at what Marshall created and gave to the world. I hope this book is an accurate reflection of some of the lesser known aspects of his work, and that writing this book gives Marshall's wisdom more visibility in the world.

Among the most amazing gifts I received from Marshall are the people I have met through my work, both colleagues and students. I want to mention three in particular.

Dominic Barter, who found the jewel of Nonviolent Communication (NVC) as he began exploring restorative justice in Brazil and created what I believe is NVC's first systemic application – Restorative Circles[146] – pushed me for years to see the difference between teaching NVC and applying it directly in life. My work will never be the same as a result of these conversations. Seeing an example of embedding nonviolent principles in systems transformed my work and brought it to a new level. Without this shift in my perception, it would not have been possible for me to envision in such detail the future world and how we could move towards it.

---

[146] See www.restorativecircles.org for more information.

Kit Miller, who was the director of Bay Area Nonviolent Communication for five years, invited me to draw out the parallels between NVC and Gandhi's work, an invitation which ultimately shifted my work from "teaching NVC" to "teaching nonviolence through the lens of NVC." I am all the richer for this transformation.

Anne Bourrit, through her endlessly gentle listening and encouragement, allowed all these shifts to settle and mature into one whole. Our conversations remain a sanctuary of love and understanding for me.

Nichola Torbett has been my Tuesday walking buddy for six rich years now. Our conversations inform much of what I write and more, ranging through theology, philosophy, and the deepest meanings of nonviolence. Much of what I have come to distill about leadership and power was sifted through her careful and loving mind and heart.

Lynda Smith accompanied the writing of this book from the very start, and held my hand in the early phases of self-doubt, confusion, and overwhelm. I never want to do any project again without her support.

Dave Belden, editor, friend, and respectful critic, has supported this project even before it became clear what it was going to become. Digesting, discussing, and attending to all his comments on earlier drafts has made this book significantly better than it was and was worth all the effort and pain that it entailed. I have grown personally from our exchanges, as well as becoming more equipped to express my ideas in ways that more people can understand and relate to.

In the time between the publication of my first book and this one, I endured a deeply destabilizing loss when my sister, friend, and closest colleague Inbal died after seven years of living with ovarian cancer. Publishing this book is my first major accomplishment done without her cheering and participation. My other sister, Arnina, who lives in Israel, is one of the tangible pillars of my life that makes it at all possible to continue without Inbal.

Ali Miller and Mili Raj joined the team again for this book, working on proofreading and cover design, respectively. Their contribution was so extraordinary before, that I couldn't imagine doing this one without them.

For some months, while I was writing this book, I read some of the stories of the future during my residential training programs. The many people who chose to stay up late at night after intensive training days to listen to a story supported me in having the faith to continue and finish this monumental task. I could see on their faces and hear in their words that my stories, in particular, tapped into some deep longing for an alternative. This gave me the courage to remain true to what has been burning in me, in some ways, since my early childhood. I finished and am publishing this book in the hopes that the stories, analysis, and practices that I offer here can hasten the emergence of a nonviolent, collaborative future.

Full Table of Contents

Index

About the Author

For over twenty years, Miki Kashtan has been pursuing a passionate vision of a world that works for all, learning, developing, and teaching principles and practices that make such a vision a true possibility. A co-founder of Bay Area Nonviolent Communication (BayNVC.org) and certified trainer with the international Center for Nonviolent Communication, she has inspired and taught people on five continents through mediation, meeting facilitation, consulting, retreats, and training for organizations and committed individuals. She is the author of *Spinning Threads of Radical Aliveness: Transcending the Legacy of Separation in Our Individual Lives* and *The Little Book of Courageous Living*. Miki blogs at *The Fearless Heart* and her articles have appeared in *The New York Times, Tikkun, Waging Nonviolence, Peace and Conflict, Shareable*, and elsewhere. An Israeli native and New York transplant, she has lived in Berkeley and Oakland, California, since 1989. She holds a Ph.D. in Sociology from UC Berkeley.

If you would like to support Miki's work, and especially her goal of moving more of her work into a gift economy mode, please donate to her Circle of Support, under the "You Can Help" menu at TheFearlessHeart.org. You can also pay for copies of this book for her to give to others who cannot purchase it, by donating at TheFearlessHeart.org and selecting Miki's Book Fund.

Printed in the USA
CPSIA information can be obtained
at www.ICGtesting.com
LVHW022138011123
762768LV00037B/279